Contributions to Economics

The series *Contributions to Economics* provides an outlet for innovative research in all areas of economics. Books published in the series are primarily monographs and multiple author works that present new research results on a clearly defined topic, but contributed volumes and conference proceedings are also considered. All books are published in print and ebook and disseminated and promoted globally. The series and the volumes published in it are indexed by Scopus and ISI (selected volumes).

More information about this series at http://www.springer.com/series/1262

Joshua Hall • Kim Holder
Editors

Off-Campus Study, Study Abroad, and Study Away in Economics

Leaving the Blackboard Behind

Editors
Joshua Hall
John Chambers College of Business and Economics
West Virginia University
Morgantown, WV, USA

Kim Holder
Richards College of Business
University of West Georgia
Carrollton, GA, USA

ISSN 1431-1933 ISSN 2197-7178 (electronic)
Contributions to Economics
ISBN 978-3-030-73830-3 ISBN 978-3-030-73831-0 (eBook)
https://doi.org/10.1007/978-3-030-73831-0

© The Editor(s) (if applicable) and The Author(s), under exclusive license to Springer Nature Switzerland AG 2021
This work is subject to copyright. All rights are solely and exclusively licensed by the Publisher, whether the whole or part of the material is concerned, specifically the rights of translation, reprinting, reuse of illustrations, recitation, broadcasting, reproduction on microfilms or in any other physical way, and transmission or information storage and retrieval, electronic adaptation, computer software, or by similar or dissimilar methodology now known or hereafter developed.
The use of general descriptive names, registered names, trademarks, service marks, etc. in this publication does not imply, even in the absence of a specific statement, that such names are exempt from the relevant protective laws and regulations and therefore free for general use.
The publisher, the authors, and the editors are safe to assume that the advice and information in this book are believed to be true and accurate at the date of publication. Neither the publisher nor the authors or the editors give a warranty, expressed or implied, with respect to the material contained herein or for any errors or omissions that may have been made. The publisher remains neutral with regard to jurisdictional claims in published maps and institutional affiliations.

This Springer imprint is published by the registered company Springer Nature Switzerland AG
The registered company address is: Gewerbestrasse 11, 6330 Cham, Switzerland

Acknowledgements

Joshua Hall would like to acknowledge the research assistance of Hamilton Hall and the financial support of the Center for Free Enterprise in the John Chambers College of Business at West Virginia University.

Kim Holder would like to acknowledge the support of the Center for Economic Education and Financial Literacy at the University of West Georgia.

Contents

1 Exploring Your Own Local Economy Using Adam Smith 1
Laura Grube

2 Extra-Curricular Undergraduate Student Field Trips 19
Cecil E. Bohanon

3 Economic Journeys in Alaska 27
Alice Louise Kassens

4 Off-Campus Colloquia as Immersive Study and Active Learning: Capitaf, Milton and Rose Friedman's Home 33
Signè Thomas and Samuel R. Staley

5 Faculty Professional Development Through International Experiences 53
Rebecca L. Moryl

6 Educating in Theory and in Practice: The Fund for American Studies 61
Anne Rathbone Bradley

7 International Internships: Their Value and a Guide to Setting Them Up 73
Matthew C. Rousu and Scott Manning

8 Teaching the Economics of Poverty and Discrimination as a Study Abroad in South Africa 83
Claudia Strow and Brian Strow

9 Teaching Economics of Poverty as a Global Classroom Course in Ghana 97
Brian Hollar

10 Business in Emerging Markets: The Case of Morocco 107
Nadia Nafar

11 The Chinese Menu: How to Discover the Key Ingredients of Market Systems Through a Study Abroad Program 119
Craig J. Richardson

12 Sports, Culture, and the Economy: Baseball in the Dominican Republic 135
Michelle A. Vachris

13 Short Term Study Abroad: Renewable Energy in Germany and Switzerland 147
Laura Lamontagne

14 Study Abroad in Germany: *Sie Müssen Arbeiten*, but It Is Not that Hard 157
Jason Beck and Michael Toma

15 Schumpeter in Vienna: A Study Abroad Course 175
John T. Dalton and Andrew J. Logan

16 Engaging Economics: 'The Innocents Abroad' in Rome and Italy ... 191
David E. R. Gay

17 Developing Study Abroad Opportunities in Economics and Finance: Guidance from a Faculty-Led Program in Madrid, Spain .. 205
Gregory M. Randolph and Michael T. Tasto

18 Exploring How Place Can Enhance Learning in Short Course Study Abroads 219
Ryan M. Yonk

19 A Study Abroad Experience in Ireland: The Celtic Tiger Before and After the Global Financial Crisis 237
Dennis W. Jansen

20 Multidisciplinary Agricultural Study Abroad in Uruguay 249
Levi A. Russell

21 The World as a Living Economics Classroom: Lessons from 'Economies in Transition', a Faculty-Led Study Abroad Course in Central and Eastern Europe 255
Olga Nicoara and Andrew Economopoulos

22 Using Study Abroad to Teach the Fundamentals of a Market Economy in Comparative Settings 273
William N. Trumbull

23 Study Abroad in the Transitional Economies 287
Travis Wiseman

Contributors

Jason Beck Georgia Southern University, Savannah, GA, USA

Cecil E. Bohanon Ball State University, Muncie, IN, USA

Anne Rathbone Bradley The Fund for American Studies, Washington, DC, USA

John T. Dalton Wake Forest University, Winston-Salem, NC, USA

Andrew Economopoulos Ursinus College, Collegeville, PA, USA

David E.R. Gay University of Arkansas, Fayetteville, AR, USA

Laura Grube Beloit College, Beloit, WI, USA

Brian Hollar Marymount University, Arlington, VA, USA

Dennis W. Jansen Texas A&M University, College Station, TX, USA

Alice Louise Kassens Roanoke College, Salem, VA, USA

Laura Lamontagne Framingham State University, Framingham, MA, USA

Andrew J. Logan Wake Forest University, Winston-Salem, NC, USA

Scott Manning Susquehanna University, Selinsgrove, PA, USA

Rebecca L. Moryl Emmanuel College, Boston, MA, USA

Nadia Nafar Virginia Wesleyan University, Virginia Beach, VA, USA

Olga Nicoara Ursinus College, Collegeville, PA, USA

Gregory M. Randolph Southern New Hampshire University, Manchester, NH, USA

Craig J. Richardson Winston-Salem State University, Winston-Salem, NC, USA

Matthew C. Rousu Susquehanna University, Selinsgrove, PA, USA

Levi A. Russell The University of Kansas, Lawrence, KS, USA

Samuel R. Staley Florida State University, Tallahassee, FL, USA

Brian Strow Palm Beach Atlantic University, West Palm Beach, FL, USA

Claudia Strow Palm Beach Atlantic University, West Palm Beach, FL, USA

Michael T. Tasto Southern New Hampshire University, Manchester, NH, USA

Signè Thomas Trinity College, Hartford, CT, USA

Michael Toma Georgia Southern University, Savannah, GA, USA

William N. Trumbull The Citadel, Charleston, SC, USA

Michelle A. Vachris Virginia Wesleyan University, Virginia Beach, VA, USA

Travis Wiseman Department of Finance and Economics, Mississippi State University, Mississippi State, MS, USA

Ryan M. Yonk American Institute for Economic Research, Great Barrington, MA, USA

Chapter 1
Exploring Your Own Local Economy Using Adam Smith

Laura Grube

Abstract In this paper, I describe a course, "The Beloit Economy and Adam Smith," which I designed for a first-year initiative program at Beloit College in Beloit, Wisconsin. The course, as the title suggests, includes readings from Smith's *An Inquiry into the Nature and Causes of the Wealth of Nations*, as well as experiential or community-based learning experiences. These experiences include tours of the local community and visits to local businesses.

1.1 Introduction

Smith teaches us economics by looking at the world and asking questions. Why are pins—such a simple, "trifling manufacture"—produced through eighteen distinct steps and the cooperation of ten men, rather than a single person making the pin from start to finish (Smith 1981, p.14)? Why is it, in contrast, that in small villages in the Highlands of Scotland workers do not perform a series of simple tasks, but instead juggle even multiple occupations? Or, as Smith says, "every farmer must be butcher, baker and brewer for his own family" (Smith 1981, p. 31). Smith's descriptions call upon our economic imagination. We are transported to a pin factory and provided a description of the division of labor (as if Smith himself had visited the factory and taken notes on the activity he observed). It becomes clear that division of labor increases output, and we're persuaded by his reasoning that this happens through (1) increases in dexterity, (2) avoidance of switching costs, and (3) the creation of better-suited tools to aid production. His critical examination of the everyday, appeals to concrete examples and reason (a persuasion that doesn't involve mathematical abstraction), and descriptions that call upon the economic imagination, make Smith's writing a fun and accessible introduction to economics.

L. Grube (✉)
Beloit College, Beloit, WI, USA
e-mail: grubel@beloit.edu

© The Author(s), under exclusive license to Springer Nature Switzerland AG 2021
J. Hall, K. Holder (eds.), *Off-Campus Study, Study Abroad, and Study Away in Economics*, Contributions to Economics,
https://doi.org/10.1007/978-3-030-73831-0_1

For these reasons, I often assign passages from Smith's *An Inquiry into the Nature and Causes of the Wealth of Nations* (hereafter, WON) in my Principles of Economics course. In fall 2018, I had the opportunity to take Smith's writings farther and create a new course to contribute to our campus-wide First Year Initiative (hereafter, FYI). I chose to combine passages from Smith's WON with a study of our local economy (Beloit, WI) and included several community excursions. On the surface, this combination may seem strange. After all, isn't the point of teaching economic history (via Smith's WON) as Boulding (1983, pp. 233–234, emphasis added) states, "to give the student a sense of an extended present and indeed an extended place *beyond his own backyard*?' (1971: 233–4, emphasis added). Or, you might wonder, how can one make meaningful comparisons across such different contexts—eighteenth century Europe (Scotland) and twenty-first century Beloit, Wisconsin? My thinking in combining WON with a study of our own 'backyard economy' was to try to mimic Smith's method of inquiry—that is, for the students to ask questions about the (immediate) world around them. I wanted students to develop a habit of mind in which they are asking questions, interrogating what may appear as mundane, and conducting research to find answers. I should note that for most of the students, the environment was new because they were coming from other states or other countries. Second, I wanted to take the basic economic theory from WON and show how the theories still apply today. By asking students to apply ideas to new contexts, we know that students retain the material better and gain further understanding. Finally, in full disclosure, one of the key goals of the FYI is to acquaint students with the campus and larger community (and I really like reading Smith).

My learning goals for the course were:

- Students will become acquainted with the mission, values, and expectations of Beloit College as a residential liberal arts learning community.
- Students will learn about the industrial history and current economy of Beloit.
- Students will begin to grasp 'the economic way of thinking' and become familiar with economic terms and language.
- Students will further develop their reading, writing, and verbal communication skills.

These learning goals are informed by the learning goals of the FYI program.[1] Although I taught this course as a first-year seminar at a small liberal arts college with a class of 15 students, I hope that faculty at other institutions may

---

[1] The learning goals for the First Year Initiative Program are: (1) Encounter and Exploration—offers students an introduction to our campus community, our mission, and our curriculum; (2) Agency—provides a strong emphasis on helping students find their own path through college, giving them the tools and support they need to follow it successfully; (3) Higher-Order Communication Skills—helps students to become more aware of expectations for effective communication at the college level by providing concrete strategies for developing as writers and speakers as well as opportunities for improvement; and (4) Social Identities—acquaints students with the presence, interests, and needs of various communities within and beyond Beloit College—local, national, and international—while asking students to reflect upon, analyze and evaluate their own position in relation to communities of which they are (and of which they aspire to be) a part.

1 Exploring Your Own Local Economy Using Adam Smith

also be able to carry out a similar course, or incorporate some of the aspects of the course. This course may be especially appealing to:

- Faculty (in economics or history) teaching a first-year seminar course;
- Faculty located on campuses in which students come from many different places across the U.S. and world and may not know about the particular town where the college/university is located;
- Faculty interested to offer an interdisciplinary elective course; or
- Teachers/faculty who want a way to get students out of the classroom and in-to the community.

In the remainder of the paper I make an argument (or rather, rely on others' arguments) for assigning Smith and for incorporating experiential/community-based learning into pedagogy. I then describe the course layout and devote time to a discussion of business visits. Next, I share important logistical considerations. I discuss student learning (tying back to course objectives) and evaluation of student performance as well as the feedback from the students about the course.

1.2 Lessons from Adam Smith

Why read Adam Smith? Smith is, of course, considered the 'founder' of the field of economics. Students who go on to take other courses in economics, or are more casual consumers of economics (for example, reading news articles) will inevitably come across a reference to Smith. Boulding (1983) has summarized various views on the value of reading 'the ancients,' or the value of studying the history of economic thought.[2] Boulding argues that Smith's WON is seminal, in that almost all modern contributions can be linked back to some idea contained in WON. Smith is part of what Boulding describes as the "extended present, which shows no signs of coming to an end" (Boulding 1983, p. 231). Indeed, we can continue to find new insights in Smith. Buchanan (2008) points out that important parts of Smith's theory were lost in neoclassical economics. For example, Buchanan references Smith's chapter three, "the division of labor is limited by the extent of the market," and notes that neoclassical models of market process lack this key insight that there exists an "interdependence between the two sides of the market" (Buchanan 2008, p. 24). That is, suppliers make pins available for clothing makers, however, they are also limited in what and how they make the pins depending on the size of the demand.

---

[2]One view is that all important things were said in the past, and that 'the moderns' (M) are "feebler repetitions of the past" ($M < A$, where A refers to 'the ancients') (Boulding 1983, p. 225). A second view is that the ancients and the moderns are of equal value ($A = M$). And a third view is that "man continuously transcends his previous achievements and that therefore the moderns exceed the ancients and indeed make them obsolete, so that the moderns include all that the ancients have to say" ($A < M$) (Boulding 1983, p. 226).

Another reason to read Smith's WON is that he puts front and center the most important ideas in economics—(1) the true source of wealth and economic growth, (2) the market system led by an invisible hand, and, (3) the consistent application of self-interest to explain robust political economy. Smith argued against mercantilists (i.e. economic nationalists) who saw economic activity as a fixed pie and sought to accumulate precious metals in order to maximize the nation's wealth. Instead, Smith argued that wealth should be defined as access to goods and services for all people in an economy. Through division of labor (or specialization) and trade, we can produce and obtain for ourselves more goods and services—or increased economic growth and prosperity. Second, the market economy, rather than a source of chaos, is a system in which individuals, endowed with natural liberty, pursue their self-interest, and in doing so, tend to guide resources to their highest valued use and contribute to the social good. This is the 'invisible hand.' Third, Smith appeals to our reason and to our basic intuitions about human nature. For example, in all trade, it makes sense for those with the lowest cost to make the good. So why then do we sometimes not allow this to happen? When barriers to trade are constructed, it is obviously to the advantage of the home producer (who has lobbied for protection to maximize his own profits).[3] Smith warns that self-interested business people can capture political favor, and this should be avoided.

Relatedly, for an undergraduate student, WON is also appealing because of its breadth. Smith covers so much ground in WON that it could be considered an introduction to social science, more generally. Students who are not particularly enthralled by the origin and use of money (Book 1, chapter 4), will also find passages on why some countries are rich and others poor? (Book 3, chapter 1), or the educational system for youth and what youth ought to study (Book 5, chapter 1).

Not only does Smith incorporate the most important ideas from economics, but he does so in a way that is surprisingly easy to read (especially given that it was written in the eighteenth century). As Boulding (1983, p. 235) notes, it is self-contained and understandable without very much background knowledge in economics. After all, Smith is writing to an educated reader, but certainly not one with a graduate degree in economics (such a degree did not exist). Smith is also writing before mathematics became the dominant form of reasoning in economics. Again, Smith's style of explanation is to examine the world around him and ask questions. Consider, for example, a lesson in economic growth in which a student is presented with Smith's passage on the pin factory, versus a lesson in economic growth using the Solow Growth Model. The first provides a concrete object –a pin– and describes in plain language the process of making this pin. The description easily taps into the reader's imagination. The reader is persuaded by the simple and logical argument. In contrast, the Solow Growth Model requires that the reader

---

[3] "To give the monopoly of the home-market to the produce of domestick industry, in any particular art of manufacture, is in some measure to direct private people in what manner they ought to employ their capitals, and must, in almost all cases, be either a useless or a hurtful regulation. If the produce of domestick can be brought there as cheap as that of foreign industry, the regulation is evidently useless. If it cannot, it must generally be hurtful (Smith 1981, p. 456)."

accept abstract and highly aggregated counts of capital, labor, and technology. The reader must grasp the meaning of a Cobb-Douglas function.

Overall, Smith is an excellent introduction to economics because of his relevance and keen insights, his focus on the important, big ideas in economics, and his accessibility. Although I argue that Smith is relatively easy to read, there are several strategies that a thoughtful instructor can employ to help maximize student learning and understanding.

1.2.1 Critical Reading

Admittedly, Smith's WON can be intimidating. Volume I alone is over 500 pages. Although there are many resources on how to help students be better readers, I share below my own strategies and lean heavily on the work of Bean (2011). Bean has an excellent chapter in which he discusses common challenges and strategies to help students read difficult texts. Some of the challenges that he identifies that are particularly relevant for WON are, students' resistance to the Time-on-Task required for deep reading, difficulty in adjusting reading strategies to different genres (or writing styles), and difficulty in perceiving the structure of an argument as they read (Bean 2011, pp. 163–165). There were a few key ways in which I sought to mitigate these challenges.

First, I required that all students purchase the same edition of the book. I selected the edition available through Liberty Fund because it is inexpensive (the two volumes together is $20). Having the same book allowed us to reference page numbers and explore the architecture of the book together. For example, not only did we consider the organization by books, then chapters, but we also noted the paragraph numbers provided in the margins. Further, when there are unfamiliar words or phrases, we were able to interrogate them together. Together, this helped students become comfortable with the format of the book and the style of writing.

Second, I encouraged the students to write notes in the book (as well as in a notebook). I asked students to underline what they thought were key passages, circle items that they didn't understand, etc. I made it clear that 'skimming' was not what we were interested in, and that they may have to re-read the same sentence or paragraph multiple times. To make this less daunting, I assigned fewer pages rather than more pages. The reading assignments ranged from 4 to 30 pages, however, I tried to aim for no more than 15 pages. I wanted the students to invest the time in understanding everything they read. Reading carefully takes time.

Third, I put together a reading guide for each assigned reading. Bean (2011) suggests reading guides as a strategy to help students become better readers. The reading guides asked a variety of different types of questions. Some questions asked students to define a word, helped to fill in cultural context, required students to paraphrase a passage, or to summarize an argument. As Bean (2011) notes, the reading guides were intended to encourage engagement and reflection with the reading.

1.3 Experiential and Community-Based Learning

In addition to reading passages from Smith's WON, students also learned about the economy of Beloit, Wisconsin, both in the past and today. It made sense that we would venture out into the local economy to learn more. I did this by asking students to conduct research on businesses in the local economy (some current, some of the past) and then to present that research at the physical location of the business during a class walking tour. I also arranged visits to local companies in which students learned about the history of the company, what they produce, and how (one to illustrate division of labor and manufacturing; the other to think about international trade).

Pedagogically, these types of activities are referred to in a variety of ways, including experiential learning or community-based learning. Experiential learning is not new and can be traced back to the contributions of Dewey's (1938) *Experience and Education*. Dewey discusses the differences between learning from texts and teachers only versus learning through experience. Or, stated another way, the "acquisition of isolated skills and techniques" versus acquisition of skills and techniques "which make direct vital appeal" and "acquaintance with a changing world" (Dewey 1938, pp. 19–20). Several decades later, Kolb (1984) promoted experiential learning, emphasizing, "the linkages that can be developed between the classroom and the 'real world' ...[Experiential learning] stresses the role of formal education in lifelong learning and the development of individuals to their full potential as citizens, family members, and human beings" (Kolb 1984, p. 4). Most recently, Eyler (2009, p. 24) has defined experiential learning as learning "which takes students into the community, helps students both to bridge classroom study and life in the world and to transform inert knowledge into knowledge-in-use." She also refers to experiential learning as facilitating the move from 'theory to practice.' Experiential learning is used to describe a range of activities, including undergraduate research, hands-on laboratory experiments, field exercises, internships, service-learning, and study abroad. Experiential learning tends to be used as a more general term, covering a diversity of different practices, compared to 'community-based learning.'

Community-based learning is a relatively new term and has similarly been described in a variety of ways, however, tends to promote more specific practices. Mooney and Edwards (2001, p. 181) define community-based learning as "an education where thought and action come together in classroom and real-life settings." Jakubowski and Burman (2004, p. 161) specifically use the term experiential: community-based learning is "experiential, action-oriented forms of learning." Wickersham et al. (2016, p. 18) define community-based learning as "learning in which significant field work is guided by and grounded in academic reflection." Within the literature, community-based learning tends to refer to more sustained activities, such as internships, service-learning, and study abroad.

It is worth noting that embedded in community-based learning (and some experiential learning opportunities) is a certain set of values. One important belief is that the types of knowledge obtained outside of the classroom are as important as knowledge learned on a black board. As Westerberg and Wickersham (2015, p. 73) state, a commitment to community-based learning (or what the authors refer to as liberal arts in practice) "arises out of a belief that opportunities to learn are not the singular province of classroom learning. Instead, a student's education in the classroom can be enriched beyond it, that the important learning we do in the classroom is tested and challenged beyond it." Outside of the classroom students may learn lessons on how to conduct oneself in different contexts, or students may come to understand how the market structures they learn in microeconomics play out in real life or bring about specific regulation that companies cannot ignore. If community-based learning emphasizes that learning can take place in many different contexts, individuals outside of formal educators also have important lessons to offer.

The rise in experiential learning and community-based learning is certainly tied to our evolving knowledge of how people learn and evidence that these practices facilitate learning. Researchers and scholars have shown that experiential learning and community-based learning increases a students' ability to retain new knowledge, their capacity to transfer knowledge to new contexts, and the development of critical thinking skills. All of these contribute to the cultivation of lifelong learners. As Eyler (2009) explains, new knowledge must be presented and shown how it is relevant (or applied) in order for it to be retained. In other words, we must condition knowledge, so that students can understand how it relates to other information and when it is useful. For example, if students are presented with a list of several different statistical tests, they must also see the logic for when to apply which test. This capacity to transfer knowledge to new contexts illustrates a deeper understanding, and simultaneously reinforces what the learner knows. Eyler (2009, p. 26–27) states, "Unless students learn explicitly to recognize when their knowledge might be useful, can recall that knowledge, and know how to apply it, they will fail to transfer what they know; their understanding is incomplete."

Critical thinking is a further outcome of experiential and community-based learning that can be defined in various ways. Westerberg and Wickersham (2015, p. 74) explain, "Critical thinking requires the ability to consider options, prioritize, and contextualize information. Critical thinkers both raise and answers questions…Critical thinking is a progressive skill, which when mastered, puts the student in charge." The authors view critical thinking as the transfer of knowledge, taken to the next level. This next level is outside the classroom, where the obvious punching in of the appropriate statistical test may be blurred; or where the application of knowledge also involves input from other people, or careful consideration of how it is presented.

1.4 Course Layout

A course is constructed with close attention to the learning goals. Fundamentally, the FYI course is about encouraging students to be curious and critically examine the world around them, including their local communities. This tone must be established from the very beginning of the course. In the first week of class, students left the classroom to explore the City of Beloit.

A large portion of the course is focused on examining the community at the level of city or town (in Beloit, this is a city with a population of 35,000 people and eighteen square miles). During the first week of class I placed students into small groups –3 or 4– and asked them to conduct research on a company in Beloit. All companies were (or had been) located close to campus, so we could visit the sites as part of a walking tour. I selected four businesses, two of which are currently operating and two that are not (currently operating: Fairbanks Morse and Irontek; not currently operating: Beloit Corporation and Alliant Energy at the Powerhouse site). The project gets the students into the library, and it is helpful to organize a presentation of library resources and how to use those resources in advance of the project. More importantly, it got the students off-campus, in some cases, to find more information, and I had all the groups present on their businesses at the business site as part of a walking tour the Friday of the first week of class. Here is the details for the Beloit Business Research Project.

Assignment, Beloit Business Research Project
Questions to answer (at a minimum):

- Who were the founders and why did they open this business in Beloit?
- When was the business active? (lifespan) What was Beloit like at that point in history? (e.g. population, other context, such as world wars may be relevant)
- What did the business make?
- How many people were employed and doing what type of work? (other things that might be relevant: who were the workers? Particular racial/ethnic groups? What education did they have?)
- If the business ended, why? Or if the business has changed over time, how?
- What else should we know about the business?
- Is the business tied to Beloit College in any way?

Outputs:

- Paper: 2–3 page explanation of the business answering the above questions
- Presentation: A 10 min explanation to be delivered on site

After studying a collection of local companies, we explored our campus community, which is approximately 1200 students and fifty acres. I relied on our college archivist, who has several versions of presentations about the history of the college and also caters those to the specific interests of students in the course. We paired the PowerPoint presentation with a historical walking tour of campus. Some of the highlights from the presentation include information about when the college was founded (versus when Wisconsin became a state, 1846 and 1848, respectively), when African American students, women, and international students first attended

1 Exploring Your Own Local Economy Using Adam Smith

the college, and how economic and political events shaped students' experiences (during the Great Depression, some student paid tuition in agricultural products). The presentation and historical walking tour offered a contrasting view of campus, compared to the information that students were presented with at all-campus new student events and tours offered by orientation leaders that focus solely on the instrumental value to the student (e.g. where the financial aid office is located or where they can buy coffee at 10 pm).

These first two activities—conducting research on a specific local business and learning about the college community—take up the first two to three weeks of the semester. During the fourth week, then, we begin our reading of Smith's WON. I selected what I view as the most important ideas in WON, with an eye to what I imagine the students will also be interested in. Those topics are:

- Introduction to Smith: Moral Philosopher and Economist
- The Division of Labor (Book 1, Chapter 1, "Of the division of labor" pp. 13–24 and Book 1, Chapter 2, "Of the principles which give occasion to the division of labor" pp. 25–30)
- Exchange and International Trade (Book 1, chapter 3, "The division of labor is limited by the extent of the market" pp. 31–36 and chapter 2, "Of restraints upon the importation from foreign countries of such goods as can be produced at home" pp. 452–72)
- What is Money? (Book 1, Chapter 4, "Of the origin and use of money" pp. 37–46, also, p. 320; pp. 337–338, p. 341)
- A Theory of Wages (Book 1, chapter 8, "Of the wages of labor" pp. 82–98 (paragraph 40)
- Economic Development and the Urban/Rural Divide (Book 3, Chapter 1, "On the natural progress of opulence" pp. 376–380)
- Education and Human Capital (Book 5, Chapter 1, Article 2, "Of the expense of the institutions for the education of youth" pp. 758–788)

For each topic, there are three components. The first is the Smith reading. I assign a reading guide for students to complete with each WON reading assignment. The reading guide asks a range of different types of questions, and overall, my goal is to get the student to engage more deeply with the reading. Some questions ask the student to define a word, to summarize (in their own words) a particular passage, to consider why Smith brings in certain information or examples, or to explain why something is important. The following class meeting we discuss the reading. Second, I present the relevant economic theory, borrowing from my principles lectures. I emphasize the importance of Smith's contribution, and then show how the topic has been slightly formalized, or extended. Third, I tie in an example from our local economy (and sometimes national or international examples). This third aspect, again, I tried to incorporate community-based learning. Our trips to local businesses were incorporated as we made our way through Smith.

For example, for international trade, I had students read approximately twenty pages from Smith. We then considered how trade (domestic and international) is mutually beneficial. We examined the impact of tariffs using supply and demand.

We considered some information about which countries are the largest trade partners with the U.S. We looked at what goods the U.S. exports today. There are several companies in Beloit that engage in international trade. We focused on Kerry Ingredients, a food company headquartered in Ireland with offices in Beloit, WI. We were able to tour the business, hearing about the company's history, walking through laboratories where new flavors are developed, and getting an overview of all the various roles within the company. Two Beloit alumni were also able to join us for a question and answer period. The reading guide for the international trade section follows:

> Reading Guide for International Trade (Book 4, Chapter 2, "Of restraints upon the importation from foreign countries of such goods as can be produced at home" pp. 452–72)

> - When faced with equal profits, why does Smith say that merchants prefer to trade at home? (And not internationally?)
> - This chapter contains the famous 'invisible hand' phrase. Find the quote and write it below. Explain what is being described with the invisible hand. (hint, is it a concept we've discussed previously?)
> - According to Smith, who petitions for monopoly privileges? (Through tariffs) Which industries specifically?
> - According to Smith, when is protectionism (e.g. tariffs) acceptable?
> - What would Smith say about today's trade war?

By chance, the Economics Department hosted the international economist Dani Rodrik on campus the semester of the course. Rodrik's research is on the topic of international trade and globalization. Rodrik was able to visit the FYI course.

1.5 Visiting Area Businesses

Several students identified visiting area businesses as their favorite aspect of the course. Business visits, an example of experiential or community-based learning, can be a high impact practice. It can also be one of the most challenging aspects to pull off (students also expressed that these visits could have been even further integrated with the Smith content). It does matter where you go, i.e. which business you select, and there's very intentional work required before and after the visit to ensure maximum student learning. A visit that is not well-integrated into a course, or does not explicitly and repeatedly make connections between classroom learning and the visit, will not be as effective (and may even be confusing as students wonder why time was devoted to the trip).

The two businesses which we visited as part of the FYI course are both food companies.[4] Manufactured products, because of their concreteness, can sometimes

---

[4] Admittedly, we completed just two business visits during the semester. Some of my knowledge here comes from organizing business visits for a department annual event, which I've led for the past 5 years. For that event we have visited various businesses in Chicago, including Groupon,

1 Exploring Your Own Local Economy Using Adam Smith

be easier for students to connect with. When students recognize the brand—Frito Lay, for example—they're all in. There does have to be a connection between the business you visit and the course content you're covering. For the Frito Lay visit, I tied this to Smith's chapter on division of labor (chap 1) and also division of labor is limited by the extent of the market (chap 3).

We completed the relevant Smith readings before the class visit. In preparation for the visit, I asked students to go to the Frito Lay website and do some reading about the company. I asked that they look up when the company was founded, several examples of chips/other snacks that they make, information about the volume of production, etc. Students had to submit these answers and three questions that they came up with on their own about the company to me on the day of the visit (I actually had them submit two copies so that they had one in hand for the trip). I told students that they were doing this preparation, in part, so that they could ask questions during our visit.

The visit began with a 40 min factory tour.[5] We were guided through the production lines by a young engineer, who shared information about her educational background and what she does on the floor. What was most striking about the tour, especially comparing this to the pin factory example in Smith, was the absence of laborers. Every part of the making of a potato chip was mechanized. Computer screens throughout reported on the workings of the machines and were monitored by people on the floor. Following the factory tour, we listened to a presentation about Frito Lay and had the opportunity to ask questions. This part of the visit was approximately 30 min.

For the following course meeting, I asked the students to do a reflection paper on how this business visit was connected to Smith (specifically the theory presented in chap 1 and chap 3) and something that they found surprising about the visit. In class, I asked students to volunteer to share their reflection papers. I had completed a similar assignment, and in a PowerPoint, I had decided to focus on technology/mechanization. I pulled in two aspects from Smith's chapters 1 and 3. The first was the third way that division of labor increases output: the adoption of new technology/machines. Here, Smith talks about a child laborer who innovates and makes his job obsolete.[6] Smith recognizes that people make improvements to

---

The Center for Neighborhood Technology, the Fulton Street Business Incubator (now Make City), Studio Gang, and Legacy.com (founded by a Beloit alumnus and trustee of the College).

[5] For readers interested to learn about how potato chips are made and unable to tour a factory, see Roberts (2011).

[6] Smith (1981, Book 1, Chapter 1, Paragraph 8) notes that division of labor increases output by increases in dexterity, a reduction in switching costs, and the invention of machines. Elaborating on the third reason, "In the first fire-engines, a boy was constantly employed to open and shut alternately the communication between the boiler and the cylinder, according as the piston either ascended or descended. One of those boys, who loved to play with his companions, observed that, by tying a string from the handle of the valve which opened this communication, to another part of the machine, the valve would open and shut without his assistance, and leave him at liberty to divert himself with his play-fellows. One of the greatest improvements that has been made upon

the production process, for example, by adopting a new technology/machine. Still, the example of the boy and the mechanization at Frito Lay seem vastly different. The idea that the division of labor is limited by the extent of the market points us in the direction of scale—economies of scale—as a key factor. When Frito Lay can sell hundreds of thousands, even millions of bags of potato chips, then it becomes cost effective to use a machine (which may cost a million dollars). To further reinforce the connection between classroom learning and business visits, instructors may also make exam questions related to these points.

Visits to businesses can be a meaningful learning experience if students prepare in advance, can actively engage during the visit (by asking questions), and have an opportunity to reflect and connect classroom learning and the experiential learning afterwards. By doing these things, we can ensure the learning that Eyler (2009) and others describe. A business visit shows the relevance of classroom (in this case, WON) learning. At the same time, it puts that classroom learning in a new context. As Westerberg and Wickersham (2015) explain, we are asking students to take book learning off the shelf and apply it in 'the real world.' By doing so, we help students to reinforce and retain the material.

1.6 The Logistics

I taught this course as a first-year seminar with 15 students. A FYI course is required of all incoming students. In order to match students into these courses, students are given the title of the course and a single paragraph description of each course. They then rank their preferences, and students are placed in a course that was among their top three selections. In general then, the students had some interest in economics.[7] Otherwise, the students were extremely diverse; one third of the class were international students (from India, Nepal, and Ghana), two students were from Beloit, WI, and the other students were from all over the country (Maine, Oregon, Illinois).

I made use of resources on campus in the library as well as the college archives. In the weeks before fall courses began, I reached out to our librarians to ask whether someone could offer an introduction to the library and guidance on how to start our particular research project on a local business of the past or present. In the first week then, I took the FYI course to the library, where a librarian shared the generic presentation on resources available, how to search the library catalogue, etc., and showed students a research guide that she had constructed for their particular research project. The guide included specific sources (news articles) related to the economic/business history of Beloit.

---

this machine, since it was first invented, was in this manner the discovery of a boy who wanted to save his own labour."

[7]Reviewing the class list, approximately half of the students went on to major in economics.

1 Exploring Your Own Local Economy Using Adam Smith

I had also reached out to the college archivist before classes began, and he shared a general presentation on the history of the College. He made some modifications to his presentation to emphasize economic conditions (for example, noting that during the Great Depression some students paid tuition in agricultural products) and interests represented in the course (for example, he noted changes to athletics over time, as there were both baseball and football players in the course).

As a resident of Beloit, WI, I was able to use my existing knowledge of businesses in the area and my own contacts to arrange visits to local companies. If an instructor does not have these contacts, a good place to start could be the campus office which assists with student internships (or the development office, if there is someone who specializes in corporate partnerships), or the local chamber of commerce. I found the businesses were eager to welcome visitors.[8]

There were not any added costs to running the course. Because we had a reasonably small class, we relied on my personal vehicle and student cars to get us to the local businesses that were farther from campus.

Of course, the development of the course is time-intensive, and there may be funds available through your college or university to assist with new course development, or the incorporation of high impact practices into teaching.

1.7 Student Learning and Evaluation

I did organize the course around a series of learning goals, which were: (1) Students will become acquainted with the mission, values, and expectations of Beloit College as a residential liberal arts learning community; (2) Students will learn about the industrial history of Beloit; (3) Students will begin to grasp 'the economic way of thinking' and become familiar with economic terms and language; and (4) Students will further develop their reading, writing, and verbal communication skills. Another learning goal that I had for the course which I did not explicitly mention in the syllabus was to get students excited about economics! Based on my own informal perceptions of the course, student performance in the course, and the course evaluations, I believe that there was student learning in these areas, and that I also was successful in getting students interested or more interested in the discipline of economics.

My evaluation of student learning in the course was comprised of five categories. Students were evaluated based on reflection papers ($6.25\% \times 4$), quizzes ($10\% \times 3$), projects (one 5% and second 10%), reading guides and other homework (20%), and participation (10%). For each category of evaluation, students had at least two assignments. I wanted to be sure that if students struggled with one quiz, for example, they had an opportunity to reflect on their performance and make

---

[8]Prepare students by asking them to come up with 3–5 questions to ask at the business. Also send a follow-up thank you note—include students.

appropriate changes to apply to another quiz. The diversity of evaluation methods reflected the course learning goals. For example, because the course aimed to help students further develop their writing skills, I assigned four reflection papers (each 500 words, or approximately one page single-spaced) throughout the semester. These reflection papers were also an opportunity to reflect on the content of the course. The general format asked students to focus in on a particular Smith reading, summarize the reading, and then explain how it is still relevant today. There was (as expected) the greatest variation in essays for the first essay, and I met with several students one-on-one to discuss the essay and asked them to make some changes and re-submit. Essays three and four were stronger in terms of structure, incorporating passages from the text, grammar, and detail around current application.

In order to ensure that students were practicing reading skills and learning the content along the way, I put together reading guides for each assigned Smith reading and other homework assignments, similar to the one provided earlier.

In general, student performance did improve over time, as is evident in grades received. Admittedly, especially in the context of a first-semester, first-year course, there is content learning taking place, but there is also the process of students becoming more familiar with expectations and students developing strategies to manage time, study more effectively, and seek out help when they need it. Indeed, the first learning goal of the course recognizes this period of adjustment.

Student learning and what students took from the course is also evident in course evaluations. Course evaluations were completed by 14/15 students in the course. The course evaluations are a combination of particular questions about how the student believes they performed in the course, the course, and the course instructor with responses ranging from 1 (not at all) to 7 (very much so) and general comments on how the student believes they performed in the course, the course, the course instructor, and whether they would recommend the course. Pulling some key questions in regards to the course, students reported that the assignments were useful (6.29/7), the readings were valuable (6.29/7), "overall, this was an excellent course" (6.36/7) and that "I learned a great deal in this course" (6.43/7). In regards to my unofficial goal of the course, students tended to agree that it "stimulated my interest in the subject" (6.29/7).

The general comments about the course are consistent with the numerical scores. I tried to locate general themes in the open comments, and found that students often discussed (1) how the course helped them transition to college, (2) how the course helped them make connections with peers, (3) how they learned about the college and/or town, and (4) overall comments.

- how the course helped them transition to college

  - "This has helped me adjust to college. I think this course was a lot more strict than others and proved a good transition."
  - "I feel more prepared for more serious classes now that I have completed this FYI course. I am very happy to have a place where I was able to prepare myself for what I will need in my future classes."

- "The course challenged me and pushed me out of my comfort zone but after awhile I got use[d] to it and it became a lot easier for me and I started to see major improvements."

- how the course helped them make connections with peers:
  - "I am definitely a lot closer with my peers in FYI which helped coming in to college easier."
  - "It was fun. Made friends, helped me get adjusted to the environment. The course material was really fun."
  - "I also met many new people during my first few weeks here at Beloit; this class helped me meet those people."

- how they learned about the college and/or town:
  - "It is equally a good introduction to college life and classes. It taught me a lot about Beloit College and the City of Beloit."
  - "It also helped me realize how many resources this place has. Beloit has so many amazing businesses and I would not have been able to know more about them if it were not for this FYI. The course included many interesting readings about Adam Smith, which I personally enjoyed a lot. The visits to various places like Frito Lay, Kerry ingredients etc. were so much fun and gave me so many opportunities to learn about how these businesses function."
  - "The strength of this FYI was that I had the opportunity to know the campus and the facilities it provided with the help of programs such as the tour of the history of the campus, library, CELEB, projects on business places of the city, etc."

- overall comments:
  - This course helped me realize I want to be an Economics major while I'm here at Beloit. It's a very interactive FYI and the relationships you build by the guidance of the instructor has put me in a successful position to succeed."
  - "It was able to make me think a great deal. I now have more interest in economics. I wasn't planning on taking an ECON class but now I am."
  - "Yes, during this course, I acclimatized to Beloit extremely well, while learning about many of Smith's main ideas. This course stimulated my interest in economics so much that I am taking an economics course next semester. This course kept me interested, did not stress me, and will be of use to me in the future. This was a great course."

Finally, looking back at the class list and current majors of the students, approximately three-quarters of the students have declared economics majors. I take this as further evidence that the course was an effective introduction to economics!

1.8 Conclusion

"Exploring your own local economy using Adam Smith" was a fun course to create and allowed me to learn more about my own local economy and incorporate more of Smith into a course than I have before. Based on course evaluations, the students also greatly enjoyed the course. If I were to teach the course again, there are a few changes that I would make.

First, I would add at least one reading from Smith's (1982) *Theory of Moral Sentiments* (hereafter, TMS). In my initial introduction to Smith (through a PowerPoint) I mention TMS and share a few key passages. Actually assigning a passage from TMS would further drive home Smith's assumptions about human nature, possibly address common student concerns about economics, and encourage students to explore a philosophy course.

Second, although we spent considerable time talking about how to read Smith, we spent much less time discussing writing. As a learning goal of the course and FYI program, this could have been emphasized more. After receiving the first reflection paper, it was clear that further instruction was needed. Because I had already assigned the paper, I opted to meet with students who were struggling one-on-one. In hindsight, a class focused on how to incorporate evidence and how to structure a paper in advance of the writing assignment would have been helpful.

Third, two students commented that the visits to local businesses could have been more carefully tied back to Smith. I agree. Here, devoting a class to 'debrief' and consider these connections would have been helpful. With more preparation, the faculty member could put together these notes and then also ask them during the business visit.

References

Bean JC (2011) Engaging ideas: the professor's guide to integrating writing, critical thinking, and active learning in the classroom. John Wiley & Sons, Hoboken

Boulding KE (1983) After Samuelson, who needs Adam Smith? Hist Polit Econ 3(2):225–237

Buchanan JM (2008) Let us understand Adam Smith. J Hist Econ Thought 30(1):21–28

Dewey J (1938) Experience and education. Macmillan, New York

Eyler J (2009) The power of experiential education. Lib Educ 95(4):24–31

Jakubowski LM, Burman P (2004) Teaching community development: a case study in community-based learning. Teach Sociol 32(2):160–176

Kolb D (1984) Experiential learning experience as the source of learning and development. Prentice-Hall, Englewood Cliffs

Mooney LA, Edwards B (2001) Experiential learning in sociology: service learning and other community-based learning initiatives. Teach Sociol 29(2):181–194

Roberts R (2011) Econtalk: O'Donohoe on potato chips and salty snacks. EconLib, Indianapolis

Smith A (1981) An inquiry into the nature and causes of the wealth of nations. Liberty Fund, Indianapolis

Smith A (1982) The theory of moral sentiments. Liberty Fund, Indianapolis

Westerberg C, Wickersham C (2015) More than community-based learning: practicing the liberal arts. In: Chamlee-Wright E (ed) Liberal learning and the art of self-governance, Routledge, New York, pp 71–90

Wickersham C, Westerberg C, Jones K, Cress M (2016) Pivot points: direct measures of the content and process of community-based learning. Teach Sociol 44(1):17–27

Chapter 2
Extra-Curricular Undergraduate Student Field Trips

Cecil E. Bohanon

Abstract Student field trips have a venerable history in business education that dates to early days of business schools. This essay shares the experience of a senior faculty member who has been a long-time advisor to his department's undergraduate Economics Club. The "how-tos" of setting up, funding and executing meaningful field trips are presented. Networking with the school's alumni base—especially those alumni who were former students of the faculty member—can be a key to success. Four examples of field trips ranging from afternoon trips to week long spring break excursions are described.

2.1 Introduction

The first four articles in the February 1913 issue of the *Journal of Political Economy* are about the curriculum and course of study at the then recently-established schools of business and commerce at universities and colleges in the United States.[1] The articles cover numerous pedagogical topics in business education, including the importance of ensuring business students obtain: "a considerable amount of contact with actual (business) conditions (Marshall 1913, p. 100)." In a footnote to the article the author, Leon C. Marshall the Dean of the then University of Chicago Business school, noted:

> The courses themselves will be run on the problem basis, as far as possible, and plans are under way for securing "case" material. In addition, the students will be taken on "field trips" and lecturers will be brought in from outside. It is recognized that *these field trips must*

---

[1] For a more extensive review of the issues colleges of business and commerce faced in their early years see Bohanon (2008).

C. E. Bohanon (✉)
Ball State University, Muncie, IN, USA
e-mail: cbohanon@bsu.edu

© The Author(s), under exclusive license to Springer Nature Switzerland AG 2021
J. Hall, K. Holder (eds.), *Off-Campus Study, Study Abroad, and Study Away in Economics*, Contributions to Economics,
https://doi.org/10.1007/978-3-030-73831-0_2

be so conducted as to make them real studies and not pleasure jaunts. It is also recognized that the outside lecturer is a real problem. However, neither field trips nor outside lectures present *insuperable difficulties.* Properly managed, they can be made to constitute two of our best pedagogical devices (Marshall 1913, p. 100). (emphasis added)

In a similar vein Dartmouth College Tuck School's future dean, H.S. Person reported:

Every possible method is employed to enable students to meet business men-lecturers-personally, and the lectures of such men are followed by a simple luncheon intended to enable the second-year men to meet the lecturers informally. Finally, the idea that thesis work shall be based upon *visits to industrial plants is encouraged by the desire that our students shall see and feel such a plant in action* (Person 1913, p. 124). (emphasis added)

The field trip, therefore, has a venerable history in business education. This article will catalogue more recent field trips taken over the last decade by this author as faculty advisor for the undergraduate student Economics Club at Ball State University in Muncie, Indiana.

The first section outlines what are in this faculty member's opinion the three basic requirements for executing an effective field trip for undergraduate students. The second section offers four examples of successful field trips. Note from the outset that all of these field trips have been for undergraduate students as a purely extracurricular activity. Nevertheless, the basic requirements for and examples of field trips are readily extendable to co-curricular activities at an undergraduate or graduate level. It is hoped that today's reader will concur with this faculty member and Dean Marshall that such trips have real value and present no "insuperable difficulties."

2.2   Basic Requirements

Educational field trips go to a location. The first and most obvious requirement is that there should be a *contact/sponsor* at the location to facilitate the group's activity. The purpose of the field trip is tied to the location and should usually entail formal participation by someone at that location. However, this latter requirement does not hold absolutely. A faculty member could, for example, self-direct a field trip to a museum taking students to exhibits to make points. Or simply release students in the museum and have them report back. However, even in the most accessible public venues, (think Art or History Museums, Public Parks etc.) it is useful to make contact with someone at the institution. Informing managers of a visit by a large group is a matter of simple courtesy. More important, such contact can often, if not usually, facilitate special programming by the institution that enhances the students' experience, often unlocking access to resources not typically available to the general public. Of course, a contact/sponsor is essential to gain entry to a private or public workplace, or to meet with an individual dignitary.

So where does a faculty member find these contact/sponsors? Many larger institutions such as Federal Reserve Banks or Museums have programs dedicated to accommodating student groups. Communications with those who facilitate these groups well in advance of the planned trip is essential. In addition, this faculty member has found that many of his university's alumni are quite willing to host student groups. This is especially true if the faculty member had the alumnus(a) as a student. Several years ago, this faculty member was cleaning the office and came across a class list from 20 years earlier. Several of these former students were contacted and were very happy to facilitate visits to their workplace by current students. In addition, the faculty member spearheading student trips can often find opportunities through their professional and social network. Many professionals are willing to host student groups and help design the field trip.

A second issue for a student field trip is *funding*. Even the afternoon trip to the local factory or non-profit agency requires access to transportation resources that the faculty member and students neither prefer nor should be expected to cover out-of-pocket. For longer trips other expenses come into play. Often funds for such trips are available within department, college, university or student affairs budgets, although it usually takes a bit of searching and cajoling to crack them open.

It has also been the experience of this faculty member that alumni, again, often former students, have been willing to make financial contributions to these efforts. Finally, there are number of Foundations that are willing to support such endeavors. It is obviously a good idea to construct a field trip description, timeline and budget for any individual trip before approaching a funding source. This faculty member has found that including current students in the planning process is itself useful and educational.

Once a field trip has been planned at a location with a contact/sponsor and financial arrangement have been made there are a number of *logistical* issues that must be addressed to ensure its smooth operation. In this faculty members experience his University requires a list of students who are going on the field trip— even if no university transportation is being used. At this university students may be excused from other classes if the field trip is approved by the Dean. It is important to note that these lists and approvals have to be finalized at least 3 days, more often 1 week in advance. A persistent issue is obtaining student commitment to the trip. A 10% attrition rate is typical, and University procedures make it almost impossible to add students at the last minute.

Of course, the mode of transportation must be procured before the trip. Most universities and even small colleges have available motor pools. For shorter trips with smaller numbers of students, faculty or approved students can drive. For longer trips with more students the school's transportation services may provide a certified driver for the trip. This, of course, must be arranged ahead of time and be part of the field trip budget. For longer trips that require air or train travel a professional travel agent should be used, especially if the group is large.

For longer trips provisions must be made for meals. Often specific restaurants have been contacted and are able to accommodate a large group with a common meal: a buffet or limited option menu. In other cases, students have been 'on their own' for meals and have borne the financial burden for their meals. In some cases, it has been possible to give students a university determined *per diem*. All these systems work, as long as all parties are well informed as to the arrangement. For any common meal it is important that dietary restrictions be communicated and accommodated. This is easily accomplished by surveying students before the trip.

For longer trips lodging of students becomes an issue. This faculty member has always insisted on same-gender room accommodation—and never had an issue with the arrangement. It this faculty member's experience safety and convenience to the locations to be visited are the most important factors in accommodation choice. Students have been packed four-to-a-room with little negative feedback.

It is quite important for all trips to communicate behavioral expectations to the student travelers *before* the trip. This can be accomplished via emails, often more than one. It is recommended, especially for full-day or longer trips that the students meet as a group, usually the day before the trip for a briefing about the trip so behavioral expectations can be established. Clear dress guidelines should be articulated, as well as expectations about student deportment in the presence of the hosts who will be visited—such as attentiveness on the part of the students to hosts and the expectation that students will ask informed and interesting questions.

It is very important that the efforts and resources expended by the host/sponsors be recognized and appreciated. In conjunction with the students and the university the field trips of this faculty member have routinely include small gifts of university branded 'swag' for the hosts/sponsors. Handwritten thank you notes have also been promptly sent by this faculty member after the trips and students are also organized to send personal thank you notes. Typically, the faculty organizer(s) and students meet for a debriefing session after the trip to organize thank you notes, and reflect on ways to improve the experience for future groups.

2.3 Four Examples

Four examples of the Economic Club's field trips are offered ranging from the simplest to the most complex.

2.3.1 *Late Afternoon Trip to Local Factory: Progress Rail*

Progress Rail is a division of Caterpillar Corporation with a production facility in Muncie, Indiana, the location of Ball State University. The factory makes locomotives for trains sold around the world. At a regular meeting of his Rotary Club, this faculty member became aware of Progress Rail having opened a Visitor Center eager to accommodate group visits. The visitors would learn of the history, production, marketing strategy, and employment opportunities of the company. The visit was further facilitated by a recent Ball State graduate who worked at the plant.

In the Fall of 2018 this faculty member along with a colleague accompanied a dozen students to the Progress Rail facility.

The group was met by a local manager and the recent Ball State alumnus who explained the firm's operations and the market conditions it faced. Students asked questions, left resumes and were exposed to a multi-national manufacturing operation. The trip left the college campus at 3:45 in afternoon on a university bus, toured the Visitor Center, leaving at 5:15 and arriving back on campus by 5:30.

2.3.2 All Day Trip to Indianapolis

This field trip has become a tradition for the third Thursday in October. The 2019 field trip commenced at 7:30 AM as twenty-three students (including one student from the university sponsored laboratory high school) and two faculty members left the Ball State campus on a university bus. The group arrived at the Indiana State Capitol at 9 AM. The group proceeded to tour the State Capitol guided by a volunteer trained to direct such groups. They then proceeded to the Indiana State Senate chamber (not in session) where a state elected officer, a legislator and a number of professional state employees gave short lectures about the functions of their offices.

The tour has been spearheaded through the years by a Ball State alumni who had been a student of this faculty member and gone on to obtain a law degree and now serves as legal counsel to the legislature. Several students brought resumes for internships for various positions at the State Capitol. The program ended at noon and was followed by a lunch delivered to the Senate Chambers.

The afternoon portion of the trip has traditionally been spent at a cultural institution in Indianapolis. Locations have included the Indianapolis based educational institution Liberty Fund, the Indianapolis Art Museum—known as Newfield's, and the Indianapolis Zoo. In all cases officials in the organization made presentations to the students and fielded questions. This year the group visited the Ray Bradbury museum and library located on the campus of Indiana University-Purdue University in Indianapolis (IUPUI). The group was met by the museum's director who gave an overview of Bradbury and the museum. The group was then allowed peruse much of its collection including Bradbury's personal effects and memorabilia. The director was pleased to note this group was among the largest ever to visit the museum.

2.3.3 Three-Day Trip to Chicago

Like the Indianapolis trip the Chicago trip has a long history with the Economics Club. In the spring of 2003, a then current student suggested the Club take a field trip to Chicago. His family was willing and able to host a group of five students and this faculty member in their home in suburban Chicago.

The 2019 field trip was arranged well in advance and students were excused from their regular classes. The seventeen students, two faculty members, a Ball State alumnus who had been on the original trip and the alumus's 10-year-old son, left Ball State campus at 8:30 AM on Thursday morning on a chartered bus for Chicago.

Over the years as the size of the group has grown. The alumnus who had originally instigated the trip in 2003 was able to arrange access to the facilities of the Union League Club of Chicago for accommodations. The students had been apprised of the Club's dress code and were always in compliance. Breakfast at the Club for both Friday and Saturday morning were included in the stay.

Upon arriving in Chicago, the group checked into the Union League Club and proceeded to the Chicago Board of Trade (CBOE), a 5-min walk from the Club. At the CBOE the group was met by an CBOE educator who explained the nature of the exchange, details of option positions and led the group to the floor of the exchange where live trading was observed. The group then left for the Federal Reserve Bank, a few minutes away by foot, for a presentation on the activities and policies of the bank by a Federal Reserve educator. This was followed by the group touring the Fed Museum at the same location. Students ended the day with dinner on-your-own. On this trip students received a university determined per-diem for this meal.

Friday consisted of visits to various workplaces and institutions in Chicago including the headquarters of Grub Hub, the downtown office of Whirlpool Corporation and the Newberry Library. The workplace visits were hosted by Ball State alumni and other contacts this faculty and the Chicago alumni have become acquainted with over the years.

Students were given three options for visits for both morning and afternoon and were accompanied by individual faculty. The individual groups were no larger than seven. This is an ideal size from a host's perspective and allows more one-on-one interaction between the host and the students. Many hosts encouraged students to bring or send resumes to their firm. Friday evening was completed by a buffet dinner at the Union League Club. The group left from Chicago on Saturday morning and arrived at Ball State campus midafternoon.

2.3.4 Spring Break Trip to New York City and AIER

The Ball State Economics Club's most extensive field trips have occurred during the University's spring break in early March. Destinations have included New York City and Washington D.C. In 2020 a group of ten students and two faculty members spent the bulk of the break at the campus of the American Institute for Economic Research (AIER) in Great Barrington, Massachusetts. The AIER campus accommodated each student in a private room and provided meals and hospitality. Activities included a visit to the nearby Norman Rockwell Museum.

The main focus of the trip, however, was to discuss in a group format a set of readings on trade, liberty and monetary policy during six, 90-min sessions led by

AIER staff. All the student and faculty participants read over 200 pages of material in preparation. Students remarked that this is what they wished college could be like! The topics covered were:

- Session 1: Harwood and classical liberal debate
  - Readings from E.C. Harwood
- Session 2: Introduction to monetary theory
  - Readings from David Hume and Karl Menger
- Session 3: Future of money
  - Readings from Armen Alchian, George Selgin, and William Luther
- Session 4: Introduction to trade
  - Readings from Adam Smith, Frédéric Bastiat, and David Hume
- Session 5: Regulation and trade
  - Readings by David Ricardo and Henry George
- Session 6: History of economic freedom
  - Reading from Deirdre McCloskey

The time at AIER was preceded and followed by time in New York City. This time included meeting informally with Ball State alumni, visiting historical and cultural sites in New York and the group attending the Broadway production of *To Kill a Mockingbird*.

2.4 Conclusions

The financial costs of these field trips have ranged from under a hundred dollars to nearly ten thousand dollars. The Ball State Economics Club has been very fortunate to be able to offer these opportunities to students at minimal out-of-pocket expense to the students. This has occurred because of the generosity of the Department, its alumni base and outside Foundations. This faculty member's advice to other faculty who wish to cultivate similar educational opportunities is two-fold: start small and grow; and work your network.

It is also very important to report the activities in a timely manner to donors. Once this is done the best approach is to expand on what worked and ask for more! The obstacles are not "insuperable." This faculty member has found that the students who select into such activities are inevitable among the best and the brightest. He is very grateful for the support from them, his colleagues, his former students and supporting foundations for helping develop these unique educational opportunities, that have clearly gone beyond mere "pleasure jaunts" and constituted "real studies."

References

Bohanon CE (2008) Persistent themes in colleges of business. J Educ Bus. 83(4):239–245

Marshall LC (1913) The college of commerce and administration of the University of Chicago. J Polit Econ 21(2):97–110

Person HS (1913) The Amos Tuck School of Dartmouth College. J Polit Econ 21(2):117–126

Chapter 3
Economic Journeys in Alaska

Alice Louise Kassens

Abstract In May of 2015 and 2018 a group of students participated in "Economic Journeys—Alaska" an intensive learning course to Southeastern Alaska. Led by an economics professor and an assistant, the group explored three economic drivers, both current and historical, of the northernmost state: tourism, fishing, and gold. Guided by daily prompts the students journaled about their experiences, offering insight and observations through an economic lens.

3.1 Introduction

In May of 2015 and 2018 eleven students from a small liberal arts college participated in "Economic Journeys—Alaska" a one credit, intensive learning course in Southeastern Alaska during a May Term.[1] Led by an economics professor and an assistant, the group explored three of the four primary economic drivers, both current and historical, of the northernmost state: tourism, fishing, and, gold.[2] The oil industry was omitted since it is in a portion of the state not visited by the group. Guided by daily prompts the students journaled about their experiences, offering insight and observations through an economic lens. Students returned rate the course highly and their writing assignments and discussion indicate that they learn a considerable amount on the trip and develop a deep appreciation for the state and its economic forces.

---

[1]Most courses at the College are one credit. Students must pass 33.5 credits to graduate. A one credit May Term course is required of all students at the College. Some May Term options are travel courses, but all are intensive, exploratory courses covering a 2–3 week period.

[2]The institution requires all travel courses to have an adult assistant. In this case, the assistant was another member of the economics faculty and husband of the faculty leader.

A. L. Kassens (✉)
Roanoke College, Salem, VA, USA
e-mail: kassens@roanoke.edu

© The Author(s), under exclusive license to Springer Nature Switzerland AG 2021
J. Hall, K. Holder (eds.), *Off-Campus Study, Study Abroad, and Study Away in Economics*, Contributions to Economics,
https://doi.org/10.1007/978-3-030-73831-0_3

3.2 Learning Objectives

The learning objectives, noted on the course syllabus, are "[u]pon completion of the course students will be able to:

1. Display a firm grasp of economic knowledge and concepts.
2. Demonstrate proficiency in a variety of communication skills.
3. Critically reflect on their learning about economics journalism and the Alaskan economy in an intensive learning environment."

The sole prerequisite of the course is principles of microeconomics or principles of macroeconomics so that each student has a working knowledge of basic economic concepts.

3.3 Logistics

The group met at an airport hotel in Charlotte the afternoon before the flight. Students got to Charlotte on their own. Many came from campus which is a 3-h drive. Flights to the west coast are often in the early morning. It is best to have everyone gathered the day before to avoid missing a flight. The group flew to Seattle a few days prior to the embarkation, again to avoid logistical issues due to travel delays through the airline. Inexpensive, clean, and safe lodging is available through a variety of online sites. In 2018 the group stayed in rented condominiums, each housing up to six people and considerably cheaper than comparable hotels.

A cruise of the Southeastern portion of Alaska, particularly in May before the peak tourism season begins, is a cost-effective way of visiting the distant state. The ample entertainment aboard is enjoyable for the students while traveling from location to location. The group selected a tour that embarked and disembarked in the same locale which made airline reservations easier and cheaper. Students submitted $2900 for the entire 12-day trip, including airfare, hotel, food, and the ship ticket. The faculty gave over $400 back to the students to spend on the trip. The $2500 net amount included the faculty and assistant fares.[3]

3.4 Schedule and Assignments

The course is divided into two parts, travel and post-travel. The travel portion is the period in which students gather most of the content for their written submissions. When in port, the class meets in the morning to establish an agenda and discuss the

---

[3] The College's policy is that the student fee, which is due several months prior to the trip, includes the faculty member and assistant's costs. The amount also includes an administrative fee by the College.

3 Economic Journeys in Alaska

assignment and in the evening to review the day. On "at sea" days the faculty leaders schedule individual meetings with students to review and edit student assignments. Once the class returns to the mainland the course enters the second portion in which students independently edit their assignments for final submission. Students are also required to submit a take-home final exam that includes reflection and course assessment.

The course includes four assignments, three of which are graded using the grading rubric. The rubric is the same one used college-wide to evaluate writing in the social sciences. The initial drafts reviewed during the individual meetings are scored using a check system ($\checkmark-$, $\checkmark$, and $\checkmark+$). The first assignment is a trial-run in Seattle, the location of embarkation for the Alaskan journey. The final three assignments are equally weighted and are a formal part of the course assessment. A brief outline of each assignment and student responses are shown below.

1. (Seattle) Discuss the real estate market in Seattle. Comment on the economic factors driving the market.

   The class spends a few days in Seattle before embarking. Some of that time is used to prepare students for the Alaska portion of the class, including giving them a 'dry run' of an assignment. In 2018, a lunch meeting with a Seattle-area real estate agent was hosted at the Rainier Club. The agent shared the current status and history of the Seattle real estate market over lunch. Students were encouraged to ask questions and used information from the meeting and their own research to complete the assignment. While not graded, the assignment went through the same process as the remaining, graded assignments, including sharing a draft with the faculty to review individually with the student author. One of the faculty knew the Seattle real estate agent who met with our group. For those without such a connection, you might consider contacting local offices via email well in advance of the trip.

2. (JUNEAU) Discuss the economic impact of the salmon hatchery.

   The class travelled by public transportation to the Macaulay Salmon Hatchery and took a tour of the facility. The group learned about the life cycle of salmon and the role of hatcheries in maintaining the Alaskan fishing industry. Students asked the guide various questions and explored the facility after the tour taking notes along the way for their written assignment. Tours of the hatchery are open to the public for a small fee per person but contacting the hatchery ahead of time is ideal to ensure that they are open and not booked for the day by a cruise ship group.[4]

3. (SKAGWAY) Discuss the economic impact of the Klondike Gold Rush (before and after).

   Skagway played a crucial role in the Klondike Gold Rush in the nineteenth century. Today the town pays tribute to that history as a national park. The group took a private tour of Skagway. The faculty leaders contacted the park office in

---

[4]All contact information is available on their webpage: http://www.dipac.net.

Skagway prior to the trip and the tour was adjusted to focus on the economic impact of the Gold Rush. The park ranger brought black and white photos along to complement the tour. Skagway is always the favorite stop and assignment amongst the students. The tour is free of charge, but to customize the tour and reserve it just for your group, you must contact the park office well in advance.[5]

4. (KETCHIKAN) Select a several square block area near the waterfront and count the share of locally owned shops. Ask at least three people if ownership (local vs. cruise line) influences their decision to shop in a store. Why or why not? If so, are they willing to pay more for a locally owned product? Might there be different motivations for local store owners compared to those owned by the cruise line? Explain. Go into at least one of each type of store. Do you notice any differences? Explain.

Cruise lines own a large share of the prime commercial real estate along the common cruise routes in Alaska which causes some local resentment. Locally owned stores place a sticker in their window indicating resident ownership. Shops owned by the cruise line primarily employ within and shift their workers to warmer locations after the Alaskan tourism season is over. Prior to this assignment, students are instructed to remember their role as representatives of the College and respect individual requests to not answer their questions. The questions are informal and no identifying information of interviewees is collected. Students took notes on their observations and answers to their questions.

3.5 Process and Required Materials

Students are encouraged to type their assignments on a tablet or laptop but are required to bring a notebook on the trip due to both the mobile nature of the assignments and the inconsistent Internet access in Alaska. Perhaps for the first time in their lives, students found that typing on a tablet was inconvenient, and taking a pen to paper was preferable. Students are encouraged upon returning to the ship to type up and detail their handwritten notes while ideas are fresh and to prepare for the daily group discussions and recaps.

---

[5]The park office webpage provides all needed information: https://www.nps.gov/klgo/planyourvisit/walking-tours.htm.

3 Economic Journeys in Alaska

Students ranged from sophomores to seniors, with a range of writing experience. In addition to the daily feedback from the faculty leaders, students are required to purchase and bring Knight's (2010) *Journalistic Writing: Building the Skills, Honing the Craft*. Available in both paperback and electronically, the reference is concise and clear in explanation with ample examples of common writing issues such as lack of word economy. Students are encouraged to read the book in its entirety, but sections are assigned to assist in various assignments.

The faculty leaders also curated various references pertaining to the Alaska economy, primarily the current tourism and fishing industries and the historical impact of the Gold Rush. The files are shared with the students prior to leaving for Alaska using a shared electronic file. Students are encouraged to read through the items while traveling to Alaska. The readings are discussed in group meetings aboard the ship and inform the students prepare the students for their assignments.[6]

3.6 Tips

The following is a list of tips accumulated during the trips to Alaska.

1. Make a list of places students should explore, including hiking trails and museums, while on their own. Students enjoy the freedom of exploring on their own without the forced participation in group activities. For example, a tour of the Starbucks facility in Seattle was the lowest rated activity of the entire trip. Some reported that they might have done it on their own, but overall did not enjoy the organized nature of the tour.
2. Most major airlines allow bidding for blocks of tickets for groups larger than ten. Instructions for each airline are available online. The faculty organizing the Alaska trip bid in both 2015 and 2018 and saved close to $100 per student over the ticket prices offered through other discount sites.
3. Buy the plane tickets as a block so that the entire group can check in at once, saving time at check-in at the airport.
4. Arrive in the city of embarkation at least 1 day in advance. If flights to the location are cancelled, the ship will not wait for the group.
5. Cruise lines often offer discounts on cabins with three of more people. The Alaska trip got the fourth student at no additional cost for several rooms.
6. Remind students of forbidden items and activities to avoid issues with ship security.
7. Remind students that ships do not wait for tardy passengers and make a plan for students left in port.
8. Cruise ships require passports be valid for several months after embarkation. Given the time required to get or renew a passport, faculty should personally

---

[6]A good place to start is Goldsmith (2008) and various issues of *Alaska Economic Trends* by the Alaska Department of Labor and Workforce Development.

inspect student passports several months in advance of the trip. The cruise line often requires a copy of the passport during the ticketing process.

9. Create social media accounts (ex. Facebook and Instagram) for the group trip to keep parents up to date on planning prior to the trip and experiences during the trip.
10. Encourage students to pack economically but prepare for the anticipated weather in Alaska.

3.7 Conclusion

Alaska is a location not often considered for undergraduate travel courses. For a relatively small amount of money, a course that explores the current and historical underpinnings of the economy for the northern-most state is possible. The course applies economic lessons while cultivating student observation, critical thinking, and writing skills.

"Economic Journeys—Alaska" was taught in 2015 and 2018. Most of this chapter includes lessons and tips learned from the first iteration in 2015 that were applied in 2018. If the course is taught a third time, there are a few things that we would adjust. First, when using public transportation, there is often a short walk to and from the bus stop. Not all students are used to walking distances of a half mile, so tell them all in advance how much walking is involved. This will help avoid inappropriate footwear and complaints about walking. If you have students or faculty who cannot walk, you will need to investigate the best way to travel to and from the ship and to various activities. Most ships have vans to take passengers into town from the ship, but not to specific destinations (without an additional charge.)

Acknowledgments Thank you to Michael Enz (Roanoke College) who served as my assistant on the exploration trip (2014) and the two trips with students (2015 and 2018). We might all still be in Ketchikan otherwise.

References

Goldsmith S (2008) What drives the Alaska economy? Institute for Social and Economic Research, Anchorage

Knight RM (2010) Journalistic writing: building the skills, honing the craft. Marion Street Press, Portland

Chapter 4
Off-Campus Colloquia as Immersive Study and Active Learning: Capitaf, Milton and Rose Friedman's Home

Signè Thomas and Samuel R. Staley

Abstract In this paper, two facilitators of an off-campus colloquia series examine its effectiveness as an alternative to study-abroad programs. The paper evaluates a week-long seminar in political economy held in the Vermont mountains at Capitaf, the former summer home of Nobel Prize-winning economist Milton Friedman and his wife, Rose. The colloquium is structured to foster active learning by combining intensive reading and discussion of Friedman's critical writings, and immerse students in the place where the economist conducted most of his writing in the late 1960s and 1970s. More than 60 undergraduate students have experienced the program. The program has had a deep, lasting impact on students, as revealed through open-end comments and responses to post-colloquium assessments.

4.1 Introduction

Colleges and universities are under increasing pressure to demonstrate value. An important measure of value, and some might say the most important measure, is the ability to foster learning among students, particularly undergraduate students. Authentic learning is one of the principal pedagogies associated with both active and student-centered learning.

Active learning is a pedagogy that seeks to involve students directly in the learning process, as opposed to the more passive learning style of a traditional lecture. In order to be considered as 'active learning,' students must do more than just listen. For example, they must read, write, discuss, or be engaged in solving problems. Furthermore, they need to be engaged in higher-order cognitive tasks,

---

S. Thomas (✉)
Trinity College, Hartford, CT, USA
e-mail: signe.thomas@trincoll.edu

S. R. Staley
Florida State University, Tallahassee, FL, USA
e-mail: sstaley@fsu.edu

© The Author(s), under exclusive license to Springer Nature Switzerland AG 2021
J. Hall, K. Holder (eds.), *Off-Campus Study, Study Abroad, and Study Away in Economics*, Contributions to Economics,
https://doi.org/10.1007/978-3-030-73831-0_4

such as analysis, synthesis, and evaluation (Bonwell and Eison 1991; Chickering and Gamson 1987). Scholars have identified scores of tools, techniques, and strategies for promoting active learning, including tools for enabling student-centered discussion rather than lecture, using applied projects to foster deeper understanding of principles and concepts, and establishing a classroom climate supportive of experimentation and exploration (Ambrose et al. 2010; Doyle 2011).

Active learning methods tend to also foster authentic learning, if implemented with applications to the real-world in mind. Rule's (2006) editorial in *The Journal of Authentic Learning* addresses the key themes and elements of authentic learning. She found that in her analysis of forty-five articles that described authentic learning, each contained at least one of four major themes that she believes to be central to authentic learning. These major themes are: (1) real-world problems that allow the learner to practice doing the work of professionals in the discipline, with presentation of findings to audiences beyond the classroom; (2) open-ended inquiry that involves critical thinking and metacognition (analyzing one's own thinking); (3) discourse in a community of learners; and (4) student empowerment through choice to further direct their own learning (Rule 2006). The Capitaf colloquia are consistent with the second and third themes. Maina (2004) identified the following as elements inherent within authentic learning: activities mimic real world situations, learning takes place in meaningful situations that are extensions of the learner's world, and the teaching is learner-centered.

Expounding on that definition in his book *Learner-Centered Teaching: Putting the Research Learning Into Practice*, Doyle (2011) says that authentic learning embodies not only the use of real problems but also seeks to have students use methods that are used in the real world, including teamwork and collaboration, technology, and the professional presentation of processes and solutions.

Most of the active and authentic learning recommendations, however, focus on traditional courses as conventional academic offerings. Relatively little research has focused on immersive, small-group study outside the more conventional setting of a course. This chapter explores the application of active learning pedagogies to off-campus study in a domestic U.S. setting. For the past 3 years, groups of ten to twelve undergraduate students have studied the economic and political thought of Nobel Prize-winning economist Milton Friedman while residing at Capitaf, his former summer home in Vermont. The setting allows for a unique immersive experience that, based on assessments provided by students, promotes transformative learning.

The next section of this paper provides an overview of recent literature on study-away programs to provide overall context, and the sections thereafter provide an overview of Capitaf and the program. The paper concludes with a discussion of its impact on students and their learning.

4.2 Benefits of Off-Campus Study

Study abroad experiences have been an integral part of higher education for centuries. In recent years, some universities and colleges have moved toward calling these ventures 'study away' programs as they have recognized that meaningful educational experiences and growth opportunities can occur off campus without being international.

Sobania and Braskamp (2009, p. 23) explain why they prefer the term study away:

> If a common goal of diversity and multicultural programs and internationalization programs is to assist students to live effectively with difference, why do we assume only an international program experience can do this? If there are critical skills we want students to acquire and engage in, does it matter whether these are acquired internationally or locally? Thus, we argue for retiring the terms 'study abroad' and 'education abroad,' and instead adopting 'study away.'

A review of 13 studies by Kelleher (2013) found wide-ranging benefits across different study-away programs. Students considered it to be 'enriching,' 'enlightening,' and even their best life experience. A 2018 study showed that cultural competency may be enhanced through curriculum-integrated study-away opportunities. Moreover, domestic study-away and international study-away opportunities can accomplish similar student cultural competency outcomes (Abe-Hiraishi et al. 2018).

Short-term study-away experiences are becoming increasingly popular as well. These programs do not have as pressing of financial, employment, and time constraints as longer-term programs do. Short-term programs are usually less than 8 weeks, while long-term study-away tends to be for at least a semester, sometimes even a year (Zamastil-Vondrova 2005; Donnelly-Smith 2009; Mills et al. 2010; Carley et al. 2011; Slotkin et al. 2012).

In terms of pedagogy, these types of off-campus study opportunities provide enhanced environments for fostering active and authentic learning. Academic preparation can take place in more traditional settings, while the off-campus locations have the benefit of limiting distractions, fostering faculty-student and student-student interaction, and creating a classroom climate that is more inclusive, welcoming, and intellectually 'safe.' These characteristics are consistent with best practices for fostering authentic learning and effective learner-centered discussions.

Slotkin et al. (2012) also showcase blended-learning models for their short-term study-abroad programs for business students, highlighting the flexibility offered by making use of online learning prior to the trip to fulfill academic content requirements. Similarly, the Capitaf programs follow a blended model of preparation and participation. All participating students are provided with the core course materials 1 to 2 months in advance of the colloquia, and instructed to read the books prior to arriving at Capitaf.

Study-away experiences provide students with an opportunity to gain self-confidence and become more independent as they step out of their comfort zone.

An additional benefit of domestic study-away opportunities is that they are generally less expensive than study-away experiences abroad, and therefore it expands such learning and personal growth opportunities to more students.

4.3 The Capitaf Immersive Study Program

Few homes possess such significance as to have earned their own name and place in history. Just as Thomas Jefferson's Monticello and George Washington's Mount Vernon have importance to historians, Milton and Rose Friedman's Capitaf has special meaning to economists. 'Capitaf' is the name that Milton and Rose Friedman gave their home in Vermont. The house was named in honor of their book *Capitalism and Freedom* (Friedman 2002[1962]), the title of which they cleverly morphed together to create the name Capitaf. The main house is pictured in Fig. 4.1.

Milton and Rose purchased the property in Fairlee, Vermont in 1965, completed Capitaf in 1967, and sold it to the University of Chicago in 1982. The university sold the property to Robert Aliber, a faculty member at the University of Chicago Booth School of Business. In 2012, Aliber sold the property to Mark Mitchell, a former colleague of Aliber at the University of Chicago Business School. Free to Choose Network, led by Bob Chitester, recruited six individuals in founding Capitaf Partners, LLC and purchased the property in July 2016 for the purpose of scholarly economic programs. Robert Aliber had added a tennis court and built a second

Fig. 4.1 The main house where discussions take place. Source: Author's collection

Fig. 4.2 Student housing. Source: Author's collection

guest house on the property, which the Free to Choose Network adapted to serve as a dormitory for up to twelve students participating in the residential colloquia (Fig. 4.2).

Free To Choose Network has been instrumental in keeping the ideas and teachings of the Friedmans alive through various media projects and launching the colloquia series on the Capitaf property. Chitester worked directly with the Friedmans as executive producer of the award-winning *Free To Choose* television series. The book by the same name was based on transcripts of the TV series and was written by the Friedmans while at Capitaf in the summer and autumn of 1979.

Chitester adds a personal touch for those attending a Capitaf colloquium, as students hear a first-hand account of many stories of the Friedmans and of the filming of the television series. Chitester has recorded nearly two dozen videos sharing some aspects of his work with the Friedmans so students can still benefit from his first-hand accounts even when he is not able to attend a colloquium in person.

Capitaf's unique and secluded setting allows for colloquium participants to fully immerse themselves in discussion. The home, designed by the Friedmans and custom built by local contractors, contains unique artifacts and architectural elements reflecting the Friedmans' living sensibilities as well as conceptual designs inspired by Frank Lloyd Wright. The property sits along the top of a ridge and includes a beautiful view featuring the Vermont mountains, Lake Fairlee, and a pond at the bottom of the hillside. The serene and secluded location was a perfect respite from the hectic pace of teaching at the University of Chicago. It allowed the

Friedmans to focus on their writings, visit Baker Library at Dartmouth College for research, and to interact with other summer residents which included both Arthur F. Burns and John Galbraith. Envisioning a Nobel prize winning scholar writing important work becomes tangible for colloquia participants.

Each colloquium's contemporary discussions take place in the living room of the hexagonal main building that was the original home of the Friedmans. A short walk down the hill is student housing, which contains the personal library of Aaron Director, translations of Friedman's books into foreign languages, and books autographed and inscribed to Bob Chitester for his efforts creating the *Free To Choose* television series. Director, who is Rose Friedman's brother, is considered by many as the founder of the Law and Economics movement. Historic elements of Friedman's original home include the clapperboard from the filming of the *Free To Choose* t.v. series and Rose Friedman's elephant souvenir collection.

At many universities, academic credit is not offered for participating in the Capitaf colloquium itself. Nevertheless, quite a few students who attend the colloquium have already completed a semester-long course focused on the content, such as the 'Free to Choose' course offered at FSU. Hence, many of the FSU participants have read the book *Free to Choose* (Friedman and Friedman 1980), watched the public television series of the same name, and have some experience discussing policy issues prior to the colloquium. Regardless of whether students have taken such a course, all participants are provided reading materials in advance of the seminar and are expected to be familiar with the content prior to arriving at Capitaf.

4.3.1 Participation

As of May 2020, 63 students have participated in six Capitaf colloquia, with enrollments evenly split between those organized by University of Arkansas (32) and Florida State University (31). Table 4.1 provides an overview of the colloquia enrollments.

While the facilities impose a hard cap of thirteen students—based on bed space— universities can include a mix of institutions. Partnerships with other universities are encouraged even if one institution is the primary organizer. Thus, while the University of Arkansas (UA) and Florida State University (FSU) limited enrollment in their first colloquia to their respective institutions, subsequent colloquia included student representatives from Lindenwood University (LU), Ashland University (AU), Ball State University (BSU), and the University of Central Arkansas (UCA).

The mixed university enrollment structure has also been successful. In summer 2019, the University of Arkansas's colloquium included nine of their students, two from the University of Central Arkansas, and one from Ball State University in Indiana. Two of FSU's summer 2019 colloquia included mixes of university participants. FSU's May 2019 colloquium included two students from Lindenwood University in Missouri. (LU also organized a subsequent colloquium for university

Table 4.1 Colloquia enrollments, 2017–2019

Sponsoring University	Date	Participation	Participating Universities
University of Arkansas	August 2017	10	UA
University of Arkansas	August 2018	10	UA
Florida State University	August 2018	10	FSU
Florida State University	May 2019	11	FSU, LU
University of Arkansas	August 2019	12	UA, UCA, BSU
Florida State University	August 2019	10	FSU, AU

faculty later that August.) Two students from Ashland University in Ohio attended FSU's August 2019 session. Feedback has shown that students greatly valued having the perspective of students from other universities participate in the discussions.

4.3.2 Funding and Contacts

Capitaf is owned and maintained by Capitaf Partners, LLC. Free To Choose Network is a member of the LLC and has the responsibility to develop educational use of the estate. Free To Choose Network (FTCN) is a nonprofit foundation established in part to curate and promote Milton and Rose Friedman's intellectual and public policy work. As of 2019, the average cost per student to participate in a Capitaf colloquium was $2100. This fee is inclusive of lodging, meals, and site visits. Individual programs (and students) are responsible for funding their transit to Capitaf. FTCN maintains the property, conducts scheduling, and participates in each of the colloquia. FTCN representatives provide intellectual context, biographical background on the Friedmans, and details on the history and importance of the property. Colloquia are scheduled through FTCN by contacting the Founder and Executive Chairman (Bob Chitester) or the President and CEO (Robert Chatfield).

Funding models also vary depending on availability of resources and program design. University of Arkansas fully funds their students, covering the colloquium fee (which includes lodging, food, and excursions), transportation from Boston to Capitaf, plus transportation to/from their home location to Boston. Similarly, LU fully funded their students, but used a competitive process for selecting students to attend, similar to a fellowship competition.

FSU, on the other hand, pays for the colloquium fee and transportation from Boston to Capitaf, but requires students to pay for their own transportation to Boston. FSU uses a more inclusive recruiting strategy, relying on interest from classes and general notices. The transportation cost requirement puts 'skin in the game' for students who want to attend, while also providing flexibility in transportation arrangements. (One student chose to drive from Florida to Vermont, using the opportunity to sight-see along the way, extend their stay in Boston, and visit Bretton Woods.)

4.4 Colloquia Learning Objectives and Structures

The colloquium's target audience is college students, although it has also served as a unique and highly effective location for faculty, too. In terms of learning objectives, by the end of the seminar, students are expected to be able to: (a) recognize the value of economic principles and theories in evaluating and shaping public policy, (b) identify and recognize core values that underlie world views that shape approaches to political economy, (c) critically evaluate different perspectives on political economy as well as the principles on which policy recommendations are made, (d) more fully understand the intellectual foundations that may underlie or inform approaches to public policy, (e) verbally articulate personal positions and ideas on political economy, and (f) synthesize ideas, values, and principles to form a coherent understanding of political economy.

The colloquia are structured to create an inclusive, accepting, and tolerant seminar climate, a critical component of promoting deep structure learning and effective discussion (Ambrose et al. 2010, pp. 153–179; Howard 2015). Facilitators use the environment, separation from conventional campus activity, and norm setting guidelines to create this climate. The program begins with the phased arrival of students on Sunday. Faculty sometimes travel with the students by bus from Boston to Hanover, Vermont, but all students are transported by faculty from Hanover to Capitaf. This time is used to introduce faculty to students and begin establishing personal relationships. Prior to the first formal meeting (on Sunday evening), students are encouraged to socialize with each other and establish collaborative protocols for assigning beds and tasks in the guest house. Sunday night is a collective dinner where everyone, including faculty and facilitators, introduces themselves and discusses their motivations for attending the seminar. Each lunch and dinner is structured to encourage this personal interaction.

During the discussion sessions, facilitators establish clear guidelines, emphasizing that all ideas and perspectives are welcome as part of a civil and authentic discussion. While the readings are focused on Milton and Rose Friedmans' contributions to political economy which are from a free-market, classical liberal perspective, discussants should be willing, and will be encouraged, to challenge these ideas. Students are expected to refer to each other by name. A discussion queue is kept during each session to ensure all students are able to participate, although none are forced to contribute.

The pedagogy of the colloquia is centered around a modified Socratic dialogue. The students participate in guided discussion, facilitated by faculty (usually faculty from their own university, and also sometimes assisted by a member of the Free to Choose Network). Prior to coming to a Capitaf colloquium, each student reads *Capitalism and Freedom* and *Free to Choose*, and occasionally excerpts from other readings such as *Road to Serfdom* by Hayek (1944), essays from *Morality of Capitalism: What Your Professors Won't Tell You* (Palmer 2011) by authors including Mario Llosa, Vernon Smith, and John Mackey, or *Defending the Free Market: The Moral Case for A Free Market* by Robert Sirico (2012) (a Catholic priest). The Socratic discussions throughout the week provide an opportunity for students to answer open-ended questions, listen and reflect on the ideas presented by others, and then formulate and articulate their own response to the intellectual points raised. As one student wrote during his assessment: At Capitaf,

> we spend our mornings discussing Friedman's economic theories while mixing in our own experiences and opinions. These friendly debates have actually changed my opinions in countless ways as other students helped 'Bring me to the light' on many issues. We spend our afternoons relaxing on the mountaintop and our nights on the lake, and I've never experienced such a mixed group of people get along so well.

The discussions permit a type of active learning that many students are not able to experience in large lecture classes back at their university. The Socratic method combined with a Liberty Fund-style facilitation of queuing discussants enables 100% participation. A 3 min position exercise at the end of each day allows students to consider the major lessons of the day, identify open questions, and reinforce their ability to verbally articulate their thoughts while probing the perspectives and insights of other participants. The student-centered approach allowed the students to explore different perspectives and approaches to economic theory, economic reasoning, and public policy—even in chapters where the content was dated such as restraint of trade and monopoly.

Respectful and inclusive culture is essential to ensuring active participation and the ability to vet a wide range of viewpoints. The inclusive environment provided a safe space for students to challenge their own ideas and that of others, reflect, present contrarian viewpoints, and explore the deeper understanding of values, principles, and experiences. As one student wrote in an evaluation: "The atmosphere and people and ideas all came together to make an experience that I don't think could be replicated anywhere else."

4.5   Program and Discussion Structure

The structure of the week-long residential program consists of fourteen discussion sessions, each focused on specific chapters of the selected readings, daily 3-min student positions, and site visits selected to deepen the students' understanding of Milton Friedman's intellectual journey and the functioning of entrepreneurial capitalism.

Prior to each colloquium, faculty assign specific chapters to each student to present to the group to start the discussion. The student leading the discussion for a given chapter provides a brief summary of what they believe the key points are in the chapter, and poses a question to the group. This enables a student-driven discussion which encourages deep structure learning (Howard 2015) and authentic learning (Doyle 2011). Faculty are present and assist with facilitating (or when necessary, moderating) dialogue, pose supplemental questions to provoke deeper thought or to question assumptions, occasionally correct factual inaccuracies, and ensure inclusive participation.

4.5.1 Days One and Two

The first day at Capitaf is focused on settling in, meeting participants, and establishing protocols and ground rules. The students arrive on Sunday, and the first discussions of content occur promptly on Monday morning (Day 2). The faculty start off with an introduction to Friedman, Capitaf, and the readings. Next comes Session 1, where the students discuss the first chapter of *Capitalism and Freedom* ("The Relation Between Economic Freedom and Political Freedom") along with the first chapter of *Free to Choose* ("The Power of the Market"). A few questions a moderator might pose during Session 1 include:

- What does Friedman have to say about 'democratic socialism'?
- What does Friedman mean when he says that history suggests only that capitalism is a necessary condition for political freedom, but not a sufficient condition?

Session 2 is centered around the second chapter of *Capitalism and Freedom* ("The Role of Government in a Free Society") and the second chapter of *Free to Choose* ("The Tyranny of Controls"). A few discussion questions related to Session 2:

- Should the government's power to spend be limited by an amendment to the Constitution?
- Name an example of a paternalistic justification for a current policy. Why does Friedman generally oppose paternalism in policymaking?

Each session is separated by 15-min breaks. An hour is reserved for a catered lunch. After lunch, students dive into Session 3, with a focus on chapter 4 of *Capitalism and Freedom*: "International Financial and Trade Arrangements." A few questions for thought pertaining to the topic of this chapter include:

- Why were the Smoot-Hawley tariffs enacted and what was the effect of these policies?
- Would the United States benefit from getting rid of tariffs even if other countries did not remove the tariffs that they have placed on the U.S.?
- When he wrote *Capitalism and Freedom* in 1962, what did Friedman believe to be the greatest threat to economic freedom in the short run? If alive today, do you think he would consider something else to be the greatest threat?

Session 4 consists of discussion around chapter 6 from each book: "The Role of Government in Education" from *Capitalism and Freedom*, and "What's Wrong With Our Schools?" in *Free to Choose*. To stimulate discussion, the colloquium moderators might prompt the students with the following:

- Discuss the pros and cons of a school voucher program.
- How is Friedman's argument for school vouchers influenced by his belief that the lowest levels of schooling do the most to promote a stable and democratic society?

- Some believe inner-city public schools protect equality for minorities, and that open competition from a voucher system might dismantle such schools and bring harm to the goal of equality. Construct an argument for or against this assertion.

The last session of each day includes a '3 Minute Position' discussion. All students are expected to participate, but volunteers are solicited for the opening position statements. The group provides facilitated feedback. By the end of the week, each student will have had at least one turn giving a 3 Minute Position. These 3 Minute Position sessions enable the students the opportunity to formulate a cohesive argument, and gives them practice articulating their thoughts and responding to push-back from their peers. While all discussion sessions are designed to encourage critical thinking, these final sessions are explicitly designed to facilitate critical elements of deeper levels of thinking and authentic learning: synthesis, analysis, integration, and application of principles beyond the seminar.

Students are then given about 90 min for free time prior to dinner. The faculty facilitators schedule special dinner guests to visit with the students on various evenings. These dinner guests often provide practical insight into contemporary issues of political economy and, in the case of Capitaf, do not necessarily have a direct connection to the day's content. For example, speakers have included experts on zoning, health care reform, and second amendment issues. The speakers are invited for their insight, perspective, and conversation. After dinner, students have the rest of each evening to read in the library, which includes many early editions of major texts on economics and political economy, spend quiet time in reflection, discuss the day's activities, or play games. Figure 4.3 shows the authors re-reading the works of the Friedmans (and enjoying the view!) during downtime in the day.

Fig. 4.3 Authors preparing for discussion during downtime. Source: Author's collection

4.5.2 Day Three

This day consists of three discussion sessions and then the rest of the afternoon is dedicated to an excursion. Session 6 kicks off Tuesday's first scholarly session, with discussion on chapter 8 of *Capitalism and Freedom*: "Monopoly and the Social Responsibility of Business and Labor." Questions for thought related to the material covered in Session 6 include:

- What is an example of a government-supported monopoly Friedman supports and one that he opposes? Why does he support the former but not the latter?
- What is Friedman's view on corporate social responsibility? What is your view?

Session 7 consists of *Capitalism and Freedom's* chapter 9 ("Occupational Licensure") and *Free to Choose's* chapter 8 ("Who Protects the Worker?"). Discussion questions include:

- What is the typical rationale given when government officials restrict who can legally practice an occupation? What tends to actually be the source of the demand for such restrictions: concerned consumers, or individuals/businesses already practicing in the occupation?
- What is the key difference between certification versus licensing requirements? Which did Friedman believe to be the better system, and why? Which do you support, and why?
- What are secondary effects of licensing requirements? Discuss potential pros and cons in various industries.

Session 8, as in the previous day, wraps up the morning discussions with more 3 Minute Positions. After lunch, students participate in a scholarship/research oriented site visit to Dartmouth College, where Dartmouth faculty give a lecture about the times that Milton Friedman spent using the Baker Library. Faculty provide background on Friedman's relationship with Vermont and Dartmouth. The Friedmans used their home in Vermont as quiet and study times during the summers, but Milton Friedman used the Baker Library as his primary center for research. Later, as teaching responsibilities became less onerous, the Friedmans would split their time evenly between Chicago and Capitaf. Nearly all of Milton's writing was done from Vermont or New Hampshire.

4.6 Day Four

Like the day prior, Wednesday consists of three discussion sessions and another site visit during the afternoon. Session 9's focus is chapter 10 ("The Distribution of Income") of *Capitalism and Freedom*, and chapter 5 ("Created Equal") of *Free to Choose*. Questions for thought that colloquium moderators may want to ask the students to discuss include:

4 Off-Campus Colloquia as Immersive Study and Active Learning: Capitaf... 45

- In Chapter 10 of *Capitalism and Freedom*, Friedman (2002[1962], p. 51) states "A society that puts equality—in the sense of equality of outcome—ahead of freedom will end up with neither equality nor freedom. The use of force to achieve equality will destroy freedom, and the force, introduced for good purposes, will end up in the hands of people who use it to promote their own interests. On the other hand, a society that puts freedom first will, as a happy by-product, end up with both greater freedom and greater equality." Do you agree with Friedman? Why or why not? To support your stance, bring in historical examples of countries that predominantly use free markets versus those that use(d) socialism.
- What does Friedman believe to be the great achievement of capitalism? Do you agree with his assessment?

Session 10 emphasizes chapter 11 ("Social Welfare Measures") of *Capitalism and Freedom* and Chapter 4 ("Cradle to Grave") of *Free to Choose*. Questions that students may want to consider include:

- Why would Friedman prefer that the government provide an impoverished family with cash rather than publicly-funded housing?
- In the Free to Choose video that corresponds to Chapter 4: "Cradle to Grave" of *Free to Choose*, Friedman said that he believes one of the worst things about expansive government welfare programs is that it discourages private charities from giving or trying to help those in need. Why does Friedman believe private charities can better help individuals in their communities than the federal government can? Do you agree? Why or why not?

Session 11 concludes the morning discussion with the 3 Minute Position exercise immediately prior to lunch. The afternoon is spent on another site visit. At Capitaf, these visits have typically included Goodrich's Maple Farm. This family-owned maple farm is presented as an example of an innovative, entrepreneurial small business. This is also where 'Milton's Own' maple products are made. The business has pioneered many technologies that improve sugar processing. Many of the techniques and skills have been passed down by generations. The family has strategically taken advantage of shifting preferences toward healthier foods and lifestyles, building their enterprise into what is now the largest producer of pure maple sugar in the United States.

4.6.1 Day Five

Thursday consists of the last three discussion sessions. After breakfast, the students begin Session 12 where they discuss chapter 12 ("Alleviation of Poverty") from *Capitalism and Freedom*. Questions to consider include:

- Why does Friedman think fiscal stimulus by the government does not produce the desired results?

- What type of government program does Friedman propose to assist in alleviating poverty?
- What type of tax structure did Friedman favor, and why? What type of tax structure do you consider to be best? Defend your opinion.

Session 13 affords the students a final opportunity to give a 3 Minute Position. In Session 14, students discuss why socialism seems to be so appealing for some, bringing in chapter 13 ("Conclusion") of *Capitalism and Freedom*, chapter 10 ("The Tide is Turning") of *Free to Choose*, as well as a few chapters from Hayek's (1944) *Road to Serfdom*: chapter 3 ("Individualism and Collectivism") and chapter 7 ("Economic Control and Totalitarianism"). Potential discussion questions include:

- Economic planning tends to become much more difficult than theorists expect. What could cause this disconnect between theory and reality?
- Was Nazism, as Hayek insists, a type of socialism, or was it basically capitalistic in nature? Support your viewpoint.
- Can a socialist society protect individual freedoms? Suggest some safeguards you would want to implement and how they might work. Can you think of a scenario where even the safeguard measure you put in place doesn't go as planned or ends up eroded?

The students have free time the rest of the day to relax and explore the property. After dinner, the students are awarded Capitaf Certificates of Achievement and are officially recognized as 'Capitaf scholars.'

4.7 Impact on Learning

The 63 students participating in Capitaf colloquia since 2017 represent a wide range of ethnicities, genders, cultural backgrounds, and majors. While many have been economics majors, students focused on philosophy, political science, international affairs, chemical engineering, and English have also participated. One student is now pursuing a graduate degree in film!

Students have universally praised the colloquium and its structure. One female graduate student from the University of Arkansas wrote: "Of the many opportunities I have been afforded, I can easily say that Capitaf has been the best one yet. I am a better person and scholar because of the learnings you shared. I will be forever grateful to the people and learnings at Capitaf."

The location itself is transformational for many participants. For example, one female student from the University of Arkansas (UA) wrote, "It was surreal to stay in Milton Friedman's home. The view of the landscape, with the endless flowers and mountains was astounding." Another female student from Florida State University (FSU) wrote, "There is something about this house and this land that inspires passionate and robust [conversation], and not always in favor of Milton Friedman's ideas." A male student from FSU said, "The colloquium did not just meet my expectations, it blew them out of the water. It's a once in a lifetime experience. It's a horrible understatement to say that I'm glad I attended the colloquium; I'm honored beyond belief to have participated."

Capitaf is a 30-min drive to Dartmouth College and Baker Library, the site where the Friedmans did the lionshare of their research for *Capitalism and Freedom* and wrote *Free to Choose*. Students tour the library and attend a lecture on Friedman's time at Dartmouth. Thus, the setting of Milton and Rose Friedman's home allows students to connect scholarship to practice in a geographically and intellectually unique way.

For almost all, students cited that the ability to get away from their college campus enabled them to minimize distractions and immerse themselves in ideas, theory, and application—creating an unprecedented environment for learning. The site visit to the Goodrich Maple Farm also receives high marks from students as it showcases how the principles and concepts described in Friedman's writings apply in practice. The visit to Dartmouth College reinforces the value of rigorous discourse and the role research plays in formulating ideas and worldviews, as students envision Milton Friedman conducting his research. The bucolic setting of Capitaf reinforces the benefits of a deliberative practice focused on independent reflection and inquiry. The innately strong connection to the Friedmans and their works is not replicable in other settings.

Florida State University asks its students to complete a seminar assessment at the end of each colloquium. Using a standard response range of 'strongly agree' to 'strongly disagree,' 95% or more of students ($N = 18$) strongly agreed that:

- "The quality of the facility and setting was excellent."
- "My interacting with the other students at the colloquium was a pleasant and rewarding experience."
- "I'm glad I attended the colloquium."
- "I believe the colloquium at Capitaf was a unique experience compared to other colloquia/conferences."
- "Overall, the colloquium was well worth my time."

Written comments about why the colloquium was worth their time focused on the key ideas brought out during discussion, the opportunity for networking, the economic history of the location, and gaining a better understanding of political economy and how it relates to current political issues.

Students universally agreed that the setting of the Friedmans' Captaf home provided a unique environment for learning and critically evaluating the Friedmans' ideas. A few student testimonials about the importance of the seminar learning climate include:

- The atmosphere and people and ideas all came together to make an experience that I don't think could be replicated anywhere else. I feel very lucky that I was able to come and experience this completely amazing event with a group of such excellent people.

- It has been an absolute pleasure to be here. ...All of the students who are fortunate enough to be here have had their minds expanded and their views strengthened on the subjects of the benefits of the free market. Students can freely meet to discuss ideas in depth, but to travel to the mountains where Milton Friedman lived and gained inspiration adds a special quality to the overall discussion.
- Incredible setting for discussion.
- The fact that I had access to such an amazing library made for much less sleep but in a good way.
- This was a great program. I was a bit resistant about the idea of coming to Vermont in order to study the works of Dr. Friedman but after coming here, I'm happy that I did. I met a lot of great people with whom I could discuss ideas with in a relaxing setting.

4.8 Conclusion

While some might be hesitant to structure a program around the writings of one person, particularly one with a focused ideological perspective, the Capitaf experience demonstrates how such a program can result in an engaging active-learning opportunity for students. The colloquia represent practical ways the writings of a well-rounded intellectual can foster robust discussions over wide-ranging ideas and interests. Students learned to appreciate and respect alternative points of view and perspectives among their peers while also more clearly defining their own positions and worldviews. The focus on promoting student-driven discussion and critical thinking, creating a respectful space for disagreement, and enforcing rules of civility encouraged students to challenge the Friedmans' ideas while developing a deeper appreciation of his informed perspective.

Numerous students commented on the transformative impact of the colloquium on their own thinking:

> The discussions and passion led to self-reflection and some changes in my own mindset, and I hope my ideas struck others.
> The Capitaf colloquium was really the first time I was able to challenge and refine my pre-existing beliefs about the free market with such a well-informed, fun group of individuals. Leaving here, I feel much more confident in my beliefs and my ability to communicate the values of the free market.

These reflections are consistent with a seminar designed and executed to encourage authentic learning. Doyle (2011, pp. 35–36) summarizes eleven features of authentic learning as it applies to teaching at the college and university level. Although the Capitaf program captures and incorporates almost all of these features, a week-long seminar with a primarily intellectual focus is unlikely to capture all eleven features of this process. For example, having students produce a 'product' to demonstrate the successful application of the principles would be challenging when the primary focus is to deepen understanding of core principles and perspectives

4 Off-Campus Colloquia as Immersive Study and Active Learning: Capitaf...

(although numerous students recognized the practical application of their learning beyond the classroom). Similarly, the focus on intellectual inquiry does not lend itself to real-time data assessment. Doyle himself points out that an authentic learning experience does not need to have all of the eleven features he outlined, and he instead encourages the reader to utilize the list as a guide in the development of authentic learning opportunities.

The Capitaf program, fusing structure with its unique setting, scores well on most of the critical criteria for designing authentic learning programs. Relegating faculty to roles as facilitators rather than lecturers, putting students at the center of discussions, and the organic nature of the seminars provide opportunities for critical inquiry, reflection, analysis, and synthesis. Below are additional criteria identified by Doyle (2011), juxtaposed with comments voluntarily provided from student assessments of the program.

- Deals with real-world [problems]

  - I have been to over a dozen conferences. This one works because it is open, fun, and allows for real-world applications.
  - Capitaf created a welcoming dialogue between conflicting ideas by identifying economic challenges, narrowing down conflicts to singular issues, and applied lessons from *Capitalism and Freedom* to address the problems.
  - The students at Capitaf had many ideological differences and at the same time, one important similarity: a devotion to making the world a better place.

- Has value beyond the school setting

  - It is one thing to read Milton Friedman for oneself and learn from the text and it is another thing completely to be able to immerse oneself in his work and life with other curious individuals. Because of the Capitaf colloquium I was able to come to a better understanding of Friedman and consider for myself how his and Rose's ideas can and should be utilized in the real world.
  - The group entered the program completely in the dark and without any connection. By the end we appreciated each other's opinions and still meet up back in Tallahassee.
  - Not only did I learn more about policy, I also networked and gained more perspective on my professional goals.

- Is interdisciplinary

  - Never before have I taken an economics course; what I've learned here is worth more than an economics course in my opinion. The immersion is like no other, the group discussions were intriguing, and the educational experience is beyond value. This is a truly once in a lifetime experience and has been the greatest honor and privilege to have been a part of this experience.
  - Continue to mix students from other universities; it's a unique networking dynamic.

- Allows a variety of learning styles

- (The students did not write a testimonial specifically mentioning learning styles so we have no direct quotes, but the colloquia indeed incorporate multiple learning styles. Reading the assigned books prior to the colloquium allows for intrapersonal/solitary learning and visual learning. Verbal, auditory, and interpersonal/social learning is put to use during the discussions once at Capitaf. A form of physical/kinaesthetic learning takes place when engaging in activities on the Capitaf property and during the excursions.)

- Allows students to take ownership of their learning

  - Capitaf allowed me to challenge my beliefs and thoughts in a professional and academic setting. With Capitaf alone, it has tremendously [molded] me into the person and economist I am meant to become.

- Uses scaffolding to assist learning

  - The short stories and memories about Milton and his family were the best! I loved that all of the moderators/ speakers let us talk and didn't let their own opinions / emotions into the conversations unless backed by scientific evidence.
  - The moderators pressed us for more, in a good way, and brought enormous energy to the colloquium.

- Encourages students to work together and discuss how to solve problems

  - The discussions took routes I would not have expected therefore challenging [me] to think critically.
  - I strongly believe that I am leaving this experience with more insight and understanding resulting from our discussions as well as more respect and appreciation for my newfound friends' opinions.

Importantly, student responses were clear that the off-campus setting was a critical element of their learning. "After our daily intense yet engaging discussions, we could not help but feel relaxed thanks to the beautiful Green Mountain Range. This awe-inspiring property provides many activities to bond with your class and the sweet mountain air ensures you will wake refreshed and ready to fully engage."

In summary, the Capitaf colloquia provide tangible evidence that off-campus study, when properly designed and executed, can promote active and authentic learning. Facilitated dialogue and discussion promote critical thinking by challenging values and assumptions. Students learned that agreement is not necessary to more fully appreciate abstract ideas, create a more sophisticated understanding of fundamental concepts, or extend their learning to real world applications. In addition, they learned, and appreciated, the value of working with peers from diverse backgrounds and perspectives to come to a more holistic understanding of political economy. As testimony to the bonding between his peers during the week, an anonymous student whose birthday coincided with the colloquium wrote it was "one of the best birthdays of my life!"

4 Off-Campus Colloquia as Immersive Study and Active Learning: Capitaf...

Moreover, students found that Friedman's 'old' ideas were relevant to contemporary discussions and contexts. Capitaf and the Vermont mountains were more than enough to challenge them in satisfying and productive ways that could not be accomplished to the same extent on their home campus. As one student said: Capitaf was the "[b]est week of my life!"

References

Abe-Hiraishi S, Grahovec NE, Anson D, Kahanov L (2018) Increasing cultural competence: implementation of study away/abroad in an athletic training program. Athl Train Educ J 13(1):67–73

Ambrose SA, Bridges MW, DiPietro M, Lovett MC, Norman MK (2010) How learning works: seven research-based principles for smart teaching. John Wiley & Sons, San Francisco

Bonwell CC, Eison JA (1991) Active learning: creating excitement in the classroom. ERIC Clearinghouse on Higher Education, Washington

Carley S, Stuart R, Daily M (2011) Short-term study abroad: an exploratory view of business student outcomes. J Manag Policy Pract 12(2):44–53

Chickering AW, Gamson ZF (1987) Seven principles for good practice in undergraduate education. American Association for Higher Education Bulletin, pp 3–7

Donnelly-Smith L (2009) Global learning through short-term study abroad. Peer Rev 11(4):12–15

Doyle T (2011) Learner-centered teaching: putting the research on learning into practice. Stylus Publishing, LLC., Sterling

Friedman M (2002[1962]) Capitalism and freedom. University of Chicago Press, Chicago

Friedman M, Friedman RD (1980) Free to choose: a personal statement. Harcourt, Orlando

Hayek FA (1944) The road to serfdom. University of Chicago Press, Chicago

Howard JR (2015) Discussion in the college classroom: getting your students engaged and participating in person and online. John Wiley & Sons, San Francisco

Kelleher S (2013) Perceived benefits of study abroad programs for nursing students: an integrative review. J Nurs Educ 52(12):690–695

Maina FW (2004) Authentic learning: perspectives from contemporary educators. J Auth Learn 1(1):1–8

Mills LH, Deviney D, Ball B (2010) Short-term study abroad programs: a diversity of options. J Human Resour Adult Learn 6(2):1–13

Palmer TG (2011) The morality of capitalism: what your professors won't tell you. Students for Liberty and Atlas Economic Research Foundation, Ottawa

Rule A (2006) Editorial: the components of authentic learning. J Auth Learn 3(1):1–10

Sirico R (2012) Defending the free market: the moral case for a free economy. Regnery Publishing, Washington

Slotkin MH, Durie CJ, Eisenberg JR (2012) The benefits of short-term study abroad as a blended learning experience. J Int Educ Bus 5(2):163–173

Sobania N, Braskamp LA (2009) Study abroad or study away: it's not merely semantics. Peer Rev 11(4):23–26

Zamastil-Vondrova K (2005) Good faith or hard data? Justifying short-term programs. Int Educ 14(1):44–49

Chapter 5
Faculty Professional Development Through International Experiences

Rebecca L. Moryl

Abstract Much emphasis is put on the important benefits for students who engage in international study experiences. This paper outlines the potential benefits for faculty professional development through international experiences such as leading a study abroad class, teaching in an international posting, or conducting research internationally. I highlight the evidence from the literature and my own experience on the development opportunities for faculty pedagogy, career development, and research opportunities. I also recommend some resources for identifying opportunities and best practices to gain the most from your experience.

5.1 Introduction

International experiences abroad for faculty can include teaching, as well as research, and even curriculum development and administrative opportunities. International teaching opportunities, whether leading a study abroad class or short-or long-term international teaching posts, provide opportunities for both personal and professional development. This paper will provide evidence—drawn both from first-person anecdotes and from the literature—of the opportunities and benefits of international teaching, research, and curriculum program development. Professional development benefits include enhancements to pedagogical skills, expanded breadth of global content to share in the classroom, building and broadening your social media brand, as well as opportunities to apply and deepen curriculum development experience. While there are recognized obstacles to faculty teaching and studying abroad, including language barriers, tenure pressures for junior faculty, and logistical challenges for those with family commitments (Dooley et al. 2008), the potential benefits are such that instructors would do well to weigh them thoughtfully and be creative and open minded to available opportunities.

R. L. Moryl (✉)
Emmanuel College, Boston, MA, USA
e-mail: morylre@emmanuel.edu

© The Author(s), under exclusive license to Springer Nature Switzerland AG 2021
J. Hall, K. Holder (eds.), *Off-Campus Study, Study Abroad, and Study Away in Economics*, Contributions to Economics,
https://doi.org/10.1007/978-3-030-73831-0_5

Personally, I have engaged in international research and teaching thanks to the support of grant opportunities through Fulbright Program and the Marion & Jasper Whiting Foundation, as well as teaching in a study-abroad opportunity through my home institution. In 2018–2019, I spent an academic year (9 months) teaching in an MBA program at the University of Kigali in Rwanda as a Fulbright Scholar. In 2018 I taught a 3-week intensive course in Emmanuel College's Eastern Mediterranean program in Greece and Cyprus. In 2016 I spent 3 weeks in Cape Town and Johannesburg, South Africa conducting research to enhance my classroom teaching of environmental and urban economics, supported by the Whiting Foundation. The Fulbright Program is a nationally recognized opportunity, while the Whiting Foundation grant is focused on college instructors from the New England region. There are many other resources available for faculty to seek both opportunities and support for international teaching. Available resources include: iie (iie.org); NAFSA: Association of International Educators (nafsa.org); Association of International Education Administrators (aieaworld.org); Council on International Educational Exchange (ciee.org).

5.2 A Review of the Literature on the Benefits of International Teaching Experiences

While the benefits of international teaching experiences are widely and generally recognized, academic research on this topic for college-level faculty is somewhat limited. Much of the literature that does exist focuses on benefits that come from opportunities for primary and secondary level teachers in training, primarily teachers of languages gaining practical teaching experience abroad. For that group, existing research indicates that teaching abroad experiences improve teachers' desirability in the job market (Gilson and Martin 2010). Smolcic and Katunich (2017) note that cultural-immersion field experiences provide teachers opportunities both for developing sociopolitical awareness as well as for personal growth. Willard-Holt (2001) notes that teaching abroad experiences can raise an instructor's awareness of the role of cultural norms and contexts, as visiting instructors are forced to adapt to those of their host country. Savva (2017) provides specific examples of how abstract benefits such as intercultural sensitivity (Alfaro 2008) and broader global perspectives that come from teaching abroad can manifest in the classroom, suggesting that an increased willingness to adapt lessons to different cultural contexts as well as an improved communication style can result. Though Alfaro (2008) cautions that in order for these benefits to result, participants must have a desire to learn from these experiences and to build international relationships during their teach abroad experience. Biraimah and Jotia (2013, p. 433) provide insight into the experience of tertiary-level teaching abroad, finding that while the experience and learning of discipline-related content did not exceed what could be achieved through traditional

5.3 How Teaching Abroad Enhanced My Teaching Tools and Skills

The most obvious benefit from teaching abroad is this opportunity to expand your toolbox of personal experiences and anecdotes to illustrate economic concepts at work in the world. Being able to relate what you've observed firsthand brings the world alive for your students and enhances your credibility beyond what you (and they) read in articles and books. For example, I can now talk about meeting with regulators and water managers in Cape Town South Africa in the context of supply and demand side environmental policies for water management in Environmental Economics. I can speak firsthand about the politics and economics of migrant settlements in Johannesburg in Urban Economics or the use of mobile money in Kigali in International Economics. Lucas' (1997) survey of faculty at Ohio with international teaching experience supports my personal experience. He notes that the majority of respondents reported benefits from having first-hand narratives and analogies to enhance the teaching of abstract concepts in the classroom. Dooley and Rouse (2009) from their longitudinal study of faculty international experience and Hand et al. (2007) from their study both find similar benefits of improved international examples and teaching techniques. Similarly, other authors report that faculty enhanced both their curriculum content (Sandlin et al. 2013) and its cultural context (Roberts et al. 2016) through such examples. Hand et al. (2007, p. 148) further note that international teaching has "enormous potential for both faculty development, and the development of students with whom they interact".

5.4 Develop New Perspectives on Your Teaching

Teaching internationally also allows a new perspective from which to reflect on your teaching habits and pedagogical practices. In addition to developing an understanding of the cultural context in the host location, the distance from your own home context can provide you a clearer view on its own cultural context and how that impacts your understanding and instruction of concepts and issues. Roberts and Jones (2009) and Harder et al. (2012) both emphasize that to get the most benefit in terms of perspective and pedagogical awareness and growth, it is important to engage in reflection, such a memo-to-self or journal writing, before, during, and after the international teaching experience.

Similarly, the broader literature on development of successful international teaching programs designed to provide practical experience for student-teachers, particularly of languages, emphasizes the importance of reflective practices. Numerous studies (e.g. Trent (2011); Vogt (2016); Cunningham (2015); Palmer and Menard-Warwick (2012)) note that teach abroad experiences designed to develop the skills of student-teachers preparing for primary and secondary-level teaching must incorporate reflective practices to be effective. Alfaro (2008, p. 25) notes that reflective practices provide participants the opportunity to "analyze and promote a deeper understanding of international education experiences". While I found no research available on this, it is likely that a college-level faculty member seeking professional and pedagogical development from international teaching would similarly benefit from purposeful reflection on their expectations and experiences.

International experiences can provide faculty opportunities to enhance how they are perceived by their students, colleagues and administrators at their home institution. Roberts et al. (2016) note the value that the ability to share these first-hand experiences in the classroom adds to an instructor's credibility, even from short-term experiences. The authors note that these experiences also empowered faculty to speak more confidently about issues they'd observed, perhaps enhancing their professional profile at the home institution. Sandlin et al. (2013) noted that participants in international teaching experiences reported their excitement and passion for teaching were revitalized by international experience, something that is certainly perceived and valued by students and peers alike.

Meeting, interacting with, and learning from new colleagues in the host country is another benefit of international teaching experience. Roberts et al. (2016, p. 34) note that among faculty they surveyed, one of the "most memorable parts of [the international teaching] experience was getting to meet new colleagues". Similarly, I found the opportunity to learn about and exchange pedagogical practices with my host colleagues one of the most rewarding aspects of the experience

5.5 Engage in Curriculum Development/Evaluation and Faculty Training

A perhaps less recognized international opportunity than teaching is the opportunity to engage in curriculum review and development. As a part of my Fulbright application, I responded to the request for support with curriculum development and faculty training in my host country. I was able to build upon my experience with revising and developing programs at my home institution to then participate in the development of new graduate level programs in Rwanda to meet their burgeoning need for education. I was also invited to participate with host-country colleagues in preliminary reviews of programs at other Rwandan institutions who were seeking accreditation by the government educational authorities. In addition, I provided hands-on pedagogical training for faculty at two campuses of my host university. These curriculum development and faculty training opportunities are frequently mentioned in Fulbright award postings, and are also the focus of programs such as those organized by the Association of International Education Administrators. I was able to expand my experience providing hands-on pedagogical training, and in shaping curriculum to meet the requirements of accrediting bodies and the mission and goals of educational institutions. I also benefited from active exchange around pedagogical strategies, challenges and successes with colleagues and others in my host country. Such interactions are excellent opportunities to share your skills while building your professional portfolio.

5.6 Use Social Media to Connect Communities Internationally & Build Your Professional Brand

Roberts et al. (2016) also found that faculty who taught internationally expanded their technology usage in their 'home' institution in an effort to provide media examples from their international experiences in their classrooms. In my experience, instructors can more intentionally enhance their professional social media profile while simultaneously providing their students at both the home and host institutions opportunities to engage globally through social media. I did not start my professional Instagram until after my time in South Africa, but my intention with the account is to demonstrate that 'economics is everywhere.' When travelling for personal reasons, I often shared demonstrations of economic ideas that we discuss in the classroom to reinforce for former student 'followers,' and to have a catalog of examples for future classes. This continued while I was teaching in Greece and Cyprus, where my postings demonstrated the variety of applications of economics to concepts in agriculture, tourism, and pharmaceuticals.

While in Rwanda, I even more intentionally used my Instagram and Facebook accounts to remain connected to the students and community at my home institution. I was able to share economic anecdotes from my everyday life, as well as my experience teaching at my host institution, thus sharing both discipline specific content, as well as content to promote international experience and connection more generally. Once I returned from my year in Kigali, I used the same account to remain connected to students who had been in my classes in Rwanda, now sharing with them slices of life and an economic view of the world from Boston and wherever else I travelled. I was also able to pull from the catalog of Instagram posts to develop content for classes and for presentations on my experiences, a benefit also noted by Ellis (2014).

Raczkoski and Robinson (2019) find that find that one of the key motivators for faculty to engage in short-term study abroad course instruction is to provide students opportunities for interactions with international students. They suggest that faculty can use social media to build a bridge that shares these experiences in both directions—between home and host—to impact not only course content, but also to link students and other community members beyond that limited sphere. Ellis (2014) notes that in leading a study-abroad course to Estonia, he and his student participants tagged the places visited in their photos, such as the local University, and received welcome messages and interactions through the social media platform. This kind of interaction can also help to build and reinforce global connections for students, faculty and beyond. Gibson and Capdeville (2019) recommend that study abroad offices could also benefit from this kind of social media use to reach and connect with student populations across the world, supporting their missions to build intercultural connection and competencies.

Godwin-Jones (2016) notes, and my experience supports, that the students and members of your host community are just as likely to be digitally engaged as those you leave at home. This not only suggests the viability of building this virtual social media community, but also the potential value for building lasting relationships for yourself, and perhaps facilitating relationships among your student communities in different countries. I have been able to retain contact with students in Rwanda through Instagram and LinkedIn, and to faculty colleagues there via WhatsApp and Facebook as well. In this way faculty can build their professional network and their online brand using social media while teaching internationally.

5.7 Build New Research Paths and Partnerships

International experiences teaching or researching can open new research paths and build new international research partnerships. Dooley et al. (2008) note that the personal relationships established through international experiences are critical for international collaborative research. Harder et al. (2007) highlight the opportunities for professional (as well as personal) growth through engagement in international research projects. Roberts et al. (2016) found that faculty reported these international research collaborations to be an ongoing benefit of their international experience. The authors further note that international experiences seem to provide particular opportunities for multidisciplinary research, which is something that I experienced as emerging from my Fulbright time in Rwanda. Though I was posted in Kigali in a teaching-focused position, I had the opportunity to meet other Fulbrights, including a researcher working in the field of Anthropology on the Rwanda / Democratic Republic of Congo border. We discovered a common interest in economic policy and are engaged in a multidisciplinary research project focusing on a Rwandan case. These kinds of opportunities to network outside your discipline, your typical research field, and your home country are fertile ground for professional development.

5.8 Conclusion

In summary, international experiences provide faculty not only the personal gratification and development from meeting people from a new community and gaining a new perspective on your home context and behaviors, but also many opportunities for professional development. These include enhanced pedagogical tools, first-hand evidence and anecdotes for the classroom, new perspectives on your practices and cultural context, opportunities to engage in curriculum development and faculty training and exchange of ideas, opportunities to build community and your brand through social media, and potential research paths and collaborations. Instructors interested in broadening their global experience and their professional horizons would do well to seek opportunities to teach, research and work internationally.

References

Alfaro C (2008) Global student teaching experiences: stories bridging cultural and inter-cultural difference. Multicult Educ 15(4):20–26

Biraimah KL, Jotia AL (2013) The longitudinal effects of study abroad programs on teachers' content knowledge and perspectives: Fulbright-Hays group projects abroad in Botswana and Southeast Asia. J Stud Int Educ 17(4):433–454

Cunningham HB (2015) Developing intercultural competence among pre-service teachers through international student teaching. PhD Thesis, University of Pittsburgh, Pittsburgh

Lucas DM (1997) The perception of the impact of international experience on faculty of Ohio University regional campuses. PhD Thesis, Ohio University, Athens

Dooley KE, Rouse LA (2009) Longitudinal impacts of a faculty abroad program: 1994–2007. J Int Agricult Ext Educ 16(3):47–57

Dooley KE, Dooley LM, Carranza G (2008) Beliefs, barriers, and benefits of a faculty abroad experience in Mexico. J Int Agricult Ext Educ 15(3):29–38

Ellis JM (2014) Pop culture, Twitter, and study abroad: Estonia as a case study. Polit Sci Polit 47(1):204–208

Gibson AM, Capdeville E (2019) Digital identities and study abroad: teaching intercultural competence through social media literacy. J Glob Initiat 14(1):12–41

Gilson TW, Martin LC (2010) Does student teaching abroad affect teacher competencies? Perspectives from Iowa school administrators. Action Teacher Educ 31(4):3–13

Godwin-Jones R (2016) Integrating technology into study abroad. Lang Learn Technol 20(1):1–20

Hand E, Ricketts KG, Bruening TH (2007) Benefits and barriers: faculty international professional development. Proc 23rd Annual Meeting Assoc Int Agri Ext Educ 153(1):148–153

Harder A, Wingenbach GJ, Rosser M (2007) Developing international research partnerships. J Int Agric Ext Educ 14(3):77–84

Harder A, Lamm A, Roberts TG, Navarro M, Ricketts J (2012) Using a preflective activity to identify faculty beliefs prior to an international professional development experience. J Agric Educ 53(4):17–28

Palmer DK, Menard-Warwick J (2012) Short-term study abroad for Texas preservice teachers: on the road from empathy to critical awareness. Multicult Educ 19(3):17–26

Raczkoski B, Robinson J (2019) Faculty motivations for leading short-term study abroad courses. NACTA J 63(1):108–116

Roberts TG, Jones BL (2009) A brain–based, experiential learning framework to guide international experiences. Proc Assoc Int Agric Ext Educ 25:404–411

Roberts TG, Rodriguez MT, Gouldthorpe JL, Stedman NL, Harder A, Hartmann M (2016) Exploring outcomes two years after an international faculty abroad experience. J Agricul Educ 57(1):30–41

Sandlin MR, Murphrey TP, Lindner JR, Dooley KE (2013) Impacts of a faculty abroad experience on teaching style and technology use in a college of agriculture and life sciences. J Agric Educ 54(3):186–197

Savva M (2017) Learning to teach culturally and linguistically diverse students through cross-cultural experiences. Intercul Educ 28(3):269–282

Smolcic E, Katunich J (2017) Teachers crossing borders: a review of the research into cultural immersion field experience for teachers. Teach Teach Educ 62:47–59

Trent J (2011) Learning, teaching, and constructing identities: ESL pre-service teacher experiences during a short-term international experience programme. Asia Pacific J Educ 31(2):177–194

Vogt K (2016) Teaching practice abroad for developing intercultural competence in foreign language teachers. Can J Appl Linguist 19(2):85–106

Willard-Holt C (2001) The impact of a short-term international experience for preservice teachers. Teach Teach Educ 17(4):505–517

Chapter 6
Educating in Theory and in Practice: The Fund for American Studies

Anne Rathbone Bradley

Abstract The power of ideas and their connection to policy cannot and should not be underestimated. The Fund for American Studies (TFAS) was established in a time of great upheaval in American culture and politics and was founded, initially, as the Charles Edison Youth Fund in 1967. In 1987 it became The Fund for American Studies. Today, we also find ourselves living amidst social, cultural and political upheaval. Populism drives American politics, racial divisions and tensions are mounting, and American politicians are advocating for a kinder, gentler version of socialism to cure the diseases they claim ail us: injustice, inequality and power. The battle of ideas rages on and the powers fighting for loyalty are willing to sacrifice freedom and liberty in their quest. TFAS equips the next generation in that profound battle with programs that bring students to Washington, D.C. as well as international programs which combine classroom with on-the-job learning through internships. If liberty is to prevail, current and future generations of students must have both the passion to make the world a better place and be empowered with analytical tools which TFAS provides.

6.1 Introduction

TFAS was established in response to the political and social upheaval of the 1960s. As that decade was ending, there were widespread protests of government policy, and confidence in the American system of government was eroding. This was especially true for college students of the time. The counterculture and many of the youth movements of the 1960s not only rejected the American political tradition, but also actively worked to undermine and subvert the ideas and principles on which America was built.

A. R. Bradley (✉)
The Fund for American Studies, Washington, DC, USA
e-mail: abradley@tfas.org

© The Author(s), under exclusive license to Springer Nature Switzerland AG 2021
J. Hall, K. Holder (eds.), *Off-Campus Study, Study Abroad, and Study Away in Economics*, Contributions to Economics,
https://doi.org/10.1007/978-3-030-73831-0_6

Surveying this political and social landscape, Charles Edison, former governor of New Jersey, secretary of the Navy and son of the inventor Thomas Alva Edison, recognized that college students needed a balanced perspective on political and economic institutions. And in 1967, he took the first steps towards establishing the institution that is today known as The Fund for American Studies.

Edison recruited Dr. Walter H. Judd, David R. Jones, Marvin Liebman and William F. Buckley, Jr., all of whom shared his concerns. And, on February 6, 1967, the group incorporated the Charles Edison Youth Fund. But, in 1969, as they were discussing how to best reach the young people of that era, Governor Edison died suddenly. To honor him and carry on his mission, the organization was renamed the Charles Edison Memorial Youth Fund. In the summer of 1970, the Youth Fund partnered with Georgetown University to organize the inaugural Institute on Comparative Political and Economic Systems. Fifty-seven students attended.

The Fund's partnership with Georgetown University was based on a shared commitment to academic integrity and a belief in the power of ideas. The relationship was established through the diligent efforts of Professor Lev Dobriansky and a student named Robert Schadler. Dr. Dobrianky who was a professor of economics served as the academic director for summer programs from 1970–1982. Other key players were Professors George Viksnins, George Carey, Jan Karski and Anthony Bouscaren. Mike Thompson and Kathy Rothschild served in management positions under The Fund's first two presidents, David R. Jones and George H.C. Lawrence.

TFAS has been successful because its programs are based upon a solid academic foundation. Its summer programs offer 8 weeks of classes for academic credit, evening guest lectures by renowned speakers and site briefings at key government institutions. Students are assigned to internships at some of Washington's most important institutions. Semester-long programs offer the chance for students to come to Washington during the academic year and continue their education while they intern. The Fund's international programs introduce promising foreign students to the ideas of liberty and civil society.

Despite early support from John M. Olin, DeWitt Wallace, F.M. Kirby and others, budgets were extremely tight in the early years. The organization was often forced to turn away students seeking scholarships until Sen. Barry M. Goldwater agreed to the establishment of the Goldwater Scholarship Fund and a biennial dinner in his honor. This program helped hundreds of students attend TFAS programs.

In 1985, the Institute on Political Journalism (IPJ) was created in response to a declining confidence in the media. Dr. Lee Edwards, serving as the founding director, developed IPJ on the foundation of the successful conferences that Trustee Arnold Steinberg and others had organized in the 1970s and 1980s. Those conferences, which discussed free enterprise and responsible journalism, were held at Vanderbilt, Rice, Pepperdine, Washington University and other top tier schools. They featured luminaries such as Frank Shakespeare, Jack Kemp, Robert Bartley, Alan Meltzer, Al Neuharth and Art Laffer.

Renowned investigative journalist Clark Mollenhoff succeeded Edwards, lending his reputation for hard-nosed investigative journalism until his untimely death in 1991. IPJ now enrolls close to 50–75 students each summer and classes extend beyond summer to include fall and spring.

In 2013, TFAS assumed control of the Robert Novak Journalism Fellowship Program from the Phillips Foundation. The Novak Fellowships are awarded each year to journalists early in their careers who wish to pursue intensive writing projects. The goal is to create a new generation of responsible and objective journalists.

The Charles Edison Memorial Youth Fund grew and matured, and in 1985, to honor Edison's request that his name be used in association with the organization for only 20 years, the organization was renamed The Fund for American Studies. Shortly thereafter, in 1990, TFAS gained financial stability when it received a large bequest from the estate of John and Virginia Engalitcheff. With this bequest, the Board of Trustees established a permanent endowment, purchased a headquarters building and began launching new programs.

Government regulation of business grew sharply in the 1960s and 1970s and, as a result, nearly every major corporation has now established offices in Washington, D.C. to represent their interests. Recognizing the important interplay between business and government, Trustee Don Cogman led a task force that developed the Institute on Business and Government Affairs in 1990. Originally named in honor of pioneering corporate representative Bryce Harlow, this program introduces students to the processes business uses to influence legislation and regulatory policy and emphasizes the importance of honesty and integrity in all aspects of professional life.

When the Berlin Wall fell in 1989, TFAS turned its attention overseas. In 1992, Trustees Randal C. Teague and William Tucker, Dean Michael Collins and Fund Executive Vice President Roger Ream visited Central and Eastern Europe. They returned with a recommendation that a new program be developed in partnership with Charles University in Prague. The American Institute on Political and Economic Systems was established in 1993, reaching more than 100 students each summer from all the countries of the former Warsaw Pact and Soviet Union. The faculty in Prague was led from the inception of the program by Georgetown Professor Jim Lengle, and has included such outstanding scholars as Walter Berns, Peter Boettke, the late Don Lavoie, and now Adam Martin. Each summer a head of state addresses students at the closing ceremony.

Recognizing the strategic importance and rapid economic development of China and many of its Asian neighbors, TFAS established the Asia Institute for Political Economy in 2002. Trustee T. Timothy Ryan of J.P. Morgan took the initiative in proposing the program. Held in partnership with the University of Hong Kong until 2019, the program brings together young leaders from throughout Asia and the U.S. for study and discussion of the American political system and a market economy. Following the end of the 'one country, two systems' agreement in 2020, TFAS moved the program to Singapore.

The Institute for Leadership in the Americas was launched in 2008 where more than 300 students have been given the tools to defend freedom in a region where freedom is deeply threatened. Courses are accredited by University of the Andes and the alumni have taken this classroom knowledge and started free-market think thanks, been elected to office and started new political parties.

Following the untimely death of David R. Jones in 1998, the Board of Trustees chose long-time board member and general counsel Randal C. Teague to serve as its chairman. Roger Ream was elevated from executive vice president to president. A generous gift in memory of Jones from Trustee Thomas L. Phillips enabled TFAS to purchase its current headquarters building on New Hampshire Avenue.

In 2003, TFAS expanded beyond its summer Institute model and developed Capital Semester, offering fall and spring semester programs for college students. Students spend a semester away from their home campuses, studying the ideas of the American political tradition and free-market economics under TFAS faculty. The Leadership and the American Presidency (LTAP) program bring students who are passionate about making a difference through strong leadership to Washington, D.C. for an immersive look at lessons from the American presidency. TFAS partners with the Ronald Reagan Presidential Foundation and Institute to offer this unique Washington D.C. summer program for future leaders to define and strengthen their leadership skills.

The core programs are academic and internship programs for undergraduates. TFAS programs accredited by George Mason University through a partnership with the economics department which began in 2013. All TFAS students are required to take a course in economics. TFAS professors, which include Dan Houser, Don Boudreaux, Christopher Coyne, Adam Martin, and Rosolino Candela, are chosen for their passion for teaching and for their ability to communicate ideas to students representing a diverse spectrum of thought. TFAS courses are uniquely designed by our faculty to bring the ideas of liberty to life.

In 2013, TFAS established a strategic partnership with the Foundation for Teaching Economics (FTE), and in 2019, the two nonprofits formally merged, bringing FTE's programs for high school teachers and students under the TFAS umbrella of academic offerings. Through the FTE programs, TFAS introduces high school students to an economic way of thinking about national and international issues. By choosing to expand into programming for high school students and young professionals, TFAS sought to create an educational journey for its students, spanning from adolescence into adulthood.

6.2 Program Details

The Fund for American Studies (TFAS) hosts Washington, DC-based Academic Internship Programs for undergraduate students each summer, fall and spring.

TFAS programs include academic credit from George Mason University, an internship placement and furnished housing in the heart of Washington, D.C. Students participate in a variety of exclusive guest lectures, site briefings as well as professional development and networking events.

TFAS students leave Washington with 250+ hours of professional experience, an expanded network of contacts, and a greater understanding of the variety of career opportunities.

Programs subject areas:

- Public Policy + Economics
- International Affairs
- Journalism + Communications
- Business + Government Relations
- Leadership + the American Presidency

6.2.1 Academic Credits

All students are required to take 3 credits during the summer, with the option to take 1 or 2 elective courses for a total of up to 9 credits. Students enrolled in the semester program earn 12 credits. A menu of economics and government courses are offered.

Academic credit is provided by George Mason University. Students receive an official transcript from GMU at the end of the term and may transfer credit back to their home universities depending on the institution's policies.

6.2.2 Program Costs + Scholarships

Summer and semester costs cover tuition at GMU and housing. Summer program students live in furnished apartment-style residence building on the campus of George Washington University. Semester housing is provided in the Capitol Hill neighborhood.

85% of students receive full or partial scholarships from TFAS to help them offset the cost of the program. Typically 20% of summer students receive full tuition and housing scholarships. Awards are made based on financial need and merit.

6.2.3 Sample Internships

Students are guaranteed an internship placement with a federal agency, non-governmental organization, embassy, Capitol Hill office, think tank or media outlet. Examples include:

- American Legislative Exchange Council
- Citizens Against Government Waste
- Economic Innovation Group
- German Marshall Fund
- The Hill Newspaper
- Hudson Institute
- Kglobal Public Relations

- Mercatus Center
- National Endowment of Democracy
- Religious Freedom Institute
- U.S. Departments of Agriculture, Education, Health and Human Services, Justice and Transportation
- Voice of America
- The Washington Times

6.2.4 Guest Lectures and Special Events

Students hear from prominent policy and economics exports in a guest lectures held throughout the program. Past speakers have included:

- U.S. Senator Rand Paul
- Jose Pinera, former Chilean Minister of Labor and Social Security
- Judge Andrew Napolitano, Fox News
- Ilya Shapiro, Cato Institute
- Dr. Michael C. Munger, Duke University
- Charlie Cooke, National Review Online
- Chris Wilson, Pollster

Students also get to enjoy a number of special events, such as:

- Site Briefings at the White House, State Department, Capitol Hill and Federal Reserve
- Weekly Professional Development Seminars
- Alumni Networking Roundtable
- Mentor Program
- Career Exploration Panels and Discussion Groups

6.3 The Economic Way of Thinking

The Fund for American Studies champions a core set of principles—freedom, individual responsibility and free markets—which we believe define the essence of the American political tradition. We strive to have a profound effect on the lives of our students by passing on the ideas that offer the greatest opportunity for personal fulfillment and human accomplishment. We know that students come to TFAS from a diverse set of world views and college majors. Some students have never taken an economics class, a few are economics majors. What unites them is a passion for improving the world and a deep commitment to the poor and marginalized. We take that passion and combine it with the economic way of thinking. This is grounded in the truths of human nature and the economic realities of the world. If we ignore either of those, we will craft policy that can never obtain what it seeks and, in many cases, generate violent unintended consequences.

The economic way of thinking implores us to begin our analysis with these truths in mind: incentives matter for human behavior, we have limited knowledge, that knowledge is decentralized, we are self-interested, and we live in a world of scarcity. That scarcity implies that we must compete, and any student of human history knows that for most of history, we have failed to compete in peaceful ways. The long story of human history is one of plunder, exploitation and short lives. But a change occurred and with it, egalitarian consumption. Ordinary people live rich and long lives, more than ever before. If we want to improve this even further, we must understand the trajectory of the past and what caused that shift to occur. Every TFAS student is required to understand these basic truths of human nature and economic principles and then TFAS faculty can lead discussions on what policies and which economic systems will generate further improvements in human flourishing.

6.4 Results

While this is the story of the institutional growth of TFAS, its real successes come at the individual level. Its accomplishments are best measured by how well it conveys to its students the importance and substance of the ideas of liberty.

Understanding the realities of economics and the principles of human behavior is essential for changing the world. At TFAS great efforts are made to measure the impact of our programs on our participants. TFAS does not vet students for acceptance by ideology, background or school. In this regard, TFAS students represent a diverse and broad swath of the overall college population. All TFAS students are interested in crafting a better world, and they are the passionate leaders of the future. But passion alone is never enough, and economics teaches us that intentions are insufficient. We must measure policies and programs by their efficacy, they must accomplish good rather than simply desiring good things.

TFAS tests classroom programs by gauging students view on a variety of basic economic questions: does market trade improve welfare? Is capitalism wealth generating? Do minimum wages help the poor? These surveys are given to each student prior to any program participation and then again upon completion of coursework and internship service. TFAS staff and faculty evaluate these surveys to constantly improve the academic components of the programs. Because students come from such diverse backgrounds and majors and different college environments it is important to start from first principles in the classroom. TFAS faculty do not assume any advanced economic knowledge and spend the first few weeks developing that through readings, lectures, classroom discussion and hands-on experiments. The challenge of teaching in this environment is that you must make the content interesting and engaging for those with advanced economic knowledge and accessible for those who do not.

TFAS faculty believe in the combination of teaching market process theory, public choice economics, and the importance of institutions. Within this analytical framework faculty teach comparative institutional analysis through political economy in the tradition of Adam Smith. TFAS faculty use this as the background for any class taught so regardless of whether a student is taking Comparative Economic Systems, Economics for the Citizen or Public Policy, they are getting intellectual training in political economy as the foundation. This foundation is essential for any productive and relevant analysis regarding policy alternatives directed at social problems. Below is a summary of some questions asked in both the pre and post survey of each student who participates in a TFAS program, all 2019 data.

1. Which Economic System is Best for helping the poor permanently escape poverty?

   (a) Mixed Economy

      (i) Pre-test 53%; Post-test 50%

   (b) Socialism

      (i) Pre-test 11%; Post-test 6%

   (c) Communism

      (i) Pre-test 5%; Post-test 3%

   (d) Democratic Socialism

      (i) Pre-test 11%, Post-test 8%

The classes use the economic way of thinking to demonstrate the relevant alternatives for economic resource allocation. It is this that changes the students thinking about what economic system will best alleviate poverty.

Students prior perception that mixed economies, socialism, communism and democratic socialism all declined after participating in TFAS courses, from a variety of faculty. Votes for capitalism increased. Faculty spend time initially simply defining these terms: capitalism is the private ownership of the means of production and socialism is the collective or public ownership of the means of production. Considerable amounts of teaching time are dedicated to delineating how resource allocation is necessarily different under these systems and then asking questions about which system is better situation to generate egalitarian prosperity.

1. Economics is Best Defined as

   (a) The Technical understanding of how the best allocate scarce resources

      (i) Pre-test 30%; Post-test 25%

   (b) The study of human action under conditions of scarcity and uncertainty

      (i) Pre-test 44%; Post-test 67%

   (c) The study and development of models and polices that create prosperity

6 Educating in Theory and in Practice: The Fund for American Studies

  (i) Pre-test 23%; Post-test 7%

(d) The development of policies that create social justice and equality

  (i) Pre-test 2%, Post-test 1%

Students and the population in general are often unaware of what economics is, some confusing with accounting or finance. Economics is the science of human action under conditions of radical uncertainty, finite knowledge, and scarcity. We must begin with a common and proper understanding of what economics is if we are to understand what economics can tell us and the limits of economists and policy makers. The survey results demonstrate that progress was made in understanding economics.

1. Profits earned through trade are good because they create strong incentives for the entrepreneur to serve their customers

(a) True

  (i) Pre-test 77%; Post-test 90%

(b) False

  (i) Pre-test 23%; Post-test 10%

A shift in thinking is revealed in the pre and post question regarding profits and their role in economic calculation. From 77% to 90% of the students understood that profits are the mechanism by which entrepreneurs get essential feedback from customers about what they want and need. The lure of pure profit drives entrepreneurship from which sustainable economic growth germinates.

1. Market trade uses prices to guide the most productive use of scarce resources

(a) True

  (i) Pre-test 77%; Post-test 90%

(b) False

  (i) Pre-test 23%; Post-test 11%

This is another essential question about the mechanisms of markets under the forces of supply and demand. Students increased their understanding by 12% on the role of prices providing both signals about underlying levels of scarcity and that role in directing resource allocation in nimble and productive ways.

1. Markets often fail and governments are the best corrective for those failures

(a) Strongly disagree

  (i) Pre-test 12%; Post-test 17%

(b) Somewhat disagree

  (i) Pre-test 31%; Post-test 35%

70 A. R. Bradley

(c) Neutral

    (i) Pre-test 19%; Post-test 17%

(d) Somewhat agree

    (i) Pre-test 29%, Post-test 24%

(e) Strongly agree

    (i) Pre-test 8%, Post-test 7%

Economic thinking helps us understand that neither markets nor government can be perfect. All human institutions operate through human action and as such, all are flawed. Economics rather that proscribing a utopia for which we would always desperately struggle helps us understand which institutions fail and why. Then and only then can we weigh different institutional correctives. From 37 to 33% either somewhat or strongly agreeing that markets often fail, and government is the fix demonstrates that students better understand both the operation of markets and governments.

1. Markets create prosperity for all people because they provide the best incentives for cooperation and innovation

(a) Strongly disagree

    (i) Pre-test 10%; Post-test 8%

(b) Somewhat disagree

    (i) Pre-test 27%; Post-test 13%

(c) Neutral

    (i) Pre-test 13%; Post-test 12%

(d) Somewhat agree

    (i) Pre-test 32%, Post-test 44%

(e) Strongly agree

    (i) Pre-test 18%, Post-test 22%

This question helps TFAS faculty understand what prior views students have about market trade before they enter the classroom and upon leaving. Initially 50% of students both somewhat and strongly agreeing that markets create egalitarian prosperity ended in 66% both somewhat and strongly agreeing. This is an indication that faculty are helping students understand the mechanisms of a market economy. From there, the students must decide for themselves what type of economic system is best.

These sample questions from 2019 data suggest that students from a variety of college backgrounds and majors have important discussions through the readings and lectures that allow them to challenge their prior views and put them to the cost-benefit test. TFAS faculty are constantly adjusting the syllabi and course framework to ensure that they are meeting students where they are and providing an exciting and civil place for classroom discussion.

6.5 Conclusion

It is impossible to say how the life and career of an alumnus—and the lives each of them touch—would have been different without TFAS. Thankfully, because of The Fund's commitment, thousands of students have had the opportunity to learn about the principles of freedom and the power of ideas. TFAS has educated over 42,000 participants in over 140 countries through its varied programs and continues to keep them engaged and connected through its alumni program. Many TFAS alumni go on to become generous donors to current TFAS programs because they have lived the experience of combining powerful economic education with practical internship experiences.

Once students recognize how the ideas of limited government, personal responsibility and a free-market economy relate to a given policy question, they can apply these principles again and again through their careers and lives. This truly does change lives. It allows them to draw connections to the historical debates that have shaped America, and become better, more reflective citizens. It is our hope now and into the future. We live in both extraordinarily wealthy and abundant times, but we recognize that there is no destiny. Like Venezuela and Argentina, robust economic freedom which leads to political freedom and democracy can be destroyed, and that destruction first comes when we forget economic realities. If in times of crisis or when the ideas of liberty seem no longer vogue, we abandon them, we lose both our abundance and our freedom. Politics and policy are downstream from ideas and culture. TFAS has and continues to provide a setting in which students from all walks of life and all cultural backgrounds can engage in debate, dialogue, and experience what the preservation and furtherance of freedom requires.

Chapter 7
International Internships: Their Value and a Guide to Setting Them Up

Matthew C. Rousu and Scott Manning

Abstract Study abroad is recognized as a high impact practice. There can be some issues with conventional study abroad that reduce a student's learning, however. Having an internship while abroad can help increase the value of study abroad and provide the student with valuable experience that will help post-graduation. In this article, we discuss the value of international internships, discuss the program at Susquehanna University for providing them, and provide recommendations for those interested in offering these experiences to their students.

7.1 Introduction

Study abroad is widely accepted as a valuable high impact practice in higher education. Students have seen this value, as data compiled by the Institute of International Education in their Open Doors project has shown almost uninterrupted growth over the past 20 years in the number of U.S. college students studying abroad—from nearly 132,000 students in 1998 to over 341,000 in 2018 (Institute of International Education 2020).

The American Association of Colleges and Universities (AAC&U) lists some of the key benefits of study abroad. Students develop personal and social responsibility while building global awareness, exploring cultural diversity, and learning how to shift their perspective in different global contexts (Association of American Colleges and Universities 2014). More broadly, research has shown a positive correlation between study abroad and student engagement, which has implications for student success and graduation rates (Redden 2012).

M. C. Rousu (✉) · S. Manning
Susquehanna University, Selinsgrove, PA, USA
e-mail: rousu@susqu.edu; manning@susqu.edu

© The Author(s), under exclusive license to Springer Nature Switzerland AG 2021
J. Hall, K. Holder (eds.), *Off-Campus Study, Study Abroad, and Study Away in Economics*, Contributions to Economics,
https://doi.org/10.1007/978-3-030-73831-0_7

The value of study abroad has led to greater support from institutions of higher education, many mobilized by the Generation Study Abroad project organized by IIE, to dramatically increase US study abroad numbers (Institute of International Education 2020). Many institutions have developed programs to encourage study abroad, often as a choice within a portfolio of other high impact practices such as the Elon University Experiential Learning requirement. A few institutions have gone as far as to include study abroad in the curriculum for all students, either at the institutional level (examples include Goucher College and Soka University of America) or the school level (e.g., NYU's Stern School of Business and the Stamps School of Art and Design at the University of Michigan) as well as in individual academic departments at many institutions. Susquehanna University, which added such a requirement in 2009, recently celebrated 10 years of conferring undergraduate diplomas only on students with cross-cultural study away experience.

While survey data demonstrates increased participation in study abroad, research on the impact and value of study abroad has focused on identifying benefits of study abroad and whether the resources devoted to providing these experiences help improve student learning. In *Student Learning Abroad: What Our Students Are Learning, What They're Not, and What We Can Do About It*, scholars in the field of study abroad examine various claims made about the educational benefits of study abroad. Vande Berg et al. (2012, pp. 15–19) get at the heart of these claims in their examination of three common paradigms of study abroad. A 'Positivist' paradigm, which simply highlighted experiencing difference for oneself; a 'Relativist' approach, which assumes that through more immersion in a culture, students will naturally be transformed by their engagement with it; and finally, an 'Experiential/Constructivist' paradigm, in which some form of intentional learning intervention is established to help students make meaning of their experience.

The results of the multi-institutional Georgetown Consortium Project highlighted the importance of the third approach—creating intentional interventions with students—on student intercultural development and learning. The study looked at 14 different characteristics such as program type and housing type, on 61 programs. They found that programs that involved working with students to reflect on and process their experiences had the most impact on students. This mattered more than the length of time in the country, whether students lived with a host family, their peers, or who they studied with. One major critique of study abroad is that without some kind of intervention to help students focus their experience, students did not make as much intercultural progress (Paige and Vande Berg 2012, pp. 36–38).

There are other critiques. Some scholars have highlighted that study abroad relies too heavily on Positivist or Relativist approaches alone. Some students may see study abroad as simply an extended vacation. Tony Ogden has pointed out the ways in which programs abroad replicate American expectations overseas to satisfy student consumers, creating a colonialist atmosphere that rarely seeks to understand the local culture (Ogden 2007). And there are many potential pitfalls that can be found in a traditional study abroad experience which may lead to students not making progress as global learners. Students who spend their time only with their peers from home, drinking excessively, and focused only on travel are all negative stereotypes of certain study abroad students, brilliantly satirized in The Onion's (2002) "Semester Abroad Spent Drinking with Other American Students."

Having students complete an internship during their study abroad can help build in an intervention strategy to alleviate many of these concerns and provide a richer experience. In this paper, we will discuss the benefits to students of completing an internship while in a foreign country. We will also discuss the details of the program in the Sigmund Weis School of Business at Susquehanna University for placing students in internships and will provide tips and suggestions for those who wish to arrange internships for their students studying abroad.

7.2 Benefits of Internships Abroad

An internship in a foreign country is a great opportunity for students. As mentioned earlier, studying abroad is considered a high-impact practice by the AAC&U. Internships are recognized as another high impact practice (Association of American Colleges and Universities 2014) and are an increasingly common form of experiential learning. The idea behind internships is to provide students with direct experience in a work setting—usually related to their career interests—and to give them the benefit of supervision and coaching from professionals in the field. If the internship is taken for course credit, students generally complete a project or paper that is approved by a faculty member. On top of the value of the learning experience, internships can also help students when looking for employment (Porter 2019).

Completing an internship while abroad provides two high impact practices to students at once and makes study abroad more meaningful. It greatly enhances the cross-cultural learning students experience. One key goal of any study abroad program is for students to immerse themselves in a culture, and to have opportunities to reflect on their experience. An internship in a foreign country accelerates this process. Students who intern abroad will not just be tourists—they will be working with coworkers from a foreign country and with a boss who is from a foreign country. As everybody who works knows, a person often gets to know their co-workers really well—many times developing relationships with them they won't develop with others. The internship also provides students with a level of cultural intervention, as they will receive feedback and an opportunity to reflect on what they are doing during their time abroad that helps them to process their experience in helpful ways.

On top of understanding co-workers better, students also experience the work culture in a foreign country. Students in Spain may see first-hand that businesses shut down for mid-afternoon siestas. In England, we've had students join co-workers after work at the pub for a drink before everybody heads home for the day and who have learned tips about differences in email styles across countries. (Note—in the US, emails are more likely to have an excited tone and use exclamation points!)

7.3 The Program at Susquehanna University and the Sigmund Weis School of Business

7.3.1 Study Abroad at Susquehanna University

The Global Opportunities (GO) program at Susquehanna was developed during a curriculum revision project and adopted in 2008. In order to meet the new university learning goals, this central curriculum requires every student to have an off-campus cross-cultural experience, bookended by preparation and reflection on campus. The experience itself must be cross-cultural, so some students could complete it in a community within the United States that creates such an opportunity, but over 90% of students travel internationally to complete the requirement.

One key component is the preparatory course that precedes the experience and the reflection that follows it. Every student begins with a 7-week preparation class, which introduces concepts of intercultural learning as well as location-specific information. Students then complete their study abroad experience and complete another 7-week reflection course on campus. Students in this class build on what they learned and are taught ways to integrate this learning into their academic and career goals moving forward.

Because every student must complete this requirement in order to graduate the program was intentionally designed to have multiples pathways and options, even though the entire program is organized around a single set of cross-cultural learning goals (Dunlap and Manning 2020). Some students prefer a cohort model in which they travel and learn with faculty and students from our institution. Other students are looking for primarily academic experiences at an overseas university that will complement their major on campus. Increasing numbers of students are looking for experiential options: internships, volunteer activity, or other project-based learning models that give them hands-on experience with people in another cultural context.

7.3.2 Internships Through the Sigmund Weis School of Business at Susquehanna University

Seeing the value that an internship can add to study abroad, in January 2020 the Sigmund Weis School of Business at Susquehanna University became the first (and currently only) business school in the world to guarantee each student an internship in a foreign country. Susquehanna students have interned abroad, while also taking a full course load, in many different countries including Australia, England, Germany, Italy, New Zealand, and Spain. Students also have the opportunity to complete their cross-cultural experience and internship during winter or summer breaks, and students have completed internships over breaks in Hong Kong, Ireland, Singapore, and over a dozen other countries.

7 International Internships: Their Value and a Guide to Setting Them Up

The impact of these internships on students' cultural learning has been powerful, but it has also helped students on the job market. A senior-level employer at an insurance company wrote:

> After being in the workforce for 35 years, I have benefited from working with and hiring employees who have studied abroad and completed international internships as part of their undergraduate degree programs. Their distinctive experiences enhance their employability in getting their first job after graduation and ultimately to becoming key leaders of domestic and international organizations. Interning in a foreign country affords young aspiring professionals with the opportunity to develop improved intercultural skills and learned outcomes related to a wide range of skills that employers value in today's diverse and fast-paced workforce. Engaging with professionals in their local workplace in a different culture, potently a different language, challenges and prepares undergraduates to develop valuable business and personal experiences with effective communication skills, creativity, and most certainly adaptability which are all highly valued and marketable skills.

A student who interned abroad, Carly Malamud '19, who went on to law school after earning her bachelor's degree, had this to say about her internship experience:

> Gaining the experience of working in Central London has offered me numerous advantages in my personal and post-SU life. When applying for programs in law school that have international reach, having previous employment in a foreign country on my resume served as a seal of approval that I could adequately represent my law school on a multinational scale. My internship in London has also been a topic of conversation during every interview and mentor meeting I've attended, whether as a direct question about what I learned through my employment or curiosity regarding what it is like to have such a unique study abroad experience. It offers a point of interest for the other party, and gives me the opportunity to express my enthusiasm and passion for international work and travel. I am continually thankful to have had the opportunity to study and work in London.

The guaranteed international internship program was put in place in January 2020, when about 50% of students were choosing to intern abroad and with capacity for our providers to take on dozens more. The business school was able to scale up quickly from placing 5–6 students annually in internships (from 2008–2009 through 2015–2016) to 60 (in 2019–2020) by following a few steps. (For context, most years 130–150 students graduate from the business school.)

First, we leveraged a relationship with a well-known and established study abroad provider, Anglo Educational Services (AES). Susquehanna had worked with AES for over two decades, and we felt comfortable working with them. They had coordinated a London Program for the school and were willing to add on internships. All that this entailed was dropping one course from the semester abroad and replacing it with a 2-day per week internship. This started in fall 2017 and immediately increased the number of Susquehanna University students interning abroad from single-digits to over three dozen.

We then worked with our university study abroad office to build on pre-existing partnerships, first with a provider in Barcelona, then with specific universities in the UK, Australia, Italy, and New Zealand. The universities in these countries allowed students to take a semester's worth of classes abroad and also complete an internship. The School also formed a new relationship with a provider that places student interns in Singapore during summer and winter break and developed a semester-long bilateral exchange program with a university in Germany. Between the providers and the relationships with universities, the capacity to place students abroad exceeds 150 annually, allowing the school to implement the guarantee of an international internship.

7.4 Issues to Consider for Arranging Internships Abroad for Students

7.4.1 How Do Students Get the Internships?

To have students interested in interning abroad is one thing, but how do they actually receive the internship offer from a firm? This is something that either the university you work with or the study abroad provider will likely help with. We will describe the general process, but note that it will vary slightly depending on whom you work with.

Your partners—whether universities or study abroad providers—essentially match your students with firms providing internships. To do this, students must first prepare and submit a resume/CV to the provider, who will then conduct an initial remote interview. Based on the students' academic record, previous work experience, and interview, the provider will place students to have an initial interview with the potential firm. In our experience, the first interview will lead to students being hired 80–90% of the time. Sometimes, however, the match doesn't feel right for either the student or firm, and the study abroad provider or partner university will then have to match the student for an interview with a second firm. We have had a couple of cases over the years where students have been turned down 3 times, which prompts a conversation with the student about their interviewing skills. (This is not a fun conversation, but it is much better that the student learns while in college instead of when applying for a full-time job.)

7.4.2 Different Visa Requirements

Each country has its own requirements—but sometimes a different visa is needed to intern abroad than to study abroad. In our experience, our partners are great at keeping students informed on deadlines and requirements.

7.4.3 What Criteria Should You Have for Interested Students?

Interning abroad requires a different level of engagement relative to studying abroad. Because of that, you may wish to impose some criteria for interested students to minimize complications. After all, in an internship, a student could get fired or negatively impact your (or your institution's) reputation. Several providers have minimum GPA restrictions, often at 2.5 or higher. Generally speaking, the guidelines an institution has in place for students to study abroad are probably adequate for interning abroad. Ultimately, students will have to make it through the interview process, so employers have the ability to say 'no'.

7.4.4 Are Internships Paid or Unpaid? (Hint, They Are Mostly Unpaid)

Given firms are taking on a foreign college student, sometimes for 100 h or more of work, and are often committing to taking students on before they meet them in person, most internships abroad are unpaid. Further, visa requirements can differ for students who would receive a paid internship vs. an unpaid internship, complicating the ability to get a paid internship in some countries. There are exceptions to this, as our institution has seen students in some locations get paid (in Germany, for example), but one should set the expectations early for students that their 'payment' will be the university credit they earn, the experience, and the ability to put this experience on their CV.

7.4.5 Should You Partner with Universities or Study Abroad Providers?

There are two key ways that you can set up internships in foreign countries for your students, partnering with study abroad providers and partnering with universities abroad. There are several universities around the world that work to place students in internships and may be willing to place your students in internships. If your university already has institutional partnerships in place, working with your study abroad office to arrange meetings to discuss internship abroad plans for students is an easy way to start considering options. If a university can allow an internship, one typical setup would be that a student takes one less course during the semester and replaces that with a for-credit internship where a student might work for 2–3 days per week. Another setup we've seen is for students to complete coursework in a block of weeks (perhaps 10–12), then work full-time at an internship for an additional 5–6 weeks.

Table 7.1 Representative list of providers that have assisted Susquehanna University students in obtaining an internship abroad

Name	Location	Third party provider	Semester with courses	Short- term programs	Primarily internship focused
Anglo Educational Services	London, England	x	x	x	
Barcelona SAE	Barcelona, Spain	x	x	x	
Projects Abroad	Various world-wide	x		x	
Sant'Anna Institute	Sorrento, Italy	x	x	x	
The Intern Group	Various world-wide	x		x	x
University of Waikato	Waikato, New Zealand		x		
University of Chester	Chester, England		x		
Hamburg School of Bus. Admin.	Hamburg, Germany		x		x

Alternatively, you could partner with a study abroad provider. They are experts at placing students and generally have more flexibility in the types of experiences they can offer your students. Many study abroad providers can place students in semester-long internships in conjunction with a semester abroad. Other providers focus solely on internships abroad and can help if you wish to have students complete an internship abroad either during a semester when completing other coursework or doing a winter/summer break. Providers often can make things easier; however, they will charge fees for their work, naturally, so sometimes they can be more expensive.

We present a list of study abroad providers and universities that have helped Susquehanna University provide internships in Table 7.1.

7.4.6 How Long Should Students Intern Abroad?

As noted above, students on traditional study abroad can often intern during or following their semester program. However, many providers cater to students who cannot be away for a full semester whether for financial, academic, or other reasons. Students generally do not complete much, if any, coursework when interning over a winter/summer break on these programs. (Other than the university credit they receive for the internship.) For example, students might complete 80–120 h of work for a company over a 3-week time period, which would not allow much time for traditional coursework.

There is no one answer for a good length of a domestic internship. Naturally, we don't think there is one length that works for international internships, either. The students must have enough time with an employer to have had a meaningful experience. It helps if this experience is complemented by academic assignments to have further reflections on what the student learned.

7.5 Conclusion

The value of internships is widely understood to be important for student learning and for enhancing student career success following graduation. The intercultural and other soft skills that can be gained through study abroad are also increasingly seen as critical in today's job market. Adding an internship to a student's traditional study abroad experience is a logical and exciting way to accelerate high impact learning and provide a boost to their post-graduation prospects.

References

Association of American Colleges and Universities (2014) Global learning VALUE rubric. https://www.aacu.org/value/rubrics/global. Accessed 20 Apr 2020

Dunlap A, Manning S (2020) The Susquehanna model of strengths-based cross-cultural learning goals. The Global Impact Exchange: Diversity Abroad 3(2):17–19

Institute of International Education (2020) IIE generation study abroad initiative. https://www.iie.org/programs/generation-study-abroad. Accessed 20 Apr 2020

Ogden A (2007) The view from the veranda: understanding today's colonial student. Frontiers: The Interdisciplinary Journal of Study Abroad 15(1):35–56

Paige RM, Vande Berg M (2012) Why students are and are not learning abroad. In: Student learning abroad: what our students are learning, what they're not, and what we can do about it, pp 29–58

Porter R (2019) How internships impact employability and salary. College Recruiter https://www.collegerecruiter.com/blog/2019/09/30/how-internships-impact-employability-and-salary/. Accessed 20 Apr 2020

Redden E (2012) Study abroad, graduate on time. Inside Higher Ed https://www.insidehighered.com/news/2012/07/10/new-studies-link-study-abroad-time-graduation. Accessed 20 Apr 2020

The Onion (2002) Semester abroad spent drinking with other American students. The Onion https://www.theonion.com/semester-abroad-spent-drinking-with-other-american-stud-1819566321. Accessed 20 Apr 2020

Vande Berg M, Paige RM, Lou KH (2012) Student learning abroad: paradigms and assumptions. In: Student learning abroad: what our students are learning, what they're not, and what we can do about it, pp 3–28

Chapter 8
Teaching the Economics of Poverty and Discrimination as a Study Abroad in South Africa

Claudia Strow and Brian Strow

Abstract Study abroad programs can be immensely rewarding for both student and professor alike. However, the high start-up costs for teaching a study abroad course can be intimidating. This chapter describes our experience teaching the economics of poverty and discrimination in South Africa. We not only discuss the reasons for choosing South Africa as a destination, we also lay out the details for assignments, planning, budgeting, and field trips. Our aim is that this chapter will help those wishing to lead a similar program by lowering their start-up costs so that more such programs can be offered.

8.1 Introduction

The population of the United States represents a diversity of races, ethnicities, socioeconomic statuses, sexual identities, and religions. Likewise, college students come from a great variety of backgrounds, though some college campuses are more diverse than others. Most US college students do not experience extreme hunger or a lack of shelter, while for others that is their norm. Likewise, many students experience discrimination based on their race, ethnicity, gender, socioeconomic status, religion, weight, sexual identity, or other factors, while some have never been the target of discrimination. How does one even begin to approach teaching about poverty and discrimination in a classroom full of such diverse experiences? Or harder yet, how does a professor adequately address poverty and discrimination topics in a classroom of people who come from similar backgrounds or who have privileges that those in other countries could never imagine?

C. Strow (✉) · B. Strow
Palm Beach Atlantic University, West Palm Beach, FL, USA
e-mail: claudia_strow@pba.edu; brian_strow@pba.edu

© The Author(s), under exclusive license to Springer Nature Switzerland AG 2021
J. Hall, K. Holder (eds.), *Off-Campus Study, Study Abroad, and Study Away in Economics*, Contributions to Economics,
https://doi.org/10.1007/978-3-030-73831-0_8

Teaching about poverty and discrimination in a typical college classroom is limited, even with the inclusion of hands on activities, service learning projects, and modern day and historical examples. While these tools help, this learning pales in comparison to the insight and understanding that one gains from a study abroad experience in a developing nation. Admittedly, there are places in developed countries that can yield similar experiences, so we do not wish to diminish the poverty or discrimination felt here in the United States or other developed countries. Rather, we seek to aid others in their ability to teach study abroad classes in order to expand the learning opportunities available to their students.

This chapter lays out our process for teaching the economics of poverty and discrimination in South Africa as part of a 3-week study abroad program. We realize that the largest cost to teaching abroad is often developing the program, the curriculum, the connections, the budget, and the itinerary. Our aim for this chapter is to facilitate that process and equip professors for leading study abroad experiences.

8.2 Why South Africa?

South Africa's beauty, diversity, apartheid history, experience with the AIDS epidemic, and extreme inequality make it a prime location in which to study poverty and discrimination. The country is beautiful and diverse in terms of both its landscape and its populace. The varied landscape offers mountains, beaches, cities, diamond and gold mines, national parks, and big game safaris. Furthermore, South Africa is a unique study in both discrimination and reverse discrimination, poverty and wealth, government instability, slavery, and economics.

With regard to its populace, Desmond Tutu aptly referred to South Africa as the 'rainbow nation'. South Africa has thirty-five languages indigenous to the Republic, with ten designated official languages. Within the four main racial groups, there are numerous ethnicities. The two largest black African ethnicities are Zulu and Xhosa, while the two largest white ethnicities are Afrikaner and English. Coloured (an official South African characterization of mixed-race individuals) and Asian (mainly consisting of people of Indian ancestry) make up the other two largest racial groups in South Africa. Table 8.1 illustrates that, over the last century, the percentage of Coloured and Indian Africans calling South Africa home has remained fairly constant, while the relative share of black Africans is increasing, and the relative share of white Africans is decreasing.

Table 8.1 Race in South Africa. Stats SA (2015)

Group	1904	2015
Black Africans	67.5%	80.5%
Coloured Africans	8.6%	8.8%
White Africans	21.6%	8.3%
Indian Africans	2.4%	2.5%

Source: Feinstein et al. (2005, p.259)

Statistics South Africa's 2019 poverty line update defines the food poverty line at $1.24 per person per day (R18.70). This is the estimated amount a South African would need to obtain 2100 calories per day. Two other poverty lines they report are the lower bound poverty line and the upper bound poverty line. These are the food poverty line plus estimates of some basic essentials a household would need. The lower bound poverty line is at $1.80 a day (R810 per month), while the higher bound poverty line is just under $3 per day (R1277 per month). Approximately one in four South Africans live below this bleak food poverty line, while roughly half of all adult South Africans live below the upper bound line, and the majority of these households have no indoor access to sanitation or water (Stats SA 2019).[1]

We discuss these dire circumstances with our students before traveling to South Africa. And yet, these discussions cannot begin to compare to the insight gained walking through shantytown encampments that lack electricity and running water in Soweto before being immersed in the lavish wealth on display in Sandton. With one of the highest levels of income inequality in the world, the contrasts in wealth and poverty and the dire circumstances faced by many South Africans are quickly apparent to anyone visiting South Africa.

In addition to extreme inequality and poverty, South Africa has the highest HIV infection rate in the world. Approximately one in five adults in the country has HIV, and over 62% are on antiretroviral treatments (Avert 2020). South African children also contract HIV at high rates, and AIDS is responsible for over half of the country's 3.8 million orphans (UNICEF 2015). Stigma and discrimination furthers the spread of the effects of AIDS, as "in the third decade of the HIV epidemic, stigma and especially moral judgement, is still a factor that can undermine the efforts to prevent and treat HIV/AIDS" (Visser et al. 2009, p.9). South Africans on the margins of society are often discriminated against when receiving treatment for HIV, and this stigma is preventing individuals from seeking and receiving medicines and treatments to prolong their life and prevent the spread of AIDS. This dynamic of discrimination, infection, and poverty is key to understanding the full story of poverty and discrimination in South Africa.

Race and inequality discussions and considerations are present most everywhere, but are especially poignant in South Africa, where apartheid ended in 1994. The history of apartheid in South Africa, the pains in establishing a new government post-apartheid, the historical and present instances of discrimination and reverse discrimination, and the stories of both struggle and reconciliation are very much alive and felt by all who visit South Africa. Numerous opportunities exist to learn more about South Africa's troubling and discriminatory history. These include planned visits to Robben Island, the Apartheid Museum, and the District Six Museum, meetings with government leaders, and a visit to the Hector Pieterson Museum and Memorial. And yet, many of our most poignant learning opportunities in South Africa typically occur by happenstance.

---

[1]Note, at the time of publication SA Stats had not measured the poverty rate since 2015 due to a shortage of funds (Stoddard 2019).

For example, a conversation with a taxi driver of Indian decent whose relatives were brought to South Africa as slaves quickly morphs into a discussion about an ethnicity that has felt discriminated against both during and after apartheid. At the District Six Museum, we meet a black South African who had to leave her home by force under the Group Areas Act of the late 1960's. As we study recent government proposals involving the repatriation of land from current white owners without compensation, and as students meet with whites who have seen and experienced the reverse discrimination caused by racial employment and ownership quotas, discussions organically progress into an examination of how to attempt to remedy prior mistakes and injustices without creating additional discrimination.

The same statistics that make South Africa an excellent country for studying poverty and discrimination may make it seem formidable as a study abroad destination. Crime rates in South Africa are substantially higher than in other locations where we lead study abroad courses such as Australia, New Zealand, Costa Rica, and Northern Europe. As a result, group security issues play a more prominent role in course planning and design with a trip to South Africa. While we have taken students and our own four young children to South Africa on multiple occasions, members of our group have experienced credit card theft, hotel room theft, personal theft from people on the street and even extortion from local police looking for a bribe.

On the other hand, our experience has been that students have learned more on this trip than they have on other similarly planned trips to less crime-ridden destinations. The people of South Africa are incredibly friendly and hospitable, and thankfully, no one in our group has ever been a direct victim of physical violence. One doesn't have to know a foreign language beyond English to get around, and the level of public infrastructure makes it relatively easy to move a large group of students around the country with few issues.

South Africa is an attractive destination to students, as it houses numerous outdoor activities such as shark cage diving, safaris, bungee jumping, zip lining and rafting. Though these attractions may be what initially draws a student to the program, the student will almost certainly finish the program with significantly impactful academic and personal development. Further, South Africa allows the budgets of American students (and professors) to travel further than the aforementioned locations due to the typically weak value of the South African Rand.

South Africa's economic history and history of race based institutional discrimination paired with its vast diamond and gold deposits makes it a country that can both inspire and challenge one's preconceived notions of poverty and discrimination. In our opinion, these attributes far outweigh any concerns we have about security in the country. In the sections that follow, we break down our course set up and logistics, the budget, and the types of experiences and field trips we undertake in country.

8.3 Course Set Up and Logistics

We pair the course in the economics of poverty and discrimination with a second course offering on the economics of South Africa. This second course covers the economic history of South Africa and current issues in the South African economy. The two courses combine to yield a better understanding of South Africa's present and past and to allow students to earn 6 hours of credit within a 3-week travel period. The second course also helps to justify the elevated cost of a study abroad vs. taking an online or on campus course during the same time period. In order to ensure that we have enough contact hours to justify 6 hours of academic credit, each class meets for several class periods pre-departure in order to cover much of the initial course material. By meeting as a class ahead of time, we are better able to make the most of our time in country. Our course layout is broken up below into pre-departure requirements and in-country experiences.

8.3.1 Predeparture

Prior to departure, we meet once a week for 8 weeks (four per class) for 2 hours at a time. These meetings consist of lecture, discussion, readings, presentations, a paper and a midterm. Then we meet one final time in our home for dinner to help the group become even better acquainted, to tie up any lose ends, and to answer any final questions prior to departure. The tradeoff for students is that while they get twice as many credit hours earned during their 3-week January term, they do have to meet ahead of time on top of their regularly scheduled fall classes. We collect information from each student regarding when they are available and schedule classes (admittedly at some odd hours) where everyone can (and must) attend.

For the course in poverty and discrimination, we administer a survey before meeting in order to get students thinking about their existing opinions, viewpoints, and biases concerning poverty. While we administer the survey on paper in order to allow for more extended responses, survey software and online technologies such as Kahoot provide another alternative to a paper survey.

The survey questions provide an interesting reference point for our lectures. Questions asked in this initial survey are listed in the Appendix. They include questions such as 'Why are some people poor/rich?', 'In what ways do you think the government should help the poor?', 'How much money does a household need to get by?' The survey also includes questions on minimum wage, school vouchers, marriage incentives and disincentives, definitions of terms we use throughout the course, and questions about racial and geographical differences in poverty.

Following the administration of the survey, the remaining on campus class periods explore official definitions of terms and measurements related to poverty and inequality, readings on poverty, inequality, and discrimination as it relates to South Africa (or the United States and the rest of the world for comparison), trends and statistics as they related to both countries and to other countries around the globe, and an examination of policies and actions around the world that are intended to combat poverty and discrimination.[2] The course uses Schiller's (2008) *The Economics of Poverty and Discrimination* as the textbook, but relies heavily on readings to complete the picture from South Africa's perspective.

The economics of South Africa course uses the book *An Economic History of South Africa: Conquest, Discrimination and Development* by Feinstein et al. (2005) along with articles from popular press outlets regarding current economic issues in South Africa.

The pre-departure meetings also provide background to students as they work on their papers. The paper topics (and related presentations in country) are varied but cover subjects including discrimination in education, discrimination in the criminal justice system, the apartheid, healthcare, inequality, affirmative action, social safety nets, aid programs, and food insecurity. A complete list of paper topics is included in the Appendix.

The student's grade in each class is a function of the midterm (given before departure) (25%), the paper and presentation (30%), the final exam given the last day in country (25%), and the student's journal kept in country relating site visits to class discussions and readings (20%). The journal is the only item that counts towards the students' grades in both classes. All other exams and presentations are course specific, so each student takes a total four exams and is part of two papers/presentations for the two classes.

8.3.2 In Country

In country details will likely vary depending on the course's home institution and that institution's policies. The authors' home institution leaves reservations, site visits, budgeting, and other details up to the faculty. For our travel to South Africa, we have typically chosen to take a longer combination of flights, saving approximately $600 per person. We then use this cost savings to enrich the students' experiences in other areas such as on Safari or with an extra excursion to Victoria Falls in Zambia. For instance, we find that flights to South Africa out of Washington, D.C. are often substantially cheaper than those out of Atlanta. This is true even after including any other expenses of flying to D.C. We also sometimes fly into London, layover there, and then continue to Johannesburg. This route helps substantially with the budget and also allows us a chance to sightsee in London for the day. As we typically offer our South Africa classes during a January term (while it is summer

---

[2]The website https://www.saldru.uct.ac.za/income-comparison-tool/ also has an interesting income comparison tool to help students see where their household income places them among South Africans.

in South Africa), we find that flying over New Year's holiday saves further expense. Budgeting details are included in greater depth in a later section.

A sample itinerary is included in the Appendix, but our time in South Africa is spent in Johannesburg, on safari at Kapama Game Reserve, and in Cape Town. For our first study abroad to South Africa, we also visited Durban and the Drakensburg mountains.[3] However, for subsequent trips, we have chosen to omit these two destinations and instead travel to the Kingdom of Eswatini (a separate country completely surrounded by South Africa—formerly known as Swaziland) and/or Zambia. We have met with an American citizen who is part of a missionary and economic development organization in rural Eswatini. Then we have used some of the financial savings of the cheaper flights to explore Victoria Falls in Zambia, one of the seven natural wonders of the world. Being on the border with Zimbabwe, it also opens the door for class discussions regarding the government and poverty in Zimbabwe.

Field excursions in Johannesburg include stops at the Apartheid Museum, the Hector Pieterson Museum, Nelson Mandela's earlier home, a tour of Soweto and Sandton (poor and wealthy townships located in close proximity), a talk at the Free Market Foundation, and a trip up to the observation deck of the Carleton Center (the tallest office building in Africa). We then travel to Kreuger National Park for a safari before heading to Eswatini, where we tour economic development initiatives and do a rural home visit. Next, we travel to Cape Town, the longest stop of the trip. There we visit Robben Island, District Six Museum, and the Springbok Experience Museum, which discusses discrimination in sports. Cape Town also offers numerous opportunities for meetings with business and government officials. For our trips, these typically include meetings at the Department of Economic Development and Tourism, meetings at Wesgro, and a visit to a venture capital firm. In addition to these academic excursions, the time in South Africa includes several touristy excursions such as: a tour of the wine district in the Western Cape, a South African World of Beer tour, a visit to a gold mine in Gold Reef City, a hike up Table Mountain, time shark cage diving and relaxing on the beach, and visits to Cape Point, various botanical gardens, and a penguin colony.

8.4 Budget

The budgeting process differs from university to university, but we describe below our typical expenses so that those wishing to lead a similar course will have a better idea of the various types of costs to consider. At our university,[4] students do not pay

---

[3]In Durban we visit the KwaMuhle Museum, tour Moses Mabhida Stadium (to show the contrast between funding soccer stadiums over other social needs and discuss the economics of hosting the World Cup tournament), and spend a day at the beach to round out the trip.

[4]The courses referenced here were taught at Western Kentucky University.

Table 8.2 Per person budget for South Africa

Item	Cost
Roundtrip air	$1300.00
Faculty overhead	$1660.00
In-country travel	$500.00
Housing	$1900.00
Excursions	$400.00
Health insurance	$30.00
Visa to Zambia	$50.00
Study abroad fee	$150.00
Meals	$5.00
Total	$5995.00

Table 8.3 Approximate hotel breakdown per night, per person

City	Hotel costs
Johannesburg	$35.00
Safari	$435.00
Eswatini	$35.00
Cape Town	$50.00
Victoria Falls	$150.00

tuition for study abroad courses, but instead must fund all costs (including salary and benefits) for the program leaders. Thus, these costs are factored into our total budget and are passed on to the students as part of their program fees.

Table 8.2 provides a summary of our typical per-person budget, while Table 8.3 gives a per-person nightly breakdown of hotel costs. Of course, prices and exchange rates change, so this is only meant to be used as an overview of what costs to include. In Johannesburg and Cape Town, we usually have four students share a two-bedroom apartment, while we have two people per hotel room in Eswatini and Victoria Falls. Safari costs are on a per person basis, as food is included for the duration of the stay.

Also, we should note that exchange rate variations play a huge role in the ability of a budget to stretch to fund extras such as shark cage diving, nicer safaris, or extra excursions and meals. Combined, we have traveled to South Africa a total of four times: 2010, 2016, 2018, and 2020. The exchange rate in March of 2010 was 7.3 ZAR to the USD. By the time we returned in 2016, it had reached a high of 16.9 ZAR per $1 (despite being below 12 ZAR per $1 when the trip budget was submitted to our study abroad office). In early 2020, the Rand was trading at 15 ZAR per USD.

As budgets for study abroad courses are typically approved almost a year in advance, extra flexibility has to be built in for fluctuations in exchange rates and changes in flight prices. Increases in the value of the US dollar can easily be spent on extras, but unexpected dips must be planned for too. One way we have built flexibility into our budgets is by advertising some excursions as optional and not promising to cover these expenses or all meals. We still build into the budget money for these excursions and a few group dinners, but make no promises up front. That way, if we find that we are able to book flights, hotels, and other expenses below budget, we can use the savings to cover these extras. In the event flight costs rise or the value of the dollar falls before tickets are able to be purchased, we can use those funds budgeted for extra excursions to instead cover the essentials. Alternatively, we can make changes in our accommodations to fit the budget.

In the case of our January 2016 study abroad to South Africa, former President Zuma unexpectedly fired his finance Minister Nhlanhla Nene in the month prior to our trip. His replacement David van Rooyen only lasted a few days before Zuma also replaced him. As a result, the value of the Rand fell drastically. Not only did this provide an interesting course discussion on the importance of government stability, but this also meant our budget went a great deal further on this study abroad. In the months prior to our return in January of 2018, former President Zuma once again fired his finance minister, which sent the Rand plummeting. In both cases, this greatly lowered our expenses in country. As our university does not allow repayment to the student of excess funds (instead they are "absorbed" by the university), we build in a budget for meals and extras that can be expanded to cover situations such as this. That way, the students' money is still spent on the students.

8.5 Final Thoughts

We believe in the benefits of studying abroad so much that we have offered programs to South Africa, Costa Rica, Australia, New Zealand and Northern Europe. We have also participated in semester long study abroad programs at Harlaxton Manor in Grantham, England and on Semester at Sea (run by Colorado State University) traveling throughout Asia and Africa. We know personally how rewarding it is for faculty to leave the traditional classroom and interact with students within the broader classroom that is our world. However, we also know all too well the trials experienced by faculty as they walk a program from its inception to its culmination abroad. Thus, we have written this chapter to help in the development process. Although our details here relate to our South Africa study abroad, many of the details can be used to plan a similar experience elsewhere. It is our hope that these pages will serve as an inspiration for those trying to decide whether to take the plunge and lead a study abroad so that more faculty and students can benefit from the incredible experiences offered outside of the United States.

Appendix

Preliminary Survey: Initial Impressions About Poverty

This survey is designed to gather your initial impressions about poverty and discrimination. You do not need to put your name on this. We will refer back to results from this quiz throughout the semester to compare your thoughts with opinions of the general public and findings from current research.

1. What are the most common reasons why some people are poor?
2. What are the most common reasons why some people are rich?
3. In what ways do you think the government should help the poor? (Circle all that you agree with)

   (a) Better education or greater government subsidy of education
   (b) Government assistance in skills training
   (c) More or better jobs and job opportunities
   (d) Financial aid/welfare
   (e) Subsidized housing
   (f) Better/more health care coverage
   (g) Better/more child care assistance
   (h) More social programs and services
   (i) Tax breaks or lower taxes
   (j) More opportunities such as . . .
   (k) Raise the minimum wage
   (l) other

4. I believe that the federal minimum wage in the US should be

   (a) raised
   (b) lowered
   (c) abolished
   (d) kept the same

5. True/False and explain: The government should enact marriage incentives as a method to limit poverty.
6. School Vouchers would better the educational opportunities of

   (a) only the poor
   (b) only the rich
   (c) only those in religious schools
   (d) only other select students
   (e) all students receiving vouchers
   (f) students in numerous groups listed above
   (g) no one

7. True/False: Persons in South Africa are poor for similar reasons as persons in the US.
8. Privatization of social security would enhance social security benefits for

   (a) the rich workers more so than the poor workers
   (b) poor workers more than rich workers
   (c) all workers evenly
   (d) no-one

(e) all workers, but at a different rate
(f) none of the above

9. I feel the best poverty policy is one that (check any/all you feel should be covered)

(a) offers benefits such as free or reduced price housing, food, clothing
(b) offers work training and childcare for impoverished individuals
(c) creates government funded jobs for poor individuals
(d) gives poor individuals a monthly check
(e) other

10. Define the following terms: poor, equity, efficiency, equality, income, wealth
11. Do you consider yourself rich? Do you believe you will one day be rich? Why or why not?
12. What 'necessities' must one be able to afford to not be considered poor in the US? Ex. electricity, running water, ...
13. How much money is needed a year for a family of 4 (2 adults 2 children) to:

(a) just get by in the US?
(b) live reasonably comfortably?
(c) be considered rich?

14. Nearly one-fourth of African Americans and Hispanic Americans is considered poor as compared to 1 out of 13 Caucasian Americans. Why do you think this discrepancy exists?
15. Circle the letter of any you feel is poor. Who of the following is poor?

(a) A homeless schizophrenic with $500,000 in the bank
(b) A young woman living with wealthy aunt in a beautiful home who enjoys accompanying aunt and doing some shopping and helping her around house. This aunt gives her money when needed, typically $3,000 per year and room and board.
(c) Similar woman to the person in (b) getting room and board and paid $3000 for similar chores for aunt but doesn't enjoy aunt's company.
(d) PhD student making $25,000/year stipend from her university as a teaching assistant.
(e) McDonald's employee making $25,000/year.
(f) Elderly woman in a $500,000 house making very little who is unable to heat house fully and skips meals due to money but doesn't want to move since all of her friends and family there.

16. In what ways do you believe poverty is different in South Africa and the US?
17. What similarities do you believe exist between the poor in the US and South Africa?

Sample Paper and Presentation Topics

1. Inequality in the US and South Africa
2. Unemployment in South Africa
3. Poverty in South Africa vs. Appalachia
4. Discrimination in the US Prison Justice System
5. Racial Discrimination in South Africa Since Apartheid
6. Economics of the South African Beer Industry
7. Economics of Labor Unions in South Africa
8. Discrimination against Women in South Africa
9. South African Poverty Relief Programs
10. Economics of the Gold Mining Industry
11. Economic of the Diamond Industry
12. South African Infrastructure
13. Zimbabwean Immigration to South Africa
14. The Impact of HIV on Eswatini's and South Africa's Economies
15. Aid Solutions to help the Poor
16. Economics of Game Preserves
17. Tourism and South Africa's Economy
18. The Role of Sports in South Africa's Economy
19. Education in the US vs. South Africa
20. Economics of the South African Wine Industry
21. Health Care and the South African Economy

Sample Itinerary for January Economics of South Africa

1. Day 1. Flight
2. Day 2. Layover/Flight
3. Day 3. Time change and arrival in South Africa
4. Day 4. Full day tour of Carleton Center, Soweto, and the Apartheid Museum
5. Day 5. Meetings at the Free Market Foundation and tour South African Brewers World of Beer
6. Day 6. Gold Reef City 'Jozi's Story of Gold' tour followed by free time in the theme park
7. Day 7. Travel to Kapama River Lodge, Kapama Private Game Reserve, game drive (3–4 h)
8. Day 8. Morning and afternoon/night game drives (3–4 h each)
9. Day 9. Morning Game drive followed by travel to Estwatini Swaiziland
10. Day 10. Tour of Cabrini Ministries (school and medical clinic), lunch with local officials, and a home visit in rural Eswatini
11. Day 11. Travel to Cape Town and free time in Cape Town

12. Day 12. Robben Island Tour (The Prison Home of Nelson Mandela and others) and Springbok Experience Museum
13. Day 13. Shark Cage Diving with Marine Dynamics
14. Day 14. Morning meetings at Wesgrow and the Department of Economic Development and Tourism—Afternoon Table Mountain hike/cable car
15. Day 15. Morning meeting at venture capital firm Glenheim Ltd. Friedrich Naumann Foundation. Afternoon at the District 6 Museum (a visit to the Castle of Good Hope is also possible)
16. Day 16. Wine Country Tour with shuttle (4 wineries). Tsiba Tsiba Tours
17. Day 17. Cape Point, Kirstenbosch Botanical Garden, and the Penguin Colony at Simon's Bay
18. Day 18. Flight to Zambia and settle in at Victoria Falls (Note: Purchase Double entry visa to allow walking into Zimbabwe)
19. Day 19. Victoria Falls and final exam
20. Days 20 & 21. Flights back to the US with an overnight on the plane

References

Avert (2020) HIV and AIDS in South Africa. Avert 15 April

Feinstein CH, et al. (2005) An economic history of South Africa: conquest, discrimination, and development. Cambridge University Press, New York

Schiller BR (2008) The economics of poverty and discrimination. Pearson Education, Upper Saddle River

Stats SA (2015) Midyear Population Estimates. Statistics South Africa, Statistical release P0302. https://www.statssa.gov.za/publications/P0302/P03022015.pdf

Stats SA (2019) Five facts about poverty in South Africa. Statistics South Africa, Salvokop

Stoddard E (2019) Stats SA poverty surveys derailed by cash crunch. Business Maverick 6 August

UNICEF (2015) Biennial Report South Africa 2014–2015. UNICEF, Pretoria

Visser MJ, Makin JD, Vandormael A, Sikkema KJ, Forsyth BW (2009) HIV/AIDS stigma in a South African community. AIDS Care 21(2):197–206

Chapter 9
Teaching Economics of Poverty as a Global Classroom Course in Ghana

Brian Hollar

Abstract Sub-Saharan Africa is home to the majority of people living in extreme poverty and is the region of the world that faces the largest challenges to economic growth. In the spring semester of 2018, I took my Economics of Poverty class to Accra, Ghana over spring break. This paper discusses why study abroad in Africa is important for economics students, why Ghana is a particularly good first African experience, and how my trip was planned and structured. This paper is intended to serve as an aid to other faculty thinking about making a similar trip with their students.

9.1 Introduction

A key part of any economics education is learning about the wealth and poverty of nations around the world and across history. This knowledge provides students with an appropriate background to understand the importance of economic growth and the transformative impact it can have on human flourishing. As part of this education, economics students learn many statistics about economic growth and standards of living, but the numbers often fail to fully convey the human reality that lies behind them. To help remedy this, I taught a course in the Economics of Poverty at Marymount University with a study abroad component that traveled to Accra, Ghana for a week over spring break in 2018. The purpose of this trip was to have students get a firsthand glimpse of what life in the developing world is actually like.

The course was designed as a normal, on-campus course which traveled from Arlington, Virginia to Accra, Ghana during our week-long spring break. While in Accra, we worked with partners at the University of Ghana and our students attended lectures given by the university's economics and sociology faculty. We also visited

---

B. Hollar (✉)
Marymount University, Arlington, VA, USA
e-mail: brian.hollar@marymount.edu

© The Author(s), under exclusive license to Springer Nature Switzerland AG 2021
J. Hall, K. Holder (eds.), *Off-Campus Study, Study Abroad, and Study Away in Economics*, Contributions to Economics,
https://doi.org/10.1007/978-3-030-73831-0_9

non-profit agencies; and various cultural and historical sites. The travel portion of the course was also designed to give students some free time to explore some aspects of Ghanaian culture on their own.

Prior to departure, my students engaged in a variety of assignments, readings, and projects to give them a sufficient background in theories of economic growth, productivity, and standard of living. During our lectures and site visits, students had ample opportunity to ask questions to Ghanaian faculty and staff about how what they were learning in Ghana connected to what we had learned in Virginia. This interchange proved to be one of the best learning experiences of the trip. And after we returned, students engaged in further class discussion and projects that challenged them to come up with policy suggestions to try to boost the economic growth of Ghana and lower the poverty rate. The class then spent time critiquing each recommendation and finding the difficulties in incentives and implementation of each recommendation. Through these experiences, students came away with a deep understanding of the complexity of these challenges.

9.2 Why Africa? Why Ghana?

Africa is currently home to the majority of the world's poor (Fig. 9.1). In 2015, 56% of all people living on less than $1.90 per day lived in Sub-Saharan Africa. The region is the only area where the absolute number of people living in extreme poverty is still growing (Roser and Ortiz-Ospina 2013). This raises the puzzle of why economic growth has taken hold in so many other parts of the world, but seems to have left much of Africa behind? As Lucas Jr (1988, p. 5) said: "Once one starts to think about [these issues], it is hard to think about anything else." To understand the most critical issues regarding global poverty today, it is critical to understand Africa.

While many American students study abroad each year, the vast majority of this travel is confined to Europe and Latin America (Metzler 2002). Despite being home to over 1 billion people (The World Bank Group 2020), Sub-Saharan Africa remains one of the least common destinations for American students. As shown in Fig. 9.2, only 4.2% of US students choose Sub-Saharan Africa as a destination to study in the 2017–2018 academic year (Institute of International Education: Open Doors 2020).

Traveling to Africa provided an opportunity to take students to a region of the world they might not otherwise go, connect ideas from class to real-world reality, and to expose students to a part of the world they have little familiarity with and many misconceptions about. My hope was that this experience will help students gain a better understanding of Africa, the challenges of poverty alleviation, the importance of economic growth, and a broader view of the world as a whole.

As Fig. 9.3 illustrates, Ghana was the second most popular destination for US students studying abroad in Africa in 2017–2018 (Institute of International Education: Open Doors 2020). Ghana is a relatively safe, stable, and accessible English-speaking country that provides a good first-experience in Africa. There is a

9 Teaching Economics of Poverty as a Global Classroom Course in Ghana

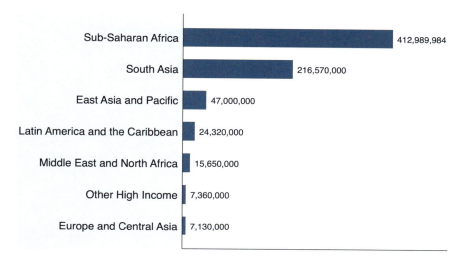

Fig. 9.1 Total population living in extreme poverty by region. Source: Roser and Ortiz-Ospina (2013). Extreme poverty defined as living on less than $1.90 per day in 2011 PPP prices

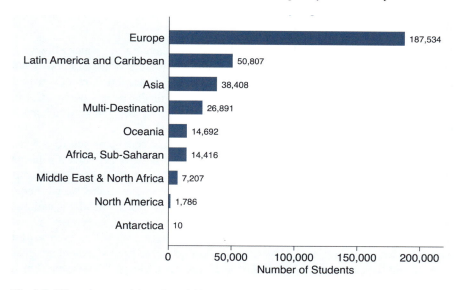

Fig. 9.2 US students studying abroad 2017–2018. Source: Institute of International Education: Open Doors (2020)

rich heritage, friendly people, history of the slave trade that connects directly to America, and reasonably good infrastructure for traveling. There is also a wide diversity of standards of living that can be seen within and around Accra. Ghana also has a thriving culture of music and dance which held tremendous appeal to my

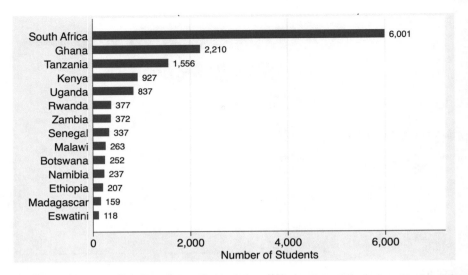

Fig. 9.3 Where US students study abroad when in Africa, 2017–2018. Source: Institute of International Education: Open Doors (2020). Figure only includes countries with more than 100 US students

students. Southern Ghana also has good roads (with heavy traffic) which allows for day or overnight trips from Accra to Cape Coast and Kakum National Park. Accra can be reached by direct daily flights from Europe, which simplified travel logistics. Accra is also home to the University of Ghana, one of the largest universities in Africa. The university has a large, active student and faculty population, which made for an ideal base for our time in Ghana.

To prepare for taking students to Ghana, I traveled to Accra by myself for a week during the summer of 2017 to become familiar with the country, investigate the safety of potential destinations, explore potential sites to visit and make connections at the University of Ghana and several other non-profit organizations we partnered with. Prior to departure, I worked with the Council on International Educational Exchange (CIEE) to develop an agenda and make reservations for my visit. A staff member from Council on International Educational Exchange (CIEE) served as host and guide while I was there and took me on several day trips to surrounding areas to scout out to see if they were good experiences for students. While there, I also made several excursions on my own to become familiar with navigating the country so I would feel comfortable while there with students.

During my visit, I also explored the University of Ghana's campus (where CIEE is located). I also had a chance to make connections with several economists at the International Growth Center (IGC)—a think-tank that is also located on campus. This connection with IGC proved incredibly fruitful and developed into their researchers giving several lectures which were among the favorite academic experiences of my students on our class trip. I also had a chance to stay in two hotels to determine which would be the better choice for staying in with students.

9 Teaching Economics of Poverty as a Global Classroom Course in Ghana

While Ghana is generally a safe environment, many parts of Accra are high crime areas at night. Because of this, we ultimately decided to stay at a guarded, gated hotel that I found on my solo visit. We had a class policy that all students had to remain inside the gates of our hotel after dark unless students were with one of our Ghanaian guides. The hotel had a swimming pool that provided an outdoor meeting and recreation area for students in the evenings.

This early site visit played an important role in helping make the trip a success. Being able to experience the logistics of getting around Accra and traveling to Cape Coast gave me the necessary knowledge to tailor the schedule for my class and re-schedule several activities to reduce stress and fatigue of long days and uncertain traffic patterns. It also gave me an opportunity to forge friendships with staff at both CIEE and IGC, which helped create a friendly rapport between us and facilitated our interactions when I returned to Ghana with students.

9.3 Course Design

Marymount is a smaller university with a student population of approximately 2200 undergraduate students and relatively small class sizes. Our Economics program is also relatively small with approximately 40 Economics majors in total at the university. To increase the appeal of my Economics of Poverty course to a broad range of students, we intentionally kept the prerequisites to a minimum of one prior principles course (either microeconomics or macroeconomics). The course also satisfies an upper-level social science course that all students need to satisfy as part of our liberal arts core requirements. These steps helped ensure enrollment in the course was high enough to make the study abroad trip financially viable for the university.

Key concepts of the course include unintended consequences of economic development programs, the connection between standards of living and fertility, the importance of reliable statistics and challenges of collecting them, the negative impact of corruption, and the importance of agriculture and industry. A fundamental idea that I share with students is the connection between standards of living and the productivity of an economy. We also discuss the fundamental requirements of productivity—institutions, incentives, human capital, physical capital, and technology.[1] After returning from Ghana, we discussed each of these ideas in turn and what students thought Ghana was doing well, what challenges they have, and how this connects to the standard of living we saw. From this, we then talk about how well we think these theories fit what we observed on our trip and where they thought these theories might not capture the entire story.

---

[1] Required readings for the course include Banerjee et al. (2006); Deaton (2013); Karlan and Appel (2011); Klein and Dabney (2013); Utley (2016).

To facilitate the trip, my university partnered with the Council on International Educational Exchange (CIEE) to develop the international potion of this course. CIEE has offices all over the world, including on the campus of the University of Ghana. I have also worked with CIEE to organize student travel to the Czech Republic and Cuba and have enjoyed considerable success in working with them on each of these trips. CIEE handled most of the in-country logistics for our group including making hotel reservations, arranging faculty lecturers at the University of Ghana, planning an overnight trip and transportation to Cape Coast, scheduling visits to non-profits and an elementary school, and guiding us on tours of various parts of Accra. Without this local partner, our trip would have been challenging at best. A full itinerary of our 7 days in Ghana is included in the Appendix.

Another central component of the trip was to have students experience cultural and historical aspects of Ghana. This included trips to important sites involved with the trans-Atlantic slave trade, including a visit a former British fortress (known as a 'slave castle') in Cape Coast that was used to imprison people as their last stop before being loaded onto ships to be sold into slavery in the United States. Our guide during this visit blamed the problems of Ghanaian economic development on the legacy of slavery. This provided for wonderful opportunities to discuss this perspective with students, challenge some of the elements of this story, consider how much of it is correct, and examine what other aspects of political and geographical challenges also play a role in Ghana's current economic development.

As part of the experience, we interacted with economists at the University of Ghana who provided lectures to my students on the effects of corruption, unemployment, the difficulties of providing health services, and the challenges of developing public works for the poor around the country. One of the key challenges underscored by the lecturers was the severe problems corruption made for Ghana at all levels of the government. While the challenges of corruption on economic development are well documented in economics textbooks, hearing about this firsthand from people whose lives are daily impacted by these challenges were much more powerful lessons about these ideas than what students would get in a normal classroom environment.

While in Accra, we spent several days visiting non-profits to learn about their work. Our first visit was to the Adventist Development Relief Agency (ADRA)— an organization dedicated to providing humanitarian relief to the poor in Ghana. My students had a chance to interact with staff members and learn about ADRA various programs to help the poor in Ghana, the impact and challenges of these programs, and ask detailed questions about their work and how they measure the effectiveness of their programs. Our class also visited the International Growth Center (IGC)— a think tank that partners with the London School of Economics and University of Oxford to promote sustainable growth in developing countries. We interacted with two economists at IGC and had ample opportunities to ask questions about the largest challenges of economic development in Ghana. Our class also spent an afternoon volunteering at a local elementary school in the Nima area of Accra. We not only had a chance to interact directly with the Ghanaian children, but also to see the conditions of schools in a poorer region of Accra. For many students, visiting the school was one of the highlights of the trip.

We also were taken on a walking tour of a slum in Accra and learned about the lack of political influence the poor have with the local government. This leads to very real issues such as lack of garbage collection, inadequate policing, low quality educational services, unrepaired roads, lack of clean drinking water, and suboptimal public health services. Having students learn about these issues in the classroom 1 day and then see it firsthand the next day was a powerful learning experience for all of them.

On our last day, students had the opportunity to visit local markets to purchase souvenirs and engage with the local economy. Students were challenged to observe what types of goods were being sold, how negotiations were conducted, and how cash was the only vehicle for trade in these markets.

Each of these experiences were designed to immerse the students in experiential learning to connect the intellectual book knowledge with real world connection. The classroom learning before and after travel was designed to synergize with what we encountered in Ghana. After returning home to Virginia, we spent time debriefing and discussing each of the following issues students saw in Ghana and how it tied into economics: health, education, institutions, saving, unemployment, corruption, fertility, colonialism, and whether Ghana is rich or poor. Students were also challenged with the question of how they would spend $1 million to help improve the lives of people living in Nima (where we volunteered at the elementary school) and how they would spend $1 billion to improve poverty across Ghana. Students overwhelmingly found these questions incredibly difficult to answer after having witnessed the complex realities of life in Africa. By this metric, our trip was an educational success.

9.4 Cost for Students

Marymount University has a core mission that emphasizes "intellectual curiosity, service to others, and a global perspective." Our university takes this mission seriously and actively promotes a wide range of short-term and long-term study abroad opportunities for our students through our Center for Global Education. A key element of this is the promotion of 'Global Classroom Series' (CGS) of classes. These CGS courses are three-credit courses that meet normally throughout the semester, but travel internationally for 7 to 10 days over spring break.

In order to keep our CGS courses affordable, Marymount subsidizes the cost of the trip for students. In 2018, when I took my class to Ghana, the total cost of all CGS courses was a flat fee of $1500. This price included round-trip international airfare from DC, double occupancy accommodations, ground transportation, daily breakfast, all program activities, and emergency travel insurance.

9.5 Conclusion

Short-term study abroad courses to Africa can be a powerful learning experience for undergraduates. They provide an opportunity for students to travel to areas they may be unlikely to visit on their own in the future and provides them with a glimpse at a part of the world they may otherwise never see. To make a course like this most effective requires a site visit by the faculty to establish relationships, develop connections, and plan a successful itinerary. It is important to balance an active schedule with time for students to have a chance for rest, relaxation, and reflection for students who may be stepping outside their comfort zone. Our trip had a good balance of academic dialogue, physical activity, visiting historic and cultural sites, and volunteering with young children.

Ghana in particular is an easy first introduction to Africa. My students loved the music, culture, and dancing they encountered and made friends that they kept in touch with after they returned home. This trip helped students internalize the complex challenges of economic development and poverty alleviation. There is much that can only be learned through experience. Spending a few days in a country can often provide more insight than reading many books. Africa can seem intimidating at first to people who have never visited, but if planned well, it can be very safe, accessible, and educational. For anyone interested in learning more about global poverty and economic development, there is no better place to visit.

Appendix

1. Day 1

   (a) Orientation at CIEE
   (b) Ghana today/Ghanaian custom and etiquette/Adjusting to a new culture
   (c) Health, safety and security protocols—Followed by Q and A
   (d) Scavenger hunt on University of Ghana Campus with University of Ghana students
   (e) Welcome dinner at the study center

2. Day 2

   (a) Tour of the City of Accra/Nkrumah Mausoleum/Cultural Arts Center/Walking through Jamestown in downtown Accra
   (b) Depart to Adventist Development Relief Agency (ADRA) to interact with officials of the organization

3. Day 3

   (a) Lecture: World Bank, IMF policies and the Ghanaian Economy
   (b) Lecture: Poverty and gender in Ghana
   (c) Visit and Interact with officials at International Growth Center (IGC) of the University of Ghana to learn about the state of the Ghanaian economy

4. Day 4

  (a) Community service at Anane Memorial School in Nima
  (b) Walking tour of the Nima Community to experience urban poverty in Ghana
  (c) Lecture: Youth Unemployment and Poverty in Ghana

5. Day 5

  (a) Depart for Cape Coast for an overnight trip
  (b) Assin Manso Slave River
  (c) Cape Coast Castle
  (d) 'Courageous Conversations'—Debriefing

6. Day 6

  (a) Depart for Kakum National Park
  (b) Lunch at Hans Cottage Crocodile Pond Restaurant
  (c) Depart for Accra to arrive at 6pm

7. Day 7—Free Day! Suggested visits:

  (a) Free Day! Suggested visits: Shiashie Cultural Market, Madina Market, Cultural Arts Center
  (b) Farewell Lunch

References

Banerjee AV, Benabou R, Mookherjee D (2006) Understanding poverty. Oxford University Press, New York

Deaton A (2013) The great escape: health, wealth, and the origins of inequality. Princeton University Press, Princeton

Institute of International Education: Open Doors (2020) U.S. Study Abroad: Destinations. https://opendoorsdata.org/data/us-study-abroad/all-destinations/. Accessed 14 May 2020

Karlan D, Appel J (2011) More than good intentions: how a new economics is helping to solve global poverty. Dutton, New York

Klein G, Dabney A (2013) The cartoon introduction to statistics. Hill and Wang, New York

Lucas Jr RE (1988) On the mechanics of economic development. J Monet Econ 22(1):3–42

Metzler J (2002) Undergraduate study-abroad programs in Africa: current issues. Afr Issues 30(2):50–56

Roser M, Ortiz-Ospina E (2013) Global extreme poverty. In: Our World in Data. https://ourworldindata.org/extreme-poverty. Accessed 14 May 2020

The World Bank Group (2020) Population, total – Sub-Saharan Africa. https://data.worldbank.org/indicator/SP.POP.TOTL?locations=ZG. Accessed 14 May 2020

Utley I (2016) Ghana–Culture Smart! The Essential Guide to Customs & Culture. Kuperard, London

Chapter 10
Business in Emerging Markets: The Case of Morocco

Nadia Nafar

Abstract Business is becoming increasingly global. In an effort to broaden students' understanding of how business in conducted in different institutional environments and across cultures, I developed a course titled "Business in Emerging Markets" that uses Morocco as a case study for Virginia Wesleyan University students. In this paper, I describe the process I went through to develop the course and select a study abroad provider. I also share information regarding the course layout, reading list, the itinerary, and cost per student.

10.1 Introduction

Virginia Wesleyan University (VWU) is a small private institution located in Virginia Beach, VA. Experiential learning and student engagement are important elements in the education that students receive. VWU seeks to enhance experiential learning and promote student engagement by encouraging students to learn outside of the classroom through internships, research and study away. The term 'study away' is used to describe taking classes abroad as well as in the United States outside of VWU.

Business has become increasingly global and it has become imperative for business students to learn how to navigate different cultures and institutional environments to succeed in their careers. In an effort to promote VWU students' understanding of different cultures, I developed a study abroad course titled "Business in Emerging Markets" using Morocco as a case study.

Developing and offering a faculty led study abroad class can require a tremendous time commitment and can be a daunting experience for most professors. In this paper, I share my experience developing my business course, my course layout, reading list, itinerary and cost per student. I share this information to provide help

---

N. Nafar (✉)
Virginia Wesleyan University, Virginia Beach, VA, USA
e-mail: nnafar@vwu.edu

© The Author(s), under exclusive license to Springer Nature Switzerland AG 2021
J. Hall, K. Holder (eds.), *Off-Campus Study, Study Abroad, and Study Away in Economics*, Contributions to Economics,
https://doi.org/10.1007/978-3-030-73831-0_10

and support to professors interested in studying Morocco in particular and emerging markets in general.

This course investigates the opportunities and challenges of doing business in emerging markets. It examines the political, legal, cultural, social and economic factors that shape the business environment in such markets as well as explores different business entry mode strategies, negotiating and relationship building in emerging markets and methods to assess risks and opportunities. The course starts at VWU with an on-campus component followed by study abroad at the destination.

The course's learning objectives range from ones specific to the course to others that are common across other VWU study abroad courses. At the conclusion of the course, students should be able to:

1. Analyze a country's political, legal, economic, social and cultural environment and understand how it affects businesses.
2. Develop understanding of the trends, opportunities, and risks involved in operating in an emerging market.
3. Connect theory and practice to identify the best emerging markets' entry modes and strategies.
4. Connect theory and practice to identify the negotiating and relationship building skills necessary to operate in an emerging market.
5. Reflect on the significance of the study abroad experience for personal growth, scholarly and/or professional communities, and wider society.
6. Achieve the following intercultural Learning Outcomes:

   - Develop cultural appreciation by being exposed to a different culture and way of living.
   - Develop a sense of social responsibility, cultural tolerance, and empathy.
   - Develop awareness of their own culture.
   - Develop a sense of their role in the global community.
   - Develop a sense of their home country's role in the global community.

The first four objectives outline the information to be taught in this class. Students are to achieve these objectives through completing their text readings, reading and presenting country specific reports, attending guest lectures, visiting local businesses and engaging in discussions. Students are expected to deliver presentations, complete homework assignments, and submit a final paper. The last two learning objectives are achieved through travelling to Morocco, interacting with local Moroccan university students, meeting with host families, participating in different cultural workshops and field activities and reflecting on all of these experiences in daily blogs.

To conduct my class in Morocco, I use a study abroad provider. The provider facilitates the study abroad program by arranging transportation, accommodation, guest lectures, business visits, excursions, and cultural activities. VWU requires that the faculty member offering the study abroad course personally meets with the provider and visits the cities included in the proposed itinerary before contractually selecting the provider and agreeing to the finalized itinerary. In 2019, I received a

'Study Away Course Development' grant to visit Morocco over the summer and meet with potential providers.

During my preparations to offer the course, I connected with four different providers suggested by VWU's Study Away Director. Most of these providers required that I complete a survey describing the goals of the course and preferred itinerary. After about a couple of months, these providers submitted proposals that included a proposed itinerary and the program fee.

I ended up selecting a provider with local presence and a cultural center in Rabat, Morocco. During my visit to Morocco in summer 2019, I met the provider to discuss program offerings. I also got the opportunity to attend a calligraphy workshop offered to the American university students attending the provider's summer language program. I then had lunch with these students at a local restaurant nearby to hear about their experience working with the provider and about their homestays. After that, I attended a cooking workshop offered to American high school students also attending the provider's high school summer language program. The workshop was offered at the house of one of the host families. This gave me the opportunity to evaluate the provider's cultural activities, talk to a host family and hear from American students. All students expressed satisfaction with the study abroad provider's staff, cultural activities offered, and described how their homestays added great value to their study abroad experience.

The provider's staff informed me that selecting homestays as an option for accommodation lowers the program fee and tends to be one of the highly rated experiences that students appreciate about the program. To help students adjust to homestays, two students are assigned per family. Students get to also complete a housing survey prior to arrival and they are assigned to families that correspond to students' preferences.

10.2   Why Morocco?

Morocco is an interesting country to visit and study. Located in North Africa, Morocco benefits from a Mediterranean climate and possesses two coastlines; the Mediterranean Sea on the north and the Atlantic Ocean on the west. The country also enjoys close geographic proximity to Europe and has a unique culture that stems from its Amazigh, Arab, African, Islamic and Jewish heritage (Barbour et al. 2019).

Morocco was colonized by both France and Spain in the first half of the nineteenth century, which had a lasting impact on the country's institutions. For example, Morocco continues to mimic France when seeking to enact institutional changes and lead modernization efforts (Chauffour 2018). These efforts proved to be counter-productive as borrowing from the experience of a foreign country can lead to reforms that do not meet the immediate needs of the population and that can be challenging to implement. This risk is referred to 'modernization without development' (Fukuyama 2014).

Starting the early 2000s, Morocco embarked on a number of economic reforms to create economic growth and enhance the quality of life of its citizens. These reforms included openness to international trade, privatization of a number of public companies, strengthening of rule of law, revamping the financial system, investing in the country's infrastructure, and increasing access to education and other basic public services (Chauffour 2018).

In 2006, Morocco entered a free trade agreement with the United States. In 2011, the country adopted a new constitution, which if consistently enforced, can have a lasting positive impact on the country's institutions. The country is currently in the process of negotiating a Deep and Comprehensive Free Trade Agreement (DCFTA) with the European Union. Morocco is also seeking increased integration with the African continent to become a leading investment hub.

In an effort to restructure its strategic sectors, the Moroccan government implemented the Morocco Green Plan (2008–2020) which seeks to modernize its agriculture, mining, energy and industry sectors. The plan is on track to achieving the goal of generating 42% of the total energy capacity from renewable energies such as water, solar, and wind power. The plan's other significant goal is to position the country within the industrial global value chains by creating an 'industry ecosystem' that attracts outsourcing projects serving in automobiles, aeronautics and offshoring industries (Chauffour 2018). As of 2017, Morocco was able to secure 26 auto industry projects worth $1.45 billion from French company Renault, PSA Peugeot Citroen, and Chinese automaker BYD, among other companies (Reuters 2017). In 2016, Morocco signed an agreement with Boeing to create an industrial zone that houses 120 of the company's contractors and suppliers (Yahoo News! 2016). The goal of these industry ecosystems is to create half a million jobs by 2020 (The Borgen Project 2016).

Coupled with careful macroeconomic management policies and controlled inflation, the Moroccan government's reforms were able to eradicate extreme poverty (percentage of the population living on $1.90 per day in constant 2011 purchasing power parity (PPP) US dollars) and reduce moderate poverty (percentage of the population living on $3.20 per day in constant 2011 (PPP) US dollars) from 7.4% in 2000 to 1.6% in 2013. GDP per capita rose from $4,492 in 2000 to $7,641 in 2018 in constant 2011 (PPP) US dollars. Access to education and other basic public services have also improved during this period (The World Bank Group 2020).

Despite these initiatives and reforms, Morocco continues to face important challenges that can threaten its future stability. The Moroccan economy is still dependent on agriculture despite efforts to diversify. The unemployment rate in 2019 amounted to 9% of the total population, with heavier concentration in rural areas (The World Bank Group 2020). A high number of Moroccans continue to feel dissatisfied with their living conditions. In 2012, Morocco's High Commission for Planning found that 45% of Moroccans are not very or not at all satisfied with their life, 24% are fairly satisfied, and barely 30% are satisfied. Disposable income was a major determinant, with affluent Moroccans reporting that they are the happiest and the poorest reporting that they are unhappy (Chauffour 2018).

The reforms and initiatives undertaken provide the business community with many opportunities. However, the existing challenges represent major threats that business professionals have to navigate and take into account when making investment decisions. Given that Morocco is a safe and affordable destination, students will be able to learn about its business environment by hearing from Moroccan entrepreneurs, academics, and non-governmental organizations (NGOs) about the role that formal and informal institutions play in accelerating or hindering economic growth. Students will also use the information they learn to identify investment opportunities as well as select market entry strategies that take into account the country's risk level.

10.3   Course Layout

The course is to take place during the university's 3 week January term with 3 days on campus and a total of 15 days and 14 nights at the destination. Although the course can also be offered during the summer, offering it during the January term is more preferable as it is cheaper. Full time students that attend the university are exempt from paying tuition for classes taken in January, except for the $250 January term fee. Flights to Morocco tend to also be cheaper during January compared to the summer.

During the fall semester, students are given a list of readings and are assigned a number of readings to present. During the first 3 days we spend on campus, I lecture on the theory of doing business in emerging markets and students present their country specific readings. The goal is to enable students to be introduced to the country and class topics prior to arrival to the destination. This gives them time to process the information they learn, which enables them to link it to what they observe once at the destination. In addition to allowing students to have more time experiencing the country once there, meeting on campus is used to clarify course expectations, discuss the risks associated with study away and go over emergency protocols. Students are required to attend a pre-departure workshop given the university's Study Away Program director. The purpose of this workshop is to prepare students for their study abroad experience and familiarize them with university policies while abroad. During their time in Morocco, students visit local businesses, hear about local entrepreneurs' experiences, attend lectures offered by Moroccan university professors on contemporary Moroccan society, green energy in Morocco, and entrepreneurship as well as visit NGOs active in promoting entrepreneurship. Students get to also interact with Moroccan university students, visit five cities, and engage in different cultural activities.

It is critical that students participate in all of these activities in order to benefit from their study abroad experience. Their class grade reflects their level of participation (15%), which is based on the enthusiasm and curiosity they show during site visits, their contribution to discussions, and their timeliness in attending different course activities. They are required to write daily blogs (20%) in which they reflect on their observations and link them to the course material. They are also encouraged to accompany their blogs with photos they take. Students have to give presentations (25%) that cover country specific readings and complete homework assignments (15%) for each topic covered in class. At the conclusion of the class, students are to submit a paper (20%) where they provide a country report that includes an assessment of the country's business environment (challenges and opportunities) and come up with 3 possible US products/services that they can sell in Morocco and 3 possible Moroccan products/services that they can sell in the United States. They are required to provide reasoning for the products/services choices, entry modes, as well as assess the risks they can potentially face and how to deal with them once they start operations. Students have 2 days upon return to the US to submit the paper, with a possible extension if needed be. In addition, students have to complete an anonymous evaluation of the course (5%) in which they are asked to assess the material covered, the sites they visited, the cultural activities and excursions they did and their overall experience. The feedback is used to improve the course and the itinerary.

10.4 Reading List

The course is structured in a way that covers the theory of conducting business in emerging markets using Morocco as a case study. I use the textbook *Doing Business in Emerging Markets* by Cavusgil et al. (2012) when discussing the opportunities, challenges and strategies of conducting business in emerging markets. When exploring how these topics apply to Morocco, I use select readings from the World Bank lead economist Jean-Pierre Chauffour's (2018) book *Morocco 2040: Emerging by Investing in Intangible Capital* along with different readings provided in the press, government sites, and research institutes.

The class covers five main topics. The first topic gives an overview of emerging markets including common demographic, political and economic characteristics. Students get introduced to Morocco by completing readings on the country's history and background including its culture and economy. The second topic explores the political, legal and cultural framework in emerging markets in general and in Morocco in particular. Students are introduced to types of political systems, legal systems and cultural differences in emerging markets as well as strategies to manage them. To learn about Morocco and its political, legal and cultural framework, students read country reports and readings provided by Freedom House (2020), The World Bank Group (2020), Hofstede Insights (2020), and other articles written by entrepreneurs that conducted business in Morocco (Nhairy 2017).

In the third topic, we discuss the economic environment in emerging markets, including institutional challenges, income distribution, and workforce characteristics. To learn about the economic environment in Morocco, students read the US Department of State's (2019) *Investment Climate in Morocco* report as well as the Heritage Foundation's country economic freedom report (Miller et al. 2020).

The fourth topic explores the opportunities and trends in emerging markets. These include growth of the middle class, urban development, the rising demand for technology and telecommunications, infrastructure investments, etc. and how businesses can take advantage of these opportunities. To learn about the opportunities and trends specific to Morocco, students learn about the Morocco-US free trade agreement, explore investment opportunities provided by Moroccan Investment Development Agency (2020), read the Morocco Commercial Guide provided by the International Trade Administration (2020) as well as different articles in the press.

The fifth topic examines the entry modes and strategies to employ in emerging markets. These include trade-based entry strategies, contract-based entry strategies, investment entry modes and the different factors to consider when selecting an entry mode. For information on the entry modes that apply to Morocco, students read the Morocco Commercial Guide provided by International Trade Administration (2020).

10.5 Itinerary

We spend the first 3 days of the January term at the university. During this time, students attend lectures, deliver presentations, and receive pre-departure orientation from the study away program director. On the fourth day, we depart from Norfolk, Virginia to Casablanca, Morocco. Once we arrive to Casablanca's airport, we meet the provider at the airport to be transported to Rabat, which is a 45-min drive away from Casablanca.

Rabat is the capital of Morocco. It is a safe city where students can be exposed to modern Morocco as well as provides easy access to the city's historic district such as the Kasbah and old medina. Students also get the opportunity to do a day trip to Casablanca as well as do overnight excursions to Marrakech, Essaouira, and Chefchaouen.

While in Rabat, students stay in homestays with Moroccan families. Prior to coming to Morocco, students complete a housing survey. The provider uses the survey to place students with the families that match students' preferences. The Moroccan families that work with the provider are vetted, have experience hosting foreign students, and have at least one English speaker living at home. This would typically be a college aged son or a daughter that lives at home and is fluent in English. Two students are assigned per family. Choosing homestays while in Rabat lowers the accommodation costs as well as gives the students the opportunity to live and interact with a Moroccan family, which deepens student's understanding and appreciation of the local culture. Students stay in hotels when visiting other cities.

The tentative itinerary below lists in greater detail the course's different academic and cultural activities.

- Day 1: VWU

  - Overview of emerging markets
  - Political, legal, and cultural framework in emerging markets
  - Morocco history and background
  - The political, legal, and cultural environment in Morocco

- Day 2: VWU

  - The economic environment in emerging markets
  - The economic environment in Morocco and market support institutions
  - Pre-departure workshop offered by the university's study away program director

- Day 3: VWU

  - Opportunities and trends in emerging markets
  - Morocco's business and investment opportunities
  - Entry modes and strategies in emerging markets
  - Entry mode strategies in Morocco

- Day 4: Travel Day
- Day 5: Rabat

  - On-site orientation on cultural issues, health and safety protocol and local logistics
  - Guided city tour of Rabat: Visit the Roman ruins of Challah, Hassan Tower and Andalusian Gardens of L'Oudaya
  - Meet host families

- Day 6: Rabat

  - Guest speaker: Contemporary Moroccan society
  - Business visit: Oulja artisans
  - Visit to the silver complex located in the old section of the city, with over 23 silver and gold stores selling beautiful jewelry
  - Tea break at the Andalusian Gardens of L'Oudaya with local university students to discuss religion, sexuality, economics, education and politics in Morocco

- Day 7: Rabat

  - Calligraphy workshop: a workshop to learn Arabic calligraphy skills and the history and variations of calligraphy
  - Scavenger hunt in Rabat with local university students to learn the way around town while interacting with local peers
  - Museum of Modern Art visit

10 Business in Emerging Markets: The Case of Morocco

- Day 8: Rabat to Chefchaouen
  - Chefchaouen city guided tour
  - Business visit: Honey cooperative
  - Discussion: entrepreneurship and education in rural areas
  - Attend workshops on leather, carpet-weaving or brass with local artisans
- Day 9: Chefchaouen to Rabat
  - Organic farm visit: Visit to an organic farm
  - Discussion: Agriculture in Morocco
  - Break to enjoy a typical Moroccan tea time with virgin olive oil, honey, fresh bread, and different organic jams
- Day 10: Rabat to Marrakech
  - Marrakech city guided tour
  - Business visit: Carpet cooperative visit
  - Free evening in Marrakech
- Day 11: Marrakech
  - Visit to local village in the Amazigh Ourika Valley, located in the foothills of the High Atlas Mountains
  - Business visit: Argan Oil cooperative
  - Lunch in the valley
  - Optional hike into the surrounding village and camel rides
- Day 12: Marrakech to Essaouira
  - Essaouira guided city tour
  - Business visit: Jewelry cooperative
- Day 13: Essaouira to Rabat
  - Guest Speaker: Alternative (green) energy solutions in Morocco
- Day 14: Casablanca
  - Guided tour of Hassan II Mosque
  - Visit to Morocco mall, the largest mall in North Africa
  - Lunch at local restaurant
- Day 15: Rabat
  - Guest speaker: Entrepreneurship in Morocco
  - Moroccan cooking class
- Day 16: Rabat
  - Visit entrepreneurship NGOs in Rabat

- Day 17: Rabat
  - Free day
- Day 18: Rabat
  - Reflection session with students
  - Farewell dinner
- Day 19: Departure to United States

10.6 Cost Per Student

This study abroad course is available to students from different majors with no pre-requisite requirement. To make the course attractive to students, the university requires all faculty led study abroad courses cost to not exceed $3500. In offering the course, I work with a provider that has local presence in Morocco. The provider facilitates a 14-night program and the fee is $2205 per student for a group of 10 to 14 students and one faculty member. The fees cover accommodations for 14 nights with breakfast, some meals, on-site orientation on cultural issues and logistics, guest lectures, local business visits, transportation from and to airport, site visits and excursions, and travel insurance and political and natural disaster evacuation package. Accommodations include double occupancy with breakfast for students and single occupancy with breakfast for faculty. The students' fees also cover one faculty member's fees.

Students are responsible for the flight cost from Norfolk to Casablanca, some meals, and money for souvenirs. The flight cost is generally under $1000 during January. I also budget for an emergency fund of $50 per student.

For full-time students that attend the university in the fall and spring semesters, the January term tuition is waived and students pay a $250 January term fee. Students have to also spend about three nights on campus before departure and they pay the pro-rated housing cost of about $25 per night. Students can apply to receive grants and funding from the university to help with study abroad costs.

10.7 Conclusion

In this paper, I share my experience developing a study abroad business course in Morocco. I describe the process I went through selecting a study away provider as well as provide the course layout, reading list, itinerary, and cost per student.

As business becomes increasingly global, it is important for students to understand how business is conducted in different institutional environments and across cultures. While developing a faculty led business course requires intense time and energy commitment, the experience can be life enriching for students and faculty.

Exposing students to different cultures can help them broaden their prospects and can ultimately lead them to have better cross cultural understanding, which can serve them well in their personal and professional lives.

Acknowledgments This course was expected to be offered for the first time in January 2021. Due the Covid-19 global pandemic, the course was postponed till January 2022. In Summer 2019, I visited Morocco to select the study abroad provider and itinerary. In academic year 2019/2020, I developed the course syllabus and got the course approved by Virginia Wesleyan University. This paper describes the process I went through to develop the course and lists the course layout, readings, itinerary and cost per student.

References

Barbour N, Brown LC, Swearingen WD, Miller SG, Laroui A (2019) Morocco. Encyclopaedia Britannica https://www.britannica.com/place/Morocco. Accessed 20 May 2020

Cavusgil ST, Ghauri PN, Akcal AA (2012) Doing business in emerging markets. Sage, Newbury Park

Chauffour JP (2018) Morocco 2040: emerging by investing in intangible capital. International Bank for Reconstruction and Development/The World Bank, Washington

Freedom House (2020) Freedom in the World 2020: Morocco. Freedom House, Washington

Fukuyama F (2014) Political order and political decay: from the industrial revolution to the globalization of democracy. Macmillan, New York

Hofstede Insights (2020) Country comparison: Morocco and the USA https://www.hofstede-insights.com/country-comparison/morocco,the-usa/. Accessed 20 May 2020

International Trade Administration (2020) Doing business in Morocco. International Trade Administration, Washington

Miller T, Kim AB, Roberts JM (2020) 2020 Index of economic freedom. The Heritage Foundation, Washington

Moroccan Investment Development Agency (2020) Investment opportunities. Kingdom of Morocco, Rabat

Nhairy S (2017) What running a business in Morocco has taught me. Entrepreneur https://www.entrepreneur.com/article/305953. Accessed 20 May 2020

Reuters (2017) Morocco Announces Auto Industry Deals Worth $ 1.45 Bln https://www.reuters.com/article/morocco-economy-autos-idUSL8N1OB691. Accessed 20 May 2020

The Borgen Project (2016) Boeing ecosystem: striking manufacturing deal with Morocco. The Borgen Project, Tacoma

The World Bank Group (2020) Data: Morocco https://data.worldbank.org/country/morocco. Accessed 20 May 2020

US Department of State (2019) 2019 Investment Climate Statements: Morocco. US Department of State, Washington

Yahoo News! (2016) Morocco signs deal for major Boeing hub https://news.yahoo.com/morocco-signs-deal-major-boeing-hub-190035392.html. Accessed 20 May 2020

Chapter 11
The Chinese Menu: How to Discover the Key Ingredients of Market Systems Through a Study Abroad Program

Craig J. Richardson

Abstract China's politicians describe often their economy as 'capitalism with Chinese characteristics'—yet there is debate about the underlying drivers of this state capitalism model. Is it government's guiding hand or the invisible hand of the free market that allows it to flourish? This paper argues that a travel course to China allows students to discover first-hand both the strengths and weaknesses of this system, through exposure to Chinese academics, migrant worker camps, factories, museums, villages and cities. By the end of the course, students also gain a greater appreciation of the strengths and weaknesses of democratic based market systems.

11.1 Introduction

I have Nobel Laureate Professor Douglas North to thank as a reason why I took a group of students to China for the first time in 2006. We never met; it was because of an article he published in *The Wall Street Journal* called "The Chinese Menu (for Development)" (North 2005). North argued that different regions of the world have different institutional structures—and they may evolve with different modes of exchange. "The key is creating an institutional structure derived from your particular cultural institutions that provide the proper incentives- not slavishly imitating Western institutions," North wrote. He argued there was no one set menu for growth—it was a 'Chinese menu.' Indeed, North pointed out that China grew strongly, yet it "still does not have well-specified property rights."

This article irked me because it challenged my understanding of economic development—I believed that there *were* some non-negotiable menu items in every economy, just as every loaf of bread contains flour, yeast, salt and water. Property rights was one of my essential ingredients on a specified list of a well-functioning economy. Indeed, my decade-long research in Zimbabwe had made me even more

C. J. Richardson (✉)
Winston-Salem State University, Winston-Salem, NC, USA
e-mail: richardsoncr@wssu.edu

© The Author(s), under exclusive license to Springer Nature Switzerland AG 2021
J. Hall, K. Holder (eds.), *Off-Campus Study, Study Abroad, and Study Away in Economics*, Contributions to Economics,
https://doi.org/10.1007/978-3-030-73831-0_11

convinced of this supposition. During the early 2000s, Zimbabwe was one of the fastest collapsing economies in the world due to its abandonment of property rights during its disastrous land reform program. It provided a powerful case in showing how important property rights are as a linchpin for an economy (Richardson 2005).

North's article threw down a gauntlet of sorts and sparked my interest in traveling to China to investigate this claim for myself. What better way to do this than to take students along and turn it into a course that investigated China's economy? The thread of the journey with my students would be to investigate the key ingredients that we economists typically hold dear: free markets, a stable money supply, low government intervention and secure property rights, and compare how they operate versus within China.

The crux of the travel course was to ask the following questions:

- Why was China growing much faster than the United States, and what role did property rights play in this development?
- Was China's system of "capitalism with Chinese characteristics" sustainable over the long term?
- Were there weak spots in the Chinese menu for development that we would discover through our travels?
- What would we discover about the strengths and weaknesses of the United States' version of free market capitalism with its reliance on democracy?

Prior to leaving, students read articles and books on China's history and economic development, studied notions of economic freedom and how to measure it, using freedom index indicators, and got a better understanding of China's current business environment.[1] Students were intrigued to learn about its culture that heralded inventions and creativity hundreds of years before Mao's Communist revolution, the hardships and millions of deaths caused by communal farming systems during the Communist era, the 1978 economic reforms through Deng Xiaoping, the entrance into the World Trade Organization in 2001, the subsequent explosion of economic activity since the 1990s, and GDP growing two to three times as fast as the United States.

Upon doing some initial research in preparing for the course, North's supposition that China doesn't have 'well-specified property rights' appears correct when looking at the hundreds of millions of Chinese living in poverty in rural areas. Since the mid-1980s, an estimated 40 million peasant farmers have had their land expropriated for commercial development, for a tiny fraction of the land's value. The Washington-based Property Rights Alliance constructed an International Property Rights Index, and between 2007 and 2019 never got above a ranking of 45 out of 121 countries (Levy-Carciente 2015).

---

[1] Students read Chang (2009), Coase and Wang (2013), Fu and Balasubramanyam (2003), Gifford (2008), Levinson (2016), North (2005), Pan (2005), Richardson (2011), and Whalley and Xian (2010).

11 The Chinese Menu: How to Discover the Key Ingredients of Market... 121

Yet China's economy has boomed, and foreign direct investment continues to pour into the country, rising from $2 billion in 1990 to $90 billion to $139 billion by 2018 (Statista 2020). This raises a compelling question: Why, over such a long time frame, are foreign investors taking such risks without secure property rights? What makes China different?

The answer, as we would find during our travels to China, is that North's declaration of China's attenuated property rights *only applies to the regions where economic growth is the weakest*. In fact, as our students learned from economists while on the trip, economic growth has depended upon a property-rights system with varying degrees of security for different groups in society. The more the property rights system emulates the Western model, the faster the growth.

The engine of economic growth is not a Chinese menu, as students would discover, but much closer to a European/American recipe card. Along other lines, however, there are special nuances about the Chinese system of markets that bear closer study- some of which accelerate growth and others which slow it down. As we discovered, it was a combination of readings, seminars in China and real-world experiences that created the best dish for understanding China's unique system of economic development.

11.2 The Real Story About Property Rights in China

North's claim that China's property rights system was different than the United States was true up to a point. Further explanation was needed since the answer was a bit more complicated. A key aspect of the course was to introduce students to China's three-tier system of property rights, which depends on where the property is located and who owns it. Foreign investors have the most secure property rights, city residents have better protection, and peasant farmers have the least protection. During my three trips abroad in 2006, 2013 and 2015, students were able to meet at least two of the three groups and interact with them, along with getting information from Chinese economics professors about the nuances of property rights in China.

11.2.1 The Foreign Investors

In Shanghai in 2013, we met with the local district mayor, who introduced us to a research park built exclusively for foreign entrepreneurs wanting to start companies in China. They paid no rent and enjoyed high quality office space for the first 6 months. One entrepreneur from the Netherlands was making solar panels. Because of the welcoming attitudes and strong protection against expropriation built into Chinese law, foreigners have developed a high level of trust with the Chinese. China nurtures this relationship for other good reasons as well. They felt very strongly about building factories in China, through joint ventures which are strongly encouraged, or on their own.

Although laborers in China's foreign-owned companies make up only 3% of the workforce, they are nine times more productive, and contributed some 40% of overall GDP growth in 2004 (Whalley and Xian 2010). This was an indication of how Western practices have had a large impact on Chinese economic growth. On another trip, we visited a large Volkswagen production plant, with state-of-the art robotic welders and painting machines. The point here to be made was that China was not all about cheap labor-foreign investment was coming here in capital intensive industries as well, with relatively few workers, because the cost of shipping was low and the Chinese government worked with foreign investors to assure them of a low regulatory environment relative to the West. China's issuing of long-term leases to multi-national companies helped assure them and led to enormous investments in capital for their factories.

11.2.2 City Dwellers

The property-rights protections for city dwellers are significantly greater. City residents often receive a special designation, known as 'urban dweller' status. Upon getting this designation, a city resident may enter into the housing market and purchase a long-term lease from the Communist government (typically 70 years). Note that in China, the government owns all the land. It is the buildings upon the land which can be 'owned' by citizens though the ownership rights are not held with an infinite time frame as they are in Western style economies. Such leases are fully transferable and can be used as collateral for borrowing. Although city dwellers are still subject to eminent-domain types of land claims, they must be compensated for their dwelling with fair market value, or allowed to buy dwelling at another, similar location. Perhaps the government recognizes, from a pure profit-motive perspective, that there is far more to lose by expropriating, say, office buildings, rather than rice paddies. The potential for foreign-capital flight would be very high indeed. Most of the people we met during our trip fell into this category of city dweller.

Our tour guide illustrated this by giving us a tour of her condo she had purchased a few years earlier. She explained to us that with her lease, she could pass this condo onto her children. I asked her, "What will happen when the 70-year lease expires?" She smiled, raised up her hands and said, "I'll be dead by then, that's not my problem." One of the issues with long-term leases is that they raise a bit of uncertainty as to what the government will do as the expiration date nears. "What will be the new lease rate?" every new owner of a building must ask. This uncertainty will lower the market price of a dwelling or any building, which is the price of government control over property. Here was another way students were learning first hand how markets in the West functioned differently than markets in China.

11.2.3 Rural Residents

Rural residents have the fewest property rights of all. Since the Communist party owns the land, farmers have little ability to leverage any equity to borrow for say, a tractor. This is not uncommon in many countries around the world, where billions of dollars of 'dead capital' remain locked up through a lack of property rights (deSoto 2003).

There is a twist with the Chinese system. The residents generally operate under the auspice of what is known as a town-village enterprise, or TVE. A TVE is a land collective that lets farmers receive the fruit of their labors but decides from year to year how land will be allocated. The mayors or managers of the TVEs are directed by China's central government to be self-supporting; no one expects government bailouts from Beijing. The town-village enterprise (TVE) is a decided improvement over communal farming, which led to the loss of millions of lives in the 1960s, but it still keeps rural farmers from gaining much ground, economically speaking.

Interestingly, Town Village Enterprises act as if they were for-profit corporations, with peasants in the role of de facto employees, rather than property owners. TVEs compete with each other in wooing foreign investors, promising them tax breaks and land. A foreign company can generate far more tax revenue and many more jobs than a rice-paddy farmer, so the Chinese government gives them more attention. Fu and Balasubramanyam (2003) demonstrate that TVEs played a significant role in the Chinese economy since the 1978 economic reforms, and are much efficient than state owned enterprises.

Our students learned time and time again that the Chinese government tends to 'follow the money' rather than a set of prescribed guidelines around the sanctity of individual rights and private property, as is typical for democracies in the West. This is part of the reason for their more rapid economic growth, where environmental groups, tighter regulatory regimes and a court system that allows people to sue against unjust takings invariably stymie more rapid growth. We thus showed that democracy, for all its benefits, in some cases can lead to stagnating growth as the economy matures (Olson 1984).

The property-rights system is thus centered on the interlocking relationship between the TVE and the foreign investor, and it has worked with a brutish efficiency that has not been thwarted by special interests, such as environmental or health organizations, or by labor unions. Foreign investors rely on TVEs to enforce land rights, while TVEs depend on foreigners for tax revenue. This goes far to explain why foreign companies do not hesitate to invest in China and have few worries about losing their investment by government expropriation.

As we learned from Chinese economists during our visit, it is not uncommon for a farmer to discover bulldozers readying his land for a new factory. His compensation, perhaps $5000, is a fraction of the hundreds of thousands of dollars that the Town Village Enterprise may receive from the foreign investor for rights to the property. The displaced farmer must then find a job in the city or at the factory. Across the countryside, peasant farmers are more openly rebelling against such actions, and anger is rising. During the 2000s farmers led tens of thousands of riots or protest (Pan 2005).

During our trip in January 2006, students travelled to a very poor rural farming village where villagers lived in one room houses and heated their homes with bundles of twigs. In one home we saw, their worldly possessions included a small transistor radio, a large bed for the family of four, two sets of clothing for each family member and a small number of dishes and pots. They could see first-hand the issues with insecure property rights, with little incentive to become more productive. In one of the most memorable and unscripted events of the trip, the farmer invited our students to play ping pong with him outside on a rectangular cement slab set up on bricks, bearing a ragged green net. With smiles all around, it was a true moment in 'ping pong diplomacy.' This interaction was listed for all students as one of the top three memories of the entire trip.

11.3 From Rural Life to Migration: The Migrant Worker

Millions of rural residents, many who were fed up with the TVE arrangement, decided to migrate to the cities to find better work. It is important to first understand a bit more about migrant workers here in China. Unlike the United States, where we can freely migrate to other cities to take jobs and eventually settle with our families, in China things operate quite differently. Every Chinese citizen is registered for a particular area of the country, in what is called a *hukou* system. They cannot legally become official residents in a new city unless given permission from the government. So when workers in China migrate, they must live in company provided temporary housing that gives them a lower social status. The workers can work and live there as long as a contract exists but must return home otherwise or somehow evade detection. They or their families cannot get access to government-provided health or education from areas outside their household registration zone.

For U.S. citizens, this lack of freedom may seem shocking, but from the Chinese government's perspective, it is more like envisioning the country as a corporation. Labor flows between different areas of the country are managed to maximize economic growth and stability. To put this in our perspective, people who work for large corporations in the U.S. are not able to move on a whim to regional offices in other cities. Rather, the labor pool is managed to assure a steady output of labor personnel at each corporate location. By contrast, the Chinese might compare the alternative to Calcutta, India, where the chaotic and uncontrolled influx of desperate villagers from the countryside has led to shockingly poor living conditions in the cities. These are the scenes China's ruling government wishes to avoid.

On the other hand, migrant workers are free to move from construction site to site, picking the company that pays the highest combination of wages and benefits. In that sense, the market should theoretically allow for workers' living conditions to improve over time, especially in a rapidly growing economy. Jian Chang, a Hong-Kong based economist at Barclays, has noted that the millions of migrant workers have "increasingly high expectations and more life options" in a 2013 *Wall Street Journal* article on China's labor shortages (Chu 2013).

11 The Chinese Menu: How to Discover the Key Ingredients of Market. . . 125

Given all this, what are the conditions for migrant workers? I wanted our students to observe this firsthand. In the end, we finally gained permission from the company through a series of lucky connections with our travel provider, the Council for International Educational Exchange (CIEE). During the study abroad trip in 2015, we visited a building site known as Rongxin & Greenland International outside of Shanghai, which was a partnership between the privately owned Rongxin company and the state-owned Greenland International. Both companies have dozens of expensive building projects across the country. In the modern lobby, a detailed scale model glowed under soft lighting, and allowed visitors to view the project from every angle. We could see a planned series of apartment towers, a hospital complex and nicely trimmed green spaces.

Most visitors never go to where the workers live, but for me this was the most interesting part for our students and me to see. Turning down a gravel road, we headed towards what appeared a typical construction site. A 10-foot wall surrounded the dormitories, and we were warmly greeted by a manager. Walking on the concrete pavement inside the compound, we saw several dozen dorm style rooms on two levels, Motel 6 style, and doors were propped open in some. Peeking inside one of them, two to three bunk beds allowed a half dozen men a place to live and sleep. The rooms, while small and not air-conditioned, nonetheless were clean and well kept. A small company store stocked cold drinks, snacks and other sundries at prices not out of the ordinary. In all, the company employs 500 migrant workers for this project alone.

Workers on break came over to greet us with big smiles. They were dressed with relatively new clothes that one would find at Walmart or Target, and nice tennis shoes. But most surprisingly, many of them had smartphones. On our short tour, we saw the company provided cafeteria, which was clean and well lit. Twenty percent of the workers had wives living on site, according to the manager, and the cafeteria transformed into a school for the children between meal times.

In response to our questions, the workers told us they had come here because the pay was so much better than the villages they had left behind. In many cases there was 'no work' or just subsistence rice farming. Here they could make far more money and send some money home. Later, I found out from one of the company managers exactly how much money these workers made, how many hours they worked and compensation for overtime. The pay, it turns out, was surprisingly high, particularly for a developing country.

Laborers at this construction site work 25 days a month, on average, and earn roughly 45,000 yuan, or $7260 a year if they are unskilled, according to the company. However, it is important to adjust for the cheaper cost of living in China. Using purchasing power parity (PPP) estimation can help give a better sense of these numbers. That same salary would be equivalent to earning about $12,100 in the United States, using World Bank conversion factors. Highly skilled workers, such as construction crane operators, do far better, earning up to $19,355 per year (or 120,000 yuan), while a PPP adjustment makes their annual salary in U.S. terms about $32,300. This is indeed a far cry from working in a rice paddy field, where villagers might only earn $500–$1000 a year. Overtime is also generous: if workers work more than 10 h, they get an extra half day's payment. And working more than 12 h earns them a whole extra day's payment.[2]

While these wages are higher than the country average for migrant construction workers, the wage growth rate for all migrant workers has been remarkably rapid in recent years. By 2018 wages were 3721 yuan per month, about $530 monthly at current exchange rates. This compares to about 5000 yuan *a year* for a typical Chinese farmer, or about $60 a month (Statista 2020).

11.4   Is China's Growth Sustainable?

This was another question our students explored and I asked them to keep this in mind as we stayed in China. China's model has worked remarkably well in bringing about the fastest economic transformation of any society in history. For the past 20 years, its GDP growth averaged 10%, while the United States averaged less than 3%. The Chinese economy is now 550% larger than it was in 1990. In contrast, the U.S. economy grew only 70% over the same time frame (but is still four times larger than China's). In 2010, the People's Republic surpassed Japan to become the second largest economy in the world (World Bank 2020).

China has succeeded by running its economy like a corporation, with government and business working in tandem to achieve economic growth and business profits. Unlike the U.S., group opposition to urban projects is forbidden by law, further speeding up the construction process. An important government role is to build a state-of-the-art infrastructure that serves its industrial base. Shanghai, for example, built twelve new subway lines in 15 years, a far cry from the cost overruns for railway projects in the United States as well as the inevitable lawsuits by NIMBY advocates.

Often unquestioned in projections about China is a key phrase: 'at the current rate of growth.' This assumption can create woefully bad predictions. If we used the growth rate of a 2-year-old child to predict her height at 16, we might conclude she would reach 10 feet. But growth rates for people and countries drop as they mature. As a result, two girls, aged 2 and 16, tend to converge in height–even if the younger one never catches up. The same holds for poor and rich countries' income levels.

This leads to a dilemma: How can a poor country acquire capital? China neatly solves this problem by saving an astonishing 53% of its GDP (World Bank 2020). This is the highest rate in the world, even though China's 2009 per capita income is only $6,800, using purchasing power parity adjustments by the World Bank (2020). As China grows, its higher GDP results in even more savings and investment, leading to a so-called 'virtuous cycle' of upward spiraling income. But as China becomes richer, it also faces the inevitable diminishing returns to capital and worker productivity, as well as a shortage of skilled workers. These are significant (and oft-

---

[2]This account of our migrant worker visit is heavily drawn from Richardson (2015b).

discussed) reasons why China's growth will slow in the future. But dig deeper and an array of other significant challenges weigh more heavily in the short term, which are a direct result of its focus on low-cost manufacturing. China has a culture that does not cultivate innovation or creativity, and there is a lack of understanding of how to build brand value.

Innovation is the work of outsiders with fresh, even daring perspectives. The ice industry did not invent the refrigerator. Shipping companies did not devise the universal container. And yearbook publishers did not create Facebook. New inventions upend old ways of doing things and cause disruptions throughout the system (Richardson 1999). Hundreds of years before its Communist-led government, China led the world with a flurry of inventions that include the compass, fireworks, papermaking, hydraulics, sophisticated drugs, multi-stage rockets, golf, and paper money.

In today's 'China, Inc.' it is not surprising that few innovative products emerge. The government prizes security, conformity, and control. The Internet is closely monitored, and networking sites such as Facebook and Twitter are banned. Individuals, working under this system of state-capitalism, are more likely to keep their heads down than to risk loss of their livelihoods by opposing the aims of the government. As in conservative corporate environments, ideas that may seem unorthodox are more difficult to share. In one sense, the 'China, Inc.' model of economic growth resembles Wal-Mart's business strategy. Both focus on cheap suppliers, inexpensive overhead, and low wages, but neither adds much value to the products they sell. Both seek growth though the rapid scaling up of sales volume to offset their typically low profit margins. Neither embraces innovation, which helps explain why a close-knit relationship has developed between the two as manufacturer and retailer. Market saturation slowed Wal-Mart's growth in store square footage from 8% annually during 2002–2006 to less than 4% annually in 2007 to 2009. Its stock price also has stagnated for 15 years after 20 years of brisk increases. Unlike innovative companies, Wal-Mart has not reinvented itself in any substantial way (Richardson 2011).

China as it too floods with world with low-end products not known for their quality. Other countries and companies understand that building product value through innovation is how long-term economic growth typically is sustained. Switzerland made almost 22 million watches in 2008, for example, roughly 4% of China's sales of 559 million watches. China's average price was a mere $2 per watch, whereas Switzerland's price was $528. As a result, Switzerland received over ten times as much revenue as China, $11.5 billion versus $1.1 billion. The Swiss understand how to create value out of more than the sum of parts. Along with a reputation for high quality, they have established a brand by law for the entire country. Swiss Made appears on the face of every Swiss watch. Chinese watches, or other products for that matter, have no such identity (Richardson 2011).

As students quickly saw, hordes of sellers were openly hawking $2 counterfeit watches, $5 fake designer clothes and shoes. Many of them were accosted with famous name watches, suitcases and clothes for a tiny fraction of the price and told stories to each other about the attention to detail, even in the tags and stickers on the clothing. They saw firsthand that Chinese manufacturers lack vital marketing skills. Chinese companies instead blatantly steal existing brands: Pizza Hut becomes Pizza Huh, Starbucks becomes Buckstarr, and Nike becomes Nire, with nearly identical logos as well.

I noted that these unimaginative shortcuts create a fraction of the value of the true brand. Apple, in contrast, delivers huge value by its brand's cachet. For example, when it debuted, the iPhone4 retailed for $600. China's sole contribution was the assembly of the individual components, which ties up only 7% of the phone's cost. Apple makes a 60% profit margin, which it partially reinvests by creating memorable ads, new software applications, and eye-catching store spaces (Richardson 2011).

11.5   Logistical Planning for the Course

Travel abroad courses take an enormous amount of effort to market and launch successfully. An on-campus International Studies program is a great asset as well to remind you of the nitty gritty details such as passports, travel visas, trip insurance and short-term medical insurance. On the academic side, a well-planned study abroad course must be like a ten-course meal- lots of different types of experiences without having an overburdened amount of any one element. Having also directed two study abroad programs with no overseas support, I can say it is much easier, particularly in a place so far away, to work with a reputable on-site provider who can handle transportation, scheduling of events, arranging of speakers, meals, medical emergencies and places to stay. The most work for the faculty member involves the time spent prior to leaving campus, where the list of key experiences is detailed and worked into a day by day schedule.

It is important to remember that the leader of a faculty member is going to bring along a set of different personalities—some will be extroverts, others shyer. Some will tire more easily than others. Some will seek excitement though interacting on the streets with locals whereas others will enjoy solace in a quiet museum. A successful travel abroad program should recognize the needs of different personalities and not just be a reflection of the faculty leader's personality. One needs to constantly listen and monitor the faces of students in the morning and throughout the day to sense the feel of the group, while at the same time recognizing that life begins 'outside the comfort zone.' By this I mean that at times students need some gentle nudging try strange new foods, or go in small groups to different areas of the city. If we are teaching the benefits of individual freedom as a takeaway, then it is important not to be a control freak during the trip.

To that end, each day I typically had an academic component such as a guest lecture, or a museum visit (typically in the morning), and a more experiential component in the afternoon such as a field trip to a factory. Building in some free time is essential as overscheduled trips leave students feeling exhausted and irritable. In addition, creating ways to interact with ordinary people as much as possible creates lifelong memories.

For my last two trips to China in 2013 and 2015 with a group of MBA students, I worked with the Council on International Educational Exchange (CIEE). It is impossible to understate the amount of trust and goodwill that is essential when working with an overseas provider. If something goes wrong, a strong working relationship with people who are seasoned professionals is essential. Establishing a friendly rapport on the phone prior to leaving is far better than uncomfortable surprises once one reaches the shores of a foreign land.

In planning the trip, I wrote down a wish list of topics, the places I wanted to go, the themes of the course and potential to take side journeys off the typical beaten path (such as the migrant worker camp). The staff was unfailingly helpful in everything from getting tickets for performances, lining up dinner reservations, having rooms ready and getting top-notch lecturers from area universities. Our bus driver was at our command for 12 h a day. As a character in movie once said, 'Spontaneity has its time and place.' Sometimes the unexpected creates the best memories.

We stayed at the CIEE Global Institute—Shanghai, which is located on East China Normal University (ECNU)'s downtown Putuo campus. It is known as the 'Garden University' for its beautiful grounds by the Liwa River. Our dormitory building had modest but clean rooms. The university grounds felt like an oasis at night with its large playing fields, pedestrian walkways and mature, leafy trees. It was an excellent place to unwind after a busy day amid the hectic crowds of Shanghai. This notion of 'quiet reflection time and space' is important to consider for keeping students' spirits high during the trip.

Another important thing: CIEE had a well-developed plan for all types of medical emergencies, from getting ill, to physical injury to flying out of the country for severe illness. Having that assurance in one's back pocket in the event of an emergency is vitally important, particularly in a foreign country where one is unfamiliar with the best hospitals and unable to converse in the language. The mantra for a study abroad program logistics should be: keep the moving parts as few as possible so everyone can focus on the main objectives and bring everyone home safely. My outsourcing of nearly all the on-site logistics made this experience immensely less stressful and allowed me to focus my energy on learning outcomes of the course. The complete details are shared in the Appendix.

11.6 Cost

Affordability can be a key impediment to international travel. Travel to Asia is quite a bit cheaper than Europe and CIEE provided a very reasonable cost for the entire trip of $1675 per student excluding airfare, as seen in Table 11.1 below. In addition, I received a $10,000 grant to help offset the students' travel costs from the Charles Koch Foundation, so the true cost to the students was only $2525. I worked with a

Table 11.1 Breakdown of travel abroad expenses, China 2015

Item	Per person	Overall total (10 students)
Flight	$1850	$18,163
Program cost	$1675	$16,750
Total	$3525	$34,913

local travel agency to book the flights, which I recommend if your students are not seasoned travelers. Some of our students had never been on an airplane before so preparing them for 20 plus hours in the air requires some advance discussion.

The CIEE flat fee covered all transfers, transportation (both rail and bus), events, performances, class sessions, boat trips, lodging and two meals a day. It was a true 'soup to nuts' program, and this included all my fees and a single room. (My flight was paid out of an additional school grant.) As a result, I was freed from the headaches and worries of the mundane, and could focus on the fun parts—interacting with my students, Chinese economists, government leaders, bus tour guides and leading discussions as we walked through the city or on long bus rides.

11.7 Academic Structure of the Course

Prior to leaving for China, over 3 weeks our class met twice a week. For two and a half hours we discussed two assigned articles on China and/or the growth of globalization, as well as an assigned book, and a data source such at the Heritage's Foundation Freedom Index.[3] In addition, about 30–40 min of each session was used to talk about preparing for the trip, including everything from cultural norms, medical situations, packing tips and strategies for making one's way across the city on one's own. The itinerary once we arrived in China was structured around three things each day: gaining an appreciation of the cultural aspect of China (e.g. an hour spent on calligraphy/language), an academic lecture from a top academic, and an out of classroom experience.

With regard to the latter, here's an example of how I tried to leverage every experience into a larger lesson. One evening, I took the students to the famous YuYuan outdoor marketplace consisting of hundreds of small shops selling nearly identical trinkets in downtown Shanghai. I didn't just say, "Have fun shopping!" among the throngs of shoppers. Instead, I used the fast-paced business environment to create a friendly contest among the students. Under a time constraint –dinner in 2 h– I formed two-person teams to search for and then purchase a model of a famous terra cotta warrior statue, standing just six inches high. They each had a photo of the statue, and little did they know that dozens of shops were selling the exact same statue. The team with the lowest price after bargaining with a street seller won a prize at dinner. This taught the teams that although the statue was widely available at

---

[3] https://www.heritage.org/index/.

different markets, transactions costs and willingness to wait lead to sharply different prices. This is a very a different situation than in the United States, where we rarely negotiate for items except for cars and homes. The youngest of the MBA students negotiated down nearly 99% of the list price, due to her willingness to spend an hour hopping from shop to shop, pitting the store owners against each other with only a calculator to communicate the price. I later wrote about the experience in a *Wall Street Journal* op-ed, titled, "An Econ Lesson in a Shanghai Market" (Richardson 2015a).

In another unforgettable experience, we entered a large city park on a Sunday to visit the famous marriage market, whereby parents of children eligible for marriage place large white placards along the walking paths for all to see. Each of the hundreds of cards detail the specifications of a potential wife or husband, with details including height, weight, income, education and family background. Instead of romance, it is more like trading used cars. Students witnessed parents doing all the negotiation for their son or daughter, trying to get the best deal for marriage of their child. This became a great discussion for the students, especially when they convinced me to stand up on the wall with my 'specifications' written in Chinese, whereupon I was immediately surrounded by several dozen interested parties, with one calling his niece in Hong Kong about the 'professor with a ticket to the U.S.'. Needless to say, that slightly embarrassing experience for me led to many stories and laughter by the students later on in the trip.

Thus, the key to a successful teaching lesson is to hitch an insight to an emotional experience, using a foreign culture as the backdrop for questioning one's own assumptions about how the world works. This can leave a lifelong imprint, which is the overall point of a study abroad class. The more one leverages the high emotional pitch of a study abroad program to specific lessons and insights, the more likely that student will remember with great clarity what you teach them.

When the students returned, they had 2 weeks to work on their deliverables: a 12–15 page research question that addressed the main objective questions of the course, complete with references from our readings and academic content gained while in China; a book review from a book about China of their choice and their journal. Although re-entry can be exhausting time to write, I encouraged the students to shape their papers on the long bus rides while in China, and met with them individually as we travelled in the bus from one venue to another. It was a good time to get one on one time with each of them, sitting beside them on the bus. In this way, they could produce far better written products when they arrived back in the United States.

11.8 Conclusion

At the end of the course, the students had a newfound appreciation for the tremendous gains the Chinese have made in getting 400 million people out of poverty with their system of state capitalism, yet also a keen sense of the tremendous disparities that exist between the well-off and the poor rural residents. The ever-present thick smog, dirty working conditions and lack of interest in preservation made us better appreciate how we lived in the United States. At the same time, the Chinese know how to build large and impressive train and subway systems, airports, and highways at much faster speed than in the United States, leading to an infrastructure that supports quick economic growth. We learned how democracy can help as well as hinder economies, when special interest groups play a role in hindering economic growth.

The big unknown question is if China's modus operandi of poaching and outsourcing ideas will work in the long run. Trust is essential in business relationships, and these relationships can quickly sour when knowledge is taken without adequate compensation. Indeed, various economic studies have shown that a country's GDP growth is positively influenced by the degree to which its citizens can be trusted (Fukuyama 1996). If China's focus on increasing profits comes at the cost of losing trust with its foreign partners, then future cooperative arrangements seem less likely, and China's options for outsourcing innovation will diminish. In any case, China's prospects for high future growth are questionable. Its lack of innovation and impending market saturation, as well as its lack of branding spell an inevitable slowdown, unless its business strategies markedly change, as we are seeing already in the past 5 years.

The study abroad programs gave both the students and me a much better insight into China's treatment of property rights, economic investment, key drivers of GDP and the sustainability of that course. After the experience, we also better understood the strengths and weaknesses of our own system in the United States. There is no good substitute for this type of experiential learning experience, that will stick with the students for years to come.

Appendix

- Day 1

  - Arrive in Shanghai late afternoon
  - Check into hotel near East China Normal University
  - Optional: Explore campus, neighborhood surroundings
  - Group Dinner near campus

- Day 2

  - Orientation, East China Normal University campus
  - Communicative Chinese Class
  - City Tour (Including Pearl Tower/History of Shanghai museum and Museum of City Planning)
  - Official Welcome Dinner and Chinese Acrobatic Show

11 The Chinese Menu: How to Discover the Key Ingredients of Market. . .

- Day 3

  - Lecture: China's Model of Communism Today
  - China Museum—gain appreciating of 5000 year old history of China
  - Tea Ceremony—understanding historical context of tea markets and connection with global economy
  - Dinner at Traditional Sichuan Restaurant with Face-Changing Folklore Show

- Day 4

  - Lecture: Growth of Chinese Economy
  - Steel plant Factory Tour
  - Yu Yuan Garden—small scale business environment, close to perfect competition
  - Group Dinner at restaurant overlooking Yuyuan Garden

- Day 5

  - Trip to Suzhou—origin of Silk Road—on 180 mph bullet train (50 miles in 20 min!)
  - Visit to Humble Ambassador Gardens via pedicab
  - Small silk manufacturing plant, silk museum, walk along canals

- Day 6

  - Migrant Worker Village Tour
  - Return to Shanghai

- Day 7

  - Shanghai Chamber of Commerce—what it means to operate a business in a Chinese economy
  - Visit to Volkswagen manufacturing plant
  - Visit to the Bund and Nanjing Road—largest retail shopping district in Shanghai
  - Group Dinner at 6th on the Bund

- Day 8

  - Lecture: Demographic Shifts—how women entering the labor market has changed the economy
  - Lecture: Americans in China—the experience of being African American

- Day 9

  - Visit to park to observe marriage market: the selection of mates through an auction process
  - Shanghai Port visit and lecture—the explosion of globalization through the invention of the container
  - Farewell Dinner and Night Cruise on the Huang Pu River

- Day 10

  - Depart for USA that afternoon and arrive late evening

References

Chang LT (2009) Factory girls: from village to city in a changing China. Random House, New York

Chu K (2013) China: a billion strong but short on workers. Wall Street J. Published May 1, 2013

Coase R, Wang N (2013) How China became capitalist. Cato Institute, Policy Report, Washington

deSoto H (2003) The mystery of capital. Basic Books, New York

Fu X, Balasubramanyam V (2003) Township and village enterprises in China. J Dev Stud 39(4):27–46

Fukuyama F (1996) Trust. Free Press, New York

Gifford R (2008) China road: a journey into the future of a rising power. Random House, New York

Levinson M (2016) The box: how the shipping container made the world smaller and the world economy bigger-with a new chapter by the author. Princeton University Press, Princeton

Levy-Carciente S (2015) International property rights index. Property Rights Alliance, Washington

North D (2005) The Chinese menu (for development). Wall Street J. Published April 7, 2005

Olson M (1984) The rise and decline of nations. Yale University Press, New Haven

Pan E (2005) China's angry peasants. Council on Foreign Relations, New York

Richardson C (1999) Digital Darwinism: is e-tail the death of retail as we know it? Entrepreneur

Richardson CJ (2005) The loss of property rights and the collapse of Zimbabwe. Cato J 25(2):541–555

Richardson C (2011) Is China's growth rate sustainable? *AIER Economic Bulletin* 51(1):1–3

Richardson C (2015a) An econ lesson in a Shanghai market. Wall Street J. Published July 6, 2015

Richardson C (2015b) Migrant workers in China: the untold story. RealClearMarkets. Published 30 June 2015

Statista (2020) Global No.1 Business Data Platform. Statista, https://www.statista.com/ Accessed 20 May 2020

Whalley J, Xian X (2010) China's FDI and non-FDI economies and the sustainability of future high Chinese growth. China Eco Rev 21(1):123–135

World Bank (2020) World Bank open data. World Bank, Washington

Chapter 12
Sports, Culture, and the Economy: Baseball in the Dominican Republic

Michelle A. Vachris

Abstract Many universities are promoting study abroad programs due to the life-changing experience of students being exposed to other cultures. Being comfortable in the global marketplace is also valuable for student success in the workplace. More and more, students in Business and Economics would like these experiences, so faculty are encouraged to develop and implement courses. This paper describes the Virginia Wesleyan University course Sports, Culture, and the Economy: Baseball in the Dominican Republic as an example for faculty considering a short-term study abroad course.

12.1 Introduction

Experiential learning is a key pillar of the liberal arts education at Virginia Wesleyan University (VWU), a small private institution located in Virginia Beach, Virginia. These experiences come in the form of internships, undergraduate research, and study away. While most of the study away programs involve travel abroad, we use the more general term 'study away' because some of our opportunities occur within the United States, such as our programs in Hawaii, Alaska, and New York City.

The commitment to study away is backed up by a strong support system for faculty and students. Our Study Away Program is housed in The Lighthouse, an office dedicated to all forms of experiential learning. The Director of the Study Away Program offers formal and informal guidance for faculty and students. Students participate in semester long and summer long programs provided by other institutions, and shorter programs that are led by VWU faculty. These short-term programs are held during our January term or during the first part of the summer. The focus of this paper is a short-term course on "Sports, Culture, and the Economy: Baseball in the Dominican Republic."

M. A. Vachris (✉)
Virginia Wesleyan University, Virginia Beach, VA, USA
e-mail: mvachris@vwu.edu

© The Author(s), under exclusive license to Springer Nature Switzerland AG 2021
J. Hall, K. Holder (eds.), *Off-Campus Study, Study Abroad, and Study Away in Economics*, Contributions to Economics,
https://doi.org/10.1007/978-3-030-73831-0_12

While Virginia Wesleyan University supports study away experiences for all of its students, we are particularly interested in increasing study away for majors that have not had many students participating in VWU programs, such as Business. To that end, I always invite our Study Away Director to visit my classes early in the semester to give a short presentation on the various options for students. Our Study Away Program has also encouraged Business faculty to develop study away courses that would particularly appeal to Business students, and this office provided extensive support to me as I developed my course.

Another underrepresented group in study away programs generally is male students. Data from the Institute of International Education (2019) show that study abroad programs have typically consisted of two-thirds women and one-third men since at least 2006. According our most recent assessment data, 29% of the VWU students enrolled in study away programs are male, whereas men make up forty-one percent of our total student body (Lighthouse 2019). Fischer (2012) explores reasons why male students may not have high levels of participation in study abroad programs. Previously, it was assumed that female students were more likely to study abroad because they tended to major in disciplines (like the Humanities) that held more study abroad courses, but Fisher argues that is not the case today. More and more programs are being offered in fields traditional dominated by male students (such and Business and STEM), but even in these study abroad programs, females are more likely to enroll. Fisher argues that men are more likely to study abroad when the program is perceived as a resume builder that will help them professionally, and they are more likely to sign up for a program along with their friends.

One Lighthouse initiative that may address the latter reason is our Buddy Grant program that encourages students to sign up for study away courses together. Open to all students, this program is so new that we do not have the data to adequately assess the outcome. To address the former reason for low male participation rates, it may help to offer courses that focus on networking and real-world value, such as Sports, Culture, and the Economy. Not only does this course cover real-world applications of business practices in sports, students are also able to network with Major and Minor League Baseball staff. Furthermore, this course is cross-listed with a course in our Sports and Recreation Management Program; these students would also be interested in the applied nature of the course.

12.2 Course Development and Description

To provide for flexibility in offering the course, I chose to create a general course shell called "Sports, Culture, and the Economy" with the following course description:

> The course Sports, Culture, and the Economy will provide students the opportunity to study the impact of a major sport on the economy and culture of the country. During this study

away course, students will be immersed in the industry of the sport and will examine the importance of the sport for the country's economy and culture.

The advantage of this general shell approach is that the location and sport to be studied can be varied without having to process a new course through the University curriculum review process. The initial offering of this course will use the more specific reference to Baseball in the Dominican Republic as follows:

Sports, Culture, and the Economy: Baseball and the Dominican Republic

The course Sports, Culture, and the Economy will provide students the opportunity to study the impact of a major sport on the economy and culture of the country. During this study away course, students will be immersed in the industry of the sport and will examine the importance of the sport for the country's economy and culture. For the Baseball and the Dominican Republic version of this course, students will study how baseball permeates the culture and influences the economy of the Dominican Republic, which is an important source of talent for Major League Baseball. This course also aims to prepare Virginia Wesleyan University students for business and service-oriented professions by giving them hands-on experiences with culturally and ethnically diverse populations.

The general course is designed to be offered as a 15-day course suitable for the Winter (January) term or as a short course over the summer. For Baseball in the Dominican Republic, it makes sense to offer it in the January term because the baseball season there is from mid-October to late January. For other sports or countries, a summer offering may be preferable, again the general shell course provides for this flexibility.

The Learning Objectives of the course include some that are specific to this course and some that are common across many VWU study away courses. Specifically, students completing this course should be able to:

1. Understand the industry of the sport.
2. Understand the cultural and economic impacts of a major sport on the visiting country.
3. Develop cultural appreciation by being exposed to a different culture and way of living.
4. Develop awareness of their own culture.
5. Develop a sense of their role in the global community.
6. Develop a sense of social responsibility, cultural tolerance, and empathy.
7. Develop a sense of the interdependence between the US and the visiting country.

The first two objectives are particular to this course. Students are first introduced to the basics of the supply and demand model and the business of baseball. The course then covers both the microeconomics of baseball labor markets as well as the macroeconomics of the impact of baseball on the economy of the Dominican Republic. For these topics students are assigned a set of readings from books like *Diamond Dollars: The Economics of Winning in Baseball* by Gennaro (2013); *Circling the Bases: Essays on the Challenges and Prospects of the Sports Industry* by Zimbalist (2011); and *The Economics of Professional Sports* by Rockerbie (2019). The choice of readings is specifically designed to be understood by students not familiar with baseball or economics, as there are no prerequisite courses required.

The remaining five learning objectives are general study away objectives having to do with raising cultural awareness. These are achieved by having students travel and interact with people in the destination country. During the country visit, students also engage in a service learning project relating to the sport in support of these objectives.

The course is designed for the 300-level with no prerequisites, and is intended for upper level students. The 300-level designation also reflects the intensity of the workload. Some assignments are completed before the trip, such as a test on the economics concepts. During the trip, students research their term papers and maintain blog entries. Their participation and reflection paper on the service learning project happens during the trip as well. Finally, students write and present their research paper upon return.

12.3 Dominican Republic Itinerary

The proposed itinerary for the course includes a visit to the Dominican Republic and pre- and post- travel sessions on campus. This itinerary, structured over 15 days, can be found in the Appendix. The pre-travel sessions begin by covering expectations and logistics for study away. Four full class sessions are used to introduce students to the business of baseball, the microeconomics of baseball labor markets, and the macroeconomic impact of baseball tourism. One important component of this course is to help students understand the interdependence between the U.S. and the destination country (Learning Objective 7). Most of the foreign-born players in Major League Baseball come from the Dominican Republic. According to Major League Baseball (2019), Major League Baseball began releasing data on foreign-born players in 1995 and the Dominican Republic has topped the list every year. In 2019, players born in the Dominican Republic accounted for 40.6% of all foreign-born players listed on opening day rosters and 11.6% of all Major League players Major League Baseball (2019). Clearly Major League Baseball is dependent on the Dominican Republic.

To that end, the course includes pre- and post- travel visits to our local Triple A baseball team, the Norfolk Tides who are affiliated with the Baltimore Orioles. Before travelling to the Dominican Republic, we take a tour of their stadium, Harbor Park, and associated facilities. This visit helps to introduce students to the business and sport of baseball. Upon returning from the study away trip, we again visit Harbor Park to interview staff from the Tides in order for students to apply what they observed and learned in the Dominican Republic to the U.S. organization. For example, students can learn about the support programs available for foreign-born and/or non-English speaking players. The Lighthouse provides us with transportation for these local visits.

During our stay in the Dominican Republic, we visit baseball related sites as well as general tourist attractions in an attempt to understand how baseball fits in with the overall tourism industry and economy. We visit a baseball museum to appreciate the effect of baseball on the culture of the Dominican Republic and the history of the sport there. One baseball museum was developed by MLB star Bartolo Colon

12 Sports, Culture, and the Economy: Baseball in the Dominican Republic

in his birth town of Altamira. During this visit, students can experience not only an overview of Dominican baseball, but also how players that made it big are investing back into their communities. This type of tour helps students make the connections between the culture of the sport, the business of the sport, and the economic impact of the sport.

The baseball specific visits also include a tour of a Baseball Academy where we can meet with local players and coaches. Further illustrating the interdependency of MLB and the Dominican Republic is the fact that every MLB team has an academy there (Rojas 2015). The academies, which often include dormitories for players and coaches, also feature playing fields, weightroom and training facilities, clubhouses, classrooms and recreational areas for participating players. These academies provide training to young players and assist them in transitioning into Major League Baseball with classes in the English language and American culture McKenna (2017).

While Major League Baseball is interested in the talent of the Dominican Republic players, Meyer and Kuhn (2008) explain that this investment is also economically beneficial to the teams in terms of the lower development training, signing bonuses, and wages relative to those in the U.S. These academies and the rest of the baseball industry there contribute to the growing Dominican Republic economy.

In addition to the academy visit, we also visit a Major League Baseball office to meet with MLB staff. By meeting with people in the industry, students can learn more about the business and labor markets of baseball. We participate in a low key baseball game with local players and attend a professional game. Finally, as mentioned earlier, a service learning project is included in the course. Our focus is on youth development, and we volunteer with a local baseball organization.

12.3.1 The Study Abroad Provider

It is important to note that the itinerary described above was developed by a provider that specializes in organizing faculty-led study abroad programs. When planning a course, faculty need to decide whether to outsource the logistics to a provider, or to organize things themselves. What are some things to consider when making this decision?

First, how familiar are you with the destination? Many faculty members may be from a foreign country or have well established contacts there. In that case, it may be preferable to plan your own itinerary and handle the logistics on your own. In my case, the course was set in a country I had not visited, nor do I speak the native language. With no local contacts, it made sense to contract with a provider who had an established program on Baseball in the Dominican Republic. Virginia Wesleyan University's Study Away Program has relationships with several vendors who provided me with sample itineraries and quotes to review. Once I chose the itinerary that most closely matched my vision for the course, I worked with that provider to tweak the program even more to my specific learning objectives. It may be the case that once I run the course several times, I may make connections there and then feel more comfortable running the course myself.

Our Dominican Republic itinerary includes first flying into Santo Domingo where we stay for three nights. Then we venture to Hato Mayor for one night for the service learning project and spend the next night in Santiago. We then return to Santo Domingo for two nights before flying home. This type of travel schedule was made easier by outsourcing the logistics to a tour company. Faculty who may be organizing things themselves may wish to consider travelling to one city and using that site as a base for day trips. There is a trade-off then. The group can remain at one hotel for the entire visit, which cuts down on the moving in and out of hotels, but that means more time in a bus or van each day.

12.4 Cost per Student

Another important consideration for the decision of whether or not to use a provider is the cost. Obviously using a provider will increase the cost per student. The Study Away Program at VWU recommends that each course fee not exceed $3500. Note that this fee would cover all travel costs except spending money and some meals. Tuition is on top of the travel fee. If the trip involves international travel, then global health insurance must also be included in the budget. Travel costs of the faculty members and any chaperones are factored into the per student cost.

Students at VWU are eligible to apply for University funding to help pay for their study away experience. We offer need based grants for any study away course and additional tuition discounts for summer courses. Students in our Batten Honors Program are guaranteed funding for Honors study away courses, and our Global Scholars Program provides funding for a full semester abroad. These latter two sources of funding do not apply to the Sports, Culture, and the Economy course as it is not part of the Honors curriculum and it is not a full semester program.

12.5 Course Development Timeline

Developing and implementing a study away course takes about one and one-half to 2 years. Table 12.1 outlines the steps recommended in our Study Away Handbook. The first step is to develop a preliminary syllabus and itinerary. This involves a lot of research on the part of the faculty member and may involve obtaining and reviewing quotes from study abroad providers. Our Study Away Program Director provides assistance to faculty interested in developing a course, providing both formal and one-on-one training. For the course to appear in the catalog, it must go through the curriculum review process. Once the course is approved, we submit the syllabus and preliminary budget as well as University paperwork to our Study Away Program.

12 Sports, Culture, and the Economy: Baseball in the Dominican Republic

Table 12.1 VWU study away timeline

Months prior to course	Task
18–24 months	Develop a preliminary syllabus and itinerary
9–18 months	Submit course for approval through the curriculum review process
9–18 months	Submit to Study Away Program director:
	1. Study away course information form
	2. Syllabus
	3. Documentation of approval by the curriculum review process
	4. Preliminary budget worksheet
9–12 months	Travel to course destination(s) to develop lesson plans, research sites, create an itinerary, and research logistics
9–12 months	Develop a detailed course budget
3–12 months	Advertise the course and recruit students
	Develop flyers and other promotional materials
	Participate in Study Away Fairs
4–6 months	Submit final syllabus, itinerary, and budget

These items (due in April of the academic year *before* the course is offered) get the course officially in the system of the Study Away Program and make the course eligible for students to apply for study away course grants.

To better prepare the course, faculty make an exploratory trip to the destination. Funding for these visits are applied for in January and travel must be completed by the end of June. During this trip the faculty member completes a shortened version of the planned itinerary and is hosted by the provider if one is being used. This visit enables the faculty member to preview the course on site. My exploratory visit was scheduled for June 2020, but has been postponed due to Covid-19 related travel restrictions. After the visit, the budget will be finalized so that students can be billed the appropriate amount.

Once the course is developed, the itinerary is set, and budgets are finalized, then begins the very important task of marketing the course to students. Our Study Away Program recommends that marketing begin 1 year prior to offering the course. This gives students time to consider the program and arrange for financing. The Study Away Program provides support for marketing in the form of holding Study Away Fairs and preparing promotional materials. The office also lists the courses on their website and social media accounts. It is useful for the faculty member to hold information sessions for the course where students can learn about the course and the destination and have their questions answered. Serving food from the destination at these meetings is a plus. Finally, faculty typically promote their courses via social media, at departmental and student organization events, and in one-on-one recruiting of students. This hands on promotion is especially important for a course that is offered for the first time. Once the course gains a reputation as a good experience, then the marketing requirements are not as strong.

Students must apply to be registered for the study away course, and each instructor sets her own acceptance criteria. University-wide suggestions include a minimum GPA requirement and a review of any Honor Code, Student Conduct, and Sexual Misconduct violations. Additionally, students are asked to provide a short essay and references. For Sports, Culture, and the Economy, I also require junior or senior level status. Each student is interviewed by the faculty member after the application is received. Once the student is accepted into the course, they must complete a Study Away Course Contract that outlines their rights and responsibilities. This extensive screening process for study away programs are part of the overall system for ensuring the safety of faculty and students participating in these courses.

12.6 Safety

Virginia Wesleyan University's system for ensuring the safety of students and faculty studying away includes the above mentioned screening process and many other support programs provided by The Lighthouse. Each study away destination is assessed for safety and security levels before and during the program. During the pre-travel class sessions, students are briefed on health and safety measures for travel. Faculty and students travelling internationally are required to have international health insurance and to enroll in the U.S. State Department's Smart Traveler Enrollment Program.

We have protocols in place to address emergencies that might occur during a trip. This is one of the reasons why we require at least two faculty members to be present for the whole trip. These protocols were especially helpful during the Covid-19 pandemic that required our study away programs to return to campus. While such disruptions are rare, it is comforting to know that there are safety procedures in place.

12.7 Conclusion

The VWU study away course, Sports, Culture, and the Economy, allows students to learn about the business aspects of a sport and to experience the cultural and economic importance of the sport in another country. Specifically, the Dominican Republic version of the course immerses students in the culture of baseball that is so important to the Dominican Republic and Major League Baseball. The external study abroad provider with whom we contracted takes care of the logistics and has the connections to the baseball industry to set up an itinerary that enables our students to meet the learning objectives of the course. The pre- and post-travel visits with our local Minor League team help students further explore the interdependent baseball relationship between the United States and the Dominican Republic. The subject manner and practical application of the course material may appeal to male students who are underrepresented in study abroad programs as a whole. While the prospect of developing and implementing a study abroad trip may be daunting, it is

12 Sports, Culture, and the Economy: Baseball in the Dominican Republic

an investment that can provide students and faculty with highly valuable educational experiences.

Acknowledgments The author would like to thank Dr. Takeyra Collins Coats and Dr. Jill Sturts, Assistant Professors of Sport and Recreation Professions, VWU for their work to help develop the cross-listed course described in this chapter.

Appendix

Sample Schedule for Fifteen Day January Term Class

- Day 1 at VWU: Baseball and the Dominican Republic.
- Day 2 at VWU: The business of baseball.
- Day 3 at VWU: Baseball labor markets.
- Day 4 at VWU: The economic impact of baseball tourism.
- Day 5 at Norfolk: Tour of Harbor Park stadium.
- Day 6 at VWU: Departure for Santo Domingo, DR.
  - Check-in, relax and refresh.
  - Historical and Cultural Walking Tour. The Dominican Republic's capital city, Santo Domingo is also the most modern and dynamic metropolis in the Caribbean. La Capital, as it is affectionately called, epitomizes the pulse of Dominican culture, where the old and the new converge seamlessly from centuries old architecture and history, to large shopping malls, art galleries, an electric nightlife, and a booming gastronomy scene.
- Day 7 at Santo Domingo.
  - Baseball Academy Tour. Learn about what it takes to become a pro. Visit the facilities and find out what the training regimes look like for local players. Interact with local players and coaches.
  - Baseball Game. Students will be able to play a friendly match of baseball with the locals.
  - Boca Chica Beach. Stretching a near mile long with brilliant, white sand, this bustling stretch is well protected by a large coral reef, and its shallow turquoise waters.
- Day 8 at Santo Domingo
  - Three Eyes National Park. 'Los Tres Ojos' is a national park with a set of three caves that can be explored. The limestone caves feature stalactites and stalagmites and springs, right in the heart of Santo Domingo.
  - MLB Office Visit. Major League Baseball continues to build its educational initiative in a country where thousands of adolescents and youth have the dream of becoming Major League players. While many prospects know

someone who has signed a professional contract, the vast majority knows that the journey upward through the system is steep.
- Professional Baseball Game. The group will attend a professional baseball match and experience the passion and enthusiasm that the game is all about.

- Day 9 at Hato Mayor.

  1. Travel 2 h to Hato Mayor.
  2. Service Learning Project. Students will volunteer with the local organization in a project that promotes Youth Development.

- Day 10 at Santiago.

  1. Travel 3.5 h to Santiago.
  2. Historical and Cultural Walking Tour. With a history that dates back to 1495, the second largest Dominican city holds an alluring charm, with its historical landmarks, excellent food scene, lofty mountain ranges, beautiful parks, an innate craze for baseball.

- Day 11 at Bonao.

  1. Travel 2 h to Bonao.
  2. Jima Waterfalls. Discover the natural wonders of the pristine Jima river. The Jima Waterfalls are found in the outskirts of the city of Bonao, and right at the foot of the Caribbean's tallest mountain range, the Central Mountain Range. We set off on a soft hike through a nature trail that takes us through the heart of the rainforest, along the trail lie many natural pools, all perfect for taking a relaxing swim before reaching our final destination, a magnificent 50 foot tall waterfall. We end the hike by eating a delicious lunch at the river's nearby community, which gives you the opportunity to have a real Dominican home cooked meal.

- Day 12 at Santo Domingo: Return to VWU.
- Day 13 at Norfork, VA: Interviews with Stadium staff.
- Day 14 at VWU: Work on paper.
- Day 15 at VWU: Final paper submission and presentations.

References

Fischer K (2012) In study abroad, men are hard to find. Chronicle of Higher Education 19 February

Gennaro V (2013) Diamond dollars: The economics of winning in baseball. Diamond Analytics, Purchase, NY

Institute of International Education (2019) Open doors report on international exchange education. Institute of International Education, New York

Lighthouse (2019) Study away program annual assessment 2018–2019. Virginia Wesleyan University, Virginia Beach

Major League Baseball (2019) MLB rosters feature 251 international players. MLBcom News 29 March

McKenna T (2017) The path to the sugar mill or the path to millions: MLB baseball academies' effect on the Dominican Republic. Baseb Res J 46(1):95–100

Meyer CA, Kuhn S (2008) Effects of Major League Baseball on economic development in the Dominican Republic. George Mason University Working Paper in Economics, No. 18-05

Rockerbie D (2019) The economics of professional sports. CreateSpace Independent Publishing Platform, Scotts Valley

Rojas E (2015) Baseball academies thrive in the Dominican Republic. ESPNDeportescom 1 July

Zimbalist A (2011) Circling the bases: Essays on the challenges and prospects of the sports industry. Temple University Press, Philadelphia

Chapter 13
Short Term Study Abroad: Renewable Energy in Germany and Switzerland

Laura Lamontagne

Abstract A short term study abroad may be preferable to students who do not wish to go abroad for an extended period of time or not have the flexibility within their major for an entire semester abroad. In the summer 2015 I organized a short term study abroad trip to study renewable energy while traveling through Germany and Switzerland. The goal of the course was to provide students with an introduction to energy markets with a specific emphasis on renewable energy and applications to the German Renewable Energy Act. This paper details the process of developing the course and experiences while traveling abroad with a group of 10 students.

13.1 Introduction

In the summer of 2015 I had the opportunity to run a short term study abroad trip while working at Christopher Newport University. The course was titled "Renewable Energy Economics & Policy Analysis" and conducted while traveling through Germany and Switzerland. The objective was for students to apply economic theory to the production of renewable energy by examining energy markets at the local, national and international level and examine specific policies designed to promote the production of renewables. Students learned how fundamental economic concepts drive energy production and how various local and national institutions affect energy markets. The goal of the course was to provide students with an introduction to energy markets with a specific emphasis on renewable energy and applications to the German Renewable Energy Act, Erneuerbare-Energien-Gesetz or EEG.

As a global leader in investments in renewable energy, Germany provided an ideal setting to study emerging renewable energy markets. The Germany Renewable Energy Act, originally passed in 2000, aimed to motivate the transition to renewable energy through the use of a feed-in-tariff (Lang and Lang 2015). A feed-in-tariff

---

L. Lamontagne (✉)
Framingham State University, Framingham, MA, USA
e-mail: llamontagne@framingham.edu

© The Author(s), under exclusive license to Springer Nature Switzerland AG 2021
J. Hall, K. Holder (eds.), *Off-Campus Study, Study Abroad, and Study Away in Economics*, Contributions to Economics,
https://doi.org/10.1007/978-3-030-73831-0_13

provides energy producers a cost based price for any renewable energy supplied to the electric grid. This incentive can be applied to any electric utilities, homeowners, or private businesses that produce renewable energy. The German Renewable Energy Act was pioneering in that it allowed utilities to participate on a wide scale basis, and the purchase price of electricity was based on generation cost, resulting in different prices paid to producers for various investments in renewable infrastructure. By traveling to Germany, students were able to witness the direct results of this policy. Over the course of the 10 day trip students were able to visit the International Solar Energy Society, visit family owned farms that have invested in wind turbines and have directly benefited from the feed-in-tariffs, and visit a large scale hydro-electric facility.

This course was conducted across 4 pre-departure meetings and 10 days traveling through Germany and Switzerland. The 4 pre-departure meetings served to review basic economic concepts, provide an introduction to externalities, and to present a detailed description of the German Renewable Energy Act and feed-in-tariffs. By covering these topics pre-departure, students were able to focus and apply these topics while at site visits. It also allowed for extra free time while traveling to enjoy the cultural components abroad.

The purpose of this paper is to provide a detailed description of both the course content and trip logistics to assist in the development of a short term study abroad program. A short term study abroad trip can be as short as 2 weeks to upwards of a month and typically offered during a university's summer session. A short term trip may be preferable to some students who do not wish to go abroad for an extended period of time or for students with large major requirements that leave little wiggle room for an entire semester abroad. Despite spending an abbreviated time abroad research shows that a short term program still enhances participants understanding and awareness of other cultures and languages, appreciation of the impact of other cultures on the world, and awareness of their own identity (Gaia 2015). This paper will detail the organization that is required to get the program approved, course content, a detailed itinerary, and trials that occurred while traveling with my students.

13.2 Pre-departure Organization

Designing and coordinating the logistics of a short term study abroad can be particularly cumbersome. Organizing travel, lodgings, site visits, and guest lectures is a daunting task that may dissuade some faculty members from creating a program. Often a faculty member will secure funding to travel a year in advance to scout potential site visits and organize details of the trip. I was able to streamline this process by coordinating with Education First (EF) Tours.

13 Short Term Study Abroad: Renewable Energy in Germany and Switzerland

EF Tours, based out of Cambridge, Massachusetts, is an international education travel agent that specializes in short term study abroad trips. In the College Study division there are over 30 pre-designed itineraries organized by discipline that can be catered to specific goals and course objectives. The Renewable Energy in Germany and Switzerland can be found under the Science and Technology programs. However, working with the program coordinator assigned to my trip I was able to ensure the visits and guest lectures could be applied to an upper level economics course.

There were many additional benefits to using a third party to coordinate the trip. EF Tours created a secure, password protected portal for the trip where students could access all necessary paperwork and submit payments through. Each time students logged into their account they could see their remaining balance, intermediate due dates, number of days remaining until departure, suggested packing lists and other trip details. Removing this burden from the faculty organizer was a huge relief in order to focus on course materials and design.

In addition to flights and lodging, all on site transportation was arranged by EF Tours and a Tour Director was assigned to our group. The guide provided by EF Tours was with us from the moment we were picked up at the airport until our departure. His role was to manage all logistics including hotel check-ins, local transportation, and help with any language barriers. This allowed me to focus directly on my students and the course material while on site.

The final cost of the trip to students was $3671. This included roundtrip airfare, lodging, on-tour transportation, daily breakfast and most dinners, and site visits and guest lectures, and the full time tour director. In order to reduce the price of the trip, Christopher Newport University agreed to travel with a group from Butler University. This increased our numbers to roughly 40 students and faculty combined. This size was a bit cumbersome while traveling abroad however combining tours allowed both universities to take advantage of reduced costs to students.

13.3 Course Design

The course "Renewable Energy Economics & Policy Analysis" was designed as an intermediate level economics elective offered during the summer term. The object was to provide an introduction to energy markets with a specific emphasis on renewable energy. Students applied economic theory to the production of renewable energy and analyzed specific policies designed to promote the production of renewables. The objective identified were as follows:

- Understand how basic economic concepts influence energy production and use.
- Understand how local, regional, and global intuitions affect energy markets and prices.

150

- Describe the challenges associated with the production and use of various renewable energy sources.
- Understand how restrictions implemented by various energy policies impact energy markets.
- Understand how various energy policies can provide incentives for investment in developing technologies.

The course was offered under the prefix "Econ 395: Intermediate Topics in Economics." The prerequisites for this special topics course were simple, any introductory course in economics. At Christopher Newport University, this included one of the following courses: Principles of Macro or Microeconomics, Environmental Economic Literacy, or The Economic Way of Thinking. Although some exposure to economics was necessary, the 4 pre-departure meetings served to catch some students up and provide them with the materials necessary for successful completion of the course. Additionally, by minimizing the perquisite requirement the Economics Department was able to market the study abroad opportunity not just to economics majors but the campus wide community.

Students that enrolled in the course were from a variety of majors, these included senior economics majors and sophomores that had only one previous economics course. This made teaching an upper level economics elective a challenge, however this had been accounted for in the course design. Prior to departure, there were four 2 h class sessions. These classes were offered once a week during the last month of the spring semester. The sessions served a dual purpose—they helped students with little economic background to catch up to the higher level material, provide students who had not taken the Environmental Economics elective a background in market failures and externalities, and helped to meet the contracted 42 h of course content. Since the trip was only 10 days it was difficult to meet this requirement entirely abroad. These meetings were conducted once a week during the spring semester following the return from spring break. Students filled out a survey with their schedules and I selected a time that worked best, usually in the evenings. Although our trip was not scheduled until the end of May, I found holding these meetings during the semester advantageous since students were still on campus. If these meetings were to be held in May in the days leading up to the trip, students would have needed to secure housing. What follows are the topics covered in each of the four pre-departure meetings.

- Meeting 1: Overview of energy supply & demand and basic economic concepts

  - Review of principles of microeconomics
  - Introduction to energy economics
  - Overview of trip expectations

- Meeting 2: Externalities and public policy

  - Review of externalities
  - Discussion of property rights, Pigouvian taxes, cap-and-trade, and other incentive-based policies

13 Short Term Study Abroad: Renewable Energy in Germany and Switzerland

- Meeting 3: Criteria for evaluating public policies
  - Introduction to the German Renewable Energy Act (EEG)
  - Europe's 20-20-20 strategy
- Meeting 4: Financing energy development
  - Feed-in-tariffs, energy credits
  - Renewable portfolio standards
  - Discussion on sustainability

The course requirements of the course were broken down as follows:

Pre-departure Problem Set Following the completion of the four pre-departure meetings, students were assigned an extensive homework assignment to be submitted prior to departure. The purpose of this assignment was to demonstrate proficiency of the material presented in pre-departure meetings. It was distributed at the last meeting and due 1 week before departure. A sample of questions are listed below:

- Define command and control environmental strategies and incentive based strategies. Provide examples of each.
- Explain the concept of a feed-in tariff and how it has helped promote investment in renewable technologies in Germany.
- Describe the characteristics of a natural monopoly. Why are natural monopolies, like an electric utility usually regulated?
- What are the major goals and targets of the German Renewable Energy Act?

Journal Articles Students were instructed to bring a notebook on the trip. They were expected to take notes at all site visits and write up a brief analysis. Each journal entry had two parts. First, students were expected to write a summary of the site visit and/or guest lecture that they participated in. The second part of the journal entry was to apply the day's activities to material that was covered in the pre-departure meetings. While traveling, I only expected students to keep notes on each visit. The journal entries were completed and emailed to me 2 weeks upon returning home. This gave students the time to reflect upon the visit and write a thorough and thoughtful journal. Over the day 10 trip I required 8 journal entries, one for each day except for when traveling. A sample of one journal entry is copied below.

> The residential and commercial solar installations we observed in Heidelberg were only made possible by the Energie-EG, the law passed by the German government that we studied prior to our departure. Specifically, it was the part of the law that gave assurance that the solar investors could sell their excess energy production back to the grid, and utilities would be forced to purchase it, no matter what, at a fixed feed-in tariff of 22.1 euro cents per kWh.
>
> Furthermore, though much has been made of the Renewable Energy Act in Germany, I still saw considerable signs of fossil fuel development. Of course, this makes sense because to completely wean a country off of fossil fuel would effectively be economic suicide. Still, I was surprised to see—looking off into the distance from the ramparts

of Heidelberg Castle—the smoke stacks of Mannheim Coal plant burning away. Though much had been made by our tour guide of the progressive policies of Freiburg, one of the larger cities in the county of Baden-Württemberg, some research into the statistics of the county's energy production reveal that it is not that much ahead of the rest of Germany, on average, in its renewable generation. Figures from 2013 taken by the Baden-Württemberg Statistisches Landesamt show that the renewable sources represent just 11.9% of total energy consumption, which is only 1.5% greater than the 10.5% share of renewables in energy consumption in Germany more broadly. What's more, I was surprised to learn that nuclear energy represents 15.3% of all energy consumption in Baden-Württemberg, compared to 7.7% on average in Germany nationally. With so much local resistance to nuclear power, and the effective dominance of the Green party in local politics, I would have thought that renewable sources would play a much larger role than they do, and that nuclear would at the very least be a smaller player due to local public discontent.[1]

Final Paper Upon return home students wrote a research paper on a topic of their choice. The paper should provide a critical evaluation of a specific site visit, energy market or policy or a topic covered while traveling. There was a great degree of freedom given to students on their chosen topics and structure of the paper. Prior to the end of the trip, students were to discuss their topic with the trip leader during down time on busses or before/after dinner in the evenings. The paper was to be approximately 3000 words. Some of the topics chosen included tradeable renewable energy credits, large vs small scale hydropower, renewable portfolio standards and further examples of feed-in-tariffs.

13.4 While Abroad

Each day typically consisted of one site visit followed by a 'class meeting' upon return to the hotel. Depending on the individual trip, visits lasted between 2–6 h. On each visit, students were expected to actively interact with the guides and planned activities while taking notes for their journal entries. Class meetings were held most days, time permitting. This time was used to apply the material presented on the visit to the material covered in the pre-departure meetings. Additionally, students proposed final paper topics based on these visits. Each class lasted approximately 1 h.

- Day 1: Flight to Frankfurt, Germany
- Day 2: Heidelberg

  - Arrive in Frankfurt. Immediately travel to Heidelberg
  - Walking tour of Heidelberg
  - Heidelberg Castle

---

[1] Special thanks to Thomas Hall for providing a copy of his journal.

13 Short Term Study Abroad: Renewable Energy in Germany and Switzerland

- – One hour afternoon class[2]
- – Welcome dinner.

- Day 3: Heidelberg

  - – Visit Solarpark Bruhrain. Completed in 2007, the park is home to 29,250 modules which provide enough electricity for approximately 1500 households
  - – One hour afternoon class

- Day 4: Freiburg

  - – Travel to Freiburg.
  - – Visit to the Innovation Academy, a non-profit association that focuses on issues of climate protection, for the following activities: guest lecture on sustainable development, visit to the Heliotrop, and visit to the solar housing estate

- Day 5: Frieburg

  - – Solar energy tour of Frieburg
  - – One hour afternoon class
  - – Excursion to Breitnau Bio Energy Village

- Day 6: Lake Constance

  - – Travel to Lake Constance
  - – Bodensee Solar lake cruise
  - – Lecture on renewable and lake preservation

- Day 7: Lucerne

  - – Travel to Lucerne
  - – Walking tour of Lucerne
  - – Excursion to Mount Pilatus

- Day 8: Lucerne

  - – Guided tour of Grimsel power plant
  - – One hour afternoon class

- Day 9: Lucerne

  - – Guided tour of Entlebuch Biosphere
  - – Free afternoon in Lucerne
  - – Farewell dinner

- Day 10: Departure flight from Zurich to United States

---

[2]Students participate in a 1 h class conducted by trip leaders to recap various excursions. These lessons are in the form of lectures and discussions and pertain to the day's activities and relation to course material. They are conducted at the beginning or end of each day, time permitting.

13.5 Trials Abroad

As with any travel one should expect the unexpected. Prior to departure there were several group meetings to discuss all aspects of the trip. Multiple emails were sent reminding students about passport requirements, packing lists, dress codes for site visits, and conduct expectations. Despite the preparation my group experienced a multitude of unforeseen circumstances that called for flexibility and adaptation while traveling.

The first interruption occurred at the very beginning on the trip on day one. Our initial itinerary departed from Norfolk, Virginia to Atlanta, GA for a brief layover before traveling to Frankfurt, Germany. On the first leg of our journey, thunderstorms prevented our flight from landing in Atlanta. We rerouted to Savannah, GA to refuel before returning to Atlanta. By this time we had missed our connection to Frankfurt and had to spend the night in Atlanta. The support from EF Tours was greatly appreciated working out the rescheduling logistics. The next flight to Frankfurt out of Atlanta was entirely booked so our group flew to Detroit, MI the following day before catching an overnight flight to Frankfurt. The airline helped to obtain hotel vouchers for the night but in some instances, students were tripled up in their rooms for the evening.

During this chaotic travel experience, several students had not packed according to suggested guidelines. Some students did not pack a carry on with a change of clothes and one student packed necessary medication in checked luggage. These problems were solved with the help of the airline tracking the bag in question and an emergency trip to Target before settling in the hotel for the night. However, based on my experiences, I suggest meeting at least 3 h prior to departure. Not only will this allow students who may be running late extra time but also to run through checklists that include, but not limited to, passports, medications, and correct packing methods. There is extra time to repack luggage or remedy any other unforeseen circumstances.

Once our group reached our destination, the stress from our hectic travel experience quickly faded as we caught up with our planned itinerary. Our next unforeseen hiccup concerned the internet connectivity. EF Tours had booked hotels that offered complimentary internet access. However, in order to reduce costs these hotels were smaller boutique hotels outside of the cities we were visiting. When 40 students simultaneously check into and log online to check emails, call home, conduct research, or stream videos the internet bandwidth was not large enough to support the demand. It would take several minutes to load a single webpage or simply not work at all. Although this issue was brought to EF Tours, there was little that could be done during the trip as the hotels were already booked and prepaid. The only solution to this was to take advantage of public wi-fi at various cafes and restaurants during our free time. Students nearly always searched out a McDonalds, Starbucks or other familiar fast food chain to use the free wi-fi. My recommendation is to find the nicest hotel or cafe and purchase a coffee, snack, or other beverage. The waiter will almost always provide you with the lounge's password protected wi-fi. This is a more secure option and usually far more comfortable than a plastic booth at McDonalds.

Despite a handful of hiccups, both students and faculty were able to roll with the punches and make the best of all of the unforeseen circumstances. When taking students abroad it's crucial to know ahead of time that any situation can arise and you will need to be prepared to handle almost anything.

13.6 Conclusion

Developing and running a short term study abroad program requires a significant commitment on behalf of the faculty member. It is considerably more work to organize the course in a remote location, secure necessary university approvals, recruit students to register for the trip, and teach on location than it is to prepare a traditional course in the classroom. However, for all of the extra effort involved with offering such a course comes with extra reward. For the majority of my students, this was their first time traveling outside of the country. Students' learning extended well beyond the classroom. In addition to learning the required course content, students were able to experience new cultures, see new regions of the world, and experience all the highs and lows of travel. Many of the students on this trip keep in contact several years later.

From my experiences running my first study abroad program, I have learned a lot myself and am better prepared to run a future program. Although I would consider my first trip a success there are several changes I would make in the future. In order to see as much as possible, our group traveled to new locations almost daily. The most time spent in a single hotel was 2 consecutive nights. There was a significant amount of time lost to traveling between locations for such a short trip. For a future trip, I would limit the number of locations to reduce travel time and further take advantage of what a village or city has to offer. Additionally, despite reviewing packing lists, codes of conduct, and course expectations for what seems like countless times, it never hurts to review them one more time. This may have reduced some stress at the start of our trip.

Despite a few hiccups along the way, the experience for both myself and my students was invaluable. Given another opportunity, I am eager to offer a similar program again in the future.

References

Gaia AC (2015) Short-term faculty-led study abroad programs enhance cultural exchange and self-awareness. Int Educ J Comp Perspect 14(1):21–31

Lang M, Lang A (2015) The 2014 German renewable energy sources act revision–from feed-in tariffs to direct marketing to competitive bidding. J Energy Nat Resour Law 33(2):131–146

Chapter 14
Study Abroad in Germany: *Sie Müssen Arbeiten*, but It Is Not that Hard

Jason Beck and Michael Toma

Abstract Universities nationwide and the AACSB have emphasized internationalization in business school curricula, but large up-front planning and development costs my hinder faculty from designing and executing study abroad programs. This paper discusses the opportunities and benefits of a 2-week study abroad program to Germany and offers practical logistical information related to program design and implementation.

14.1 Introduction

Since at least the 1990s, American Assembly of Collegiate Schools of Business (AACSB) accreditation has required internationalization (American Assembly of Collegiate Schools of Business 1993) and in recent AACSB *BizEd* publications, between one-fifth and one-third of business school recruiting advertisements include references to 'international' and/or 'global' (American Assembly of Collegiate Schools of Business 2019, 2020). Short-term study abroad programs are often more viable for students who are unable to commit to an entire semester or year overseas, but who still have an interest in experiencing a foreign culture and bridging the program to their business school curriculum. Concurrently with satisfying student preferences, short-term study abroad programs also serve the dual purpose of internationalizing the business school curriculum and can serve to satisfy AACSB accreditation guidelines.

Given the business school administrative incentive structure established by AACSB guidelines and student preferences for short-term study abroad programs, creating such a program might be of interest to business school faculty, but can be inhibited by significant start-up costs. The reality is that effort will be required to develop the program, but it certainly can be done in a way that satisfies student

---

J. Beck (✉) · M. Toma
Georgia Southern University, Savannah, GA, USA
e-mail: jbeck@georgiasouthern.edu; mtoma@georgiasouthern.edu

© The Author(s), under exclusive license to Springer Nature Switzerland AG 2021
J. Hall, K. Holder (eds.), *Off-Campus Study, Study Abroad, and Study Away in Economics*, Contributions to Economics,
https://doi.org/10.1007/978-3-030-73831-0_14

preferences and/or constraints caused by tight household finances. The text below offers guidelines useful in overcoming the start-up costs for a short-term study abroad program focused on Germany, with the option to also incorporate several nearby countries.

An overview of two routes for self-directed (without a private study abroad travel company) study abroad programs in Germany is provided for faculty interested in developing such a program. While the culture, history and experience that is Germany certainly makes the country a highly desirable location for a study abroad program, the opportunities to infuse the program with business and economics course content are numerous and straightforward.

In Sect. 14.2, we present a brief summary of the benefits to students of study abroad programs. In Sect. 14.3 we discuss the strengths of Germany as a destination for a 2-week program and provide ideas for two separate routes, highlighting some of the attractive draws and connections to academic content associated with the locations. Section 14.4 discusses travel logistics including budgetary information and information related to designing daily program itineraries. Section 14.5 concludes.

14.2 Benefits of Study Abroad to Students

International education, in general, has been promoted and supported by the Institute of International Education (IIE) since 1919, and annual data on both international students studying in the U.S. and participation of American students in study abroad programs has been reported for seventy years in IIE's annual *Open Doors* report. With respect to business programs, the intentional internationalization of business and economics curricula has been the subject of discussion and investigation for over 40 years (Porter and McKibbin 1988; Knight 1994; Webb et al. 1999). Praetzel et al. (1996, p. 1) comment that it is "one of the most discussed and highly agreed upon curricular issues for business and economic programs" and lament the lack of implementation plans (Porter and McKibbin 1988; Praetzel 1999; Arpan et al. 1993) even though the AACSB requires business school curricula to include global issues (American Assembly of Collegiate Schools of Business 1993).

While much progress has been made since the 1990s, less than 10% of 2.6 million recent graduates of American business schools study abroad (Institute of International Education 2019). Annually, *Open Doors* reports the number of international students in the U.S. and indicates that for the 2017/2018 academic year 341,751 American students participated in study abroad programs for academic credit, with Europe constituting the majority (54.9%) of the destination locations (Institute of International Education 2019). Of these, roughly 71,000 (or 20.8%) were in a business or management program of study. This compares to 10.9% of study abroad participants in business and management programs in 1985/1986.

One of the more obvious means of internationalizing business school curriculum is incorporating study abroad programs into degree programs. Recruiting efforts for these programs often include the ubiquitous Top-Five Reasons lists with pictures of exciting-looking foreign landmarks, people, and food as well as student testimonials supporting various claims in the Top-Five list. Perhaps it is the hyped nature of the recruiting material and the lack of rigorous assessment of study abroad programs that have given rise to detractors of study abroad programs (Mangan 1997; Terzuolo 2018). However, beyond the glitzy components, the marketing material generally emphasizes developing cultural competence, enhancing communication skills, personal development, and improving career outcomes. This is generally consistent with Varela's (2017) meta-analysis of 72 study-abroad investigations finding evidence in support of marketing material claims. In summary, Varela (2017) finds study abroad programs enhance cognitive skills (language acquisitions), attitudinal learning (intercultural competence), and behavioral learning (intercultural adaption). With respect to the latter two attributes, programs as short as several weeks are found to have the same impact as longer term programs.

Outcomes with respect to probability of employment and career development are less difficult to assess than amorphous conceptual benefits such as cultural competence (Harder et al. 2015). This research tends to rely on survey data of study abroad program participants. Di Pietro (2015) finds a statistically significant and large effect on the probability of employment within 3 years of graduation for Italian students participating in study abroad programs. Doorbar (2003) presents findings suggesting improved employment prospects are likely for students with better interpersonal skills and that human resources managers are more likely to think that students who participated in study abroad programs have better interpersonal skills. This is consistent with surveys of employers querying as to attributes of candidates that increases the likelihood of hire (Hodge and Lear 2011). Research advocating for study abroad programs emphasizes the alignment of employers' desired skill-sets and how those skill-sets are enhanced by participation in study abroad programs (Institute of International Education 2017).

Orahood et al. (2004) find that participation in study abroad programs affects career goals in that students are more inclined to consider working for global company, to work overseas, are more likely to list the study abroad experience on resumes, and discuss it during an interview. Institute of International Education (2017) found that roughly 50% of study abroad participants believed it contributed to their receiving an offer for a job they currently have or held in the past. Further, former study abroad participants believed that in addition to affecting their initial hire, the international experience also contributed to promotions during their career.

In summary, study abroad programs enhance professional development, cultural competency, and employability.

14.3 But Why Study Abroad in Germany?

In addition to much the publicized factors such as culture, history, arts, diversity, and ease of travel, Germany is also accommodating to English-speakers and safe.[1] Iconic imagery of Berlin, Heidelberg, Munich, and beer and pretzels often catch the attention of students considering a study abroad program.

Beyond this marketing glitz, Germany provides fertile ground for a variety of business and economics-related study abroad content. Germany has a powerful, diverse, and trade-oriented economy. Iconic German brands such as BMW, Mercedes-Bends, Volkswagen, Audi, and Bayer, to name a few, offer opportunities for site visits and exploration of international business practices. It is the largest of the European economies, fifth largest in the world, and is the third largest exporting nation in the world behind China and the United States (Central Intelligence Agency 2020).

The history and culture of Germany provide opportunities to delve into economic aspects of the great European conflicts of the twentieth century. Economic history leading to World War II and the post-war East vs. West division provide extensive content for coursework, lectures, guest speakers, and site visits. Important cultural and historic monuments are testimony to the complex history of Germany in the twentieth century.

Germany's architectural diversity is quite stunning. The list of imperial palaces, Gothic cathedrals, castles, monuments, Roman ruins, and pre-romanesque architecture is impressive and make for excellent site visits and socio-economic discussion content for the study abroad program. Various elements of economic history give rise to these architectural landmarks and monuments to ancient and modern commerce.

Germany's membership in the European Union (EU) offers opportunities to explore international business and political relations. German business practices and business culture can vary substantially from those of its EU partners.

Two study abroad program routes are outlined next that combine a series of cities encompassing and highlighting German commerce, history, culture, political integration, and more. The North-West Route highlights Germany's post-war integration into a larger economic and political alliance in Europe. The alternative South-East Route can be used to highlight Germany's tourism economy and/or post-communist economic transition. We present a city-by-city rundown of these routes, both of which include extensive exposure to Germany's economy, history, culture, and diversity. The descriptions of the German cities on the routes are based on a framework obtained from the website study-in-germany.de, which includes a wealth of information and an A to Z overview of German cities popular as study abroad

---

[1] In addition to the reasons cited above, reasons for longer term study include low-cost, high-quality, and varied programs of study (Educations 2019; Study-in-Germany 2019; ExploreInsiders 2019; Van Wagenberg 2020).

destinations. Germany's transportation system is modern, quick, and highly efficient which facilitates travel along the two routes.[2]

14.3.1 North-West Route: Hamburg, Cologne, Brussels, Trier, Luxembourg, Frankfurt

The North-West Route originates in Hamburg with stops in, or day-trips to, Cologne, Brussels, Trier, Luxembourg City, and ends in Frankfurt. This itinerary features cities and experiences highlighting Germany's economy, trade, integration with the European Union, as well as economic history dating to the Roman Empire, the medieval Hanseatic League, and the post-war German 'economic miracle.'

Hamburg is on the north coast of Germany between the North Sea and the Baltic Sea. This strategic location made it ideal for membership in the medieval (primarily 13th to 15th centuries) Hanseatic League of trading cities on the Baltic Sea and Rhineland area including the Low Countries and England. The historical economic significance of the city remains today, as Hamburg is Germany's principal port, home to aircraft manufacturer Airbus, and an important media center. The opportunities for infusing the economic history of regional trade alongside contemporary international trade through Hamburg are clear. Hamburg is the site of major corporations in addition to Airbus, thus also providing site visit and guest lecture opportunities focusing on international commerce.

The second city on the North-West Route is Cologne, roughly 250 miles from Hamburg in western Germany near the Low Countries. Cologne is perhaps best thought of as a place to witness the so-called 'economic miracle' of post-war Germany's economic re-development. The city was subjected to 262 Allied air raids during the war and much of the city's core was destroyed. Now displacing the ruins is a modern cosmopolitan city emphasizing a vibrant mix of culture, arts, and music alongside a re-emergent manufacturing and media center. The 700,000 year old Cologne cathedral was damaged during the war but was not destroyed, despite its location near a strategic bridge spanning the Rhine River and its proximity to important war-material manufacturing districts.

The Belgian city of Brussels is 130 miles west of Cologne and while a bit of a stretch, it can be done as a day-trip. Brussels owes its existence, dating from the tenth century, to its location on the north/south flowing Senne River and its location on east/west crossroads of trade connecting the Low Countries to the Rhine River valley. Brussels' modern global importance dates to post-war Europe and the founding of the precursor to the European Union. The city now serves as

---

[2]Although reading the train, subway, trolley, and bus timetables for first-time visitors can be a daunting experience, remember this: if it does not appear make sense and appears wrong, that means it has not been interpreted correctly. The logic is there, keep looking; the system is remarkably efficient.

the *de facto* and administrative headquarters of Europe, serving as the seat of the European Parliament and the European Commission. While the Parliament's focus is international governance, the Commission's focus is budgetary and regulatory. For study abroad programs, this is an important academic linchpin of Brussels; international regulation and budgetary administration has the ability to affect the economic wellbeing and economic development of the union's member countries. Naturally, Brussels has evolved alongside the EU as a global hub of business and international relations. With respect to the economy of Belgium, Brussels is its financial center and tourism focal point.

The western city of Trier in the Mosel River valley (about 160 miles southeast of Brussels) is an excellent example of a destination that combines economic, cultural, and historical elements. The Mosel River valley supports the wine-making industry in a complementary basin to the great Rhine River varietals. As Germany's oldest city, it was founded 300 years before the Roman Empire established it as an important regional capital and important trading hub. It is home to the largest collection of Roman historical sites in Germany, including several well-preserved UNESCO World Heritage sites such as the Roman Black Gate, amphitheater, and baths, as well as Germany's oldest cathedral (from 1270) and other ancient structures. As an added bonus for economics programs, Karl Marx was born in Trier in 1818.

Luxembourg is 30 miles from Trier, which makes for an excellent day-trip from the old Roman regional capital. Luxembourg's history dates to the tenth century and its twentieth century economic foundation was steel-making. As that industry waned, the city emerged as an important investment management center in Europe and is the second wealthiest country in the world on a per capita basis. It also is the seat of many of the EU's important administrative institutions including those related to the justice system, auditing, parliament, investment banking, and economic stability.

The final stop on the North-West Route is Frankfurt, 150 miles northeast of Trier. Also known as Frankfurt-Am-Main, this city is a modern important financial powerhouse in Germany. It is home to 150 international banks as well as the DAX, Germany's stock exchange. Although time may be limited here prior to departure and return to the U.S., the city's skyline will remind some of New York's Manhattan Island, giving it the nickname "Mainhattan." The German central bank and the EU's central bank are headquartered in Frankfurt. The academic connection to international finance and monetary policy is impossible to miss.

If time and budgetary considerations allow, consider adding Heidelberg (155 miles east of Luxembourg, and about an hour south of Frankfurt) as a 2-day stop prior to departure from Germany via Frankfurt. Germany's tourism economy is on full display here, largely owing to its long history, beautiful river valley and hilly terrain, and most importantly, it was not bombed during WWII. The city is home Germany's oldest university (dated 1386), is a hub of German philosophical thought and culture, and hosts castle ruins situated scenically on a hilltop that dominates the medieval city core.

14.3.2 The South-East Route: Berlin, Wolfenbuettel, Prague, Munich

The South-East Route originates in Berlin with stops in Wolfenbuettel, Prague, and Munich. This itinerary features cities and experiences highlighting Germany's East/West history, post-communist and transitional economics, manufacturing prowess, and the economics of tourism. Germany's post-war division, subsequent reunification, and continuing strengths and challenges rooted in the East vs. West divide are readily apparent throughout Germany, but perhaps not more so than in Germany's capital city of Berlin. In addition to visits to iconic sites such as the Brandenburg Gate, Berlin Wall remnants, and the eastern TV-tower to emphasize historical aspects of Berlin, the economic rejuvenation of the former East Berlin is on display in thriving entertainment districts and "bohemian" enclaves easily accessible by a short subway, train, or street-car ride from the core of central Berlin. The cultural diversity and the bustle of a young, vibrant capital city serve as attractors to Berlin's many tourists. Academic content abounds here with comparative economics, re-unification and regional economic development, and tourism economics as leading candidates to infuse the study abroad curriculum.

Wolfenbuettel, 150 miles west of Berlin, has the largest concentration of centuries-old timber-framed buildings in Germany that serve as an important tourism driver for the city. It was largely undamaged by bombings in WWII and the historic church and castle complement the tourist amenities. The city's Herzog August Library hosts the world's largest collection of books and documents, accumulated over a 400 year period, printed prior to 1501. Wolfenbuettelis home to Jaegermeister, and a visit to the distillery often generates interesting discussion of international marketing strategy.

Prague's 1000 year history and preservation of important architectural landmarks led to the entire city center being designated as a UNSECO World Heritage site in 1992. The (real) Budweiser brewery tour provides an interesting mix of modern brewing and bottling technology along with a good bit of international marketing and international legal dispute over the use of the 'Budweiser' name. Prague also played an important role in the East/West rivalry in Europe. Communist rule ended in the former Czechoslovakia in 1989 when the Velvet Revolution transformed the country into a democracy in 1990. The country split in 1993 with Prague becoming the capital of the Czech Republic.

After Prague, head 225 miles southwest to visit Germany's southern-most major city, a mix of manufacturing excellence, Bavarian charm, and high-tech industry in Munich. The city, third largest in Germany, is the economic engine of the region and hosts globally known brands such as BMW, Siemens, Audi, and Allianz. The city is also a cultural center for the arts and museums, is home to Germany's two largest breweries, and is well-known for its beer gardens! The scientific prowess of the city's innovative class has transformed the former heavy industrial city into a high-tech hub supported by two of Germany's most highly regarded universities.

From Munich, a day-trip to King Ludwig II's Neuschwanstein Castle in the Bavarian Alps is a study in the efficiency of the German transportation system and tourism economics, and is breathtaking cultural experience. It also happens to be a study in failed public finance policy because King Ludwig II famously bankrupted the kingdom building the Disney-like castle during the mid to late 1880s.

14.4 Planning and Logistics

From a logistics point of view, Germany is an excellent choice for a study abroad destination. Large air transportation hubs facilitate international travel, English is widely understood, and travel between and within cities is usually convenient.[3] Furthermore, Germany is not particularly expensive, is relatively safe, and has good access to quality healthcare services should the need arise. This section discusses the logistical aspects of a Germany study abroad program in more detail.

While many different study abroad formats exist, this discussion focuses on a relatively short, faculty-led program that would most easily occur over a few weeks in the summer. Longer study abroad experiences, such as ones where students spend the entire summer or semester abroad, are certainly valuable but can be impractical for many students. Beyond the intimidation factor of being away from home for so long, semester-long programs can sometimes complicate a student's graduation progression, and lengthy summer programs can interfere with students' ability to work and earn income over the summer months. Since program costs increase linearly with additional days but, in our experience, marginal benefit diminishes after a few weeks, a program duration of 10–14 days seems optimal for this format.[4] Keeping the program at or under 2 weeks also minimizes student homesickness; something program directors should anticipate in some participants. We find that departing about a week after the conclusion of the spring semester works well. For many universities, this will be mid-May. The weather in Germany at this time is typically good and it will precede the busier summer tourist season when larger crowds and higher prices can negatively impact the experience.[5]

For faculty with more budgeted funds than time and experience, be aware that there are many tour companies which specialize in arranging study abroad experiences. While these services can be extremely helpful, they ultimately increase the cost of the program thus making it more difficult for students to afford.

Promotion and recruitment should be well underway by the middle of the fall semester with a deadline for an initial deposit around late January. We recommend aiming to recruit about eight students per participating faculty member, and,

---

[3]The authors both have a working knowledge of very basic German. While this does occasionally come in handy, it is not necessary.

[4]Interis et al. (2018) use survey data to conclude that a 3 week duration is most preferred.

[5]The average high in Berlin in May is 66 °F with 2.2 in. of precipitation.

14 Study Abroad in Germany: *Sie Müssen Arbeiten*, but It Is Not that Hard

if possible, to take two faculty. An ideal program would thus involve 18 total participants: 16 students and 2 faculty members. A group this size allows the program to take advantage of economies to scale but is still manageable. Groups larger than that may find it difficult to secure accommodations, arrange restaurant and tour reservations, and be generally more difficult to manage.

Since recruiting sufficient student participation for the program to 'make' can sometimes be a concern, having a completely separate pool of majors to recruit from can be helpful. Pairing a Germany program with other business school disciplines is easy, but we have also successfully run programs in cooperation with political science, various health science disciplines, and even the natural sciences. It is often surprisingly easy to tailor a specific site visit to two different disciplines.[6] And on days where this is not practical, the group still benefits from the economies of scale in the overall logistics of the program.

Regarding accommodations, our programs to Germany have almost exclusively utilized hostels. European hostels can vary widely in quality, but it is usually possible to find good, or even excellent, accommodation for about 50 euros (roughly $55) per student per night. An ideal choice would have good access to public transportation, have four to six beds per room for students, single rooms for faculty, and offer an included (or low cost) light breakfast onsite. Travel websites can be valuable sources of information regarding conditions such as cleanliness and safety.[7] The larger four-bed and six-bed rooms help keep costs down, and students consistently tell us that they prefer to be in larger rooms with several of their classmates.[8] Furthermore, having more students in fewer (but larger) rooms helps with coordination and may increase safety. Another advantage of hostels is that your students will have the opportunity to mix with other youth travelers from all over the world.

Since adjustments often need to be made, providing the students with too much specific detail before departure tends to do more harm than good as original and revised information can conflict. Providing students with a general itinerary, in broad stokes, before departure is better, with final details for each day provided at the 'debrief' session of the preceding day. Since our programs have always been two weeks or shorter, student free time has been limited to evenings, with scheduled

---

[6]For example, one year the economics study abroad program partnered with the chemistry department. A site visit to a cooperative pharmaceutical company began with a general tour of the facility, but then the two groups of students had separate programs. The chemistry students dove deeper into the science of the pharmaceuticals while the economics students were able to meet and talk with employees that dealt with pricing and the German regulatory environment. See Carpenter and Beck (2020) for a discussion of the chemistry program details.

[7]You may find that students (and parents) are often unnecessarily wary of hostels. Upon arrival, we recommend taking a few photos yourself to use in recruitment for future programs. Your personal experience and photos will be much more reassuring to future potential participants than information from the hostel's website.

[8]"It helps us all feel like we're in it together," reported one recent participant.

Table 14.1 Sample day's itinerary for Hamburg Germany

Time	Activity
8:00–8:30 a.m.	Group breakfast and discussion of day's activities
8:30–9:00 a.m.	Transportation via subway to first site
9:00–11:30 a.m.	Morning activity-Holstein Brewery
11:30 a.m.–12:00 p.m.	Transportation via subway to central part of city
12:00–1:00 p.m.	Group lunch and informal discussion of morning activity
1:00–1:50 p.m.	Lecture/group discussion and 15 min student presentation
1:50–2:00 p.m.	Brief walk to afternoon activity
2:00–4:30 p.m.	Afternoon activity-bike tour of city
4:30–5:00 p.m.	Transportation back to hostel
5:00–5:30 p.m.	Debrief and logistical instructions for next day
7 p.m.	Optional group dinner

activities typically running from morning through late afternoon. See Table 14.1 for a sample day's itinerary.

Being over-prepared for the day's activities is highly recommended. For example, planning out the public transportation route in detail beforehand and knowing what to expect upon arrival at destinations is worth the investment of your time. In this new and potentially intimidating environment, students will take their cues from the faculty member. A program director who appears to have everything under control generates credibility and improves morale. While the occasional mistake is unavoidable, students will not fully 'buy in' to a program (be emotionally invested and compliant) if their confidence in the program director is low. Furthermore, we (and Marine 2013) anecdotally observe a positive correlation between smooth program execution and good student behavior.

Although the planned day's timeline may be tight, study abroad experiences involve frequent bouts of waiting which can be utilized. For instance, a delayed bus may leave the group with an unexpected block of time. Or perhaps the group finds itself on an uncrowded train ride allowing for some spontaneous class discussion. We create a sequential series of small, stand-alone topics and instruct students to have the next one in the cue 'loaded and ready' to be discussed at any time. If an unexpected opportunity comes up, it is utilized this way thus allowing us to weave in additional course content as the opportunities present. As we cover one of these topics, the students automatically know that by the following day, they should have the next topic prepared to actively discuss. Since the program is relatively short, it is important to utilize the limited time as efficiently as possible to maximize student engagement and instruction.

While Germany is a relatively safe destination, safety is always a concern when traveling. Most of the students on our programs have had limited experience outside the U.S. so helping them make wise choices is an important part of the faculty member's role. At our university, the Office of International Studies conducts a required pre-trip workshop on safety. As shown in Table 14.1, group activities

14 Study Abroad in Germany: *Sie Müssen Arbeiten*, but It Is Not that Hard

constitute the entire day, but students have free time in the evening to allocate to course work and explore on their own. You will find that many participants will choose to congregate in the common area of the hostel, but others will venture out and enjoy the evening, seeing the sights, and meeting the locals. Since even in groups, students may find themselves lost or in otherwise uncomfortable situations, we provide each student with a 'carry card'. The 'carry card' is a small laminated card (about the size of a business card) with all hostel addresses as well as emergency contact information. These are given to each student at the beginning of the program and they are told to have them on their person at all times (we have periodic 'carry card' checks with small rewards for compliance).

14.4.1 Budgeting

The cost of a study abroad program to Germany can vary greatly with the duration, the specific cites visited, and the exchange rate. But in our experience, we have found that we can provide an excellent 2-week program for about $3600 per student. This figure includes everything except tuition, some meals, and students' personal spending money.[9]

Program directors are advised to expect the unexpected, hence the need for the contingency fund in Table 14.2. We recommend between $150 and $250 per student. As the end of the program draws near, unused balances in the contingency fund can be used to cover additional meals for the students or spontaneous 'pick-me-ups' (for instance, an ice cream or coffee break). And, of course, returning any remaining balances back to the students can be a pleasant surprise for them. Regardless, it is much easier to return unused funds than cut the budget during the program to deal

Table 14.2 Per student program cost breakdown

Item	Cost
Roundtrip Flight	$1200
Accommodation (roughly $55/night for 12 nights in country)	$660
Activities (roughly $50 per day for 12 days)	$600
Overhead for faculty costs	$400
Meals (one meal provided by program per day at $15/meal, 12 days)	$180
Intra-city Transportation	$60
Inter-city Transportation	$300
Contingency Fund	$200
Total	$3600

[9]Students will ask you how much they should bring for spending money. We usually suggest $500 with the obvious caveat that the appropriate amount will vary wildly by the student's spending habits.

with unanticipated expenses. We recommend an end-of-day exercise in which the program director journals the amount of funds expended and balances remaining so that unexpectedly high or low daily expenses can be noted and upcoming expenses can be modified if necessary and when possible. It is never a good idea to just 'ballpark' fund balances for the remaining portion of the program.

Regarding intra-city transportation, it is often possible to find multi-day, unlimited-use group public transportation tickets for a reasonable price. For instance, a 3-day, five-person group ticket in Berlin is around $26 and can be purchased from vending kiosks. This implies a cost of about $2 per day for each participant. For day-trips, group tickets on select regional rail lines are also often available making visits to nearby cites quite affordable. Long distance travel can, however, be a significant expense. Anecdotally, it appears that fares are noticeably less expensive 2–3 months in advance and thus it is best to book these tickets well ahead of time both to get favorable fares and to avoid unpleasant budgetary surprises as departure draws near.

14.4.2 Planning Timeline

Planning should begin at least 9 months before departure. See Table 14.3 for a suggested planning timetable for a program that would run in the latter half of May.

Table 14.3 Planning timetable for a mid-May departure

Date	Tasks
September	Work with your International Studies Office to prepare all necessary paperwork
	Determine cities to be included on the program
Early-October	Draft budget
	Prepare marketing materials
	Begin recruitment
Mid-October through January	Recruitment
Late January	Deadline for deposits for program participants
Early February	Book flights, inter-city transportation, and accommodations (popular tours may need to be booked by this time as well)
	Passports application (if applicable)
March	Finish booking remainder of activities
April	Reading list and course information provided to students Orientation
May	Departure

14.4.3 Planning the Itinerary

Germany is probably too large to try and explore all the regions in 2 weeks.[10] Each relocation will consume at least a half of a day, and the process of packing up, moving out, and resettling can be fatiguing. Thus, we typically aim for no more than three or four total cities over the 2 weeks. Keep in mind that additional cities, including ones in adjacent countries, can often be accessed via easily arranged day-trips thus increasing the breadth of the experience.

Our program to Germany have either taken the North-West Route (sample itinerary in Table A.1) which includes day-trips to Luxembourg City and Brussels, or the South-East Route (sample itinerary in Table A.2, which includes three nights in Prague.

14.5 Conclusion

Our goal has been to provide a framework useful in reducing start-up costs and other potential barriers faced by business and economics faculty who have an interest in developing a study abroad program to Germany. An outline is provided of two relatively short-term programs, each emphasizing varying aspects of the diverse experience that is Germany, with useful information about linking elements of the study abroad program to business and economics curriculum. Further, we offer guidance and advice regarding planning for the program and logistical issues that will need to be addressed to develop an efficient, well-run program that is not bedeviled by budgetary shortfalls. The study abroad programs can be exceptional experiences for students and faculty alike, all while satisfying AACSB requirements of internationalizing undergraduate education in business and economics.

---

[10]Germany is approximately 140,000 square miles, which is roughly the size of Montana.

Appendix

Table A.1 Sample itinerary for North-West Route

Day	Activities
Day 1—Travel Day	Depart for Hamburg in evening
Day 2—Hamburg	Arrive and check-in
	Welcome and information session
	Welcome dinner
Day 3—Hamburg	Holstein Brewery visit
	Lecture #1
	Bike tour of city
Day 4—Hamburg	Port of Hamburg
	Lecture #2
	'Dialog in the Dark'
Day 5—Cologne	Depart Hamburg for Cologne
	Check in
	Lecture #3
	Walking tour of the city
Day 6—Cologne	DSM Pharmaceutical Plant (day-trip to Maastricht, Germany)
	Lecture #4
Day 7—Cologne	Day-trip to Brussels
	Walking tour of Brussels
	Site visit to European Union Headquarters
Day 8—Trier	Depart Cologne for Trier
	Check in
	Tour of city Roman ruins
	Lecture #5
	Vineyard tour
Day 9—Trier	Excursion to Berg Eltz and Chochem Castle
	Lecture #6
Day 10—Trier	Day-trip to Luxembourg City
	Lecture #7
Day 11—Frankfurt	Depart Trier for Frankfort
	Check in
	Lecture #8
Day 12—Frankfurt	Financial District
	Farewell dinner
Day 13—Travel Day	Depart Frankfurt for home

14 Study Abroad in Germany: *Sie Müssen Arbeiten*, but It Is Not that Hard

Table A.2 Sample itinerary for South-East Route

Day	Activities
Day 1—Travel Day	Depart for Berlin in evening
Day 2—Berlin	Arrive and check-in
	Welcome and information session
	Welcome dinner
Day 3—Berlin	Museum Island
	Lecture #1
	Bike tour of city
Day 4- Berlin	Checkpoint Charlie
	Bradenburg Gate
	Berlin Wall remnants
	Alexander Platz/TV Tower
	DDR Museum
	Lecture #2
Day 5—Berlin	Depart Berlin for Wolfenbuettel
	Check in
	Jaegermeister Tour
	Herzog August Library
	Lecture #3
Day 6—Prague	Depart Wolfenbuettel for Prague
	Lecture #4
	Walking tour of city
	Winery tour
Day 7—Prague	Excursion to Kunta Hora
	Lecture #5
Day 8—Prague	Prague Castle
	St. Vitus Cathedral
	Lecture #6
Day 9—Munich	Depart Prague for Munich
	Check in
	Lecture #7
Day 10—Munich	Bike tour of city
	BMW factory tour
	Ayinger Brewery Tour
Day 11—Munich	Clariant Werk chemical production facility (day-trip to Burgkirchen)
	Lecture #8
Day 12—Munich	Guided trip to Neuschwanstein Castle
	Farewell dinner
Day 13—Travel Day	Depart Munich for home

References

American Assembly of Collegiate Schools of Business (1993) Standards for business and accounting accreditation. American Assembly of Collegiate Schools of Business, St Louis

American Assembly of Collegiate Schools of Business (2019) Radical impact. BizEd 18:1–74

American Assembly of Collegiate Schools of Business (2020) Inclusive cultures. BizEd 19:1–74

Arpan J, Folks W, Kwok C (1993) International business in the 1990s: a global survey. Academy of International Business, East Lansing

Carpenter S, Beck J (2020) Fermentation chemistry: a study abroad course. J Chem Educ 97(3):873–877

Central Intelligence Agency (2020) CIA World Factbook. Central Intelligence Agency, Washington

Di Pietro G (2015) Do study abroad programs enhance the employability of graduates? Educ Financ Policy 10(2):223–243

Doorbar A (2003) The US study abroad market: What are the barriers to purchase. IIE Networker Fall:58–60

Educations (2019) Top 10 reasons to study abroad in Germany. https://www.educations.com/articles-and-advice/ten-reasons-to-study-abroad-in-germany-13664 Accessed 4 Dec

ExploreInsiders (2019) Top Reasons Germany Is the Best Destination for Studying Abroad. https://www.exploreinsiders.com/study-in-germany/. Accessed 4 Dec

Harder A, Andenoro A, Roberts T, Stedman N, Newberry III M, Parker S, Rodriguez M (2015) Does study abroad increase employability? NACTA J 59(1):41–48

Hodge KA, Lear JL (2011) Employment skills for 21st century workplace: the gap between faculty and student perceptions. J Career Tech Educ 26(2):28–41

Institute of International Education (2017) Gaining an employment edge: the impact of study abroad on 21st century skills & career prospects in the United States. Institute of International Education, New York

Institute of International Education (2019) Open doors report on international exchange education. Institute of International Education, New York

Interis MG, Rezek J, Bloom K, Campbell A (2018) Assessing the value of short-term study abroad programmes to students. Appl Econ 50(17):1919–1933

Knight J (1994) Internationalization: elements and checkpoints. Canadian Bureau for International Education, Ottawa

Mangan KS (1997) Business schools promote international focus, but critics see more hype than substance. The Chronicle of Higher Education, September 12

Marine SS (2013) Designing a study abroad course in chemistry: information from three different courses to Europe. J Chem Educ 90(2):178–182

Orahood T, Kruze L, Pearson DE (2004) The impact of study abroad on business students' career goals. Front Interdiscip J Study Abroad 10(1):117–130

Porter LW, McKibbin LE (1988) Management education and development: drift or thrust into the 21st century? McGraw Hill, New York

Praetzel GD (1999) Pedagogical recommendations for internationalizing the undergraduate business curriculum. Int Adv Econ Res 5(1):137–146

Praetzel GD, Curcio J, Dilorenzo J (1996) Making study abroad a reality for all students. Int Adv Econ Res 2(2):174–182

Study-in-Germany (2019) Five reasons to study in Germany. https://www.study-in-germany.de/en/plan-your-studies/5-reasons-to-study-in-germany_70674.php. Accessed 4 Dec

Terzuolo ER (2018) Intercultural development in study abroad: Influence of student and program characteristics. Int J Intercult Relat 65(June):86–95

Van Wagenberg H (2020) Five reasons to study abroad in Germany. https://www.goabroad.com/articles/study-abroad/five-reasons-to-study-abroad-in-germany. Accessed 4 Dec

Varela OE (2017) Learning outcomes of study-abroad programs: a meta-analysis. Acad Manag Learn Edu 16(4):531–561

Webb MS, Mayer KR, Pioche V, Allen LC (1999) Internationalization of American business education. Manag Int Rev 39(4):379–397

Chapter 15
Schumpeter in Vienna: A Study Abroad Course

John T. Dalton and Andrew J. Logan

Abstract This paper builds upon the work of Dalton and Logan (Rev Austrian Econ, 2020a) by describing the motivation for and mechanics of teaching a course dedicated to Schumpeter as a study abroad program in the city of Vienna. We argue that the qualities Vienna possesses, both historical and contemporary, make a good laboratory for exploring Schumpeter's ideas and that the process of encountering a new culture through a study abroad course is the best way to internalize his theory of innovation. To do so, our paper first outlines the course content before describing the linkages between "techno-romantic" Vienna and Schumpeter's intellectual development. We then describe specific examples for how instructors can use Vienna as a laboratory for teaching Schumpeter's ideas. We close by sharing preparatory details for instructors and offering the perspective of a student who took this course in the summer of 2018.

15.1 Introduction

Studying abroad immerses students in new ways of living, exposing them to a deluge of innovations on a daily basis. Although the innovations are not new to the home country, students, as foreigners, perceive them as such, which means studying abroad may be one of the best ways for students to internalize the role of innovation in shaping an economy. Innovation and its accompanying ideas of entrepreneurship and creative destruction are central concepts in economics for understanding the dynamics of economic growth, the ultimate driver of increases in standards of living, the ur-question of economics since the time of Adam Smith. What better way then for students to learn the importance of these ideas than a class dedicated to the

---

J. T. Dalton (✉) · A. J. Logan
Wake Forest University, Winston-Salem, NC, USA
e-mail: daltonjt@wfu.edu; logaaj17@wfu.edu

© The Author(s), under exclusive license to Springer Nature Switzerland AG 2021
J. Hall, K. Holder (eds.), *Off-Campus Study, Study Abroad, and Study Away in Economics*, Contributions to Economics,
https://doi.org/10.1007/978-3-030-73831-0_15

Prophet of Innovation himself, Joseph Schumpeter, in Vienna, Austria?[1] This paper describes such a course.

The experience on which this paper is based began as a study abroad course on the "Life and Economics of Joseph A. Schumpeter" held in Vienna, Austria during the summer of 2018. The course took place at a property in Vienna owned by Wake Forest University, called the Flow House, which regularly hosts faculty and students from the university on study abroad programs. Although the first iteration of the course on Schumpeter was specifically designed for study abroad, the intention was to continue teaching a version of the course back at Wake Forest and to begin a research agenda on Schumpeter based on the teaching experience. The course has been taught a second time at Wake Forest, and the research agenda has so far resulted in a series of papers.[2] The current paper is a chance to reflect on the initial study abroad course in the summer of 2018, coupled with the ensuing 2 years of teaching and research as a way to refine the content, to provide a guide for instructors considering teaching a study abroad course on Schumpeter. For those not yet considering to teach a course on Schumpeter abroad, our paper is designed to convince you of the value of doing so.

The paper provides a description of the study abroad course on Schumpeter and how Vienna, Schumpeter's hometown, can be leveraged as the backdrop for the course to contextualize Schumpeter's theories. Schumpeter's ideas related to innovation, entrepreneurship, creative destruction, and the optimal role of government in society, i.e. capitalism versus socialism, all remain highly relevant for the study of economics. We have already highlighted the importance of these ideas for understanding economic growth; understanding contemporary public policy debates surrounding capitalism versus socialism is another topic that benefits from knowing Schumpeter. Indeed, academics recognize Schumpeter's contributions in the form of increasing citations, even outstripping those to Keynes (Diamond 2009a; Dalton and Gaeto 2018). Unfortunately, innovation, entrepreneurship, and creative destruction remain undertaught (Diamond 2007; Gwartney 2012; Phipps et al. 2012), so there is a great need for more Schumpeter in the economics curriculum. The first part of the paper, the description of the course, helps to fill this gap.

After describing the course, we turn to how instructors can use Vienna as a laboratory for exploring Schumpeter's ideas. Historical and contemporary Vienna provide many examples illustrating the course's main ideas of innovation, entrepreneurship, creative destruction, and capitalism versus socialism. We center our discussion of Vienna primarily around how the city can be used to help students grasp the ideas of innovation, entrepreneurship, and creative destruction, as these ideas are most closely related to our argument of study abroad as exposure to innovation on a daily basis. However, we do provide a brief discussion of how the city's history

---

[1]Prophet of Innovation is the moniker McCraw (2007) gives Schumpeter in the title of his biography.

[2]See Dalton and Gaeto (2018), Dalton and Logan (2020c), Dalton and Logan (2020a), and Dalton and Logan (2020b) for details.

can be used to contextualize the debate over capitalism versus socialism. The next section of the paper provides tips for instructors preparing a study abroad course on Schumpeter in Vienna. We provide additional resources for teaching Schumpeter and learning the history of Vienna for use in the classroom. We also include a brief discussion of the city's logistics. The paper then concludes by providing a student's perspective on studying Schumpeter in Vienna as a study abroad experience, along with a reflection on how the course fits into the student's overall education as an undergraduate economics major.[3] This first-hand account allows instructors to evaluate the value of teaching Schumpeter abroad from a student's perspective.

This paper most closely relates to Dalton and Logan (2020a). Dalton and Logan (2020a) provide a description of a discussion-based course on Schumpeter. Using a dialogue between professor and student before, during, and after the course, the paper describes the structure of the course and specific details related to content. Dalton and Logan (2020a) also includes a syllabus, sources for class materials, and a list of over forty discussion questions for the class. Whereas this current paper focuses on study abroad and Vienna as a backdrop to a course on Schumpeter, Dalton and Logan (2020a) is written for a general audience interested in teaching more Schumpeter, whether at home or abroad, and goes more in depth into course content than we do here. This paper also relates to two pedagogical papers written specifically about Schumpeter, Diamond (2009b) and Dalton and Logan (2020b). Diamond (2009b) shows how different video clips can be used to teach creative destruction, whereas Dalton and Logan (2020b) shows how the movie *Joy* can be used to teach Schumpeter's theories of innovation and entrepreneurship. Lastly, this paper relates to two papers written on teaching economics courses abroad. McCannon (2011) describes a course on Austrian economics taught at the same Wake Forest University facility in Vienna. Indeed, the course described in McCannon (2011) planted one of the first seeds for the idea of teaching Schumpeter in Vienna. Strow (2016) provides suggestions for teaching on a range of economic topics in Costa Rica. Strow (2016) points out the lack of papers on study abroad courses in economics. We help to fill this gap.

15.2 A Study Abroad Course on Schumpeter

A course dedicated to Schumpeter is valuable for two reasons. First, the ideas Schumpeter wrestles with are especially relevant for the present day. In an era marked by technological change and disruption, his analysis of creative destruction is a useful way to make sense of the whirlwind changes our society is facing both economically and politically. Students often have a personal relationship to his ideas, be they through childhood memories of strolling through now shuttered

---

[3] Andrew J. Logan was a student in Professor Dalton's Schumpeter course in Vienna during the summer of 2018.

Blockbusters or the political disruption caused by social media. Schumpeter's diagnosis of the problems of democracy and capitalism also resonate for students, many of whom are young voters still forming their own political opinions. Dalton and Logan (2020a) argues that a discussion-based course on Schumpeter can serve as a model for civil dialogue on contentious topics like those Schumpeter's own writing tackles. Second, Schumpeter's work is rich and complex, and a class dedicated to unraveling his ideas allows students to tease out their many nuances. For example, the class would have sufficient context to engage in discussions about whether Schumpeter was being satirical when discussing the feasibility of socialism. Situating the course in Vienna aids in this process, as the course design makes use of the city as Schumpeter's "intellectual home" to illustrate key concepts and provide context for his experiences and ideas.

Broadly, the course design identifies and critically analyzes Schumpeter's response to the following three questions: (1) What are the key characteristics of capitalism? (2) What does the future of capitalism hold? and (3) How does democratic governance fit into that future? To answer each question, the course has students read parts of three books. The first book is Thomas McCraw's *Prophet of Innovation: Joseph Schumpeter and Creative Destruction* (McCraw (2007)), an accessible Schumpeter biography that provides a comprehensive look at how Schumpeter's tumultuous personal life shaped his thinking on capitalism, especially his theory of creative destruction. The second book is *The Theory of Economic Development*, written by Schumpeter himself (Schumpeter (1934)). We focus on Chap. 2 of the book that elucidates Schumpeter's view of economic growth as a dynamic process that relies on credit, entrepreneurs, and "new combinations," or what we now call innovation. The third book students read is Schumpeter's *Capitalism, Socialism and Democracy* (Schumpeter (1950)), which incorporates his work in *The Theory of Economic Development* and extends it to analyzing the relationship capitalism has with democratic governance, capitalism's feasibility relative to a socialist economic system, and what the future holds for capitalism. Schumpeter's answers are startling and insightful and provide fertile ground for discussion and debate. Dalton and Logan (2020a) showcases what such classroom discussion might look like. All three books are available to students as inexpensive paperbacks.

Students begin the course by watching the 2016 documentary *The Man Who Discovered Capitalism*. The documentary provides an overview of Schumpeter's life, his key economic ideas, and their relevance for today. We find that the documentary is a useful motivation for the first section of the class, which delves into Schumpeter's life with a special emphasis on the time he spent learning economics in Vienna. Students read McCraw (2007) and do 'Schumpeter selfies' at key landmarks around the city of Vienna that relate to formative years he spent in the city, such as the apartment building in which Schumpeter lived while growing up and the commemorative plaques of economics professors in the courtyard of the University of Vienna. The course then shifts to discussing Schumpeter's ideas in depth, beginning with his theory of innovation and entrepreneurship. To do so, students read Chap. 2 of Schumpeter's *The Theory of Economic Development*.

Class discussions focus on identifying the characteristics of the Schumpeterian new combination, the qualities of the entrepreneurs that bring such innovations to market, and how the interrelated mechanisms of credit, entrepreneurs, and new combinations create economic growth. To reinforce the course material, students watch the 2015 film *Joy*, which Dalton and Logan (2020b) argues is effective at showing Schumpeter's theory of innovation and entrepreneurship in practice, and then tackle the case studies of Netflix/Blockbuster and Uber/taxicabs, one a complete example of creative destruction and one, at the time of this writing, an ongoing example. The course then progresses to *Capitalism, Socialism and Democracy*, wrestling with each of the book's first four parts: Marx, Capitalism, Socialism, and Democracy, in turn.[4] Dalton and Logan (2020a) provides sample discussion questions and classroom deliberation to help provide a reference for where discussion in this section might lead. In our experience, students connect best with discussions of the feasibility of socialism, the ability of capitalism to coexist with democracy, and the impact of creative destruction on their daily lives. Recognizing that, the course concludes with teams of students giving group lectures to the class highlighting different real world examples of creative destruction. Project topics have been diverse as students use it to engage with their specific interests. As an example, the projects have ranged from the effects of the introduction of the light bulb on the oil lamp market to the guided missile's effect on the manned bomber industry.

15.3 Vienna as Schumpeterian Laboratory

Schumpeter's personal and intellectual growth was heavily shaped by the years he spent in Vienna. Born in the small Czech village of Triesch in the Austro-Hungarian empire to an upper middle class family, Schumpeter's father died when he was only four. In pursuit of a better life for her son in Austria-Hungary's rigid, class-defined society, Schumpeter's mother, Johanna, remarried to a noble military commander 30 years her senior for status and money. Recognizing young Schumpeter's precociousness and eager to help him succeed, Johanna moved the Schumpeter family to Vienna, the capital of the Hapsburg empire and one of the great intellectual centers of Europe. There, Schumpeter attended the Theresianum, a rigorous preparatory school designed to train the next generation of imperial civil servants and leaders. The Theresianum sits near the Ringstrasse, or simply "the Ring," a circular boulevard that wraps around key administrative buildings and works of monumental architecture. Schumpeter's family apartment was also situated near the Ring only a hundred yards away from Parliament; biographer Thomas McCraw notes how his daily walk to school would have taught lessons

---

[4]The last part of *Capitalism, Socialism and Democracy* presents a history of socialist parties. Since this part of the book is the least essential for teaching Schumpeter's theories, the course leaves out this part of the book.

about architecture, art, and politics just from the effects of proximity (McCraw 2007, p. 14). After graduating from the Theresianum, Schumpeter next enrolled in the University of Vienna, where he developed the special talent he had for economics. At the time, the University of Vienna was one of the best places to study economics in the entire world. Under the tutelage of mentors like Eugen von Böhm-Bawerk, Schumpeter was exposed to competing theories of capitalism at a time when Vienna and the Austro-Hungarian empire were industrializing, a process that would bring about the kind of radical change that would inspire Schumpeter's theories on capitalism and usher in a "techno-romantic" Vienna.[5]

The phrase techno-romantic captures the clash between technological change and capitalist society, on the one hand, and imperial and aristocratic society, on the other, taking place in turn of the century Vienna, the period in which Schumpeter grew up. As we have argued elsewhere (Dalton and Logan (2020c)), this period of immense social and economic transformation helps explain Schumpeter's focus on understanding economic dynamics, both in terms of its origins, entrepreneurs, and its consequences, innovation and creative destruction. As a social scientist trying to explain the world around him, Vienna was Schumpeter's laboratory. Of course, visitors to Vienna today cannot witness in real time the transformations that unfolded during Schumpeter's time in the city, but visitors can find evidence of many of the transformations, such as the physical enshrined in architecture and art. Indeed, one of the main reasons to teach a study abroad course on Schumpeter in Vienna is that Schumpeter's Vienna is so well preserved. Students can experience the Vienna of Schumpeter's time and better contextualize his ideas.

Consider two examples, Otto Wagner and Gustav Klimt. They lived and worked in Vienna during Schumpeter's time. Wagner and Klimt both died in 1918, with Wagner being approximately 20 years senior to Klimt. Both men are quintessential Schumpeterian entrepreneurs whose legacies of creative destruction are on full display to the modern visitor of Vienna. Wagner was an architect and urban planner who worked primarily in the art nouveau style. His buildings, such as the Austrian Postal Savings Bank, can be seen today in the city. Most visitors to Vienna, however, encounter Wagner's legacy when riding the subway. Wagner was chosen by the city government to lead a team in expanding and redesigning the city's transportation network during a time of rapid population growth. Wagner designed the infrastructure, such as the stations and bridges, in the Renaissance style and bathed the structures in a distinct white and green color, which, today, are easily noticeable throughout the city. The most famous structure in the Wagner subway network is considered the station at Karlsplatz. The students on Wake Forest's study abroad programs in Vienna encounter Wagner's legacy every time they take the subway, as the local station is a Wagner station. The Wagner subway illustrates techno-romantic Vienna by the obvious merger of the old and the new—the Renaissance style and color scheme from another era coupled with the functionality

---

[5]The use of the phrase techno-romantic to describe Vienna during this period comes from McCraw (2007, p. 34).

of a modern subway system. This same combination of old and new in the Wagner subway illustrates Schumpeter's idea of innovation as new combinations. Finally, the story of the Wagner subway can be used as an example of creative destruction, as old parts of the city were torn down to make room for the new and one type of transportation, rail, replaced another, such as horsepower.

Klimt's domain was painting. He arguably became Vienna's most famous painter and his paintings, such as *The Kiss*, are recognized by people throughout the world today. His artwork can be viewed throughout the city, but the largest collection, including *The Kiss*, resides in the galleries at the Oberes Belvedere. There are different ways instructors can use Klimt as an example of techno-romantic Vienna and Schumpeter's ideas. The most straightforward is just to view paintings from Klimt's so-called "Golden Phase," such as *The Kiss* or *Judith and the Head of Holofernes*. Even the most untrained eye immediately recognizes Klimt's innovation of combining gold leaf with portraiture. What the untrained eye does not recognize, and here the instructor can provide a deeper look at Klimt as an example of techno-romantic Vienna and Schumpeter's ideas, is the context from which this artistic period of Klimt's evolved. Klimt began his career as a more traditional artist in the prevailing styles by working on large murals, including in the Burgtheater, or Imperial Court Theater. But, as his style developed, Klimt began to push artistic boundaries as far as he could, including his more sexualized renditions of *Philosophy*, *Medicine*, and *Jurisprudence* commissioned by the University of Vienna.[6] The outcry against these "pornographic" paintings was immediate and far reaching for Klimt, including not displaying the paintings and Klimt refusing to take public commissions for the rest of his life. Klimt continued to innovate in his painting but only for private consumption. This episode highlights the very real clash between new and old ways of being taking place in techno-romantic Vienna. Klimt's struggles against the status quo also illustrate Schumpeter's theory of the entrepreneur as a special economic agent. Schumpeter stresses entrepreneurs must have the psychological characteristics necessary to go against the prevailing tendencies in society, to break free of routine and risk condemnation in order to bring their vision of the world into reality. Schumpeter writes of the obstacles entrepreneurs face, including resistance from the outside world, such as that faced by Klimt after his paintings for the University of Vienna were unveiled. The example of Klimt brings Schumpeter's ideas to life for students studying in Vienna.

Of course, being able to observe historical examples of Schumpeter's ideas is not the only way Vienna enhances the learning experience of students. Contemporary Vienna, a modern, multicultural city, offers much for students interested in seeing Schumpeter's ideas come to life. At its heart, a study abroad experience is about observing and learning from innovation. Why? The theory of innovation developed in Schumpeter (1934) can help us understand. Schumpeter described innovation as new combinations of existing resources. Schumpeter argued these new

---

[6]Unfortunately, these paintings did not survive World War II, but their images can still be viewed online.

combinations could take five different forms: (1) a new good or quality of a good, (2) a new method of production, (3) opening a new market, (4) finding a new source of supply, or (5) carrying out a new organization of an industry. New combinations are typically embodied in firms. In so far as students are encountering a new culture for the first time, which is overwhelmingly the case and the motivating factor for most study abroad students, then students observe the very act of creation, the birth of new innovations all around them. It does not matter if these innovations are not new, not new to the Viennese, for example. What matters is that the innovations are new to the student, to the foreigner. In this way, living abroad, encountering a new culture for the first time, may in fact be the absolute best way to internalize Schumpeter's theory of innovation.

Living in Vienna provides an abundance of opportunities to internalize Schumpeter's theory of innovation: traditional meals served in restaurants, like Tafelspitz, Gulasch, and Wiener Schnitzel; street food, like the Käsekrainer sausage; Kaffee und Kuchen, or coffee and cake; eating ice cream at an ice cream parlor with its seating spilling onto the sidewalk; a glass of wine at a local Heuriger; a mug of Glühwein at a Christmas market; a bottle of Ottakringer beer; a night of music, opera, and theater at the Musikverein, Staatsoper, and Burgtheater, respectively; viewing modern art in the Museumsquartier, or simply relaxing on its unique outdoor furniture; listening to live classical music played by a local musician in the shadow of the Hofburg; horse drawn carriage tours of the old city; different architectural styles, including that of the Hundertwasserhaus and all its eccentricities; the stillness of Vienna's churches and cathedral, Stephansdom; and long, meandering walks. But, even the mundane, like grocery shopping: How do I untether the cart? Shouldn't the eggs be refrigerated? And, the milk? I've entered the store, haven't bought anything, and now want to leave. How do I get out? Instructors can incorporate these examples and more from life in Vienna to show students the continuing relevance of Schumpeter's theory of innovation. Students will internalize the ideas much better having been exposed to them on a daily basis.

In addition to discussing Viennese innovation with students in the classroom, we also recommend instructors take students on a field trip to see the innovations together as a class. There are many possible itineraries, but we suggest what we call the Naschmarkt-Secession-Café Museum tour of innovation. This tour has the following advantages: (1) it is logistically easy, (2) students observe many different examples of Viennese innovation, both historical and contemporary, and (3) the tour provides a full range of sensory experiences to engage students' minds.

The tour begins in the Naschmarkt by getting off at the subway station Kettenbrückengasse on the U4, or green subway line. The Naschmarkt is the largest outdoor food market in Vienna. Its pathways are flanked by grocers, street food venders, cafés, and restaurants, all mixed together to form a beautiful chaos. Austrian, Turkish, and Asian cuisines feature prominently. Walk in a northeast direction for the entire length of the Naschmarkt. As you walk, sample something you have never tried, maybe the famous Turkish street food, döner kebab. Challenge your students to do the same, as the Naschmarkt has something new for any budget. Food is a perfect example of Schumpeter's definition of innovation as new combinations, and students should easily be able to relate to the idea of food as innovation. Pay attention also to the different forms of business organization, another example of innovation. From the aggressive hawking of the Turkish vendors with their kebabs to the inviting demeanor of the staff at a sushi stall, the Naschmarkt contains many different styles of salesmanship. Notice the way food is displayed and packaged by the grocers. Can you smell the fresh dates? The cheeses, sausages, and sauerkraut? The candied treats? Think about the entrepreneurs who created the food stalls. Ask your students what it would take to create such a business. Schumpeter (1934) identifies three main obstacles entrepreneurs face: (1) uncertainty, (2) subjective reluctance on the part of the entrepreneur, and (3) resistance from outside forces (remember Klimt), such as legal and political obstacles, social mores, customs, etc. Which of these do students think is the greatest obstacle faced by entrepreneurs wanting to create a Naschmarkt business? Beyond the connection to Schumpeter's theories, the Naschmarkt provides many other opportunities to observe economics in action. How do prices vary across the different sellers? Does the quality of the goods matter? Or, is the location of the seller within the Naschmarkt more important for prices? Is there any evidence of collusion? For students who have never applied an economics framework for trying to understand a lively market like the Naschmarkt, the educational value of the in person experience can be substantial.

After exiting the Naschmarkt onto the street called Getreidemarkt, the Secession building will be on your left on Friedrichstraße. This part of the tour focuses on Viennese art history as examples of innovation and entrepreneurship. The Secession building was created to house the art expositions of the Vienna Secession, an art movement founded in 1897 and designed to break away from the traditional art establishment of Vienna. Both Otto Wagner and Gustav Klimt were members of the Vienna Secession, and we have discussed above how both figures embody many of Schumpeter's ideas. As a result, this stop on the tour is a good place to discuss Wagner and Klimt in more detail with the class.[7] The exterior design of the Secession building with its golden globe of foliage announces to all the intention of the builders: there is a new way of doing art. Inside the building, the main attraction is the *Beethoven Frieze*, a painting by Klimt in honor of the composer. Students can view the art and identify Klimt's innovative style.

By this point in the tour, everyone will likely be tired and need a break to sit down. The last stop on the tour, Café Museum, provides a place to relax and is just a short walk away from the Secession building. As you exit the main entrance of the Secession building, turn left and continue walking down Friedrichstraße away from the Naschmarkt. The sidewalk along Friedrichstraße merges into Operngasse, which you follow towards the city center until you reach Café Museum on your right.

---

[7]For those instructors interested in incorporating more art history to illustrate Schumpeter's ideas, then this is also a good place to introduce students to another founding member of the Vienna Secession, Josef Hoffmann. Hoffmann was an architect and interior designer, most famously associated with the Wiener Werkstätte, an artist workshop that produced pioneering modern design. Hoffmann's work, and that of other members of the Wiener Werkstätte, can be viewed at the Museum of Applied Arts in Vienna.

Vienna's café culture is world famous, and Café Museum is one of many options available to enjoy. Kaffee und Kuchen are a staple of Viennese life, and patrons are invited to sit as long as they like. Students can choose from over a dozen each of traditional Viennese coffees and cakes, most of which will be new combinations for the first time visitor. The coffee combinations range from the simple, e.g. a Kleiner Brauner (espresso and milk), to the complex, e.g. a Maria Theresia (espresso with sugar, orange liqueur, and whipped cream garnished with orange zest). The cakes are similarly diverse. Instructors may want to connect previous discussions in the course by pointing out the history of the Café Museum as an artists' café, with Gustav Klimt, Otto Wagner, and many others as frequent guests. Instructors can then synthesize what was learned on the tour by leading a discussion about Schumpeter's theory of innovation and Viennese innovation. Getting back home from Café Museum is easy with the nearby Karlsplatz subway station.

This section has focused primarily on techno-romantic Vienna as a source of Schumpeter's ideas on entrepreneurs, innovation, and creative destruction, and we have naturally drawn from historical and contemporary Vienna for examples of these theories in action. These topics coincide with more than half of the course on Schumpeter, the other primary topic of the course being the optimal role of government in society, e.g. capitalism versus socialism. We want to briefly point out that the capitalism versus socialism part of the course also benefits from being taught in Vienna. Debates surrounding capitalism versus socialism, both in terms of economics and politics, were raging in Vienna during Schumpeter's time. As we have pointed out, Schumpeter studied under the economist Böhm-Bawerk, one of the leading critics of Marxism at the time. Schumpeter attended Böhm-Bawerk's seminar on Marx, which was also attended by Otto Bauer, Rudolf Hilferding, Emil Lederer—all three of them Marxists who went on to distinguished careers—and Ludwig von Mises (McCraw 2007, p. 45). One can only imagine the level of debate. Schumpeter's command of Marxist thought mastered during this period comes through convincingly during the Marxism portion of *Capitalism, Socialism and Democracy*. Café Central, which is arguably the most famous, or at least heavily touristed, of Vienna's café's today, was another center of these debates, with Leon Trotsky regularly holding court there. The socialist politics of the period peaked during so-called "Red Vienna," the period of social democratic government following the collapse of the Habsburg monarchy. One of Red Vienna's most lasting public works projects, the Karl-Marx-Hof, an imposing housing complex, can still be viewed today. In short, the history of Vienna during Schumpeter's time serves as a useful backdrop for the capitalism versus socialism portion of the course.

15.4 Pre-departure Tips for Teaching Schumpeter in Vienna

Instructors teaching a study abroad course on Schumpeter in Vienna should concentrate on three areas of preparation before departure: (1) Schumpeter and his ideas, (2) Austrian and Viennese history and culture, and (3) the logistics of life in Vienna. The primary texts for the course (McCraw (2007), Schumpeter (1934), and Schumpeter (1950)) provide the bare minimum foundation necessary for teaching, but a more extensive background on Schumpeter and his ideas is preferable. Allen (1991), März (1991), Stolper (1994), and Swedberg (1991) are all examples of biographies of Schumpeter containing information about his life, including his formative years in Vienna, and the development of his economic ideas. Schumpeter's flamboyant personality appeals to students in a way other economists do not, so knowing the biographical details of Schumpeter the man allows instructors to bring Schumpeter to life in the classroom as a way to motivate students' interest. In terms of ideas for specific course content, Dalton and Logan (2020a) provides a wealth of information for anyone looking to teach a course on Schumpeter, whether as a study abroad course or not. Wasserman (2019) is the most recent full-length history of the Austrian school of economics. The first part of the book naturally takes place in Vienna and details the rise of the early economists, such as Carl Menger, Friedrich von Wieser, and Eugen Böhm von Bawerk, who would later be associated with what became known as the Austrian school of economics. Schumpeter features prominently in this part of the book, as the intellectual atmosphere in which he learned economics was heavily influenced by these thinkers. Wasserman (2019) gives instructors a thorough background in understanding the time and place in which Schumpeter learned economics, and parts of the book can be assigned as reading for students in the class. Lastly, although we think Schumpeter (1934) and Schumpeter (1950) expose students to the most important of Schumpeter's ideas, there are, of course, many other primary works by Schumpeter which were not used as class materials in the study abroad course. Two collections of essays, Schumpeter (1991) and Schumpeter (2009), contain some of Schumpeter's most important shorter works. As such, instructors can easily use the essays as individual modules for a course.

The Vienna of Schumpeter's life is well preserved, and it is easy to imagine what life might have been like for Schumpeter in the city by simply walking its streets, viewing the architecture and art, and visiting its many cafés. Instructors can use the city as an extension of the classroom by familiarizing themselves with its history and understanding the context in which Schumpeter lived. Zweig (1943) is the most famous book written on the final years of the Austro-Hungarian Empire, the time period in which Schumpeter lived in Vienna. Stefan Zweig, a writer, was one of the leading intellectuals in Vienna at the time, and his book paints an intimate portrait of the cultural and intellectual milieu through which Schumpeter would have moved. Morton (1979) and Morton (1989) give more historical details about particular time periods during the final years of the Austro-Hungarian Empire. Schorske (1985) provides a broad overview of life, cultural and political, in fin-de-siècle Vienna, whereas Hofmann (1988) covers the entire history of the city. For those with little background knowledge on Vienna, Schorske (1985) and Hofmann (1988) give the best overview and should be read first before our other suggestions. Lastly, Gainham (1979) provides a compelling look at Vienna through a series of biographies of figures from its history. Taken together, these readings will give an instructor a thorough grounding in the cultural, social, and political history of Vienna and will help connect the city to the content of the course. These suggested readings can also be given to students as pre-departure reading to familiarize themselves with Vienna as well.

Instructors should also familiarize themselves with the logistics of life in Vienna before departure. All the standard resources, such as travel guides and online resources, for traveling abroad should be used to prepare. The geography of Vienna is easily mastered. The modern city straddles the Danube with a canal extending south of the river. The old city rests south of the canal and is encircled by the Ring, Vienna's grand boulevard. Many of Vienna's most beautiful buildings line the Ring, including the University of Vienna, which was central to Schumpeter's education as an economist. Knowing Vienna's geography will help instructors map out their Schumpeter selfies, along with possible field trips such as the Naschmarkt-Secession-Café Museum tour of innovation. Vienna is a major destination for tourists. As a result, making online reservations for certain attractions, such as the Musikverein, Boys' Choir, and Spanish Riding School, among others, should be made months in advance. Instructors should let their students know about the demand for these attractions for students to make their own plans before departure. Lastly, instructors can purchase their public transportation tickets online before departure at https://shop.wienerlinien.at/ and recommend that students do the same.

15.5 A Student's Perspective on Schumpeter in Vienna

As a student, I got a great deal out of Professor Dalton's study abroad course in Vienna. More than anything, the experience of being in Vienna brought the course material to life in a way the four walls of a typical classroom do not. Biographer Thomas McCraw analyzes how Schumpeter's personal experiences in a rapidly changing, techno-romantic Vienna influenced his writing and thinking, and the way Professor Dalton structured our course to take full advantage of everything the city has to offer really illuminated what McCraw meant. The Schumpeter selfies in our first week did a great job of both orienting our class to a new city and showcasing Schumpeter's many personal and intellectual influences. Seeing his Vienna apartment near the Parliament building and the prestigious private high school he attended gave context for his personal and political ambitions. Innovative works of architecture such as the Secession Building and the Looshaus showcased the influence of a vibrant city in transition. Of course, no discussion of the Schumpeter selfies would be complete without a mention of my favorite spot: the University of Vienna courtyard with its plaques of famous economists like Böhm-Bawerk and Menger. Walking in the footsteps of those intellectual giants, much like Schumpeter did, was such a treat, especially since it was just earlier that day that our class had discussed their impact on Schumpeter's thought! Professor Dalton's use of the city's food and architecture to illustrate the idea of new combinations—the heart of Schumpeter's theory—was also highly effective. I particularly enjoyed the time he would take at the beginning of some class lectures to describe the various coffees and pastries at the many Vienna coffeehouses, describing the influences they combined to create a (delicious) Schumpeterian new combination. As an example, one pastry I particularly liked—the Apfelstrudel, a long piece of dough stuffed with apple filling, dusted with sugar, and often served with ice cream—was in part inspired by the Ottoman Empire's baklava.

Teaching the course in Vienna has many functional benefits; it is certainly effective at bringing Schumpeter's ideas to life. However, from my experience as a student, a study abroad course is valuable not just for the physical sights it offers but for the sense of immersion it evokes. Vienna did just that—I found that the city was incredibly conducive to learning and immersion. Vienna has a rich history that plays out in its coffeehouses, palaces, and churches, which create an appropriately dramatic setting for learning landmark theories of economics. The imperial grandiosity of Viennese architecture and the unapologetically dated norms of the coffeehouse helped knock me back to the past in a way that offered fresh inspiration and perspective on Schumpeter's ideas. The coexistence of the past with the city's many modern touches—like quaint trams and horse drawn carriages trundling down the Ring alongside modern cars—reflect a Vienna still dwelling on the threshold between the past and present, and in some ways must have been reminiscent of how Schumpeter felt living in a city in transition between a powerful imperial history and a humble democratic future. Another aspect of the city that I especially appreciated was that there were many good spots to read and study. Unlike many other cities, Viennese coffeehouses expect their patrons to be seated for several hours and enjoy books, newspapers, or good conversation over coffee and pastries. I found myself on several occasions taking advantage of this to wander into Café Schopenhauer, order a pastry, and lose myself in Schumpeter's writings for a few hours, carefully cocooned in a coffeehouse that was not seeking to hustle me out the door to make table space for the next patron. To me, the café perfectly encapsulates why Vienna and Schumpeter made such a good study abroad pairing: I was eating, drinking, and living a culture whilst learning an influential work of economics whose conclusions were shaped by countless hours of conversation spent at many of those same places almost a century ago.

Finally, Vienna's centralized location makes a good spot for a study abroad course. Since Vienna is a major rail hub, I was able to quickly and cheaply travel to the Austrian Alps and other Central European cities to gain new cultural exposure. I found this aspect of Vienna to be particularly helpful given that this summer study abroad course was my first time outside the United States, like many other students on the trip, and I wanted to make the most of it.

For other students who might be about to embark on their own journey to Vienna to study Schumpeter, I offer the following tips. First, do your research on the city to start identifying places you would like to see and experiences you would like to have. I primarily consulted Google, TripAdvisor, Lonely Planet: Vienna, and my study abroad professor for ideas. Thanks to that legwork done beforehand, I was able to connect my love of Cold War history with a special screening of the classic Cold War film *The Third Man* at the Burg Kino cinema and do a tour of the Vienna sewer system which features so prominently in the film's plot. Second, even if you do not like classical music, plan a trip to the Opera. The Opera is quintessential Vienna and a very distinctive experience—I was skeptical at first but ended up really enjoying it! Note that limited availability means tickets must be sought out well in advance. Third, pack comfortable walking shoes and at least one outfit of business casual clothes. Vienna is very much a walking city, and you will want the business casual for the opera or some upscale cafés and restaurants. Fourth (this one is Schumpeter specific), I would recommend brushing up on your notes from your principles of economics and intermediate macroeconomics classes.[8] Schumpeter is not technical at all, but the heart of his work is dedicated to describing the causes and consequences of economic growth. I found it helpful to review some of the elementary growth models (Solow and Romer) I had learned in class beforehand to get a sense of how economists had made sense of Schumpeter's work in the years since.

In all, I learned much from my study abroad experience and gained substantial insight into the life and works of Joseph Schumpeter. Even today, some of those lessons and the way they were presented in Vienna still resonate with me. For one, I came into the class quite skeptical about the value of reading an economist who used no mathematics to formulate his theory of innovation and entrepreneurship. Early on in my economics courses I had intuited that mathematics was the language used to describe economic phenomena and was not sure what value Schumpeter added to that body of work. What I came to realize is that powerful insights in economics can be made without mathematics. Schumpeter does not present any theorems and proofs to back his analysis of an entrepreneur guided by the desire to build a lasting dynasty, nor does he model the struggles entrepreneurs face when bringing their innovations to market, but that makes his analysis no less accurate or valuable. In fact, it has helped shape how I think about more mathematically oriented classes. Particularly in courses that evaluate different drivers of economic growth, Schumpeter's identification of creative destruction as the vital fact of capitalism goes a long way towards describing what goes into black boxes like Total Factor Productivity, as Dalton and Logan (2020a) discusses further. The way in which Professor Dalton formulated the innovation section of our course syllabus, with its emphasis on case studies, really drove this home for me. Our class did no econometric analysis of Blockbuster's demise or the Naschmarkt vendors, but we were still able to engage in fruitful discussions that put Schumpeter's prose in context in a way a Stata script does not. Another thing I realized from the course is how inspiring Schumpeter's intellectual breadth was and how he could be a role model for my own life. McCraw (2007, p. 488) notes how Schumpeter died with a book of plays in its original Greek at his bedside. This was a man with a rigorous classical education whose life experiences ranged from academia to politics

---

[8]The course has been taught at different levels, including with only principles of economics as being a prerequisite and with both intermediate microeconomics and intermediate macroeconomics as being prerequisites. The latter is the preferred set of prerequisites, as we believe intermediate courses prepare students to get the most out of Schumpeter's theories.

to business, and he drew upon all of those experiences in his writing. Schumpeter has inspired me to read and think more broadly, in the hopes that I too might be able to bring a breadth of knowledge to bear on research questions. I conclude my thoughts by sharing that Professor Dalton did a phenomenal job guiding our class both through a new city and Schumpeter's dense prose alike, and I am incredibly grateful for the opportunity to relate my experience.

15.6 Conclusion

Studying abroad expands a student's notion of acceptable ways of being. This is an important personal lesson for students to learn. For example, it teaches students to be more tolerant of other cultures and helps foster cooperation. But, students also learn an important economic lesson when studying abroad as well, which is to be more tolerant of economic innovation. Studying abroad teaches students innovation is not to be feared—it can be viewed as simply another way of being. This idea helps foster an openness to entrepreneurship, innovation, and creative destruction, which has important public policy implications for promoting economic growth and prosperity. Many students do not easily internalize these economic lessons from the blackboard alone, or are not entirely convinced at least, so having students immersed in the innovations accompanying any study abroad experience is a powerful learning tool.

This paper argues teaching a course on Joseph Schumpeter, the Prophet of Innovation himself, in Vienna, Austria, is an effective way to bring about this transformation in students' openness to entrepreneurship, innovation, and creative destruction. We describe the course details and encourage readers interested in a more in depth look at the course to read Dalton and Logan (2020a). We then discuss in detail how both historical and contemporary Vienna can be used to illustrate various ideas from Schumpeter's theories. The paper also provides practical tips on preparation for anyone considering teaching Schumpeter in Vienna. Lastly, we give a student's prospective on studying Schumpeter in Vienna, along with a reflection about how a course on Schumpeter fits into an overall undergraduate education in economics.

Acknowledgments We thank all the students who participated in a course on Joseph Schumpeter in the summer of 2018 for inspiring the idea of this paper. We also thank the many people, including Günter Haika, David Levy, and Mike Tyson, for helping organize a successful study abroad course in Vienna. Financial support from the Szurek Mathematical Economics Fund at Wake Forest University is gratefully acknowledged. The usual disclaimer applies.

References

Allen RL (1991) Opening doors: the life and work of Joseph Schumpeter, 2 volumes. Transaction Publishers, New Brunswick

Dalton JT, Gaeto LR (2018) Schumpeter vs. Keynes redux: "Still not dead" Working paper

Dalton JT, Logan AJ (2020a) Teaching and learning Schumpeter: a dialogue between professor and student. Rev Austrian Econ forthcoming

Dalton JT, Logan AJ (2020b) Using the movie joy to teach innovation and entrepreneurship. J Econ Educ 51(3–4):287–296

Dalton JT, Logan AJ (2020c) A vision for a dynamic world: reading *Capitalism, Socialism and Democracy* for today. Indep Rev 24(4):567–577

Diamond AM Jr (2007) The neglect of creative destruction in micro-principles texts. Hist Econ Ideas 26(4):352–356

Diamond AM Jr (2009a) Schumpeter vs. Keynes: "In the long run not all of us are dead". J Hist Econ Thought 31(4):531–541

Diamond AM Jr (2009b) Using video clips to teach creative destruction. J Private Enterprise 25(1):151–161

Gainham S (1979) The hapsburg twilight: tales from Vienna. Atheneum, New York

Gwartney J (2012) What should we be teaching in basic economics courses? J Econ Educ 43(3):300–307

Hofmann P (1988) The Viennese: splendor, twilight, and exile. Doubleday, New York

März E (1991) Joseph Schumpeter: scholar, teacher and politician. Yale University Press, New Haven

McCannon BC (2011) Teaching Austrian economics in Austria as a non-Austrian: a note. J Econ Financ Educ 10(2):1–5

McCraw TK (2007) Prophet of innovation: Joseph Schumpeter and creative destruction. The Belknap Press of Harvard University Press, Cambridge

Morton F (1979) A nervous splendor: Vienna 1888/1889. Weidenfeld and Nicolson, London

Morton F (1989) Thunder at twilight: Vienna 1913/1914. Charles Scribner's Sons, New York

Phipps BJ, Strom RJ, Baumol WJ (2012) Principles of economics without the Prince of Denmark. J Econ Educ 43(1):58–71

Schorske CE (1985) Fin-de-siècle Vienna: politics and culture. Alfred A. Knopf, New York

Schumpeter JA (1934) The theory of economic development: an inquiry into profits, capital, credit, interest, and the business cycle. Harvard University Press, Cambridge

Schumpeter JA (1950) Capitalism, socialism and democracy. Harper & Row, New York

Schumpeter JA (1991) The economics and sociology of capitalism. Princeton University Press, Princeton, edited by Richard Swedberg

Schumpeter JA (2009) Essays: on entrepreneurship, innovations, business cycles, and the evolution of capitalism. Transaction Publishers, New Brunswick, edited by Richard V. Clemence

Stolper WF (1994) Joseph Alois Schumpeter: the public life of a private man. Princeton University Press, Princeton

Strow C (2016) Teaching the economics of ecotourism, trade, healthcare, education, poverty, and immigration as a study abroad experience in Costa Rica. J Econ Financ Educ 15(3):83–94

Swedberg R (1991) Schumpeter: a biography. Princeton University Press, Princeton

Wasserman J (2019) The marginal revolutionaries: how Austrian economists fought the war of ideas. Yale University Press, New Haven

Zweig S (1943) The world of yesterday. Viking Press, New York

Chapter 16
Engaging Economics: 'The Innocents Abroad' in Rome and Italy

David E. R. Gay

Abstract Engaging students at the Rome Center (UARC) for five summers led the author to revamp the approach to remembering, comprehending, analyzing, synthesizing, and judging decisions. Individuals became adept in the seen and unseen parts of economics and, by extension, to draw inferences from architecture, painting and sculpture, by being careful, trained observers. One gradually questioned why the gondoliers no longer sang in the canals of Venice. Why pickpockets rode on Rome's bus #64. And they looked behind the obvious answers. This paper explores adapting one semester microeconomic and macroeconomic basic economics class using a modified, revised Bloom's taxonomy. Students developed an extensive class portfolio full of observations sparked by curiosity, exploration, and discovery. Beginning as innocents abroad, they did well and grew in experience. As a teacher you have each student at a special time when a student is curious, wants to explore, and discovers a new world.

16.1 Introduction

The University of Arkansas established a Rome Center in 1989 to serve the programs of the School of Architecture. The founding Director (1989–2019) was Professor Davide Vitali. The scope was expanded to serve as a university-wide campus offering year-round classes. Arkansas took the lead to establish a consortium of universities with whom to share the campus. By having a staff and key faculty in Rome, many of the core elements are handled by them, such as group introductions to Roman history and art, and field trips in city, plus an extended 3-day trip to Florence, Venice, or other appropriate area. Housing and bus or train transportation is secured by the Rome Center. Rome faculty guide groups through architectural and art history in Rome and off-city sights. The University of Arkansas

---

D. E. R. Gay (✉)
University of Arkansas, Fayetteville, AR, USA
e-mail: dgay@uark.edu

© The Author(s), under exclusive license to Springer Nature Switzerland AG 2021
J. Hall, K. Holder (eds.), *Off-Campus Study, Study Abroad, and Study Away in Economics*, Contributions to Economics,
https://doi.org/10.1007/978-3-030-73831-0_16

Rome Center (UARC) is located in the heart of the old city. It is near the bridge from Castel Sant' Angelo crossing the Tiber. Located in the Palazzo Taverna, it was associated with the Orsini family.

Knowing my Italophilic leanings, in 2013 the Sam M. Walton College of Business (WCOB) asked me to develop two courses in economics in the University Core curriculum that any student would be eligible to take. In five summer sessions (2015–2019), we offered the introductory classes of economics principles (micro, macro, and the one semester survey). A 5-week summer session from mid-May through the end of June utilized three or four faculty from Fayetteville, along with five or six Rome resident faculty. Faculty recruited students or they could not go to Rome. Normally a faculty member taught two classes (full summer salary) or one class (half salary). Classes were held 3 h for 2 days of the Monday–Thursday week. Students had four 3-day weekends with two weekends of general field trips, an open weekend, and normally a 3-day structured visit to Florence. Generally, students flew together based upon the faculty flight itineraries. A few did arrive earlier but the end of the spring semester did not encourage an early arrival due to spring term final exams and the proximity of Memorial Day. Often, they would stay longer for independent travel.

My course strategy was using engagement to define their experience. In my view, study abroad lent itself to this approach, along with an intuitive class involving observations and less emphasis upon computations. Using the title to Mark Twain's (1869) travel book as an implicit subtext meant that a class would be engaging if one promoted curiosity, or exploration, or discovery. Being innocents abroad, not only one of these characteristics was present but all three were there. Most grades involved a series of about 15 'Discoveries.' Each Discovery consisted of one's observations connecting an event with basic principles of economics. A Discovery included a cover page with jpg images of the student, followed by two pages plus of text. Ending the bulk of classwork provided a portfolio of time in Rome (and the trip to Florence). Many became quite adept with that format. I overheard one student asking another classmate, "What does he mean by that?" He responded, "He wants us to be careful observers and draw economic inferences from observations. Connect principles from our study to our field trips." The additional subtext was to be able to explain to a prospective employer, or for graduate school, what was learned in the Rome study abroad.

Study abroad changes students in particular ways. Hopefully changed for the better. Adam Smith (1776, p. 728) pointedly criticized the practice of a 3–4 year grand European tour beginning at ages 17 or 18 because a student "returns home more conceited, more unprincipled, more dissipated, and more incapable of any serious application either to study or to business..." However, it is also worth noting that he tutored the young Duke of Buccleuch in 1764–1766 on a grand tour in exchange for a lifetime salary. While in Toulouse, France, Smith noted that he was becoming bored and decided to continue writing a book about economics, as part of his follow-up to his ethics book.

Sources to prepare oneself to lead students into a summer in Italy, primarily exploring Rome and Florence, can be widespread. First, select a text, such as Heyne et al. (2014) that focuses upon principles and application is a plus. It does its job well because of the focus on concepts instead of 'number crunching.' Other alternatives are Gwartney et al. (2017) or Alchian et al. (2018). Their drawbacks are that they more than a bit long for a summer session in Italy. The Gwartney et al. (2016) text is a manageable length and is appealing to a wider audience, abroad. Students in fashion design, art history and other areas are understandably reluctant to accept a heavily quantitative focus. Even industrial engineers claimed the course added value to their program because they felt as if they typically crunch numbers and moved onward. It has been described as 'crunch and go.' They 'didn't do concepts' (an understatement). You'll select a text that is the best in terms of length, depth, complexity and recognition that your students should not be taking your campus course in Rome. There are certainly substitutes for economics among the courses, as well as among the attractions of Italy.

Second, concept support is readily available at long distance. The Federal Reserve Bank of St. Louis has podcasts on concepts, along their transcripts.[1] Additionally, there are frequently video clips that match the podcasts. Students can hear, read, and see more concepts than you will likely use. There only a few quibbles about content. Their length range about 8–10 min. They are almost godsends in summer school (or in a regular semester). Third, embed as many Italian specific examples that you can locate. Often, the *New York Times* has human interest and other examples and recurring features on Rome. Occasionally, the *Wall Street Journal* has Italian-related stories and analysis. The *New York Times* obituaries have been a source of information about business practices and Italian connected stories. Italian entrepreneurs, inventors, products made in Italy, fashion houses, and others add that special learning economic concepts illustrated in Italy.

Several sources that could assist your preparation are mentioned briefly, here. First, the UNESCO World Heritage Sites at the World Heritage Center.[2] Easier to navigate is the Italian National Tourist Board (ENIT) site and their listing and links to the Italy World Heritage Sites.[3] Second, for Rome, glossy commercial appeal is widely available in major hotels in the monthly magazine *Where Rome*.[4] Third, searchable information on the Made in Italy theme is also available on the from the Italian National Tourist Board.[5] The brief backgrounds and accomplishments of many Italian inventors and businesses responsible for many of the global Italian icons can be explored with additional searching. The list is long: Alessandro Martini (martini), Alfonso Bialetti (the iconic faceted espresso pot), Battista Pininfarina (automobile styling), Carlo Bugatti (furniture), Danilo Nannini (confectionary), Diego Della Valle (shoes and fashion), Emilio Pucci (fashion designer), Giovani

---

[1] Available at: https://www.stlouisfed.org/education/economic-lowdown-podcast-series.

[2] Available online at: https://whc.unesco.org/en/. Search for 'Italy' under the list of World Heritage sites.

[3] http://www.italia.it/en/travel-ideas/unesco-world-heritage-sites.html.

[4] https://www.magzter.com/US/Morris-Media-Network/Where-Rome/Travel/.

[5] http://www.italia.it/en/travel-ideas/made-in-italy.html.

Buitoni (pasta), Giovani Michelucci (architect), Giuseppi Borsalino (men's hats), Gianni Agnelli (Fiat), Grazia Deledda (Nobel Laureate in literature), Gualtiero Marchese (culinary), Guccio Gucci (luxury goods), Leonardo Del Vecchio (Luxottica eyewear), Luiggi Lavazza (coffee), Mario Draghe (former head of the EU Central Bank), Roberto Cavalli (fashion), Mario Moretti Polegato (GEOX footwear and apparel), Michele Ferrero (chocolates, including Nutella, and Tic Tacs), Salvatore Ferragamo (luxury shoes and fashion), and many, many others.

Gradually, the course evolved with some topics and field trips adjusted when focus and interests changed. By the fourth and fifth summers the course included a framework applying concepts, and moving beyond questions that focused upon remembering knowledge instead of higher ordered learning. Using a modified version Bloom's revised framework encouraged being a careful observer and practitioner of analysis. Included in the detailed syllabus schedule are eight examples of concepts within the modified taxonomy. They include using different aspects or levels of analysis, along with the key words to ask or to direct inquiry. For students writing an Honors Thesis or interacting with events, prior experience in compelling story-telling builds a better argument.

The opening strategy was to engage the students in discoveries—thus the name Discovery instead of assignments. Beginning by asking them to be careful observers at the local farmer market placed markets directly into their purview. Using images from the market included a .jpg with each student at the market. Followed by more than two pages of text description of what each noticed about that market-process began their portfolio. This became the talking point of carefully observing. Coupled with the advice in our text to seek the seen and unseen elements of economics set the tone. In Italy, Discoveries included the broader market in Rome at "Campo de' Fiori" and the haggling in the Florence straw-leather market. In the one class on campus we completed a hand-held face-to-face double auction. They could see the whites of the eyes in purposeful actions of others seeking a 'good deal.' It was a richly rewarding experience. Prizes were awarded by selecting a prize from several items but having to identify the runner-up. The subjective nature of cost and choice tied down opportunity cost.

16.2 The Initial Design and the Detailed Process in Italy

A quick overview of the course as proposed lets you sense the flavor of the upcoming journey. Within the framework of active learning the purpose is to tantalize the unfolding opportunities to whet one's curiosity, to encourage exploration, and to promote discoveries by each student.

The class blends the historical, cultural, and business connections of being in Rome, and Italy, with the basic lessons of microeconomics and macroeconomics combined into a one semester course for nonbusiness students. The traditional topics of a regular principles class are be Italian-enhanced for this study abroad trip. The course is keyed to studying in Italy, Rome and the excursion to Florence. The final

16 Engaging Economics: 'The Innocents Abroad' in Rome and Italy   195

arrangement of topics and events were always somewhat open-ended, as they needed to be coordinated with the other options in the Rome Center Program.

The University of Arkansas catalog depiction of ECON 2143 Basic Economics describes the course as "Surveys basic micro, macro principles and analytical tools needed to study contemporary economic problems such as inflation, unemployment, poverty, and pollution. Not open to students majoring in Economics or Business Administration."[6] The course counts as a social science course for undergraduate students.

The course is enhanced should students decide to take it for honors. A broader portfolio allows honors students to select additional projects, and to pursue all required and selected topics at a higher level of learning consistent with Bloom's Taxonomy (revised 2001) and modified for economics (more on this later). These are in the cognitive (knowledge, comprehension, and critical thinking—particularly evaluation and synthesis) and affective domains (emotional reactions—responding, valuing, and organizing).

The following topic areas and approximate timing of the 5-week class are as follows:

- Week 0 Prior to Departure (in Fayetteville). Learning by observation, the students write their first discovery (Assignment) from the Fayetteville Farmers Market. Market behavior through discovery (a double auction). Mutual benefit, market driven emergence of order, led to promote an end not part of intentions. Mapping actions that underlie searching for a good deal and sometimes finding it. Observing and debriefing. Intro to the revised, modified taxonomy. Observation and records from the Fayetteville Farmer Market—the first of the 'discoveries' and debriefing.
- Week 1 **Markets and Exchange**. Alfred Marshall's visit (1880s) to Palermo, Sicily, led to the revelation of the extent to which price change sensitivity affects our buying. Included are the factors that affect the magnitude of the elasticity connection and spending changes. Household behavior and the formation of various types of firms are included in a visit to the Museo Nazionale Romano Palazzo Massimo for some insights into early Roman life and organization of economic activity. We visit a small business (gelato shop) to observe its organization, marketing, and response to the market-place. Demand and supply shifts combine intuition and a structured approach for this most famous economic concept.
- Week 2 **Firms**. Intro to price-taking firms and to price-Making or price searching firms. "If the 'bigness' of business is 'badness,' what can be done about it?" We consider the growth of (largely) American industry and the rise of the late nineteenth century trusts. Several Italian firms are included. Marketplace protections, antitrust laws and cases (U.S., Italian, and E.U.), along with global markets enter into the array of actions and processes of competition. 'Market

---

[6]https://catalog.uark.edu/undergraduatecatalog/coursesofinstruction/econ/.

196 D. E. R. Gay

failure' and 'government failure' are included in the context of understanding policy limitations. Pollution and other externality issues are part of 'market failure.' The extent to which the Rockefellers may have been similar to the Medici will be explored in the visit to Florence. Begin macroeconomic analysis focus of the overall economy.

- Week 3 **Micro and Intro to Macro**. Exploration of aggregate economic activity: national income, national output, and Employment. We examine measurement issues, trends, and analysis of economic outcomes. Fiscal policy will be introduced. We review the economic conditions conducive to economic growth and the distribution of income.
- Week 4 **Aggregates and Banking and Inflation**. We consider explanations of inflation, the money supply and currency debasement. Usually, we visit to the Italian Central Bank. Italian and U.S. banking history have similarities which are emphasized later. In their Money Museum we explore currency, its debasement, and some of the effects of inflation and a monopoly on production of money.
- Week 5. **Selected topics and International Trade**. Returning to market behavior and the closing of the cognitive domain, we briefly enter the emotional power of the affective domain in economic story telling. The interrelated nature of markets brings revenues, tariffs, and quotas into review. The power of vested interests to concentrate benefits in the hands of the few and hiding or dispersing costs across the many. The seen and unseen parts of economics recur with government success and failure along with market success and failure. Finally, the ethics of the market are contrasted with mundane morality. Prepare for the final exam this week.

Grading followed the University of Arkansas scale of 90%+ for 'excellent' or 'A' results, and so forth. Students were expected to keep and maintain a proper portfolio of 'discoveries' for class use and beyond (about 50%). There were a series of brief quizzes (about 20%), classroom checks (about 10% if graded), and a comprehensive final exam (about 20%). The successful completion of an appropriate portfolio analytical record, in a timely manner, finished the academic requirements.

We explored aspects of the eight (+) concepts highlighted by the Federal Reserve Bank of St. Louis podcasts, transcripts, and videos. Usually about 8–10 min in length, they generally provide an underpinning for our text. The economic concepts connect to our field trips, general UARC-wide trips and activities. We used the framework provided by Bloom's revised, modified taxonomy (Anderson et al. 2001). It was explicit in class and in discussion and feedback. Often referred to as levels, they were aspects of reasoning that would assist with their discoveries, and later with term papers or honors theses.

Bloom's revised taxonomy (Anderson et al. 2001) used action elements applied to concepts, as illustrated in the concept of elasticity. Suggested descriptors are in the second column, along with suggested FAQs or elements to focus and to distinguish among approached. The revised taxonomy is modified by switching the last two characteristics so that the creativity is next to last and evaluation is the last/highest aspect or level. Then it fits economics. Improving their storytelling ability helps students to focus on cognitive skills and to differentiate what they are doing. Using their cognitive skills better leads to separating and honing their emotional punch. The baroque artists (such as sixteenth to seventeenth century luminaries Caravaggio, Gian Lorenzo Bernini, Artemisia Gentileschi, Rembrandt van Rijn) knew how to stir emotion. An emotional appeal connected to cognitive skills can provide a memorable punch line. This is done in the last week.

The economic concepts that were fit into the classification applied to eight aspects. They were (1) seen and unseen aspects of supply, demand, and market behavior, (2) elasticity, (3) costs that matter, (4) price-taking firms, (5) price-making (or price-searching) firms, (6) overall macroeconomics, (7) macroeconomics and inflation, and (8) seen and unseen market success and failure, government success and failure.

Table 16.1 illustrates how the framework can be used to discuss and work through the concept of elasticity in its seen and unseen aspects.

16.3   Curiosity, Exploration, and Discovery

A class tends to go well when there is curiosity, or exploration, or discovery. In Study abroad there is not just one of these attributes, all three are present. That combination can help our 'innocents abroad' have an exceptional experience. It happens frequently. Being careful observers and drawing inferences about economic behavior from principles make discoveries, or connections. Usually they know more economics than they give themselves credit.

As mentioned earlier, before departing campus, we complete an exploration and Discovery at the local Farmer's Market. The students observed the operation of the market and reported their findings (using the front page for images) and more than two pages of findings. Each Discovery was submitted to the course management system. This became an introduction to being a careful observer. I shared the day at the market as they visited. Before departing, we had one class to debrief the Farmer's Market and then to conduct a double-oral auction. Using a hand-held version, each student acted either as a buyer or as a seller.

Students did not receive more of the syllabus after the Farmer Market until we arrived in at the University of Arkansas Rome Center. Thereafter they received update a week or two ahead of class and field trips. The flexibility in the timing was necessary because timing and options depended upon factors known after we arrived in Rome. Syllabus construction is extensively detailed to provide many prompts and connections to the subject, the overall framework, the general schedule, and to make connections to our class-specific field trips and independent Discoveries.

Students produce a booklet length collection of economic observations, images, in an Italian context for many aspects of economics. The 'discoveries' are normally due ahead of the following class, unless otherwise noted. Discoveries must be

Table 16.1 Bloom's revised, modified taxonomy framed for elasticies or sensitivities

Building cognitive skills	Keywords and frequently asked questions (FAQ)
Remembering/Knowledge	Define, recall, name, list, recognize, ...
	Can the student list factors, describe three characteristics, or locate the basic elements or define elasticity of demand?
	[Define elasticity of demand, its formula, coefficient, interpretation, and significance...]
	Alfred Marshall's trip to Palermo, Sicily
Understanding/Comprehension	Interpret, summarize, relate, demonstrate, ...
	Can the student focus/summarize on the formula, coefficient of comparison, and its interpretation?
	Contrast with the St. Louis Fed version? How should it be adjusted?
	[Computations or numerical relations with interpretation.]
	FAQ: If P increases and demand is inelastic, what is expected to happen to spending? Justify
Applying	Diagram, employ, draw, construct, use information, ...
	Can the student use the elasticity of demand in a familiar setting?
	Single, day-pass, week-pass, or month pass for Rome?
	[Which elasticity of demand value (elastic >1, inelastic<1, or unitary=1) is reflected?]
Analyzing—to take apart or to disassemble	Compare, separate, combine, categorize, detect, ...
	Can the student separate the three factors influencing the magnitude of elasticity of demand?
	Results vary according to (1) available substitutes, (2) proportion of budget, and/or (3) time.
	[What are common descriptions for elasticity of demand compared to other elasticities (income)?]
Syntheses/Creating	Design, construct, plan, ...
	Can the student create an estimate based upon the underlying elasticity calculation?
	The jump from detecting the underlying pattern leads to creating, for example, advertising elasticity
Evaluating	Critique, judge, justify a decision, ...
	Which are the best products to tax with an understanding of the expected sensitivity?
	If it's a locality, like New York City, how does that alter the evaluation?
	[Which elasticity is likely best for taxation purposes? For reducing usage?]

16 Engaging Economics: 'The Innocents Abroad' in Rome and Italy

submitted on time, on topic, within length (or reductions apply).[7] Expectations for all students relate to the modified, revised Bloom's taxonomy, described in classes and on in the online class learning system. I followed it because it helps students to compose better essays (clarity, illustration, context, comparison, synthesis, and affective learning).

The prompt for a market discovery looked something like this:

> Observe, describe, and identify how the market operates. Explore the displays of product, location of the stands, signage, interaction between buyers and sellers, for example. Connect these to economic actions. This should be 2+ pages of text. Page one includes your .jpg taken at the market (with you in the image), followed by pages 2 and 3+ of text. This is the course format.

The discoveries fit into the overall UARC scheduling, along with certain field trips for the class, as well as discoveries during free time. Students were instructed to use the podcasts, class lectures, and the class text as background to fit their discovery into the taxonomy aspects or levels to build their portfolio. Topically, the course followed this order for the term:

1. Arkansas: Intro to Me (to be shared if you permit)
2. Arkansas: Farmer's Market (subsequent debriefing sets the framework for applying the taxonomy to future discoveries)
3. Rome: Household Management and Commerce
4. Rome: Small Business at a Gelateria (Gelateria del Teatro near campus, or La Romana 'near' Palazzo Massimo)
5. Rome: The Vatican Museums aim for one aspect of their administration, a painting, and a sculpture
6. Rome: At your own timing select a lunch or dinner
7. Rome: Revisit a small business
8. Rome: The Rome Market at Campo de'Fiori involves space sharing, general merchandise, and timing with surrounding business
9. Rome: The Renzo Piano designed auditoria at Parco della Musica, site of the 1960 Olympics
10. Rome: Central Bank of Italy focus on the Money Museum introduces a history of inflation (debasement of the currency) along with a banking history similar to the United States
11. Rome (optional): the ruins at Pompeii, or Herculaneum, or Oplontis
12. Florence: Uffizi Gallery
13. Florence: Ferragamo Museum
14. Florence (optional): The exterior of the Orsanmichele Church
15. Florence: The outdoor "straw/leather" market with bargaining
16. Rome: The Affective Domain, or stirring emotion with the Baroque, along with thoughtful reflection upon the economic emphasis of their study abroad

---

[7]Late? = 0. Art history? = 0 Too brief? Check format settings. Score reductions apply (about 33–100%).

There are many backups and options. Among the ones used, here is a sampling: (1) Caravaggio paintings and their use of lighting in the French Church, (2) the Baths of Diocletian and (3) the Church of Santa Maria degli Angeli e dei Martiri—both near the Museum of the Romans at Palazzo Massimo, (4) Trajan's Markets and Museum near Trajan's Column, (5) Villa D'Este in Tivoli, (6) Palazzo Altemps Museum near campus, (7) Museum of the Risorgimento and exhibitions at the Vittoriano, (8) the Palazzo delle Esposizione, (9) Museum Ara Pacis near campus, (10) the exhibits at the Scudere del Quirinale, (11) the Palazzo Barberini Museum, and (12) the Cinecittà movie studios and museum.

16.4 Lessons from Discoveries and Study Abroad

Study abroad changed me during those five summers in ways that were unexpected. Never have I written so many letters of recommendation. When asked to write letters to medical school, my response was "wouldn't it be better for your biological sciences professor to do that?" Invariably the response would be "Perhaps, but you know me well." That was true. The strangest surprise was asking my students to write reference about the Rome program and taking econ as one of their two classes. Of course, that sort of inquiry meant that they needed to be comfortable to respond with yes, or no. They often became the best recruiters and I shared (with their permission), names and contacts. Somehow, I'd gotten away from the notion that I wanted their candid responses to share their experiences with other students. Upon entering a classroom to recruit next year's students it helped to leave the slide with names and contact information, and major in clear view. In some engineering classes connecting principles of economics in their social science block meant economics was not just a business class, but how it fit into their curriculum.

Beginning by being a careful observer helped to stoke curiosity. Some immediately looked beneath the surface and discerned that purposeful individuals searching for good deals looked again to find better deals. The decision to buy depended upon a process or procedure to sniff out a good enough deal. Buyers and sellers interacted with each searching for better alternatives. Some explored alternatives in the institutional arrangement of the market. There were many questions. Shelf life? Personal consumption? Transformed into other products? Switch between? Going better with something else? Food stamps? Closing time? Why did some venders have a line? Signage? Arrangement? Appearances? They carefully observed and describe. We debriefed.

In our only class before departure, we initiated buying and selling with a double auction. Buyers were instructed to seek their best deal with any leftover money reflecting how well they'd bought. Sellers were instructed to sell for cost, of higher, with an excess of revenue above cost as a measure of how well they had done. In other words, don't spend more money than you have or don't sell at a loss. Prizes were later awarded based upon how each buyer and each seller did with this metric (and additional prizes would also be awarded based upon other metrics).

16 Engaging Economics: 'The Innocents Abroad' in Rome and Italy

The debriefing and discussion highlighted many general observations, such as, purposeful individuals seeking good deals often found them, and intentions did not matter (exchange created value) without changing outcomes, and high cost sellers or low moneyed buyers were not competitive, and repeat business, and there are substitutes for virtually everything, and ways to assist those whose economic conditions were limiting, and opportunity costs as the highest foregone alternative. Finally, all of this introduced the seen and unseen markets early in the text. Look at the surface and try to discern factors that lie behind or underlie actions in the marketplace.

Prizes were awarded based upon how well buyers had bought without spending all that they could while sellers were rewarded for receiving cost or higher. In that instant, both parties to a completed exchange benefited. Mutual advantage. When asked whom they were trying to help, most, if not all, said themselves. Actually, it didn't matter whom they professed to help. Both benefited. Thinking of yourself or thinking of others simply did not matter. Motives were not important. Almost as significant was a realization that prices tended to have lower variance as successive rounds occurred. With more information in successive rounds the prices tended to converge. Prices agreed by the buyer and seller were recorded and were visible in each round. Often you could reveal a sealed envelope containing the predicted price (plus or minus) and the expected number of exchanges. They were led as if by an invisible hand to promote an end that was no part of their intentions.

Awarding prizes from selecting between candy, fruits, or a dollar bill by selecting the first choice but also announcing the runner-up item nailed opportunity cost. Behind each potential exchange was a series of prior exchanges that led to the current exchange. Looking beyond the seen elements to the unseen ones meant cooperation and competition occurred long before any item entered a market. The market success favored the high valued buyer and the lower cost sellers. It was tougher to trade if you didn't have as much to spend or were a higher cost seller.

We explored several ways to help the low valued buyer to buy in the future. Options included (1) a price control to squash the higher valued buyers and to reduce opportunities for others, (2) to seek a higher valued skill in order to have more to spend, (3) taxing others to enable higher disposable income, (4) take up a collection to enable the one with little in his/her wallet to have more to spend.

Thus, by curiosity, exploration, and discovery they continued to realize that they knew more that they professed. For example, asked how many pairs of shoes they brought in their luggage, they were asked to explain why they didn't bring three more pairs? Of course, we continued that way for 5 weeks and beyond.

Here are several examples that illustrate coupling cognitive and emotional firepower. Among the Rome examples selected are "Apollo and Daphne," by Lorenzo Bernini (1598–1680) in the Borghese Galleria, the abduction of Persephone by Pluto, lord of the underworld (Hades), the "Boy With Basket of Fruit," masking a series of decisions and transactions about a choice being a 'good deal' or being a 'good enough' deal, and the "Sick Bacchus," by Michelangelo Merisi da Caravaggio (1571–1610). A summary of inferences could include: (1) potential exchange not expected to be mutually beneficial, (2) the unexpected, unanticipated desirable effects of an event, (3) the trail of events leading to final selection of goods, or (4) the urge to subsidize spillover benefits (health care or to require inoculation against communicable childhood disease) or deal with spillover costs.

Economics and art can engage students through evidence, inference, context alone and a wider context to reposition their observations into the affective domain to enlist the power of emotions to tell an economic story. The student 'discoveries' led the them to the final discovery at the Borghese Gallery. Its contents were collected by Cardinal Scipione Borghese (1577–1633). He couldn't become a Pope of the Catholic Church, but he did amass an incredible collection of paintings and sculpture.

The statue of Apollo and Daphne illustrates (1) part of the transformative influence of the affective domain. Gian Lorenzo Bernini (1598–1680) created a life-size, marble, Baroque statue of the mythical Greek Apollo and Daphne. Apollo, chasing Daphne, is closing on his objective. In her flight she has called upon the gods to save her from his intentions. Alas, her plea did not specify how she was to be saved and she is becoming a tree sprouting twigs and branches from her fingers and beginning to sink roots into the ground becoming a laurel tree. Apollo is oblivious to her transformation, for the moment. Quite soon he will discover that the object of his expected net gain will not likely provide a 'good deal' for him. Ah, the surprises of involuntary exchange appear. The sculpture clearly emphasizes that their union would not be expected to be mutually beneficial.

Another powerful Bernini sculpture is in the main second floor room. It also illustrates (2) the anticipated consequence of mutual advantage that has gotten off track. The sculpture is Bernini's depiction of the abduction of Persephone by Pluto, lord of the underworld (Hades). His designs upon Persephone are far from benevolent or mutually beneficial. She draws back in her despair will his hands grasp her body. The placement of Pluto's fingers on her marble thighs reveals indentations around the fingers as if they are sinking into her (marble) flesh. A marble tear is falling down her distressed face. Pluto's three headed dog from the underworld is howling near her feet. The power of that confrontation almost makes the sculpture leap off the pedestal in its emotion. Bernini's work is also known as "The Rape of Persephone."

The Caravaggio (Michelangelo Merisi 1571–1610) collection in Galleria Borghese includes the "Boy with Basket of Fruit," which can illustrate the interconnected marketplace that led to the range of fruit visible in the painting. The supply chain associated with the fruit underlines the extended order of the market, along with the temporal nature of the fruit as it continues to reveal evidence of rotting. Caravaggio's use of light highlights the degree of liveliness in the subjects and objects.

The "Young Sick Bacchus" reveals a ghastly pale subject with a greenish, sickly caste. To what extent can the sickliness be an object of individual actions, unexpected results, spillover costs, or can there be possible remedies? Alternative subjects highlighted by Caravaggio, or his followers, abound in Rome. The Caravaggio paintings in San Luigi dei Francesi, the French Church in Rome (1518–1589), are noteworthy and have economic interpretations focusing upon individual choices with the use of lighting that highlights individuals.

16.5 Concluding Observations

This course is part of an ongoing strategy to connect learning with exploration and discovery. It reflects a four-pronged strategy involving (1) finding where to start a course (with a skills inventory), (2) engaging the cognitive domain through topical areas, and (3) adding the zest or zip to economic storytelling through the effective use of the affective domain. For example, one can describe the policy of the Federal Reserve Board to pursue a 2% rate of inflation. Another way to describe the policy is to couple the annual average family income as $60,000 and a 2% inflation is $1200 or about an average of $100 per month. Monetary value shrinks to reflect the inflation. It's almost as if someone slips a $100 bill each month out of your wallet. However, it's not obvious because you're not billed in any explicit way. Which of the two illustrations has more punch?

Acknowledgments The author thanks his students for being open to other perspectives and drawing inferences from observations. Special thanks are due to Davide Vitali, first Director of the UA Rome Center (1989–2019), the second Director Francesco Bedeschi, and the UARC Faculty and Staff for their kindness and good will. D.S. Long, UA Study Abroad Director and editor Josh Hall provided helpful comments and suggestions. Louise Rozier provided guidance and friendship for 30 years. The UA WCOB Global Engagement Office has supported these opportunities. The usual caveat applies.

References

Alchian AA, Allen WR, Jordan JL (2018) Universal economics. Liberty Fund, Indianapolis, IN
Anderson L, Krathwohl D, Airasian P, Cruikshank K, Mayer R, Pintrich P, Raths J, Wittrock M (2001) A taxonomy for learning, teaching, and assessing: A revision of Bloom's taxonomy of educational objectives. Pearson, Upper Saddle River, NJ
Gwartney JD, Stroup R, Lee D, Ferrarini TH, Calhoun J (2016) Common sense economics: What everyone should know about wealth and prosperity. St Martin's Press, New York, NY
Gwartney JD, Stroup RL, Sobel RS, Macpherson DA (2017) Economics: Private and public choice. Cengage, Boston, MA
Heyne PT, Boettke PJ, Prychitko DL (2014) The economic way of thinking. Pearson, Boston, MA
Smith A (1776) An inquiry into the nature and causes of the wealth of nations. Modern Library, New York, NY
Twain M (1869) The innocents abroad, or the new pilgrims' progress. American Publishing Company, Hartford, CT

Chapter 17
Developing Study Abroad Opportunities in Economics and Finance: Guidance from a Faculty-Led Program in Madrid, Spain

Gregory M. Randolph and Michael T. Tasto

Abstract As universities have focused more attention on study abroad opportunities for students in recent years, an increasing number of students have studied abroad through short-term programs. While short-term trips associated with a class have the potential to offer great learning experiences for students, faculty face high startup costs in the design of programs and students may not experience an improvement in intercultural competence without a focus on design principles. This chapter provides faculty with a program development guide for a faculty-led course in Madrid, Spain. Initial preparation, curriculum design, marketing and enrollment, teaching, trip management, and assessment of the program are discussed in detail. Additionally, guidance is provided to assist students in the development of intercultural competence and assessment throughout the course.

17.1 Introduction

Study abroad programs provide potentially life-changing experiences for undergraduate students. In addition to offering opportunities to enhance intercultural competence, students can build soft skills, apply discipline-specific content in real world settings, and improve their job prospects through study abroad opportunities. Students can also earn credit toward the completion of their degree while visiting countries and destinations that they may never experience otherwise. Recognizing the importance of global citizenship and intercultural competence, universities across the U.S. have increasingly encouraged students to study abroad. For example, the Institute of International Education's Generation Study Abroad Initiative has attracted over 800 institutional partners committed to increasing study abroad

---

G. M. Randolph (✉) · M. T. Tasto
Southern New Hampshire University, Manchester, NH, USA
e-mail: g.randolph@snhu.edu; m.tasto@snhu.edu

© The Author(s), under exclusive license to Springer Nature Switzerland AG 2021
J. Hall, K. Holder (eds.), *Off-Campus Study, Study Abroad, and Study Away in Economics*, Contributions to Economics,
https://doi.org/10.1007/978-3-030-73831-0_17

opportunities since the inception of the program in 2014 (Institute of International Education 2019a).

Short-term study abroad programs, defined as experiences that last less than 8 weeks or occur during summer terms, have become more popular recently as universities look to expand study abroad options. While the number of U.S. students studying abroad has grown in recent years, almost 65% of all students studying abroad participated in short-term programs in the 2017/2018 academic year compared to approximately 55% of students studying abroad in 2008/2009 (Institute of International Education 2010, 2015, 2019b).

Short-term study abroad programs may be more appealing to students for financial reasons since shorter trips are typically more affordable. The short-term programs also allow students to travel abroad while maintaining their on-campus schedule, continuing to participate in university activities including athletics and clubs, and keeping employment options open as many students work throughout their college careers. Compared to a semester or yearlong study abroad program, short-term study abroad programs are typically less intimidating for students who have not previously traveled abroad. Short-term study abroad programs also often have the additional benefit of being directed by faculty members on campus. Faculty members can design experiences to help students get the most out of a short-term program by creating a class experience that encourages intercultural learning and connecting discipline-specific content to the trip. Students and their parents may also feel more comfortable with travel abroad when students are accompanied by a faculty member with travel experience who can provide a safe and structured travel opportunity for students.

Despite the general recognition of the value of study abroad and the commitment on behalf of many universities to enhancing study abroad participation, numerous challenges may prevent further development of study abroad opportunities. While 1.9% of all students reported participation in study abroad during the 2017/2018 academic year, this is a relatively modest increase from the 2013/2014 academic year when 1.6% of students participated (Institute of International Education 2015, 2019b). Fischer (2019) cites a lack of faculty incentive and absence of recognition of international program development as part of promotion considerations as contributing factors in the relatively modest study abroad numbers. While short-term faculty-led programs provide potential to further expand access to study abroad, the programs require a serious time commitment on behalf of the faculty and staff involved, as well as a financial commitment from administration to fund the startup. Faculty must select a location and prepare for a trip far in advance, design a course, recruit students, complete necessary trip documentation and plans, deliver a course, and travel with students. Additionally, these trips typically occur when faculty have a break from teaching and displace time normally utilized to catch up on other work.

While the emphasis on short-term programs has increased in recent years, there are still relatively few academic resources designed to assist faculty in the development of a faculty-led study abroad program in specific fields. Sachau et al. (2010) and Keese and O'Brien (2011) offer advice for the design and delivery of short-term study abroad programs in general and note the lack of articles specifically intended to assist faculty with developing and managing short-term study abroad programs. While recent research has provided additional advice for faculty (Bain and Yaklin 2019; Pittenger et al. 2019), Strow (2016) highlights a lack of publications that provide guidance on the development of study abroad courses in the field of economics in particular and provides faculty with advice on developing a course involving a trip to Costa Rica. Faculty members looking to offer faculty-led short-term study abroad options for their students could benefit from better guidance on effectively designing and offering these programs. The challenges associated with designing and delivering study abroad courses may be a contributing factor in the relatively limited growth of study abroad participation.

Given the expansion of short-term study abroad programs, research has also focused on the extent to which short-term study abroad programs contribute to student acquisition of intercultural competence. A number of articles related to short-term study abroad programs have noted that research regarding their efficacy is continuing to develop and there is some debate in the literature regarding their overall contribution to intercultural learning (Gaia 2015; Niehaus et al. 2018; Mule et al. 2018). Numerous studies indicate that short-term study abroad programs can improve intercultural competence (Chieffo and Griffiths 2004; Gaia 2015; Walters et al. 2017). Other studies suggest that short-term programs may not provide students with an opportunity to develop intercultural competence in comparison to longer-term trips (Medina-López-Portillo 2004), do not necessarily increase self-identification as global citizens (Mule et al. 2018) and may provide only a trivial experience for students if not designed correctly to foster intercultural competence (Di Gregorio 2015).

This chapter provides guidance for faculty members seeking to effectively design short-term faculty-led study abroad programs in economics or finance that both engage students in discipline-specific content and assist students in developing intercultural competence. We draw on our experience with the design and delivery of a short-term faculty-led program in Madrid, Spain to offer advice on the initial preparation and selection of a location, curriculum design, marketing and course registration, management of the student experience during the trip, and follow-up activities and assessment after returning from the trip. Additionally, aspects of the program that were designed to specifically promote contributions toward student development of intercultural competence are highlighted throughout the paper. We intentionally attempted to engage in cultural mentoring behaviors outlined in Niehaus et al. (2018). Cultural mentoring actions include expectation setting, explaining host culture, exploring self in culture, and facilitating connections.

17.2 Selection of Location and Initial Preparations

Faculty who want to offer a short-term faculty-led study abroad program for students will first have to select a destination for the trip. There are many locations around the world that could provide students with great opportunities to travel and learn. However, it makes sense to consider the goals of the course, cost, student interest, and the faculty member's ability to facilitate the learning experience in the selection of location. After considering the needs of our students, we selected Madrid, Spain for a variety of reasons. Spain offered an opportunity for students to experience a new culture in a location that students and their parents viewed as an attractive and safe location. There is no shortage of amazing art, architecture, music, food, and literature to explore in the city. Both the historical and recent economic and political landscape of Spain is of great interest to students of economics and finance. Madrid also provides a relatively affordable location for students departing from the East Coast of the U.S. Airfare is generally reasonable, modestly priced food is available in the city, affordable public transportation is available, and many of the major attractions in the city are easily accessible to the public. Finally, students can visit Spain with just a U.S. passport. It is no surprise that Spain is the third most popular location for U.S. study abroad programs (Institute of International Education 2019b).

Another decision that faculty will need to determine early in the process is whether to partner with a host institution or other organization in the destination location to assist with the study abroad experience. Alternatively, faculty may prefer to design, plan, and lead the trip on their own. We decided to partner with Nebrija University in Madrid due to the high-quality experience that the university could provide for our students and the commitment to excellence that our contacts at the university displayed throughout the planning process. Our partners in the International Programs Office at Nebrija University secured hotel accommodations at a great price in a central location in Madrid with all meals included. The university offered a variety of class sessions on topics including Spanish culture, Spanish politics, income inequality, the Spanish financial sector, and the business environment in Spain. They were able to schedule workshops for our students to work with Spanish students and international students studying in Spain on the Nebrija University campus. Nebrija University also scheduled visits to cultural, business, and government sites based on the needs of our students. University staff accompanied students on several trips to assist with language translation when necessary. We selected field trips including the Prado Museum, the Official Institute of Credit, and the National Commission of Markets and Competencies. It is important to discuss the cost of the partnership in detail, but the university was able to provide very reasonable pricing for the student experience. The International Programs Office staff and faculty helped to provide a great experience for our students and offered several opportunities that would be challenging or difficult to recreate on our own. If faculty decide not to partner with a local university or organization, we strongly suggest researching housing, food, field trips, opportunities to interact with local students, and transportation in detail well in advance of the trip.

In order to prepare for the trip, we suggest a site visit to the destination approximately one year prior to the student trip if feasible. While it is possible to travel with students to a location for the first time, we found that a brief site visit provided us with an opportunity to identify a number of great opportunities for students and better plan the overall experience. Fortunately, Southern New Hampshire University (SNHU) provided support for us to stop in Madrid for two nights as part of another university-sponsored trip. This afforded us with an opportunity to meet with the host university, visit the campus, and examine the hotel. It was much easier to discuss trip details in person with our host university and plan an itinerary on location even though we stayed in the city for less than two full days. We were also able to explore field trip opportunities for students and become familiar with key locations so that we could assist students in navigating the city upon arrival. We would suggest becoming familiar with the location of the nearest U.S. embassy and a local hospital just in case of an emergency.

17.3 Course Curriculum Design and Teaching Before the Trip

One of the major underlying aspects of a faculty-led program is the actual course that students will register to take as part of their curricular requirements. Many colleges and universities offer faculty some flexibility when trying out new courses. At our institution, we can teach a course one time as a 'Special Topics' course. It can only be offered only once without going through the proper curriculum approval process, which can typically take 3–5 months. Once the course is approved, it can be published in the next catalog publication, so that students can view the course offering and then register to take the course. It is important to keep your institution's catalog publication date in mind, so that you can plan accordingly for this lengthy process. In addition, the course needs to be in the catalog the semester before you plan to offer the faculty-led program, as that is when student registration occurs.

The ability to teach a course one time as a special topics course alleviates the many hurdles described above. This also allows you to test which course aspects work well, before submitting your syllabus and course for approval. Syllabus design is critically important as it outlines the foundation and expectations of the course and faculty-led program. The syllabus is the contract between you and your students. Immediately following our first trip to Madrid with 15 students, we realized that the design of our syllabus was missing some incentives and disincentives. For example, on the last day of structured activities, one of our students decided to sleep-in and not participate, partially because it would not have a major impact on their grade. As a result, we revised our syllabus to place more weight on activities and participation. We also did not have ample disincentives for bad behavior, so we revised our syllabus to allow the instructor to remove a student and not allow them to participate in the structured activities. Since we already placed greater weights on those specific aspects, not participating will now have a detrimental impact on their grade. Our general rule was to have any incentive or disincentive cost a student a letter grade (10%). We felt that the cost of a letter grade was an easy concept for students to realize and incentivize them to change their behavior.

It is important to consider designing faculty-led programs that fit into students' academic programs when creating your course. The minimum number of students to run a course at our institution is ten. Getting students to register for your faculty-led program is important and your course must be practical and useful in terms of getting students closer to graduation, in addition to being appealing, intellectually challenging, and affordable. To add value for students, we created two separate courses that are nearly identical, but with different prefixes. Both courses were submitted through the curriculum approval process. We created two courses:

- ECO 455: Experiential International Economics
- FIN 455: Experiential International Finance

These courses allow students to register for either an upper-level economics or upper-level finance course, satisfying the degree requirements for more students in our school of business, rather than just our department's majors. Of course, any student in our university could always register for the course, but it would use up one of their free electives. As you could imagine, our faculty-led program to Madrid might look more appealing to business administration students trying to satisfy a 300–400 level finance elective requirement. We attempted to design our course objectives to reflect both the goals of developing intercultural competence and discipline-specific knowledge. Niehaus et al. (2019) provide an assessment of course objectives in short-term study abroad courses, finding that faculty may tend to emphasize discipline-specific content over intercultural competence. Even when course outcomes focus on intercultural competence, many faculty instructors seem to focus on knowledge over skills and attitudes. We recommend reviewing the article when designing course outcomes.

Through trial and error, we have rearranged how we teach this course. The highlight of our course for students is the trip to Madrid occurring over spring break. However, prior to the trip, we meet with students on Wednesday from 5:00 to 6:00 pm.[1] We designed these classes to meet some of our course objectives, discuss both discipline-specific concepts and intercultural concepts, and take care of administrative issues. Two half-hour time slots are dedicated for our study abroad and student life offices to discuss the rules and regulations related to international travel expectations of students. In our other class meetings, we review the five academic components of the class, which are:

- Component 1—Why are you here?

  - Please write an essay explaining why you are going on this trip. What are you looking forward to most? What concerns (if any) do you have? What finance

---

[1]Interestingly, a unique aspect of this course design results from not requiring a dedicated classroom assignment. Our university has a break from undergrad during the day to graduate at night—thus between 5:00 and 6:00 pm there are many classrooms readily available, so we are not taking up a dedicated classroom for the entire semester. These cost savings should be highlighted, when promoting your program to administration.

concepts are you interested in exploring during this class/trip? What plans (if any) do you have to work in a field related to finance? (2–3 pages)

- Component 2—Spanish culture and analysis of business practices in Spain

  - Identify three important cultural aspects from Spain that you find interesting. These can be anything from food traditions, family traditions, religion, historical, etc. Discuss the similarities/differences between culture in the U.S. Additionally, please find scholarly articles that identify a business trend in Spain using the Shapiro Library Resources. Reflect on your thoughts on the articles, why the trend is important, and how businesses can capitalize on the trend going forward. How are the trends similar and/or different to trends in other European countries and the U.S.? (3 pages)

- Component 3—Journal

  - Keep track of your experiences in Madrid in a journal. You will want to document your experiences with faculty and students on campus, trips to businesses, and other experiences. You will want to describe your thoughts/feelings regarding these experiences. At a minimum, you are required to write a $1/2$ page summary of each day of classes at Nebrija and each tour/visit. Feel free to include additional travel or research that you would like to consider for the future based on your experiences in Madrid. Additionally, find and document exchange rates for US Currency at five different banks while in Madrid on 3 separate days. (minimum 5 Pages)

- Component 4—Reflection

  - Complete a reflection paper regarding your experience in Madrid. What did you learn? What did you find surprising? Would you do anything differently? What advice would you provide for other students regarding travel abroad? How will you apply what you learned going forward? You have flexibility with this assignment to discuss your experience. As an alternative, you can create a 5-min video documenting your experience that can be shared with other members of the SNHU community. (minimum 3 pages)

The pedagogy of teaching languages invokes students to participate in activities that spark conversation, laughter, and engagement. These Spanish classes encouraged our students to talk to each other, learn the basics of the Spanish language, and build friendships before departing for the trip. They also helped students learn more about the culture of Spain and feel more comfortable about knowing what to expect upon arrival. Increased familiarity of the native language created confidence and excitement among our students, a component that had been missing from our earlier design. Again, this design alteration was a major improvement for our course.

Cultural diversity and education are important issues on our campus and emphasized by university administrators. Given the importance of intercultural competence, we devoted time in our classes to discuss student expectations for the Madrid trip and Spanish culture. We also encouraged students to read *Ghosts of*

Spain: Travels Through Spain and Its Silent Past (Tremlett 2008) before the trip to provide students with a better understanding of Spain's recent history. This faculty-led program could represent a pathway to achieving the goal of increasing cultural awareness. To assess whether that happens, we utilize a CQ (Cultural Intelligence) assessment tool.[2] The tool is administered through a survey of questions targeting student awareness, attitude, or beliefs before and after the experience. The post-test measures the effectiveness of our design and experiences. To make sure students took this seriously, we allocated 5% of their final grade to completing the pretest and post-test.

17.4 Marketing for Course Registration

Successful faculty-led programs offer potentially life-changing opportunities that open doors previously unknown for students who participate in the course. This cannot occur if the course is low-enrolled and does not run. Our institution has a minimum of ten students to register for the course, and there is an additional $2500 'lab' fee attached to registering for this course. We recommend 12–15 students and 2 faculty members.[3]

At our university, there are trips that do not run because of low enrollment. It is critically important that the marketing of your faculty-led program is a priority before and during the registration period. Imagine all the planning and effort that you have invested into creating this faculty-led program, and then find out that the program will not run because not enough students register for the course.

The faculty-led program you create must offer value to the students and there are many different opportunities to add value in the design phase, as discussed earlier. Prior to registration is when you can highlight all of the great things that your study abroad course offers. The structure of the fall term does not easily lend itself to many extended studying abroad opportunities. Thanksgiving break is the exception, but the week is often dedicated primarily for family gatherings and relatively close to the end of the fall semester. Consequently, most of the faculty-led programs at our institution occur over spring break or after final exams in May. This means the fall registration period is when most students will be registering for their study abroad course.

The study abroad and marketing office typically provide stand up posters or fliers that highlight the different options available to students. While this does provide exposure, it does not necessarily highlight or recruit specifically for your faculty-

---

[2] Available at: https://culturalq.com/products-services/assessments/cqselfassessments/.

[3] The rationale for 12 students results from transportation costs for the group (to and from the campus and airport), increasing from $600 to $1200 for 15 or more. If there were a lot of students interested, we might increase the number, but we would do so in groups of two (for roommate purposes).

led program. One way to increase registrations is to visit other classes and give a brief 5-min explanation of your faculty-led program. Another way, that we have found to be more successful, is by e-mailing specific groups of students organized by their major. To assist in sparking interest and urgency, we let them know there are a limited number of spots available and students are accepted on a first-come, first-served basis.

This past year our school of business organized an information session for all students interested in attending a faculty-led program. At this information session, five different faculty-led programs were presented to interested students. We do not feel this was too effective at increasing our program registrations and it also was not well attended. Alternatively, we suggest holding 1–2 information sessions exclusively for your students. Offering pizza and soda at the meeting is a good idea. Finally, speaking with students on an individual basis can help ease some of that early anxiety and fears about embarking on international travel.

A variety of faculty-led programs to different locations potentially provides a nice benefit to a university through increased overall enrollments. When parents and prospective students come to campus to learn about the university and academic programs, we have found that parents absolutely love faculty-led programs. Parents are generally concerned about student safety when considering an individualized study abroad experience for a semester in a foreign country. When they hear about faculty members are leading a group of students on a structured, academically inspired, and supervised short-burst trip abroad during spring break, parents are generally more comfortable and excited about the opportunity.

17.5 Madrid Trip and Advice for Travel

As with most things, prudent planning results in a greater likelihood of success. Most of the planning for your faculty-led program draws from the structure created in your course syllabus. We include a detailed itinerary for each day starting with our departure from campus and ending on our return to campus.

The detailed itinerary is important for a variety of reasons. The itinerary outlines your expectations of the students, provides them guidance on where and when they need to be at certain places, and provides the basic organizational framework for your entire trip. Obviously, schedules and events are always subject to change, but setting expectations and following through on them creates a reliable atmosphere, which reduces student anxiety. Students need to know what is expected of them and the consequences for not meeting those expectations. There can be many pitfalls associated in traveling with students internationally. Some are foreseeable while others are not. We provide our recommendations in this section based upon our experience.

Initially, our university had not planned on providing transportation to the airport from our campus and instead asked everyone to meet up at the airport. This had the potential for many unnecessary complications and starting off the trip on a bad note. You can imagine students getting lost, stuck in traffic, going to the wrong terminal, and some ultimately missing the flight and/or trip entirely. We asked and received support from our school of business to organize transportation departing from our parking lot.[4] The same transportation was also waiting to pick us up when we returned.

To avoid any complications with students taking other courses and potential midterm exams, we designed the departure time to be Friday night, arriving in Madrid on Saturday. We then departed from Madrid and arrived back in Boston the following Saturday. This schedule allows the students 11/2 days to adjust to Spain and 11/2 days to adjust to being back in the U.S., before classes start on Monday. There is an opportunity to reduce transportation costs if all faculty-led programs coordinated their departure and arrival times. All students and faculty participating could potentially take a bigger bus to and from the airport. At this time, some programs do not have organized transportation, some leave during the middle of the week (before spring break begins), and some come back after spring break. Students always ask how much money they should bring on the trip with them. When we designed the faculty-led program, we included their airfare, transportation, hotel, all meals, subway pass, and excursions expenses into the extra $2500 charge for the course. That means students could feasibly attend this trip with no additional expenses. Our general suggestion for students was to budget approximately $200 in additional spending, depending upon how many souvenirs they would like to buy or if they want to eat out at other places outside the hotel cafeteria.

Our original itinerary set aside 1 h for lunch. We realized that this was not feasible, and it needed to be closer to 2 h. We found ourselves rushing to hastily go back and forth from the local host university or meet our contacts on time at a site visit. The cafeteria (adjacent to the hotel in Madrid) provided all the meals that were included (breakfast, lunch, and dinner). The food was not particularly great, but it did provide the necessary nutrition. Most students ended up going out to one of Madrid's amazing restaurants for dinner, while towards the end of the trip we found some students who were a little strapped for cash joining us for dinner at the hotel cafeteria. Again, while the food was not spectacular, it did offer students a free option and a check-in time where they knew they could talk to us about anything.

The check-in times are important for regrouping and catching up with everyone regarding their experience. Prior to leaving on the trip, students were paired up with roommates for the hotel, not only because we needed to have two students in each room, but also for safety when going out at night. The expectation was that our students would not be going out alone. Every morning, we would have a check-in before venturing out to a site visit or to the local host university. Most students were prompt at the beginning of the trip, but as the week progressed, waking up on time became an issue. Roommates typically looked out for each other. However, initially we were knocking on doors trying to get everyone to wake up. In retrospect, this is

---

[4]The SNHU Manchester, NH (main campus) is approximately 1 h away from Logan International Airport in Boston. Schools in metropolitan areas may not face a similar transportation issue.

17 Developing Study Abroad Opportunities in Economics and Finance...

not something we would advise faculty to do. Students need to be held accountable and act responsible. Consequently, we revised the grade weights for participating in activities (incentives/disincentives in our syllabus) to enforce our expectations. Their actions now more directly influence their letter grade, and in the case that the impact on their grade is not severe enough, we would remind the student that we have the authority to send them back to the US early and at their own expense, if they did not change their behavior.

Additionally, faculty should be prepared to encourage students to engage with meaningful interactions with individuals in the host country throughout the trip. Students may tend to stick together and avoid interactions due to language barriers and/or a fear of interacting with people in a different country. Scheduling devoted time for students to interact with students in the host country is one option to ensure students engage with members of the community during the trip.

A few final recommendations regarding the traveling portion are to always remind the faculty to do a headcount. It is the quickest way to make sure you have everyone all in one place at the same time. Relying on the students to know if their classmates are all present is not reliable. It is a good idea to start a group text message for easy communication. We suggest that you enter names into your phone so that you know who is writing the text messages. Cellular communication is only effective if your students have their phones turned on while abroad, which is why we require students to set up a plan with their provider prior to departure.

17.6 Post-Trip and Assessment

Students and faculty members will likely be exhausted upon return from the trip. Depending on the timing of the study abroad experience, students and faculty may need to immediately return to classes shortly after returning from the trip. While there may be more flexibility during the summer, it is important to consider other student and faculty obligations after the conclusion of the travel. Our trip occurs during the week of spring break, which leaves students with just 6 or 7 weeks of class remaining. Regardless of the timing of your trip, it is likely advisable to provide a break for students to recover, readjust, and process the trip before engaging additional work or conversation. However, we have found that students are typically excited about the travel and happy to meet to discuss the experience. You could consider scheduling an additional meeting time for all students or potentially meet with students individually or in small groups once everyone has a chance to recover.

In our experience, the reflection assignment is an extremely important component of the course. This assignment provides students with an important opportunity to explore their personal experience in the host country culture and connect experiences in the host country to previous experiences in the U.S. We encourage students to review their journal assignment, in which they have documented their trip in detail throughout their time in the host country, while completing the reflection assignment as it can be easy to overlook experiences and feelings after the fact. Students are offered a substantial amount of time (up to 1 month) to complete the assignment given the time that it may take to fully appreciate the experience and competing responsibilities that students have when returning to the U.S. We also offer the opportunity for students to submit a brief video (YouTube clip) as their reflection assessment, which we utilize to show future students the class and trip that they may be able to experience.

Students are also asked to complete the follow-up Cultural Intelligence assessment, which is designed to measure changes in the effectiveness of student capabilities in diverse situations after traveling abroad. It may be important to remind students to submit these assignments as some students may have many other obligations. This is an important assessment requirement at our institution, which is why we offer 5% of the course grade to this assessment.

It is important to provide quality feedback on the final reflection, either in writing or through conversation. Some students may prefer discussing the experience directly with faculty members while others will feel more comfortable providing more detail in writing (some reflections were 20+ pages). Students often make important connections in the reflections based on our experience. Faculty will also need to determine how to best follow up with students after the conclusion of the class. Since we work at a university with relatively small classes, we were able to chat with almost all of the students who attended our trip individually after the conclusion of the study abroad program. Many students will likely be interested in discussing specific aspects of the experience, which provides a great opportunity for faculty to help facilitate connections between student experiences at home and abroad. Additionally, it is a good idea to follow up with students after the trip to suggest additional opportunities to build intercultural competence. Rowan-Kenyon and Niehaus (2011) find that short-term study abroad programs may encourage students to take advantage of longer-term study abroad options and additional opportunities to build on their travel experience. One of our students, who had been initially worried about international travel in general, decided to study abroad for a full semester after our first short-term program. This is a sure testament to the effect that faculty-led programs can change the direction of a student's life.

17.7 Conclusion

Universities have attempted to expand access to study abroad programs and increasing numbers of students are traveling abroad on an annual basis, but there is still a great deal of work to be done to encourage more students to engage in study abroad opportunities. Study abroad has the potential to deliver numerous benefits including helping students to develop intercultural competence, enhance valuable skills that can assist in the job market, and develop a lifelong love of travel. While short-term faculty-led study abroad programs require a great deal of effort on behalf of faculty members and serious attention must be paid to the development of intercultural competence in the design of programs, the opportunities for students are absolutely worth the effort in our opinion. Additionally, while some faculty may be intimidated by the responsibility for student safety in another country, careful planning and collaboration with university partners can alleviate many potential problems.

We hope that this chapter provides assistance and encouragement for faculty members looking to design and offer short-term faculty-led study abroad programs. In our experience, the short-term program provides many students who could not travel as part of their degree program with some of the benefits of studying abroad in a longer-term program without the cost or time commitment and also encourages students to engage in travel opportunities after the completion of the program. In addition to being a great experience for students in our class, we also learned a great deal through the experience and continue to discuss the study abroad trips with students in other classes. We also hope that faculty members continue to share their experience with faculty-led programs to provide guidance for others. Finally, we encourage additional research on the effectiveness of short-term faculty-led trips and further exploration of options aimed at increasing opportunities in study abroad programs, particularly for students of color, lower-income students, and first-generation students who are currently underrepresented in study abroad programs.

References

Bain SF, Yaklin LE (2019) Study abroad: Striving for transformative impact. Res High Educ J 36:1–5. https://www.aabri.com/rhej.html

Chieffo L, Griffiths L (2004) Large-scale assessment of student attitudes after a short-term study abroad program. Frontiers 10(1):165–177

Di Gregorio D (2015) Fostering experiential learning in faculty-led study-abroad programmes. In: The Palgrave handbook of experiential learning in international business. Springer, London

Fischer K (2019) How international education's golden age lost its sheen. Chronicle High Educ 5:56

Gaia AC (2015) Short-term faculty-led study abroad programs enhance cultural exchange and self-awareness. Int Educ J Comp Perspect 14(1):21–31

Institute of International Education (2010) Open Doors fast facts. Institute of International Education, New York, NY

Institute of International Education (2015) Open Doors fast facts. Institute of International Education, New York, NY

Institute of International Education (2019a) IIE Generation study abroad initiative. Institute of International Education, New York, NY

Institute of International Education (2019b) Open Doors fast facts. Institute of International Education, New York, NY

Keese JR, O'Brien J (2011) Learn by going: Critical issues for faculty-led study-abroad programs. The California Geographer

Medina-López-Portillo A (2004) Intercultural learning assessment: The link between program duration and the development of intercultural sensitivity. Frontiers 10(1):179–199

Mule L, Aloisio K, Audley S (2018) Short-term, faculty-led study abroad and global citizenship identification: insights from a global engagement program. Frontiers 30(3):20–37

Niehaus E, Reading J, Nelson MJ, Wegener A, Arthur A (2018) Faculty engagement in cultural mentoring as instructors of short-term study abroad courses. Frontiers 30(2):77–91. https://www.frontiersjournal.org/index.php/Frontiers/issue/view/35

Niehaus E, Woodman TC, Bryan A, Light A, Hill E (2019) Student learning objectives: What instructors emphasize in short-term study abroad. Frontiers 31(2):121–138. https://www.frontiersjournal.org/index.php/Frontiers/issue/view/38

Pittenger K, Parsons K, Moss J (2019) Enhancing educational experience of business students through engagement in innovative and impactful short-term study abroad program–a case study and beyond. In: Developments in business simulation and experiential learning: proceedings of the annual ABSEL conference, vol 46

Rowan-Kenyon HT, Niehaus EK (2011) One year later: The influence of short-term study abroad experiences on students. J Stud Aff Res Pract 48(2):213–228

Sachau D, Brasher N, Fee S (2010) Three models for short-term study abroad. J Manag Educ 34(5):645–670

Strow C (2016) Teaching the economics of ecotourism, trade, healthcare, education, poverty, and immigration as a study abroad experience in Costa Rica. J Econ Finance Educ 15(3):83–94

Tremlett G (2008) Ghosts of Spain: Travels through Spain and its silent past. Bloomsbury Publishing USA, New York

Walters C, Charles J, Bingham S (2017) Impact of short-term study abroad experiences on transformative learning: A comparison of programs at 6 weeks. J Transform Educ 15(2):103–121

Chapter 18
Exploring How Place Can Enhance Learning in Short Course Study Abroads

Ryan M. Yonk

Abstract I explore the role of place in study abroad experiences using a study abroad I have led multiple times, "How the Scots Invented the Modern World". This short study abroad takes students through the Scottish enlightenment and the works of Adam Smith and David Hume, while in London and Edinburgh. I explore how connecting students both to the ideas but also to the place where the ideas were developed enhances their learning. Place provides a context that can motivate students towards deeper understanding and connect students tangibly to those ideas in ways that reading and studying them alone cannot.

18.1 Introduction

Often the discussion of study abroad experiences and their value begins with story of how participating in one as a student was transformative and a highlight of the undergraduate experience for the author. I have no such story to share. In reality until I was well through graduate school and had started my first academic job I viewed study abroad experiences as vacations masquerading as academic courses. I could see little value in most of what I saw. What I heard from students about their experience abroad, especially when they described the very common short-term study abroad experiences, seemed to bolster my impression with the majority of students focused on partying in Spain, traveling across Thailand, and enjoying wine in Southern France, and how much they enjoyed traveling.

These discussions led me to believe that the experiences they had overseas were valuable and had deeply impacted them, but the way students described their experience largely presented them as devoid of content, rigor, or serious academic value. They were clearly an experience that the student had enjoyed and were often

---

R. M. Yonk (✉)
American Institute for Economic Research, Great Barrington, MA, USA
e-mail: ryan.yonk@aier.org

© The Author(s), under exclusive license to Springer Nature Switzerland AG 2021
J. Hall, K. Holder (eds.), *Off-Campus Study, Study Abroad, and Study Away in Economics*, Contributions to Economics,
https://doi.org/10.1007/978-3-030-73831-0_18

transformative in social and individual terms but seemed to have little relationship to the 'learning' the University claimed to be providing.

These discussions with students led me to the core question of this chapter, and one that I have grappled with as a faculty member that has led numerous short course study abroad experiences. Can short-term, approximately 7–14 day, study abroad experiences provide both the experiences that many students described, as well as a rigorous academic learning experience. If they can, what can be done to ensure that it happens. In this chapter I first explore the pedagogy surrounding experiential education and study abroad, then relay my experience in grappling with this question and share how I came to believe that the answer is yes it is possible. I then share a set of principles I have used in building study abroad experiences that at least attempt to ensure a positive academic and life experience for the students that participate.

18.2 Changing Perspectives

During the first semester of my first academic job, it became clear that our department wasn't currently and hadn't offered a study abroad experience and I was encouraged, to plan a short-term summer study abroad in collaboration with several other departments to demonstrate that we were actively supporting the new 'experiential' mission of the University. This encouragement coupled with some fortuitous external funds I had raised allowed a very small group of students, just two on that first study abroad, to spend 10 days in London and Scotland exploring at least nominally comparative politics and economics.

On that first study abroad, I took my impression of study abroads as lacking academic rigor with me and while we had a great time and both students expressed high levels of satisfaction with the experience, I was left with a nagging sense that something was missing and that the experience could have been much better. Those students had left the country for the first time and that experience was valuable, but as I reflected became clear to me that had to be a better way to both design and execute a study abroad that could combine the experience of being abroad with academic learning.

As in often the case in departments once you've done something once, you are now the expert and I was again encouraged to plan a study abroad during my second year. Armed with the intuition I had developed from that first trip I started the planning process focused on what I thought the students should learn on the study abroad. This second trip was to Athens and Rome and was designed to be an overview of the influence of the Greeks and Romans on modern conceptions of government, democracy and the philosophy.

It was on this trip that I started to develop both a respect for the potential of short course study abroads to have academic value. I also began to develop a set of principles that I believe provide students with both the experience of being abroad and navigating a foreign culture alongside rigorous academic learning. Learning that is enhanced by the location rather than the new experience serving as a distraction from it.

Since these first study abroads I have planned and led numerous additional formal study abroad and travel based short courses. The entirety of my experience in this area is leading short courses of 7–14 days most often immediately after the end of spring semester and so my suggestions and experience should be viewed with that lens in mind. The semester long study abroad experiences differ in both form and substance and I hope others will have taken up the exploration of these longer form courses and identified principles for ensuring they serve as a valuable life and academic experience for students.

I no longer view these experiences with as much skepticism, and I no longer categorically reject the potential for academic learning. That learning, however, is predicated on a well-designed set of learning objectives where a sense of place enhances the ability of students to both experience the new location and uses that sense of place to enhance their understanding of the academic material. This change in perspective has been reinforced by my experience with experiential education generally and the process by which experiential education enhances student learning.

18.3 Understanding the Pedagogy of Study Abroad Experiences

The development of Study Abroad programs especially the short form version emerges from a focus on experiential education that has gained traction in higher education and has become the increasing focus of many initiatives at institutions across the country.

This focus on experience while newly ascendant is not a new innovation. John Dewey's seminal *Education and Experience* (Dewey 1938), laid out the basis of experiential learning theory. While all learning is experiential in some sense (in that learners incorporate knowledge according to their own experience), experiential learning theory explores learning outside traditional and abstract methods of teaching–lectures, textbooks, etc. Instead, experiential learning generally occurs through hands-on, real world experiences. Joplin (1981) lays out eight characteristics that define experiential learning: it is student rather than teacher based, personal, oriented towards process, self-evaluated, focused on holistic understanding, organized around experience, perception rather than theory based, and individual.

Although experiential learning has been viewed as occurring outside of contexts in which a student interfaces with teachers, experiential education does not necessarily require the absence of some teacher mediation (Moon 2004, pp. 76–77). The reality is that experiential education is now prolific throughout undergraduate curricula (Katula and Threnhauser 1999), and is in large part how Study Abroad experiences are marketed and justified.

Most of the discussions of experiential education generally and study abroad experiences specifically, lack course specific academic learning outcomes and often the experience itself is viewed as the outcome. My own experience with the potential value of experiential learning leaves me sympathetic to the potential value of encouraging students to have these sorts of experiences. At the root of my sympathy is my experience in developing and undergraduate research program at Utah State University in the Institute of Political Economy.[1]

That program was rooted in the idea that direct experience was key to learning the process of research and that by directly engaging in that research the academic training occurring in the classroom focused on statistics, research methods, as well as theory would be enhanced as students engaged in direct application of those skills. Experiential education like this doesn't replace the academic experience but instead becomes a testing ground for applying the academic skills.

The experiential education literature suggests that this approach can yield meaningful student learning. Craney et al. (2011), for example, asked undergraduates who had participated in social science research to rate the potential benefits of undergraduate research from one to five, depending on how strongly they agree that undergraduate research gave them that particular benefit (five being the best). Of the benefits, the following received an average rating over four: develop communication skills, formulate research questions, contribute new knowledge to society, strengthen interest in advanced study, and improve chances of admission to advanced study. The remaining benefits all rated over 3.5: develop problem-solving skills, earn prestige, provide an opportunity to publish, provide a realistic career option, and improve employability after college. These results are largely replicated in a survey reported by Lopatto (2010).

What is often forgotten is that even when surveying the students about their satisfaction, the researchers have identified learning outcomes that they think the experience should have provided. For undergraduate research these outcomes focus on research learning objectives and strongly suggest that approaches when experiences are used to supplement the academic learning environment student learning outcomes can be improved.

Likewise, a similar logic is found in work-based experiential learning and the relationship between academic learning and the experience associated with it (Chisholm et al. 2009). The value of linking academic knowledge to workplace activity is multifaceted (Lester and Costley 2010). Problems and experiences encountered on the job allow students to apply and contextualize previously abstract concepts. Internships that encourage students to take the critical thinking skills developed in their classes and begin to use them outside the context of the classroom have been demonstrated to have particular academic value (McCormick 1993). Internships that allow students to work with some autonomy offer better postgraduate employment opportunities, reduce the 'reality shock' associated with

---

[1] Some representative journal articles and books from this program include Hansen et al. (2017), Yonk et al. (2017a), Yonk et al. (2017b), and Yonk and Smith (2018).

entering the workforce, and help young professionals to conceptualize their own workforce identity (Taylor 1988). Empirical work has confirmed that students who do internships during their undergraduate degrees are both better prepared for post-graduation jobs and enjoy those jobs more (Gault et al. 2000).

What is often missing from the discussion of designing experiential education and is essential to the achievement of positive outcomes is a clear and direct link between the learning objectives of the academic programs and the experience being offered. What is common among the most successful programs is that a clear and purposeful link between the experience and the learning objective are necessary for the experience to have meaning in an academic context.

Like the other areas of experiential education, the ability of Study Abroad experiences to have value to the academic learning is predicated on a strong connection between the experience and the academic learning objectives.

The literature on short course study abroads most often touts, increased appreciation for diversity, global awareness, openness to differing ideas, as the primary outcomes of the study abroad experience (Cubillos and Ilvento 2018). While these outcomes may be desirable they are often not the claimed learning objectives of the course and there is a wide and growing literature that explores the possibility that many academic courses are not appropriate for the short study abroad format (Cubillos and Ilvento 2018). Often this short-term study abroad experiences are viewed as an opportunity to primarily experience another language, culture or circumstance rather than having strong academic purposes outside language or culturally focused courses (Lewin 2009; Cubillos and Ilvento 2018).

In contrast others have suggested that academic learning beyond these experiences in language and cultural exploration may be possible in short term study abroad experience, if they are well designed (Barkley and Barkley 2013). What is clear from the literature surrounding both experiential education generally, and the study abroad pedagogy literature specifically is the clear reality that the direct hands on approach where academic learning is combined with experiential learning can form a successful learning process.

For study abroad experiences that hands-on reality is deeply tied to the location and place where the learning is occurring, however it is common that the learning outcomes that are actually achieved are not necessarily those of the academic course that is purported as being taught. It is my view that the most successful study abroad experiences are those that are rooted in that sense of place and actively work to connect that sense of place with the academic learning goals of the course being taught.

18.4   The Role of Place as Experience in Learning

One of the few things I remember from the literature classes I took both in high school and college is that a sense of place is key to the development of good literature and serves as a way to hook the reader into the story. I recall Mrs. Anderson at the front of a high school classroom attempting to explain what place meant to a group of 11th graders who had no desire to read any of the classic literature she required and while I did not enjoy (and still don't enjoy) the writings of the Bronte sisters, having read them it is now clear to me that without the sense of place they created there would have been no story, and virtually nothing to have been learned from them. *Wuthering Heights* (Brontë 1847), for example, is intimately tied to the sense of place that the author develops, and the ability to connect to that place becomes one of the primary ways in which the story is carried on. Creating a rich sense of place becomes as essential as any of the characters an author creates, and the reader develops a connection to.

People are naturally tied to the places and experiences we have. Our understanding of the world is often directly shaped by our sense of place and our lived experience with that place. Often in academic endeavors as we attempt to understand abstract ideas we are left without a connection to the place and circumstance where the ideas were formed and developed.

Among my favorite study abroad courses to teach is one focused on the Scottish Enlightenment and the influence it had on the development of modern economics and philosophy. Many of the ideas that have influenced the modern era developed during the Scottish enlightenment (Muller 1995; Herman 2001; Broadie 2001).

One of the challenges of teaching something like the Scottish enlightenment generally and the thinking of Adam Smith and David Hume specifically is that for students their writings are divorced from them in time but also in place. Often students have little sense of the issues that drove them to write, what the source of their ideas were, and little motivation to discover them. Their ideas while powerful on paper are often esoteric and disconnected for the average undergraduate and given that disconnect many students fail to grasp their importance and do not internalize the debates that led to the thinking of Smith, Hume and others.

One of the solutions I have found to this disconnect is to inspire in students a connection both to the ideas but also to the place where these discussions were occurring. This sense of place can develop by walking where Smith and Hume walked, seeing their graves, visiting the places where they lived, taught, and were heavily influenced. This experience provides a context that when harnessed and connected well to their writings can motivate students towards a deeper understanding of their ideas and connecting students tangibly to those ideas in ways that simply reading and studying them cannot.

I first became convinced of the value of this connection to place during a study abroad focused on western civilization, where the course learning objectives were focused on understanding the influence of the thinking of the Greeks and Romans on modern politics and democracy. Having an in-depth discussion of Plato's *Republic* while standing in the Agora of Athens after having walked among the ruins of what might have been where Socrates delivered his lectures the ideas from the Republic, the Socratic dialogues were suddenly directly in front of the students. While we stood among the ruins discussing those ideas an energy and life came to them that hadn't occurred during our more standard lectures.

Similarly, in Rome discussing the role of Christianity and particularly the Pauline epistles to the development of western thought at the *Areopagus* (Mars Hill) brought context both to our discussion of the role of Christianity in Western Civilization and to our broader discussions. From the discussion that started standing at the base of the hill students began to make connections between the core ideas of Pauline Christianity, Greek notions of democracy and civicness, the role of the Roman Empire. A wide ranging and at times heated discussion emerged that pushed to students to explore the ideas in ways that were not immediately apparent in the more traditional classroom approach.

A similar situation emerged among a group of students at the cemetery at Canongate Kirkyard standing around the grave site of Adam Smith after having earlier visited the Old Calton Cemetery where David Hume and other figures of the Scottish Enlightenment are buried. The reality of the lives of these thinkers and the direct connection of being physically at their final resting places brought conversations about how they might agree, where their disagreements may have been, and why given the reality of their time and place they arrived at the conclusions they did. These conversations were lively and deep, and much more animated than those I have had in a classroom about the same subjects. This type of experience is common when there is a clear connection between place and the academic course being taught. Place when directly tied to the learning objectives becomes as valuable a tool in learning economics as it is for the novelist in crafting a story.

It is in this intersection of the direct experience of place, and in the design of the academic course that I have found an opportunity to improve the academic outcomes of a short course study abroad. My own experience and the principles I follow in the practical planning of these courses attempt to harness place as a motivating factor to draw discussion and explorations from students that may not otherwise occur.

18.5 Key Principles for a Place Focused Study Abroad

While it is clear that experiential learning can be a valuable tool and serves to enhance student learning, implementing these approaches is not necessarily intuitive or easy. Over the years I have struggled to implement them well, but through leading short course study abroads I have found a set of principles that I work to implement in planning and executing them. In general, they are consistent with the wider experiential pedagogy literature and seek to implement academic learning objectives alongside the experiences that students most often identify as being the part of study abroad they most value.

- Start with the end in mind
- Identify class material for each activity that is enhanced by the place
- Formal and informal discussion each day
- Clarity about mandatory activities
- Opportunities for free time and add on experiences

The first principle, is one that applies in every course that is being taught whether abroad or in the classroom at home, is to start with the end in mind. At first glance this would appear to be such a commonsense bit of advice as to be completely pedantic. What is powerful about it is that the tendency to simply assume things will develop that will allow students to connect place and the academic goals is both unrealistic and unlikely to yield satisfying academic results. Students will likely enjoy the trip but whether they have learned anything substantive ends up being left to chance and often leaves the instructor unsatisfied with the academic part of the trip.

In practice this means that each formal part of the trip has to be thoughtfully connected to the academic course, and clear expectations for participation and discussion laid out. When well implemented this principle brings a sense of purpose to each activity and ties the student's involvement both to attending but also to what learning is meant occur.

There is a potential risk to over plan and schedule, and what this principle suggests is not a set of busy work that students have to complete at each site, and indeed I rarely require the worksheets or journaling that some suggest as assignments. Instead I use the end I want to achieve as a guide to the discussion that occurs during the activity. With that goal in mind the I can guide the discussion, pose questions, challenge ideas and push the students to deeply consider the academic content and the experience of place together.

To implement the first principle well the second principle of a clear set of texts selected specifically because the places to be visited can enhance student interaction with them and because they are tied in some meaningful way to the place is essential. Connecting these texts directly to individual activities and experiences is key to learning.

For place to be relevant it must have clear connections to the materials students have read, and it must be possible for students to see those connections. I have led some trips where multiple disciplines are present and where several faculty members are teaching different courses, and two potential pitfalls have become clear. The first is to simply have no course material the students are required to engage during the trip, this leaves students without substance to explore and place simply becomes a tourist experience rather than an academic one.

The second is to simply assign an overall set of readings and do little to directly connect those readings to individual activities, this leaves the students in the position of grappling about what parts apply to which activities and often leaves them unable to apply the readings in a direct and effective way.

18 Exploring How Place Can Enhance Learning in Short Course Study Abroads

If the learning goals are clear, and the course materials have been well tailored to the activities connecting place with learning during formal and informal discussion is readily achieved. These discussions are essential to achieving the goals for learning in the course. Having some time each day devoted to a formal discussion led directly by the faculty member teaching the course helps to contextualize and highlight what is important for that day and provides a basis for the informal discussions that occur at each site. These informal discussions become the mechanism by which the experience of place becomes integrated with the formal academic learning. During the study abroads I have taught, we start the day by having a formal discussion over breakfast that sets context for the places we will visit and introduces the readings the students should be thinking directly about during those visits. Then at every site, or experience we pause to discuss the ideas and the experience, and when the formal discussion has been well presented and participated in the informal discussions at the individual sites and activities are at their best.

These first three principles lay out a study abroad agenda that appears intense, and it is. However, not every minute of every day can or should be focused on the mandatory activities that form the basis of these discussions. Identifying what things are essential for students to meet the academic goals of the course and making them mandatory rather than having every possible activity required provides students with both the necessary learning and the opportunity for experiencing the country directly and in a self-directed way. Clearly identifying what experiences students must participate in also allows the instructor to have clear expectations and allows grades to more easily be assigned for participation and discussion.

The opportunity for some self-directed discovery and exploration is an important part of study abroad, but not every student is comfortable with simply being turned loose. As a result, my final principle is to have potential activities alongside the option for free time beyond the mandatory events. For students who are uncomfortable with simply exploring on their own having the option to participate in activities with a group often enhances their experience, and for those who are comfortable exploring independently free time provides the experiences they often report as transformative.

My experience and approach have been that the additional activities I plan are most often the list of things I want to do that are experiences that are not necessarily connected to the academic course but that I think have value or will be fun. They aren't mandatory or included in the cost of the study abroad allows students to select the level of structure they desire. It also gives students who may be uncomfortable with exploring a new country on their own the opportunity to explore and as they gain confidence they are often more willing by the end of the trip to explore independently than they were at the beginning.

These principles: (1) Start with the end in mind, (2) Identify class material for each activity that is enhanced by place, (3) Formal and informal discussion each day, (4) Clarity about mandatory activities, (5) Opportunities for free time or add on experiences, have been particularly useful for me as I have led multiple short course study abroads. In general, these principles have left me with the belief that even short course study abroads can be academically valuable and still provide the experiences that students desire, also known as being 'fun'.

18.6 Implementing a Place Focused Study Abroad: "How the Scots Invented the Modern World"

The study abroad I have led most often has focused on the thinkers of the Scottish Enlightenment and their influence on modernity. I have generally titled the course; "How the Scots invented the Modern World."

To understand the course, a sense of the daily structure is helpful. Each day that isn't primarily a travel day starts with a mandatory discussion over breakfast typically at 8 AM. This discussion is jointly led by both the instructor and a student who is assigned to present the materials, including the assigned readings. This presentation becomes part of the grade a student receives for the course. This coupled with the participation in all mandatory activities and the informal discussions during them comprise 50% of the total grade, the remainder being a final paper. This more formal discussion asks students to directly address the assigned reading and raise questions they have regarding those readings and the ideas they present.

Following breakfast, a series of site visits begins with informal discussion occurring at each site. These discussions are focused on how the site visit relates to the themes from the readings assigned, the larger themes of the course, and whether visiting the site raises additional questions that were not immediately apparent form the readings and formal discussion. Typically, these site visits occur from 9:30 am to 12 pm with a break for lunch that often continues the discussion and sets context for afternoon and again from 1 pm to 4 pm. At around 4 pm (earlier on days where city exploration is explicitly noted) the students are free from mandatory activities. Each day a series of add on activities are available that students can choose to participate in. On the Scotland/England trip these add-ons have included tours of Royal Palaces, theater performances, trips to traditional English pubs, Scotch Whiskey tours (tasting only for those students over 21 per university regulations). Most often students break off in small groups (with a minimum of 2) and it is not uncommon for many of the participants to attend the add on activities and then do additional things in the later evenings.

Each night students are required to check in by text or email by midnight (unless other arrangements are made), and attendance at the breakfast discussion every morning is mandatory. These extracurricular add-ons and other experiences often come up during the informal discussions during the day and have served to provide additional insight as students work to draw connections between their unstructured activities and the course itself.

18 Exploring How Place Can Enhance Learning in Short Course Study Abroads

For "How the Scots invented the Modern World" most typically I have designed the trip to have 10 days in country with 2 travel days between the US and the UK. My current version of this course uses a number of books and supplemental materials. These include; *The Theory of Moral Sentiments* (TMS) and *The Wealth of Nations* (WON) by Adam Smith (1981, 1982), *How the Scots Invented the Modern World* by Arthur Herman (2001), *The Scottish Enlightenment* by Alexander Broadie (2001), and *Adam Smith: In His Time and Ours* by Jerry Z. Muller (1995). These books are supplemented with other readings that aid in understanding the Scottish Enlightenment.

Appendix Table 18.1 contains a sample course itinerary. It indicates the trip is focused around sites that are directly connected with the themes of the course and readings are assigned daily that have relevance to the sites visited with the goal of implementing principles identified above from the outset.

As is clear from this itinerary, students have a clear sense of the mandatory activities early on, for each trip the extra-curricular activities vary by what is available during the dates we are in country and what things I have identified as being of interest to me. Further students are encouraged at pre-trip meetings to obtain a good guidebook and identify things they may want to do that are not part of the academic site visits of the trip and explicitly plan for those activities well in advance.

In planning a specific trip, a more detailed daily schedule is provided so that students know exactly where things are located, how to arrive there if separated from the group, as well as any adjustments that become necessary during the trip.

As each day of the itinerary begins there is a morning discussion of the readings, the places we will visit, and the key themes, students are expected to have read the materials before the trip and have brought the books (or an e-copy) as we often refer back to them during the discussions.

Students have a clear sense of the purpose of the visits, as well as the expected discussion for the day and so as they read the assigned material they can carefully consider the discussion topics and prepare for the daily formal sessions. From those formal discussions and the informal discussions at each site along with seeing and experiencing them, students are better able to engage the material deeply and experience the power that place can have in the learning process.

18.7 Planning and Logistics

One of the most intimidating parts of leading a study abroad can be the logistics and planning, and nearly every university has an office of study abroad that aids in the planning of these sorts of trips. They can be helpful for the first-time leader. For the study abroads I have led I have taken the lead in planning and designing these trips coordinating with Study Abroad Offices but relying little on them for substantive assistance beyond aiding in the process of trip approval, payment collection, and ensuring the course is registered in the University system. I find that the greater amount of direct oversight I have, the better the study abroad trip is both academically and logistically.

All of the universities I have worked at have been public institutions where students are highly cognizant of the costs of attendance and one of the first questions my students always ask is how much does it cost? Having run the trip numerous times, the costs to students have varied. I have generally been fortunate enough to have had alternate funding to cover my travel costs, and I have generally not taken salary for leading these trips, which left students with an approximate cost of between $1000 and $1250 excluding airfare, add-on activities, and tuition. The cost of faculty travel increases the costs and unless a relatively large number of students participate can be the single largest individual line item in student costs, and thus cost prohibitive.

18.8 Conclusion

While I have no story about the transformative power of a study abroad I participated in as an undergraduate, I have come to value the opportunity that short-term study abroad courses can have when they are well designed and work to use the place where they are occurring to enhance the learning experience. Having led the same trip multiple times, much like teaching a course multiple times the "How the Scots Invented the Modern World" study abroad has improved much over the course of its delivery and the readings and discussion themes have and continue to evolve over time. But what has become clear is that the work of connecting the place to the academic content is as necessary as it is rewarding and that students can have both a rigorous academic experience and have 'fun' on these study abroads.

Appendix

Table 18.1 Sample itinerary with site visits, readings, and discussion topics

Day	Title	Site visits	Description	Readings	Discussion topics
1	Travel day		Travel to Edinburgh, Scotland		
2	Introduction to the Scottish Enlightenment	Calton Hill, Edinburg Castle, National Gallery of Scotland	Each of these sites has a particular connection with the Scottish Enlightenment and provides a strong sense of place for the discussion that will occur. That national gallery houses substantial artifacts of this era and Calton hill allows individuals to get a sense of Edinburgh proper, as does the castle	*How the Scots* pp. 38–189; *TMS*, "Account of the Life of Adam Smith"	Discussion will focus on the economic and political philosophies that emerged in Europe up until the Scottish Enlightenment and an overview of the Enlightenment itself. Subjects include: Economic and Political Thought in the Middle Ages, the origins of the Scottish Enlightenment and its philosophical roots, and how the Scottish Enlightenment changed perspectives on individual action and the exploration of knowledge as an individual endeavor.
3	Adam Smith	University of Edinburgh; Royal Exchange and Customs House	Both of these sites are closely aligned to Smiths academic and public life. It was at the University of Edinburgh that Smith taught and honed his ideas and the Royal Exchange house was the site of much of Smith's work with Government and where the implementation of many of his ideas began	*WON* Book I, Ch. 1–4; Book II Ch 3; *TMS* Part 1: Section 1 Ch 1-V; *How the Scots* pp. 189–229; *Smith in His Time* pp. 1–39	Adam Smith's life, philosophies, and legacy will be explored. Smith's impact on modern economic thinking would be difficult to underestimate, indeed most every core economic principle espoused by Smith has become part of our modern understanding and he can most appropriately be called the father of modern economics. Subjects Include: Smith's Theory of Moral Sentiments (An understanding of the Motivations of Humankind; The Wealth of Nations; Smith's Perspective on Civil Society

(continued)

Table 18.1 (continued)

Day	Title	Site visits	Description	Readings	Discussion topics
4	David Hume	David Hume City Walking Tour	David Hume's home, workplace and other significant locales have been organized into a walking tour in Edinburgh and we will work with a qualified tour guide to ensure that the relevant sites that connect directly to his thinking and perspective are visited	*Scottish Enlightenment* pp. 130–40, 7–42, and 94–108; *How the Scots* pp. 267–290	David Hume's life, philosophies, and legacy will be explored. Hume as a political economist and philosopher is among the most consistently referred to of the Scottish Enlightenment philosophers During our walking tour we will explore Hume's ideas, and his impact on modern economic and political thought in detail. Subjects Include: Hume on Liberty and Freedom; Hume's perspective on Religion and life; The Scientific Exploration of Economic Life
5	Scottish Public Policy	Scottish Parliament; Free Exploration in the Afternoon		*Scottish Enlightenment* pp. 219–231	The impact of the Scottish Enlightenment can continue to be examined in the modern era. Scottish political institutions and international relations will be explored from an economic and philosophical perspective and examined in the context of the Scottish Enlightenment
6	Travel day	Depart Edinburgh, Scotland and travel to London, England		*How Adam Smith Can Change Your Life*—full book!	

7	British Economic/Political Philosophy	Primrose Hill; City Exploration	Primrose hill provides a chance to talk about London in the context of the Scottish Enlightenment period. Looking out over London and then exploring the city with students provides a chance to better understand the city	Continued discussion on *How Adam Smith Can Change Your Life*	The city's history, economic, and philosophical environment that existed during Adam Smith's life will be discussed. Focused around the previous days reading of "How Adam Smith Can Change Your Life". This discussion will help synthesize the first half of the trip
8	Smith's Idea's in London	Kings College London; Free Exploration in the Afternoon	A campus tour of the college will be followed by a lecture and discussion on the philosophies of Adam Smith and how they influenced London from staffs at Kings College who are experts in Adam Smith	*Smith in His Time* pp. 100–112, 77–83, 140–153	Subjects Include: The Impartial Spectator; Legislator and Merchant the role of self-interest in public policy; The Visible Hand
9	Economics of the British Empire	Victoria and Albert Museum; Tower of London	These two sites provide the backdrop for a discussion the evolving British Empires economic philosophy. The tower represents early Britain and its defensive posture while the V&A represents the empire at its height of influence and power	*Scottish Enlightenment* pp. 78–113; *How the Scots* pp. 345–386	The economic philosophies and practices of the British Empire will be explored, with emphasis being placed on the emerging Scottish philosophies. Subjects Include: Mercantilism, Colonialism, The rise of the corporation

(continued)

Table 18.1 (continued)

Day	Title	Site visits	Description	Readings	Discussion topics
10	London Exploration	Buckingham Palace, National Gallery, Big Ben, Piccadilly Square, Lancaster Square, British Library	These sites are among the most iconic sites of British history and have had a historical importance to both the cultural and economic development of the UK	Magna Carta; *Smith in His Time* pp. 177–194	Discussion will focus on the cultural and political institutions of eighteenth century London as well as common law
11	Political and Economic Institutions	Parliament Tour; St. Paul's Cathedral; Globe Theatre; Millennium Bridge	These sites along with those from the 22nd represent British Society and Thinking through history and act the backdrop to our discussion of the cultural political and economic understandings of British society through time	Magna Carta; *Smith in His Time* pp. 177–194	Historic and modern public policies will be discussed. Additionally, the role of economics in religious and literary culture in eighteenth century London will be explored. A final summation of the trip's material will be presented
12	Travel Day Return Home				

References

Barkley A, Barkley M (2013) Long term knowledge from short term study abroad in Brazil and South Africa: Facilitating effective international experiences. NACTA J 57(3a):146–152

Broadie A (2001) The Scottish Enlightenment: The historical age of the historical nation. Pearson, Edinburgh

Brontë E (1847) Wuthering heights. Thomas Cautley Newby, London

Chisholm C, Harris M, Northwood D, Johrendt J (2009) The characterisation of work-based learning by consideration of the theories of experiential learning. Eur J Educ 44(3):319–337

Craney C, McKay T, Mazzeo A, Morris J, Prigodich C, De Groot R (2011) Cross-discipline perceptions of the undergraduate research experience. J High Educ 82(1):92–113

Cubillos J, Ilvento T (2018) Intercultural contact in short-term study abroad programs. Hispania 101(2):249–266

Dewey J (1938) Experience & Education. Kappa Delta Pi, Indianapolis, IN

Gault J, Redington J, Schlager T (2000) Undergraduate business internships and career success: are they related? J Mark Educ 22(1):45–53

Hansen ME, Shughart WF, Yonk RM (2017) Political party impacts on direct democracy: The 2015 Greek austerity referendum. Atlantic Econ J 45(1):5–15

Herman A (2001) How the Scots invented the modern world: The true story of how Western Europe's poorest nation created our World & Everything in it. Crown, New York

Joplin L (1981) On defining experiential education. J Exp Educ 4(1):17–20

Katula RA, Threnhauser E (1999) Experiential education in the undergraduate curriculum. Commun Educ 48(3):238–255

Lester S, Costley C (2010) Work-based learning at higher education level: Value, practice and critique. Stud High Educ 35(5):561–575

Lewin R (2009) The handbook of practice and research in study abroad: Higher education and the quest for global citizenship. Routledge, New York

Lopatto D (2010) Undergraduate research as a high-impact student experience. Peer Rev 12(2):27–30

McCormick DW (1993) Critical thinking, experiential learning, and internships. J Manag Educ 17(2):260–262

Moon JA (2004) A handbook of reflective and experiential learning: Theory and practice. Routledge, New York

Muller JZ (1995) Adam Smith in his time and ours: Designing the decent society. Princeton University Press, Princeton, NJ

Smith A (1981) An inquiry into the nature and causes of the wealth of nations. Liberty Fund, Indianapolis, IN

Smith A (1982) The theory of moral sentiments. Liberty Fund, Indianapolis, IN

Taylor MS (1988) Effects of college internships on individual participants. J Appl Psychology 73(3):393

Yonk RM, Smith JT (2018) Politics and quality of life: the role of well-being in political outcomes. Springer, New York, NY

Yonk RM, Hoffer S, Stein D (2017a) Disincentives to business development on the Navajo nation. J Dev Entrep 22(02):1750012

Yonk RM, Lofthouse J, Hansen M (2017b) The reality of American energy: the hidden costs of electricity policy. Praeger, Santa Barbara, CA

Chapter 19
A Study Abroad Experience in Ireland: The Celtic Tiger Before and After the Global Financial Crisis

Dennis W. Jansen

Abstract This chapter describes a study abroad program to Ireland, a faculty-led 5-week program that was taught on the University College Dublin campus. This program included instruction in two courses, one on Financial Economics and one on the Economic Development of Ireland. It included weekly travel to locations throughout Ireland, from an excursion to Galway that included visits to the Connemara region and the Cliffs of Moher in the Burren, to an excursion to Belfast that included visits to the Peace Walls, the various shrines in Belfast, and including travel to the north coast to see the Giant's Causeway. The program consisted of 15–20 students and one faculty instructor, and proved quite popular.

19.1   Introduction

Texas A&M University has an extensive offering of study abroad programs, although this is not shared by all University departments equally. After spending a semester as a Fulbright Scholar at National University of Ireland-Galway in Fall 2010, I decided to try my hand at a study abroad program in Ireland.

Ireland has much to recommend itself as a study abroad destination, especially for someone coming from a (very) large public flagship university in the heart of Texas. A prime consideration is language. Obviously, English is the official language, and the language of common use, in Ireland. This is important to me, a language-challenged scholar, but it is perhaps more important to my potential students. By far, the vast majority of economics majors at Texas A&M University are in the B.S. program, which has no language requirement. Students choose the B.S. program over the B.A. for exactly that reason—they trade a required econometrics course for a required language sequence of courses.

D. W. Jansen (✉)
Texas A&M University, College Station, TX, USA
e-mail: dennisjansen@tamu.edu

© The Author(s), under exclusive license to Springer Nature Switzerland AG 2021
J. Hall, K. Holder (eds.), *Off-Campus Study, Study Abroad, and Study Away in Economics*, Contributions to Economics,
https://doi.org/10.1007/978-3-030-73831-0_19

Ireland is also somewhat mysterious, a place known but not known well to the representative native Texan, representing the bulk of our undergraduate enrollment. This makes it relatively easy to garner interest in the program. Ireland is also a highly developed nation, and it is safe. There is low crime, very low violent crime, and despite past 'troubles,' there is very little fear of terrorism. All of this makes Ireland an attractive study abroad destination to students, and perhaps just as important, to their parents. This is an important consideration for any study abroad program, as the program must generate sufficient demand. Texas A&M University requires a minimum of ten students in order for a faculty-led study abroad program to be approved.

From a pedagogical standpoint, Ireland is different enough from the U.S., and different enough from Texas, so that it provides student participants with the opportunity to experience a different culture, a different society, which is perhaps the greatest benefit of a study abroad program. Certainly, Irish politics and the average resident's opinion vary quite a bit from Texas, providing students with an opportunity to broaden their horizons and their understanding of how others see us, and how we see others—through the lenses of our own cultures. Ireland provides a gentle entrée into this cross-cultural understanding.

Ireland is part of the European Union, and the Eurozone. The latter fact gives students firsthand experience with foreign exchange and prices in a different currency. This seems obvious and easy, but it is a new experience for most of our study abroad students. More importantly, Ireland is a proud member of the European Union, and the Irish tend to be strongly and loudly 'pro-Europe' while simultaneously having a special place in their hearts for the United States. The Ireland-to-U.S. migrations have cemented family ties between our two nations and can partly explain the fascination that America, and especially American politics, holds for the Irish. Moreover, this knowledge of American politics and American society, together with the slightly different prism through which another culture sees the world, provides students with that alternative world view which proves so broadening.

The membership of Ireland in the E.U. also provides a host of potential discussion items for the classroom, including issues of federalism, differences between the political and economic relationships among nations in the E.U. and states in the U.S., and so on. The Irish experience with the global financial crisis and the Great Recession provides another lesson, as the crisis had a strong negative impact on Ireland and led to a period of austerity from which they have since recovered. Ireland's growth and acclaim as the 'Celtic Tiger' in the 1990s and early 2000s provides another lesson, as Ireland has grown to surpass the United Kingdom—and much of the E.U.—in GDP per capita. These large themes can provide the basis for special topic courses or for student papers.

19.2 Academic Structure of the Program

My study abroad program was deemed a faculty-led program through Texas A&M University. Basically, this meant that I accompanied students on the program that I organized. These were strictly Texas A&M University students. I advertised the program on campus, but not externally.

Texas A&M required that I teach two three-credit-hour courses during the study abroad program, and that these two courses contain the same amount of contact hours as a course I would teach on campus in College Station, which is 35 h. The two courses I taught would count as general electives for Economics majors or minors, and as social science courses or general electives for other majors. The opportunity to focus on Ireland as a case study for economic analysis, its growth and development and its financial sector, and to contrast Ireland with the U.S., is a unique feature of this program. I was there the year before, and then just at the beginning of the financial crisis and the Great Recession, and thus my class focused on Ireland's rapid growth and development rather than on Ireland's experience with the Great Recession.

19.3 Courses

I taught two courses. One was a financial economics class that I also taught annually at Texas A&M University, and the other was a special topics course more specific to Ireland.

19.3.1 ECON 489: Special Topics: Growth and Development of the Irish Economy: History, Current Status, Future Prospects

The Department of Economics teaches several courses in economic development, but no course studying the development and economic history of a single nation. This course views Ireland as a case study, and in many ways, Ireland is ideal for this purpose. Ireland has a long history of impoverishment, terrible famines and huge out-migration, and a reliance on remittances from abroad. Post-nationhood status, it was one of the poorest countries in Europe, especially Western Europe. It is a nation that, in the last three decades, has seen its status change to become arguably the richest country in Europe, a nation branded with the moniker 'Celtic Tiger' because it achieved growth rates usually associated with the Asian Tiger economies such as South Korea and Taiwan. During this period, Ireland experienced a significant and persistent in-migration of non-Irish for the first time in its modern history, and Ireland became a source of remittances for other nations such as Poland. Most recently, it is a nation hard-hit by the Great Recession, facing a situation that, relative to its size, is more damaging than the financial crisis in the U.S.

Simultaneously studying Ireland's economy while sojourning in Ireland provides students with an immersion in the Irish economy, Irish culture and way of life that is not available in other settings. Identifying the determinants of economic growth and development in Ireland, understanding the policy debates, understanding why the Irish focus so much on relations with Europe, the Euro, and gaining a deeper knowledge of how living in a currency union and Free Trade Zone impacts daily life as well as policy debates, were all enhanced by studying in Ireland. Trips to the Connemara region north of Galway exposed students to life in Ireland as it was in past days, a relatively poor agrarian society, bringing into focus Ireland as it was, pre-Celtic Tiger. Living in Dublin gave students exposure to the vibrant and arguably premiere city in Ireland and home of the federal government. They learned first-hand about life in Ireland today, post-Celtic Tiger, and trips to various other locations in Ireland (e.g. Galway, Belfast) provided students with exposure to the great diversity in Irish society. Studying in Dublin allowed access to one of the premiere universities in Ireland, University College Dublin (UCD), as well as possible access to UCD faculty for guest lectures.

The academic objectives of the course were to provide students with an understanding of the gains from trade (the concept of comparative advantage, the terms of trade), exchange rates, exchange rate systems, and determinants of exchange rates (such as purchasing power parity), balance of payments issues (definitions, determinants, the role of a Free Trade Zone), the special case of a small, open economy (definition, impact on policy choices), monetary and fiscal policy in a currency union (impact on policy choices), and the theory of economic growth (determinants of growth, property rights and institutions). When we discussed each of these topics, we took time to apply our tools of economic analysis to Ireland, aiming to see how our understanding of each economic concept helped us understand the Irish experience. Students learned certain facts of Ireland's economic history and the tools to place those facts within a coherent and logical structure to better understand Ireland's stellar growth rates—the Celtic Tiger period—along with Ireland's current situation and constrained policy choices. The class was primarily lecture based, with readings from Weil (2009) and Easterly (2002).

19.3.2 ECON 445: Financial Economics (Study Abroad Version)

This course serves as an overview of financial economics, including financial institutions, asset pricing, portfolio management, risk management, and derivative securities. The course textbook was Bodie et al. (2012). While this course is taught nearly every semester by the Department of Economics, in Ireland it was modified to include an extended discussion of the Euro and Eurozone, and how participation in this currency union impacts Ireland. Ireland is a good case study of a country participating in a currency union but with several major trading partners—the U.S. and especially the U.K.—that do not participate in the currency union. The course spent more time on European financial institutions, especially Ireland's financial relationship with London and the rest of Europe, and less time on U.S. institutions. Living in Ireland provided students with firsthand knowledge of life in a nation firmly committed to the Euro and economic integration. Finally, our discussions of the financial crisis focused on Ireland, a nation hard-hit by the Great Recession, more so than the U.S., and on the Irish response to this crisis.

When taught in College Station, ECON 445 students are required to build and manage a semester-long hypothetical stock portfolio, to create an 'annual report' detailing the performance of this portfolio, and to present this to the class. When taught in a summer study abroad class in Ireland, this is not practical due to the shortened calendar time of the course. Instead students are required to write a paper comparing the impact of the financial crisis, and responses to the financial crisis, in Ireland and one other impacted country.

Advantages of studying in Ireland include gaining a better understanding of how the financial system in Ireland differs from the U.S., especially how participation in a Free Trade Zone and a currency union impacts financial matters and restricts policy choices. For instance, Ireland's response to the financial crisis is restricted by its lack of a monetary policy instrument, as monetary policy is determined in Frankfurt at the European Central Bank. In Dublin, students can explore the Irish Central Bank, including its limited role given Ireland's adoption of the Euro. We examined the Maastricht Treaty and other constraints placed on Irish monetary and fiscal policy as members of the Eurozone. Ireland's specific, small, open economy characteristics and the impact on Irish financial markets were discussed, and we spent time studying remittances.

Ireland was once a net exporter of labor—outmigration to various nations especially the U.K. and U.S.—and a net recipient of remittances, monies sent by emigrants back to the home country. Ireland, the Celtic Tiger, later became a net importer of labor—a large migration from other E.U. countries, e.g. Poland—and a net supplier of remittances, funds send home by immigrants to Ireland. Studying these topics in Ireland provided an immediacy absent from studying these topics in the middle of Texas. In addition, students were asked to consider Ireland as one state in the E.U., and compare Ireland to one state in the U.S., e.g. California or Texas, in order to compare and contrast Ireland's ability to respond to the recent financial crisis with California's ability to respond to the crisis in the U.S.

19.4 Why Dublin?

I had originally planned to make NUIG and Galway our home base. Galway has much to recommend it as a smaller, more intimate community and something of a college town. It has a lively music scene and nightlife for students. But in the end, I made Galway a destination for one of our weekend excursions instead of our home base.

Instead, I chose University College Dublin because it is in the capital city and because of the somewhat quirky Irish rail system. The train routes in Ireland basically originate in Dublin, on the east coast, and spread out to the various cities in Ireland like spokes on a wheel. This means that travel from Dublin to the various locales was relatively easy to arrange. Unfortunately, it meant that travel from one of the far locations, say Galway, to another location, say Cork, requires a train ride first from Galway to Dublin, and then from Dublin to Cork. There are no direct train routes from Galway to Cork. This unfortunate feature of the Irish rail system led me to investigate and eventually choose UCD as our home base. Dublin also has the advantage of more things to do, as it is both the largest city and the capital of Ireland. The Appendix contains a list I provided to the students of things to do in Dublin and places to visit in and around Dublin. This information is quite useful to the students as they explored Dublin in the afternoons and evenings of their stay.

19.5 Why UCD?

UCD was willing to provide lodging and classroom access, for a fee, and had the benefit of being located in Dublin. It is not in the city center, as is Trinity University, but it is in a suburb about 10 min by bus from the city center. UCD is a modern university campus with many amenities and with a familiar feel for students used to an American-style campus.

At UCD we were able to arrange for use of a standard small classroom equipped with the usual facilities. This was negotiated as part of our dorm rental agreement.

19.6 Excursions, Guest Speakers, and Other Activities

The program lasted 6 weeks. Class was held during weekdays, and excursions occurred almost every weekend. On class days we would often meet for 2 hours per class, with a number of breaks during the class time. What follows is my activity list for 1 year of the program. The activity list in the second year was almost identical.

- **Week 1**. First weekend, arrive and settle into housing at UCD, tour UCD; tour Dublin. (Guinness Storehouse; Literary Pub Crawl tour; Dublin Historical Tour; Trinity University, Bank of Ireland.)
- **Week 2**. Second weekend, excursion to Wicklow Mountains and Glendalough. Travel by public tour bus. Depending on availability, we would schedule a local Irish expert to discuss aspects of Ireland's culture, history, and society. This would occur during class time.

- **Week 3**. Third weekend, trip to Galway by train. Local transportation in Dublin by tram. One night in Galway hotel. Visit Cliffs of Mohar by tour bus on arrival day. Visit Connemara region by tour bus on departure day.
- **Week 4**. Fourth weekend, visit Belfast by train. Long weekend. Hotel in Belfast. One day for Black Cab tour of Belfast, including Peace Walls and various shrines to events during The Troubles. Second day for tour along the north coast, including the Giant's Causeway.
- **Week 5**. Open. Long weekend. Optional travel for students—most took advantage of the opportunity to visit another city or cities in Europe. Examples include London, Amsterdam, Paris, even Rome or Barcelona.
- **Week 6**. Departure follows.

In addition to weekend activities, there were activities scheduled during the week, and almost always activities for the late afternoon or evening. Some of these are listed as Week 1 activities above, but other activities include the following:

- Tour of the Irish Parliament, the Oireachtas. (Arranged by staff at UCD.)
- Visit Dublin theatres.
- A hurling match or a Gaelic football match. (Possibly also a rugby or soccer match).
- The Dublin greyhound racing track. (Evening event I attended with interested students.)
- A pub or other location to see Irish set-dancing.

19.7 Lodging and Meals

Lodging in Dublin was easy to arrange; we stayed in University College Dublin dorms. These are modern apartment-style rooms with in-suite facilities for each room. This constrains the study abroad program to begin after the UCS spring semester is over, but that did not impose a severe restriction on planning the program.

An important benefit of this lodging arrangement was the close contact our students had with study abroad students from other universities in the U.S. and students from other countries who were also staying in UCD dorms that summer, as well as some Irish UCD students spending the summer on campus. This contact with other students was also part of the broadening and learning experience of my study abroad program.

Similar dormitory housing would have been available at NUIG as well. Irish universities were willing and able to arrange to rent out their unused dorm space for American summer study abroad programs.

Meal service was arranged after a bit of give-and-take with UCD. They offered several choices of meal plans involving either a fixed number of meals (such as breakfast every day) or more expensive flexible plans. We chose a plan that included breakfast for every student and allowed students to seek lunch or dinner on their own, either on campus or in the community. This worked well, as students did not feel they were tied down to UCD for lunch and dinner meals.

19.8 Transportation: Ground and Air

Ireland has an extensive bus service between cities and to various tourist locations, and good train service to and from Dublin. Public transportation to most activities is feasible and desirable. Locally there is bus service from the Dublin city center to the UCD campus located in the southern outskirts of Dublin. The bus travel time is about 10 min outside of rush hour. Dublin airport is the main airport in Ireland and there is bus and taxi service to the city center. An alternative is Shannon airport on the west coast near Limerick and not far from Galway.

Students made their own arrangements to arrive at Dublin's airport. I provided an extensive document outlining transportation by coach from the airport to a bus stop at the edge of campus. I included both a route map for the coach and directions to get from the bus stop to the dorms on the UCD campus. I also included a map of the UCD campus with building names in case students were lost, and my cell phone was available to them as well. The appendix provides a short guide to transportation around Dublin.

19.9 Program Cost

This program was relatively inexpensive by the standards of Texas A&M University study abroad programs, mostly because I did the planning for excursions and negotiated good rates for lodging and meals with UCD. That said, the program was costly. In 2012 the cost was estimated to be $6800. This included tuition and fees for the two classes ($1700), estimated airfare ($1100), estimated meal expenses ($640), travel documents, textbooks, etc. ($220), lodging ($1300), excursions and in-country transportation ($580), health insurance and etc. ($150), a study abroad administrative fee ($360), and $400 to cover faculty expenses. That last charge was to cover my airfare, meals, and lodging while at UCD. Texas A&M University paid me a summer salary for organizing and teaching in this program, but the students were required to cover my travel, meal per diem, and lodging expense.

The estimate of $6800 probably severely underestimated actual student expenditures. Most students spent many evenings socializing in restaurants and pubs, and participated in many of the optional weekday events. Almost all students took advantage of their location on the edge of Europe to travel to another country on our 'long weekend' near the end of our time in Ireland, and this surely incurred additional expenses.

19.10 Summary of Experience

I thoroughly enjoyed my two summers taking students to Ireland. I welcomed the opportunity to show them the country, and I found that I very much liked getting to know them. There were 14 students with me in 2011, and just over 20 in 2012. These were students who spent part of almost every day with me for 5 weeks or more. In many ways this was the most enjoyable undergraduate teaching experience of my career. Almost all of my undergraduate teaching has been to fairly large or very large classrooms, so having a 'liberal art-type experience' while teaching for Texas A&M University's Economics Department was a treat, an experience to cherish. I would probably have continued the program for several more years if budget cuts had not led to a 70% reduction in my compensation for running the program. It turns out that such an offer was well below my reservation price!

The students who participated in this program were very enthusiastic about the opportunity to study abroad. They bonded with each other, and they bonded with me. My 2011 class proved to be my best advocates, and were great recruiters for my 2012 class. Both classes have largely kept in touch over the years, certainly in much higher proportions than any other undergraduate class I have ever taught.

Our travels around Ireland were especially popular, including our trip to Galway and our exploration of the Wicklow Mountains. The most interesting trip was no doubt our trip to Belfast. The 'Peace Walls' and shrines to those fallen in The Troubles were eye opening to me, and to the students. I am sure all of them were moved by the experience.

Through this program I feel like I provided the 'transformative experience' that Texas A&M University desires in its study abroad programs.

Appendix

Transport Around Dublin

Dublin has a good bus system. It has a train—the DART (Dublin Area Rapid Transit), with stations at the city center and places outside the city such as Malahide, Howth, Bray, Dun Laoghaire. There is also a tram (or light rail system) called the Luas, with a red line that runs from the city center to the north side, and a blue line that green line that runs from the city center to the south side. Taxis are usually available in the city centre. They can be expensive. Taxi ranks are found on O'Connell Street, Middle Abbey Street, and St. Stephens Green. Here are some useful Dublin transportation websites:

1. Dublin bus: www.dublinbus.ie
2. Bus guide: https://www.tripsavvy.com/taking-the-bus-in-dublin-1542307
3. Luas: https://luas.ie/

4. DART: http://www.irishrail.ie/
5. UCD's 'Hit the Road' website: http://ucd.hittheroad.ie/[1]

Some Things to do in Dublin

- Parks
  - St Stephen's Green Park
  - Merrion Square Park
  - The Iveagh Gardens
  - Dubh Linn Gardens at Dublin Castle
  - Phoenix Park (houses the Dublin Zoo)

- Theatre and concerts
  - Abbey Theatre (Ireland's National Theatre)
  - Gate Theatre
  - Gaiety Theatre
  - The O^2
  - Bord Gáis Energy Theatre

- Films
  - Screen Cinema
  - Savoy Cinema
  - Irish Film Institute
  - Stillorgan Cinema
  - Cineworld Dublin

Some Places to Visit in and Near Dublin

- **Howth**—reachable by DART or bus. A small fishing village. A pier, beautiful scenery, cliff walks, great restaurants, an open air market on weekends.
- **Dún Laoghaire**—reachable by DART or bus. A seaside town.
- **Bray to Greystones Cliff Walk**—DART to Bray, 6km cliff walk to Greystones.
- **Croke Park Stadium**—the home of Gaelic Games: football, hurling and camogie.
- **Temple Bar**—city centre. Cobbled streets, pubs with traditional music, nightlife.
- **George's Street Arcade**—a shopping centre located in the city centre.
- **Christ Church Cathedral**—located in the city centre.

---

[1] Shows how to travel from UCD to other locations in Dublin using the bus, Luas, or DART.

- **Guinness Storehouse**—walkable from the city centre, or take a bus.
- **Kilmainham Gaol**—Take the 79 or 79A from Aston Quay. Historic gaol that held prisoners during the Easter Rising (1916), the War of Independence, the Irish Civil War.
- **Cow's Lane Market**—outdoor market on Saturday.

References

Bodie Z, Kane A, Marcus AJ (2012) Essentials of Investments. McGraw-Hill, New York, NY
Easterly W (2002) The elusive quest for growth: economists' adventures and misadventures in the tropics. MIT Press, Cambridge, MA
Weil D (2009) Economic growth. Pearson Addison/Wesley, Upper Saddle River, NJ

Chapter 20
Multidisciplinary Agricultural Study Abroad in Uruguay

Levi A. Russell

Abstract One of the key advantages of study abroad programs is the students' exposure to a range of new experiences. Though these experiences often occur within the context of the culture of the country they are visiting, economics students can benefit from programs that result from collaboration with other academic disciplines. The University of Georgia's International Agribusiness in Diversified Livestock and Grain Production program is a collaboration between the Animal & Dairy Science and Agricultural Economics departments. Over 8 days, students traveled the country learning about business practices, production techniques, return on investment, and trade policy from the perspective of a small, exporting country.

20.1 Introduction

Study abroad programs in agriculture cover a wide range of fields. Many of these programs are multidisciplinary and enhance students' educational experiences by exposing them to an integrated approach to agricultural production in addition to the cultural experiences provided by study abroad. The University of Georgia's (UGA) International Agribusiness in Diversified Livestock and Grain Production program was intended to provide both cross-cultural and interdisciplinary experiences for students.

The program was designed to be explicitly multidisciplinary; the program is conducted by two professors from different fields within the College of Agriculture and Environmental Sciences (CAES) at UGA. The year that I led the program, another professor from the Animal and Dairy Science (ADS) department, Dr. Jacob Segers, co-taught the course with me. This ensured that students would have experts across two agricultural fields in the program and in Uruguay to enhance their experience and maximize their learning potential.

L. A. Russell (✉)
The University of Kansas, Lawrence, KS, USA
e-mail: levi.russell@ku.edu

© The Author(s), under exclusive license to Springer Nature Switzerland AG 2021
J. Hall, K. Holder (eds.), *Off-Campus Study, Study Abroad, and Study Away in Economics*, Contributions to Economics,
https://doi.org/10.1007/978-3-030-73831-0_20

This essay continues as follows: First, an explanation of Uruguay as a choice for this particular program is presented. A course layout is then followed by a discussion of the primary assignment the students completed. A breakdown of the cost per student rounds out the essay.

20.2 Why Uruguay?

The difficulty in establishing a study abroad program is well-documented in the literature (Strow 2016). In this case, however, a particular set of connections made the program much easier to administer. Though the program was established 5 years prior to my leading it in 2018, I was made aware of the founding of the program and had extensive contact with the parties involved. The host in Uruguay in 2018 was the same person who helped establish the program.

Dr. Bruno Lanfranco, Investigador Principal at Instituto Nacional de Investigación Agropecuaria (INIA), was our host in Uruguay. He helped establish the program with the UGA Agricultural and Applied Economics (AAE) department faculty in 2013. Dr. Lanfranco's relationship with the department had been in place many years before the program was established; Dr. Lanfranco earned his PhD in the AAE department at UGA. His employer, Instituto Nacional De Investigacion Agropecuaria (INIA), is a public/private agricultural partnership that provides research and educational services to agricultural producers in Uruguay. These connections have proven to be essential components of the study abroad program, both for students and faculty administering the program.

Uruguay is an agricultural powerhouse, given its size, making it a prime location for students to understand agricultural production, processing, and trade. Nearly 83% of Uruguay's land area is dedicated to agricultural production, and roughly 10% is dedicated to forestry (Food and Agricultural Organization (FAO) of the United Nations 2020). Uruguay has more than one head of beef cattle per person in the country and exported nearly 78% of the beef it produced in 2019 (United States Department of Agriculture (USDA) - Foreign Agricultural Service (FAS) 2020). Other major crops include rice, sorghum, and soybeans.

Agriculture is an astounding 5.64% of GDP in Uruguay, compared with only 0.07% in the United States (GlobalEdge at Michigan State University 2020a,b). Thus, agriculture is ubiquitous in the country, which allowed students to travel to three locations around the country and engage with a range of agricultural operations. The itinerary in the appendix lists the agricultural operations students visited.

Uruguay's massive agricultural production and its large coastline provide it with unique opportunities for international trade. In addition to its relatively large beef exports, Uruguay exports nearly all of its soybeans, and over 95% of its milled rice (United States Department of Agriculture (USDA) - Foreign Agricultural Service (FAS) 2020). Even with these relatively large exports, most of the meals during the study abroad experience featured beef.

20 Multidisciplinary Agricultural Study Abroad in Uruguay

Trade was an important topic for students during the study abroad experience in Uruguay. I recall a particularly poignant example of this when a student majoring in ADS engaged in a long conversation with a meat processing plant owner over the nuts and bolts of international trade. I have not seen a student so interested in international trade in the classroom; only a study abroad experience can provide opportunities for such interaction.

20.3 Course Layout

The Uruguay Study Abroad program consisted of three phases: pre-trip classroom learning, a week in Uruguay during spring break, and presentations and a paper to round out the semester. The course is offered annually in the Spring semester primarily to students in the College of Agricultural and Environmental Sciences.

The multidisciplinary nature of the program necessitated a series of lectures that functioned as a 'leveling' course. The schedule of weekly lectures is detailed in Table 20.1 and features agricultural business economics, beef production and supply chain economics, an overview of forage production in the southeastern U.S., U.S. government agricultural policy, and grain and oilseed production in the U.S. Program orientation and pre-flight briefings were also offered during the weekly class times.

During spring break, students and faculty flew to Uruguay and spent 8 days traveling to various sites. An overview itinerary for the week can be found in

Table 20.1 Course schedule

Week	Topic
1	Program orientation (online to facilitate family questions/concerns)
2	How do farmers and other producers make decisions
3	US beef supply chain
4	US beef industry production and marketing economics
5	US southeastern forages
6	Economics of international trade
7	Government policies and their impact on farmers, consumers, and trade
8	Grain and oilseed production in the US
9	Pre-flight briefing, confirm travel arrangements, fly to Urugay
10	Uruguay (see Table 20.2)
11	Presentations and papers
12	Presentations and papers
13	Presentations and papers
14	Presentations and papers
15	Class wrap-up
16	Class wrap-up

Table 20.2 Schedule when in Uruguay

Day	Location	Activities
1	Athens GA/Plane	Overnight flight to Montevideo
2	Montevideo	Orientation at INIA headquarters
3	Montevideo	3 h guided tour of Montevideo
4	Montevideo	Dairy production and farm tours
5	Treinta y Tres	Beef packing plant and travel to Trienta y Tres
6	Treinta y Tres	Cow-calf operations and farm tours
7	Punta del Este	Sheep farm visit, rice mill visit, INIA experimental station
8	Punta del Este	Oliver farm visit, vineyard and winery visit, cattle production
9	Montevideo/Plane	Morning free with late evening departure
10	Plane/Athens GA	Return to US

Table 20.2. After arrival early Saturday morning, students were given a chance to rest, then given an orientation by Dr. Lanfranco. Sunday Dr. Lanfranco gave the students a tour of the capitol city, Montevideo, and a tour of INIA's facilities in the city. Staying near Montevideo on Monday, students toured a local dairy and a crop farm near the coast.

On Tuesday, the group rode inland to Treinta y Tres in the eastern part of the country. On the way, we spent a significant part of the morning at a beef processing facility. Students were able to see all aspects of the slaughter, disassembly, boxing, and storage of beef products in this facility. Students were also treated to a long discussion with the plant's owner, who provided significant insight into the economic and financial aspects of the operation.

Students visited a large INIA research facility and were given a tour of the beef cattle research unit. On Wednesday, students visited a large commercial integrated beef, rice, and soybean farm. Students were treated to a game of soccer with the cowboys and a meal of bread and grilled lamb. The owner of this farm was particularly interested in talking with the students about the economics and financial aspects of his operation. He provided them with a detailed presentation of the financial history of his operation including information on revenue, expenses, and rates of return.

Traveling back toward the coast on Thursday, students visited a massive 11,000 hectare farm. The visit focused on sheep production. At this stop, I believe the AAE students learned the most about the technical aspects of agricultural production. In the afternoon, students visited a rice mill. This was the first time students were able to see a crop processing facility on the trip. This stop focused on the technical aspects of drying and determining the quality of the grain.

On Friday, the last visits near the coast featured an olive and wine grape farm and winery. Students spoke at length with the farm's owner, who had recently experienced a catastrophic loss of her crops due to high winds. Through tears, she explained the work she had done over the last several years to rebuild her trees and vines, and explained the mutual aid insurance organization that helped her rebuild.

Saturday was a free day until late in the afternoon when we returned to Montevideo for our flight back to the U.S.

Upon their return, students were encouraged to reflect on the trip and revisit any notes they took. They were required to write a lengthy essay on a key topic from the trip. Of the 15 students in the program, roughly half were Agribusiness majors. The others primarily majored in programs in the ADS department, and the essays reflected this. Students were encouraged to incorporate economic and technical aspects of the trip in their essays and the two professors split the grading.

From my experience grading these essays, the students who took the most away from the experience were those who planned to work in the livestock industry after they finished their degrees. They planned to either return to their own family farm operations or to work in the beef supply chain as business managers, veterinarians, or livestock nutritionists. The Uruguay trip gave them an up close look at a production system that differs significantly in some ways from the system in place in the U.S. A few students told me that, after seeing it working in Uruguay, they were more convinced that grass-finished beef production could be viable and expressed interest in pursuing this alternative to the current system after they graduated.

20.4 Costs and Conclusions

Study abroad programs are often quite expensive and can be a barrier to international experiences for students. The Uruguay Study Abroad program appeals to many students because of its modest cost. Since the program is only a week long in Uruguay, costs are much lower than the average semester-long program. However, students in the program still receive 3 hours of credit due to the assignments before and after the Uruguay trip. Additionally, the in-country partnership with Dr. Lanfranco and INIA keeps cost low by eliminating the need for pre-trip travel by professors to make arrangements.

In 2018, the program was budgeted at roughly 33,000 dollars. Expenses included salaries for professors, a stipend for the organizers in Uruguay, and travel expenses in Uruguay for faculty and students. The AAE and ADS departments paid faculty salaries (roughly one sixth of the total) and the UGA Office of International Education (OIE) paid roughly one third of the total. UGA OIE also provided support in the form of advertising for the program to students, as well as an online portal to manage applications and student documents.

The remaining cost of the program was billed to the 15 participants at the cost of 1000 dollars per student. Additionally, students were responsible for booking their own flights and for bringing spending money for the trip. The total trip cost is well below the average semester-long study abroad program and remains popular among UGA CAES students.

The proliferation of cultural diversity requirements along with the rising cost of higher education makes shorter, multidisciplinary study abroad programs particularly attractive. The program discussed in this paper is a great example of collaboration across disciplines and across the globe that minimizes the cost of the program and maximizes educational opportunities for students.

References

Food and Agricultural Organization (FAO) of the United Nations (2020) Country profile: Uruguay. http://www.fao.org/countryprofiles/index/en/?iso3=URY. Accessed 9 Aug 2020

GlobalEdge at Michigan State University (2020a) United States. https://globaledge.msu.edu/countries/united-states/economy. Accessed 9 Aug 2020

GlobalEdge at Michigan State University (2020b) Uruguay. https://globaledge.msu.edu/countries/uruguay/economy. Accessed 9 Aug 2020

Strow C (2016) Teaching the economics of ecotourism, trade, healthcare, education, poverty, and immigration as a study abroad experience in Costa Rica. J Econ Finance Educ 15(3):83–94

United States Department of Agriculture (USDA) - Foreign Agricultural Service (FAS) (2020) Production, supply, and distribution statistics. https://apps.fas.usda.gov/psdonline/app/index.html#/app/home/statsByCountry. Accessed 9 Aug 2020

Chapter 21
The World as a Living Economics Classroom: Lessons from 'Economies in Transition', a Faculty-Led Study Abroad Course in Central and Eastern Europe

Olga Nicoara and Andrew Economopoulos

Abstract Teaching 'Economies in Transition' as a study abroad course is an effective way to convey the role of ideas, institutions, culture, and leadership in the transition of former communist countries. Four countries in Central and Eastern Europe: Germany, Czech Republic, Hungary, and Romania, were visited. The course allowed the students to 'make the world their living economics classroom' through immersion into the history, geography, culture, and economy of these countries. This article presents the core planning process, the academic and implementation challenges, costs, and lessons learned from the experience. The key principles that guided the development of our curriculum, activities, and assessment are also presented.

21.1 Introduction

November 9th 2019 marked the thirtieth anniversary of the Fall of the Berlin Wall. Over 30 years ago, as revolutions swept across Central and Eastern Europe, the communist regimes fell one by one, culminating with the dissolution of the Soviet Union (December 26th 1991) and the end of the Cold War between the communist East and the capitalist West. The Cold War remains known in history as the world's battle for the ultimate system for the world economy, or a dispute over 'The Commanding Heights' of the economy (Yergin and Stanislaw 2002). Fundamentally, however, the war was a 'battle of ideas' or a debate over which sets of policies and institutions are best at fostering social cooperation and economic prosperity in light of economic theory and history (Hayek 1988[2011]; Boettke 1993; Lavoie 2015; Boettke 2001; Tarko 2020; Mises 1920[1990]). Indeed, at

---

O. Nicoara (✉) · A. Economopoulos
Ursinus College, Collegeville, PA, USA
e-mail: onicoara@ursinus.edu; aeconomopoulos@ursinus.edu

© The Author(s), under exclusive license to Springer Nature Switzerland AG 2021
J. Hall, K. Holder (eds.), *Off-Campus Study, Study Abroad, and Study Away in Economics*, Contributions to Economics,
https://doi.org/10.1007/978-3-030-73831-0_21

the core of humanity's experience with Soviet-Type regimes lies Adam Smith's (1776[2008]) question on what causes the wealth of nations or what types of institutional environments are best at promoting thriving and cooperative societies. Smith's question, while well-appreciated by scholars, is likely not what comes to the minds of the young American voters today.

Our students today are part of the new generation who have not only never lived through the Cold War era, but may also lack a quality history education in school (Gordon 2002), and may be more prone to falling to media and partisan influence in their voting (Hartig 2019). The twentieth-century battle of ideas carries on today, but the public discourse reveals confusion over the notions of 'communism', 'socialism' and 'capitalism'. For example, based on results of a recent Gallup survey, about 25% of Americans surveyed were not able to articulate the meaning of the term 'socialism,' only 17% of Americans today associate the term with government ownership of the means of production in society, while 23% of Americans today associate the term with 'some form of equality' (Newport 2018). By contrast, in 1949, in the aftermath of World War II and the rise of the Soviet-Type economies, 34% of Americans surveyed by Gallup associated the term with government ownership of the means of production (Newport 2018).

The Gallup survey results seem to suggest that the vast majority of Americans today are either confused about or unaware of the lessons learned from the experiments with socialism in recent human history. One could argue that the farther away we move from the times of totalitarian regimes, the easier it becomes to forget or underplay their devastating economic, political, social, and psychological consequences. This is true for individuals in countries with first-hand experiences of totalitarian regimes as their collective memories are likely to start fading away over time with each subsequent generation. The inclination to overlook or ignore the lessons from the world's history with communism is even more relevant for the populations of most countries in the world today who have experienced some form of a mixed regime based on a combination of market-oriented institutions and socialized programs.

Over the past 30 years of transition, the former centrally-planned countries (FCPCs) of Central and Eastern Europe have undertaken a variety of policies and institutional reforms. Taken together, these reforms can be seen as a natural experiment and constitute an ideal ground for investigating how institutional changes may impact the economic prosperity and well-being of individuals living in FCPCs.

For Western individuals studying economics, travelling to FCPCs is important for many reasons. First, it is more impactful for the student. The in-person interactions with FCPC eye-witnesses who have experienced different economic and political systems first-hand and can recount personal life stories can have an eye-opening effect and long lasting learning experience. Second, the FCPCs are ideal natural grounds for testing economics hypotheses. Students of economics may have many questions which are best answered by traveling to FCPCs: What is the meaning of economic totalitarianism? Does surrendering control over one's economic life lead to deprivation of control over one's political life as F. A. Hayek (1988[2011],

21 The World as a Living Economics Classroom: Lessons from 'Economies... 257

2007) cautioned? Were Soviet-type economies pervasive 'shortage economies' per János Kornai's (1992) emphasis (Shleifer and Vishny 1992)? What do people from FCPCs believe about their past and present? Do their perspectives and stories about life under communism support the various economic theories and arguments learned in economics and/or heard elsewhere?

21.1.1 Brief Background on Study Abroad Courses in 'Economies in Transition'

Traditional, medium-to-long term study abroad programs and 'student exchange programs' are numerous and widely-adopted across colleges and universities around the world. By contrast, faculty-led, short-term education abroad programs, particularly in economics, are few and/or less promoted. A Google scholar search using various key terms, including 'economics study abroad,' 'education abroad Eastern Europe', and 'study abroad economies in transition' give few search results, with many works only tangentially related to studying economics abroad, and none about studying transitional economies in Eastern Europe or economic development in Eastern Europe. A similar search on ProQuest returns just as few, or not so relevant results. This could be in part due to the high costs with program development and implementation of study abroad courses (Strow 2016) or the inherent challenges of designing and assessing undergraduate economics courses with an experiential learning environment (Allgood et al. 2015). In addition, burdensome and bureaucratic aspects involved with dealing with regulations in the field, are a natural impediment for designing and implementing economic courses with a study abroad component.

As we outline below the core planning and a supportive structure can overcome many of the impediments, and produce a rich and rewarding educational experience. The next section discusses how we filled this gap and met the academic challenges. Section 21.3 focuses on how we dealt with other implementation challenges including a chronological roadmap and details in setting up the course and meeting the standards. Section 21.4 discusses costs. Section 21.5 presents lessons learned and Sect. 21.6 concludes.

21.2 Filling in the Education-Abroad Gap in Economics: Our 'Economies in Transition' Study Abroad Course

We wanted to offer our students an authentic experience and global learning environment for the 'Economies in Transition' course. A traditional course in comparative systems focuses on understanding the political economy of the transition from centrally-planned to market-based systems after the Cold War. We argue that the ideal way to teach this course is to make 'the world our economics classroom' by taking a multi-city field trip and immerse ourselves in the history, geography, culture, society, and economy of a subset of the former-communist countries undergoing transition reforms. To have a balanced representation of former communist experiences in the region, we chose the following four countries along the North-West to South-East diagonal on the map of Europe: Germany, Czech Republic, Hungary, and Romania. The idea was to gain enough local understanding of each country's experience to be able to make informed comparisons and draw lessons.

Adapting the course to have a field component did not come without trade-offs. To make this course on-site rather than off-site (or in-classroom), several structural transformations and modifications were necessary. Rather than a general exploration of how alternative economics systems matter for explaining the performance across countries, the curricular focus needed to be directed to the specific experiences and knowledge gained from the particular places we visited. The academic emphasis of the course, therefore, was more directed by specific cities, museums, landmarks, and sites located in Germany, Czech Republic, Hungary, and Romania, than general theoretical concepts organized in a pre-designed pedagogical manner. The trade-off is that students received less of a general perspective and more of a specific in-situ driven learning experience. Another necessary modification was to pick essential questions, activities, and goals that we wanted to accomplish from the specific places we visited. The trade-off here is that we gained a more in-depth, practical, and contextualized understanding of the questions we focused on, instead of a broader, theoretical, and general perspective of the issues at hand.

Because the topics of transitional economics and development are so broad and rich, it was challenging to pick and narrow down the key questions, activities, and goals that we really wanted to focus on during our study abroad course. In this regard, a previous research by Olga Nicoara (our resident expert) was helpful in outlining the broad areas and lessons learned from the collapse of communism (Nicoara and Boettke 2015). Those lessons could be broadly summarized as: Institutions matter, culture matters, and leadership and ideas matter. These lessons served as foundation for the developing of our course syllabus. We elaborate on these lessons below as they relate to our study abroad course.[1]

21.2.1 Institutions Matter

In our traditional in-classroom economics classes, we emphasize the roles of secure property rights, dependable legal system, honest government, political stability,

---

[1] We also integrated into our syllabus the Quest Open Questions of the Ursinus College Core Curriculum (or simply, The Quest). We elaborate on how we integrated The Quest into our study abroad course in Sect. 21.3, under 'Curricular Development'.

and open and competitive markets.[2] Moreover, the importance of institutions, particularly economic institutions, for a successful post-communist transition and long-term economic growth, has been researched in numerous scholarly projects (Gwartney and Montesinos 2018; Nicoara and Boettke 2015; Djankov et al. 2003; Roháč 2013; Nicoara and Boettke 2015; Boettke et al. 2008; Boettke 1993). One way to succinctly convey the importance of institutions in the classroom is to show data on the most free and least free economies vis-à-vis their per capita GDP and growth rates.

Institutions matter, however, beyond 'objective' measures of standards of living like GDP per capita. From existing empirical projects and numerous studies, we know today that institutions that foster private property rights, the rule of law, and economic freedom more broadly, matter not only for better standards of living, economic prosperity, and growth, but also because they are strongly associated with social and health outcomes, with a high correlation with more democracy, civil liberties, political rights, life expectancy, and lower poverty rates and under-five mortality rates (Gwartney et al. 2019; Faria and Montesinos 2009; Faria et al. 2014; Montesinos-Yufa 2019). Therefore, in our study abroad course, our students observed not only the material prosperity in 'dollar-terms' but also other aspects of development including the local and urban infrastructure, public transportation, sanitation, public health (including mental health), public safety, and the freedom to start and run a productive business. Our students were required to journal their observations in each city regarding these and more aspects of transition on our course blog www.economiesintransition.com. Our students were also required to reflect upon the role of the above-mentioned institutions (or lack thereof) in the making of the current U.S. system compared to the places we visited, both now and during communism, before the Fall of the Berlin Wall.

21.2.2   Ideas and Leadership Matter

In our traditional in-classroom economics classes, we also teach that ideas matter. Since institutions are derived from ideas, we wanted our students to explore how ideas may impact the course of history and humanity. Communism, for example, was a beautiful idea, on paper, especially because of the seemingly noble intentions of its original proponents. In practice, however, communism was the greatest tragedy in the history of humanity as documented in The Black Book of Communism (Courtois et al. 1999). Our students learned all about the history and the horrors of communism as **experienced** by individuals in each of the countries visited. We did so by studying in the local Museums of Communism and Memorial Parks presenting the facts and commemorating the victims of communism.

---

[2]See the five key institutions as explained in the textbook by Cowen and Tabarrok (2017).

Similarly, ideas mattered in the post-communist transition because they motivated different choices of reforms. In turn, the different choices of reform propelled the countries into different transitional paths (Aligica and Evans 2009; Nicoara and Boettke 2015; Aslund 2013). In this process of rapid change and adaptation, good leadership was vital. Bringing ideas into political discussions and successful negotiations requires fast and clear-minded leadership. Students received lectures by local leaders (including entrepreneurs, policy leaders, NGO representatives, start-up executives, former dissidents, and professors) and had conversations with them around problems with corruption, regulatory burden, populism, political manipulation, and the details about living and starting a business in the countries visited. Our students reflected on the role of these ideas in the lives of the people they met and interacted with, including local guides, eye-witnesses, political dissidents and participants in revolutions, and their stories.

21.2.3 Culture Matters

We also usually teach that culture matters. Therefore, we wanted to explore various aspects of a society's culture, such as social trust, and some of Geert Hofstede's (2001) cultural dimensions such as individualism versus collectivism, long-term versus short-term orientation, uncertainty avoidance, etc. In particular, we wanted to observe, using local knowledge, the relevance of cultural beliefs in the success of the reforms. The relevance of culture was ignored by Western reformers who treated the transition as a merely technical/engineering problem that could be solved using a 'laundry list' of reforms established by the Washington Consensus, ignoring therefore the history and the underlying social realities in these countries. This technical-versus-cultural problem dichotomy has been long emphasized in the literature (Boettke 1998; Pejovich 2003; Nicoara 2018; Tarabar 2017; Kornai et al. 2004; Boettke et al. 2008; Krasnozhon 2013).

In addition, as the world becomes more open and interconnected thanks to the global spillovers of technological and institutional innovations which have reduced transaction costs significantly (Munger 2018; Connors et al. 2020), we wanted to explore the role of trade and integration on people's individuality. Our blog is full of anecdotes based on student's observations regarding differences in fashion (brand-name clothing and shoes), car brands, ethnic foods, etc., mostly produced elsewhere, implicitly highlighting the importance of international trade and economic activity post socialism as opposed to self-sufficiency during communism.

To the best of our knowledge, an economics course about 'Economies in Transition' with an experiential learning component as we developed it and briefly described above did not exist. From an academic point of view, there are trade-offs. However, as argued here, we demonstrate that the benefits of developing and implementing such a course far exceed the costs. In this regard, we believe that we are filling in a gap in the instructional possibilities regarding teaching comparative economic systems and economies in transition. We hope our course will be useful

21 The World as a Living Economics Classroom: Lessons from 'Economies...   261

for other teacher-scholars who plan to outline their own specific courses in the future. It will certainly be a benchmark to us as we plan to offer the course regularly.

21.3 Chronological Roadmap

The development of the economies in transition summer study abroad program was a 24-month process. This section provides a roadmap of the process. This process includes the setting of the vision, understanding and working with the university, meeting the standards, developing the curriculum, and working with the economics of the program.

21.3.1 Vision

The vision of the economies in transition study abroad program came about from a confluence of interests. First, the university has strongly supported opportunities for students to explore other cultures through study abroad. It was only recently that the college endorse the development of home-grown study abroad programming. Second, the department had a funding source whose goal is to promote student experiences that engage them from various perspectives that included a free market orientation. The funding source was suitable to support the study abroad program. Finally, the department recently hired a faculty member with expertise in the area of transitional economies. The new faculty member was key to the development of the vision.

As noted above, students come to the university with little understanding of the workings and experiences of communist economies. The fall of communism in the Eastern-Block provides Western students with a great opportunity to see societies working through their past and forging a new future. In the formative stages of the study abroad vision, it was essential that students should learn and experience the different experiments of former communist countries. Through the guidance of the resident expert, four countries were selected: Germany, Czech Republic, Hungary, and Romania. These countries provided a range on transitional experiences: Germany which transitioned relatively quickly to Romania which is still struggling in the transition. The on-site case study approach to learning accomplished the goal of the funding source and the university.

As a practical matter, the program had a vision that the experience would be concentrated, but significant. Given the goal of visiting four locations, 5–6 days at each location was planned. The overall experience was 22 days. This time fame had several advantages: First, it would be allowing students to gain a sufficient time in a location, but not over-welcome our stay. Students would be ready to move to the next location. Second, the program could be nestled between the end of the spring semester and the start of summer employment. For some colleges and universities, a perfect program would take place during the May term. Third, the time frame was needed to satisfy the college's credit requirements. Finally, the time frame reached an (estimated) upper bound of the affordability for students.

21.3.2 Working Within the University

The timeline for the program started with meeting the Director for Study Abroad. The Director shared university guidelines for an in-house study abroad program. For an established study abroad program, the office required an 18-month window. For a first time venture, they recommended a 24-month window. The first 6-months was drafting a syllabus. The syllabus included location and a sketch of the kinds of educational activities the program envisions. The university required any in-house study abroad program to collaborate with a Study Abroad Organization (SAO). These organizations provide on-site logistics and/or services along with emergency support for unforeseen contingencies. Once the location of the program was established, the Director could solicit proposals from SAOs that have offices in the program's location(s). The SAO requested a draft of the syllabus to better understand the program's goals and to suggest programming at the sites. Part of the process was working out a program that would meet a target price. Initial programs included a large number of services and activities provided by the SAO in which the faculty had minor academic roles. It was a 6-month process to come to an agreement between the SAO and the faculty developing the program.

While the Director of Study Abroad solicited proposals, the department submitted a proposal to the committee approving the new course. The course could fulfill various college and major requirements. The university required a more detailed syllabus than the one submitted to the SAO. (See Sect. 21.3.4 below on the curriculum development.) To be able to cast the broadest net in attracting students, the course requirements were designed to attract economics and non-economics majors while maintaining the goals of the course.

Once the SAO was selected, formal contracts were signed, and the Study Abroad Office became the back-office administrator of the program. The goal was to have a contract signed 9–12 months prior to the departure. This assured sufficient time to promote the program and to have all administrative processes in place. Students were directed to the study abroad website. Student applications were vetted. A timeline for deposits, paperwork, passports, applications for scholarships, and general orientation meetings was given to students accepted in the program. The Study Abroad Office also worked with the business office to establish the proper accounts.

21.3.3 Meeting the Standards

In the United States, education abroad programs are regulated by the Forum on Education Abroad (FEA). The organization established the Standards of Good Practice for Education Abroad in 2004 and it is recognized by the U.S. Department of Justice and Federal Trade Commission as the Standards Development Organization (SDO) for the field of education abroad. As stated in the guide for short-term education abroad programs (of 8 weeks or less) published by this SDO, their standards are considered a "benchmark for education abroad program excellence and accountability" (Forum on Education Abroad 2017, p. 2). The organization differentiates between the following approaches with regard to program responsibilities that faculty and postsecondary education institutions could choose from: (1) Full Responsibility of the program leader; (2) Shared Responsibility between program leader and campus offices; and (3) Less Responsibility: Program entrusted to an independent program provider (Forum on Education Abroad 2017). Because Ursinus College does not have campus offices abroad, we needed to explore all the options available to us to implement our study abroad course in compliance with the standards. Therefore, we integrate the three SDO choices above into a two-by-two matrix to better visualize and summarize our options in Table 21.1.

The Full Responsibility option is also known as the Do-it-Yourself approach. This is option (1) in Table 21.1 and it entails giving the faculty leader(s) the most autonomy and flexibility over all the aspects of the program. This approach poses difficulties and risks too high particularly for small colleges. At the end of the spectrum is the option to Outsource all aspect of the program to an Independent Provider(s) or a Study Abroad Organization (SAO). This is option (3) mapped in Table 21.1 and it entails the faculty leader(s) give up control, and therefore responsibility, over all aspects of the program entirely.

Therefore, in consultation with our colleagues, the Dean's office, and the Director for Study Abroad, we opted for option (2) in Table 21.1. We opted for shared responsibility of the program with two Independent Providers or SAOs to ensure that the highest standards of safety for our group were met throughout the entire trip. The SAO's responsibility was mainly to facilitate the safety procedures, the

Table 21.1 Short-term program responsibility options

		Faculty leader responsibility	
		High or full	Low or none
Campus office(s)[a] or independent provider responsibility	Low or none	Full responsibility of the program leader (1)	Not Applicable
	High or full	Shared responsibility (2)	Responsibility outsourced to independent providers (3)

[a] Ursinus College does not have campus offices abroad. Therefore, we worked with independent providers

21.3.4 Curricular Development

Our 'Economies in Transition' course was part case study, part experiential learning, and part academic. The overarching goal was for students to learn but also experience the transitions facing the countries visited. The design and materials were guided by the academic learning goals and the University's core curriculum questions. The academic learning goals were directly associated with the three big lessons from the collapse of communism: Institutions Matter, Culture Matters, and Leadership and Ideas Matter (see Sect. 21.2). The University's core curriculum questions, known as the Quest Open Questions or simply 'The Quest', are: What should matter to me? How should we live together in this World? How can we understand the World? And what will I do?

Key to curriculum was to include a significant number of writing reflections. Since students had limited exposure and knowledge of communism, it was essential to have students personally recognize the tradeoffs that could occur in a communist state. Students cannot understand what matters to themselves if they do not understand the tradeoffs. Thus, the curriculum started off with a pre-orientation reflection on the tradeoff between freedom and security. In what areas are freedom important to personal decision-making and what areas are security more important. This was followed by historical readings on the economic systems of the Eastern European countries.[3] The reflection and reading provided the foundation for the orientation. Since students came from various academic backgrounds, prior to departure, students spent two full days of on-campus orientation and instruction that focused on markets under freedom and economies under constraints. The two-day boot camp included, lecture, group discussions, Free to Choose film screenings, and a board game on gaining wealth in an economy of shortages. At the end of the orientation, students were again asked to reflect once again on the question of freedom and security.

For the portion of the program abroad, the curriculum contained five basic elements for each location:

1. Overview of the country/city,
2. Academic discussions, readings, and videos on the communist experience,
3. Local speakers on the past, present, and future,
4. Tours of key historical sites and museums,
5. Exploration by students (See Table 21.2).

---

[3]The readings included classic texts such as Bukharin and Preobrazhenskiĭ (1988[1922]) and Boettke (1993).

21 The World as a Living Economics Classroom: Lessons from 'Economies...

Table 21.2 General itinerary example

Day	Activity
1	Arrival and city tour, film screen or reading
2	Morning faculty-led session on communism, afternoon visit to a historical site/museum, reading
3	Morning meeting with guest speaker, afternoon visit with entrepreneur, reflection assignment
4	Morning debriefing and reflections, afternoon independent exploration
5	Travel to next city and city tour, blog post
6	Last country—tour of countryside and stayover
7	Last country—tour of countryside and travel to airport hotel
8	Departure to the United States

Upon arrival, the group took a tour of the city. This provided the cultural and geographical context of the living classroom. Students were asked to either watch a video or read about the country's experience under communism. While students could do the latter anywhere, the program included speakers from the country that had experienced living during the communist era. Some of the speakers were academics, while others were political activists, entrepreneurs or individuals—all who lived the experience and who can provide a contrast to the current life.[4]

The SAO arranged tours to specific historical sites or museums that exhibited life during the communist era. The exhibits portrayed both civilian and political realities. The program set aside time for students and faculty to interact and discuss their observations and to address their question. Faculty also used this time to instruct on issues that students heard or saw during their day. As an example, many of the students never travelled abroad and faced for the first time dealing with exchange rates. Some went to money changers and came back with questions. Why are the exchange rates so different between countries? How to deal with money exchangers? What is a good rate? Finally, the students were asked to journal their reflections during the stay. We gave short, and mid-length prompts during the trip. Students were asked to pick a specific observation that called their attention in one city and to keep it in mind as they journal in the next city that was visited. Students were given a couple of blocks of time to explore the city, and to video journal anything that stood out as unique to their experience. These reflections culminated into a blog post. Students had a final essay to be turned in 2 weeks after their return. Students were to do a comparative analysis of two locations visited. (See the Appendix for details on the writing assignments.)

---

[4] The program leveraged the faculty's knowledge and connections in the region. We were able to arrange speakers from the following private universities: the CEVRO Institute, the International Business School in Budapest (IBS), and American University in Bucharest. These arrangements allow the program to have greater control over topics and perspectives, and at a more reasonable cost.

The curriculum was enhanced by the resident expert connections to local universities, and other higher education centers, and think tanks with lecturers specialized in transition reforms, the history of communism, public policy and entrepreneurship in some of the countries. This allowed the curriculum to be focused and to accomplish the goals of the course. While the SAO assigned a liaison in the country to guide and direct the group to various activities, the faculty developed programming required some additional effort from the faculty to coordinate the logistics.

21.4 Costs

The target price was based on several factors. The first factor was to meet the college's requirements of having a Study Abroad Organization (SAO). The SAO provided several quotes based on the services rendered. These services included arrangement of accommodations, speakers, museum tickets, local transportation, tour guides, rental of facilities, emergency care, and local liaisons. We were willing to have students stay in various accommodations from four star hotels, to dormitory facilities to a hostel.

Given the program parameters, the SAO provided the cost per student depending upon the number of students in the program. SAO minimums were 10 students. We set a maximum number of students at 18 for two faculty. Fourteen students went on the program. The second factor was to estimate food costs. The program's goal was to gather during the evening meal to discuss the day events, and the costs for dinner would be covered by the program.[5] The goal and the reality was very different. Although the students talked about their experiences, the group dinner was also a great bonding time. The days in which students explored the city, the food costs were borne by the students. Most breakfasts were included in the accommodations, and at least one group lunch was arranged in each country.[6]

Finally, we developed a budget that included academic costs such as books, supplies, speakers, and miscellaneous expenses such as emergency fund, unexpected expenses not included in the SAO program, etc. Faculty received a stipend and all expenses paid on the trip. Our target price was $3,500 for the program plus airfare.[7] Round trip airfare from and to the United States plus a flight between Budapest and Bucharest costed $1,550. Total advertised cost was $5,100. Students received four

---

[5] In some cases, the SAO made the arrangements for a group reservation, but for most of the dinners, the faculty leaders searched for locations. Some restaurants that accepted our large group were frequented by internationals while other restaurants by locals.

[6] The SAO would normally arrange a welcoming dinner which was included in their fee. We estimated an average daily food expense based on a survey of city restaurants. In our case it was $10 breakfast, $15 lunch and $25 dinner. The SAO provided a set meal for everyone. We took the approach to give each student a budget to spend in local prices. Students preferred the choice and in most cases they were below their budget. This enabled us to splurge later in the trip.

[7] The College had external funding to promote economic explorations which allowed us to subsidize each student about $650. The actual price was $5,750 per student.

college credits but did not pay for tuition. The students could also apply for a small scholarship from the College's study abroad program. These awards ranged from $500 to $1,200.

21.5   Lessons Learned

As with most plans, the implementation is when you understand how well you planned. There were several lessons learned from our first study abroad program.

1. Having the SAO involved reduced the stress and uncertainty of dealing with logistics. All of the traveling days went smoothly and having arrangements made by the SAO for the first day allowed the group to settle into their itinerary.
2. Flexibility is essential. We realized that traveling days are not days to plan academic goals, and evening dinner was not an opportunity to have a group discussion on the day events.
3. Multiple means of payment are needed for backup. A credit card not working or a debit card being eaten by an ATM were experienced.
4. Knowing the language was not essential, but it was helpful. Many spoke English, and most directions were also given in English, but some transactions such as purchasing tickets for public transportation required a knowledge of the language. Make sure you have Google translator.
5. On the day of return there was no opportunity to celebrate the experience. A celebration of the experience was needed at the start of the next semester.
6. The end of May—beginning of June period is 'final exams period' for most students in Europe, so opportunities to engage with local students in common curricular activities over this period is limited.

21.6   Conclusion

Economies in Transition was a successful short-term study abroad course on three fronts. First, in terms of the student experience student reviews were a testament of the impact it had in their lives. Eyes were open to a new world as they interacted with a different culture, and an old world as they understood the experiences under a communist system. Second, the foundations of a successful development and implementation process include having a dedicated faculty, strong support from the University, and an experienced SAO. Third, from a liberal arts perspective, our study abroad experience enhanced the student-faculty and student-student relationships by the shared experiences between students and faculty that became indelibly imprinted in lives for the participants. The students' comments below were typical and show how this kind of course can have a significant impact on their lives:

The on-site exploration helped me to understand the difference between each country and witnessing it first-hand further solidify how a country's policies could impact the citizens and country, especially after the revolution. It was also a great way to make friends...

The intense three weeks spent abroad in Eastern Europe taught me a lot about the world and myself... being in a completely different land and experiencing a whole new variety of cultures was instantly eye-opening to me. Through the course itself, economic and political lessons have guided my understanding of how our world works to new levels.

The things I got to experience on this trip were things that no-one can learn from simply sitting in a classroom. Not only was I able to benefit from all the information and history I was getting but also the involvement of the culture of these countries is something I will not take for granted. I feel all the knowledge that I have gained on this trip will help me with the understanding of different people's lives and how we all interact.

Economies in Transition (ECON-223) has taught me more not only more about how different economies function, but also a lot more about myself.

In conclusion, we made the case that teaching 'Economies in Transition' as a study abroad course is the most effective way to convey the role of ideas, institutions, culture, and leadership in the transition of former communist countries. Above all, the study abroad course experience enriched the lives of our students in many ways, including intellectual, cultural, and personal development. Students loved learning through on-site explorations or by 'making the world their living economics classroom.' We hope our 'Economies in Transition' summer study abroad course model and experience could serve well other faculty planning to develop and lead similar short-term study abroad courses at their institutions.

Appendix

Assessment

The course included short, mid-length, and long writing assignments that focused on reflection about an experience, a reading, or an observation. The short and mid-length writing assignments were given in each country. For the short assignments the prompts were narrow in scope and typically pertained to an experience of the day. These were given to capture the moment, and were at times unplanned as a part of the curriculum. As an example, in Berlin we toured the Memorial of the Murdered Jews of Europe. The memorial was an interactive experience in which the sculpture brings art and emotion to a deeper understanding of the genocide that was committed by a totalitarian regime. Students were asked to reflect on the meaning of the memorial. Mid-length writing assignments focused on connecting the information about socialism with their experiences in their home country.

One such prompt focused on the differences in economic wellbeing of the individuals among the eastern-bloc countries and the United States. Students read articles and visited a museum on life under communism and were asked to highlight allocation choices of the various countries and reflect on how it differed at home. After each country the students posted a mid-length blog on the country. The

21 The World as a Living Economics Classroom: Lessons from 'Economies...

blog was a journal of their observations about something that you find interesting, something that has challenged your thinking, or something that you have learned. The first blog theme was to be the basis of future blogs in the other countries. The goal was to connect the experiences and observe differences between the countries. Some of the topics students covered were public transportation, pollution, and urban renewal. The longest assignment was a culmination of their experiences. At the end of the program students were to compare and contrast a particular observation for two of the countries. Students researched the topic and were to complete a standard term paper.

Both faculty were involved in the grading. One faculty member gave the final grade after consultation with the other faculty member. The rubric for writing assignments varied with the type of assignment. For short writing assignments, the grade was given a complete or incomplete. Students were given a minimum word count, and if the student showed thought, they were given credit. For mid-length and long assignments, guidance was given on what was expected.

Our assessment was overall guided by the academic learning goals and the Ursinus College Quest Open Questions. The learning goals were directly associated with the three big lessons from the collapse of communism: Institutions Matter, Culture Matters, and Leadership and Ideas Matter. The Ursinus College Quest Open Questions are the key questions of our Core Curriculum: How should we understand the World? How should we live together? What should matter to me? And what will I do? These principles were the essence of all our assessments during our Study Abroad Course.

Acknowledgments The authors would like to express gratitude for helpful feedback, suggestions, and the support of our colleagues at Ursinus College, particularly: Melissa Hardin, Meredith Goldsmith, Scott Deacle, and Hugo Montesinos. We are also grateful for the prompt help of our colleagues and collaborators in Europe: Josef Šíma, Bojár Gábor, Bogdan Glăvan, Alexandru Butiseacă, and many others who served as facilitators and who cheered for us in the first iteration of our summer study abroad journey. Financial support came from the Gladstone Whitman Summer Fellows Program.

References

Aligica PD, Evans AJ (2009) The neoliberal revolution in Eastern Europe: Economic ideas in the transition from communism. Edward Elgar Publishing, Cheltenham

Allgood S, Walstad WB, Siegfried JJ (2015) Research on teaching economics to undergraduates. J Econ Lit 53(2):285–325

Aslund A (2013) How capitalism was built: The transformation of Central and Eastern Europe, Russia, the Caucasus, and Central Asia. Cambridge University Press, New York, NY

Boettke PJ (1993) Why perestroika failed. Routledge, New York, NY

Boettke PJ (1998) Why culture matters: Economics, politics and the imprint of history. Ama-Gi J Lond Sch Econ Hayek Soc 2(1):9–16

Boettke PJ (2001) Calcuation and coordination: Essays on socialism and transitional political economy. Routledge, New York, NY

Boettke PJ, Coyne CJ, Leeson PT (2008) Institutional stickiness and the New Development Economics. Am J Econ Sociol 67(2):331–358

Bukharin NI, Preobrazhenskiĭ EA (1988[1922]) The ABC of communism: A popular explanation of the program of the communist party of Russia. University of Michigan Press, Ann Arbor, MI

Connors J, Gwartney JD, Montesinos HM (2020) The transportation-communication revolution: 50 years of dramatic change in economic development. Cato J 40(1):153–198

Courtois S, Werth N, Panné JL, Paczkowski A, Bartošek K, Margolin JL (1999) The black book of communism: Crimes, terror, repression. President and Fellows of Harvard College, Cambridge, MA

Cowen T, Tabarrok A (2017) Modern principles of economics. Worth Publishers, New York, NY

Djankov S, Glaeser E, La Porta R, Lopez-de Silanes F, Shleifer A (2003) The new comparative economics. J Comp Econ 31(4):595–619

Faria HJ, Montesinos HM (2009) Does economic freedom cause prosperity? An IV approach. Public Choice 141(1/2):103–127

Faria HJ, Montesinos-Yufa HM, Morales DR (2014) Should the modernization hypothesis survive Acemoglu, Johnson, Robinson, and Yared? Some more evidence. Econ J Watch 11(1):17–36

Forum on Education Abroad (2017) Leading short-term education abroad programs: Know the standards. Forum on Education Abroad, Carlisle, PA

Gordon G (2002) Should history class be left in the past? Gallup. Available via Gallup Poll Tuesday Briefing. https://news.gallup.com/poll/6862/should-history-class-left-past.aspx. Accessed 18 June 2020

Gwartney JD, Montesinos HM (2018) Former centrally planned economies 25 years after the fall of communism. Cato J 38:285–309

Gwartney JD, Lawson R, Hall JC, Murphy R (2019) 2019 Annual report: economic freedom of the world. The Fraser Institute, Vancouver

Hartig H (2019) Stark partisan divisions in Americans' view of socialism, capitalism. Pew Research. Available via Pew Research Center. https://www.pewresearch.org/fact-tank/2019/06/25/stark-partisan-divisions-in-americans-views-of-socialism-capitalism/. Accessed 18 June 2020

Hayek FA (1988[2011]) The fatal conceit: The errors of socialism. In: The collected works of FA Hayek book 1. University of Chicago Press, Chicago, IL

Hayek FA (2007) The road to serfdom: Text and documents. In: The collected works of FA Hayek, vol 2. University of Chicago Press/Routledge, London

Hofstede G (2001) Culture's consequences: Comparing values, behaviors, institutions, and organizations across nations. Sage Publications, Thousand Oaks, CA

Kornai J (1992) The socialist system: The political economy of communism. Oxford University Press, New York, NY

Kornai J, Rothstein B, Rose-Ackerman S (2004) Creating social trust in post-socialist transition. Palgrave Macmillan, New York, NY

Krasnozhon LA (2013) Institutional stickiness of democracy in post-communist states: Can prevailing culture explain it? Rev Austrian Econ 26(2):221–237

Lavoie D (2015) Rivalry and central planning: The socialist calculation debate reconsidered. Mercatus Center at George Mason University, Arlington, VA

Mises Lv (1920[1990]) Economic calculation in the socialist commonwealth. Ludwig von Mises Institute, Auburn, AL

Montesinos-Yufa HM (2019) On geography, institutions, human capital, and economic development. Dissertation, Florida State University

Munger MC (2018) Tomorrow 3.0: Transaction costs and the sharing economy. Cambridge University Press, Cambridge

Newport F (2018) The meaning of "socialism" to Americans today. Gallup. Available via Gallup News. https://news.gallup.com/opinion/polling-matters/243362/meaning-socialism-americans-today.aspx. Accessed 18 June 2020

Nicoara O (2018) Cultural leadership and entrepreneurship as antecedents of Estonia's singing revolution and post-communist success. Baltic J Eur Stud 8(2):65–91

Nicoara O, Boettke PJ (2015) What have we learned from the collapse of communism? In: Coyne CJ, Boettke P (eds) The Oxford handbook of austrian economics. Oxford University Press, New York, NY, pp 643–677

Pejovich S (2003) Understanding the transaction costs of transition: It's the culture, stupid. Rev Austrian Econ 16(4):347–361

Roháč D (2013) What are the lessons from post-communist transitions? Econ Aff 33(1):65–77

Shleifer A, Vishny R (1992) Pervasive shortages under socialism. RAND J Econ 23(3):237–246

Smith A (1776[2008]) An Inquiry into the nature and causes of the wealth of nations. Management Laboratory Press, Hamburg, Germany

Strow C (2016) Teaching the economics of ecotourism, trade, healthcare, education, poverty, and immigration as a study abroad experience in Costa Rica. J Econ Finance Educ 15(3):83–94

Tarabar D (2017) Culture, democracy, and market reforms: Evidence from transition countries. J Comp Econ 45(3):456–480

Tarko V (2020) Understanding post-communist transitions: The relevance of Austrian economics. Rev Austrian Econ 33(1):163–186

Yergin D, Stanislaw J (2002) The commanding heights: The battle for the world economy. PBS. Available via WGBH/PBS. http://www.pbs.org/wgbh/commandingheights/lo/index.html. Accessed 18 June 2020

Chapter 22
Using Study Abroad to Teach the Fundamentals of a Market Economy in Comparative Settings

William N. Trumbull

Abstract I describe two related courses, The Cuban Economy and The Post-Socialist Economies of Europe. Though both courses are ostensibly about socialist or post-socialist economies, my motivation is for a better understanding of the miracle of the Invisible Hand of the capitalist economic system. I also discuss the advantages of embedding study abroad in a regular semester course.

22.1 Introduction

Picture a typical college student (let's call him Tom) going to the grocery store in search of apples. He finds them there, of course. Why would he not? It does not even occur to him that they would not be there any more than it occurs to him to wonder if the sun will rise the next day. Yet, there are thousands of apple producers in the U.S. alone, tens of thousands of grocery stores, and hundreds of millions of apple consumers. And no one is in charge! What makes this daily miracle happen? Why are stores not empty of apples some days and so full of apples that there is no room for anything else on other days? Tom doesn't think to ask these questions. It's just the way it is and always (in his experience) has been.

Of course, we would like to think that Tom would realize the miracle of the market economy when he takes ECON 101 and learns that what coordinates the independent decisions of thousands of apple producers and millions of apple consumers and tens of thousands to apple intermediaries is Adam Smith's Invisible Hand. But Tom does not. Not really. He gets what a demand curve is and what a supply curve is and he can regurgitate that the market equilibrium is where those two curves meet but he has a hard time relating that to his life. Those apples are where he expects to find them because they always are. Those supply and demand curves are just textbook stuff.

W. N. Trumbull (✉)
The Citadel, Charleston, SC, USA
e-mail: wtrumbul@citadel.edu

© The Author(s), under exclusive license to Springer Nature Switzerland AG 2021
J. Hall, K. Holder (eds.), *Off-Campus Study, Study Abroad, and Study Away in Economics*, Contributions to Economics,
https://doi.org/10.1007/978-3-030-73831-0_22

As economists, we know otherwise. We know that those apples (or bread or shoes) have not always been there and that they are not always there in other places where the market economy either does not exist or where the state prevents them from freely performing their miracle. But Tom does not. He has never experienced anything other than a well-functioning market, so it is hard for him to truly see and appreciate what is happening all around him every day. What Tom needs to fully understand a well-functioning market economy is to study, and experience for himself, an economy that is not market based.

In this paper, I outline two related courses that I have taught over the years at two institutions (West Virginia University and, since 2013, The Citadel), one on the Cuban economy, a course that features a 10-day trip to Havana, the other a course on the post-socialist economies of Europe, a course that features a 10-day trip to either the Czech Republic or Poland. Unlike most short-term study-abroad experiences, the trip is part of a regular spring semester course. The trip takes place during spring break. There are many advantages to this arrangement, which I will discuss in the concluding section. But first, in the next section, I offer my thoughts on why one might consider teaching such a course even though, quite honestly, it is a lot of work.

22.2 The Pros and Cons

One might want to teach a course like these because it achieves something not possible, or more difficult to achieve, in a regular classroom setting. My primary goal in these courses is to make Tom, our typical undergraduate whose life experiences are still so limited, truly understand the miracle that is the market economy by having him experience for himself an economy in which those apples are not likely to be there, where people line up outside the bakery each morning, where store shelves are empty or, in the case of the post-socialist economies, where the students can talk to people who had to live like that and where the legacies of the socialist period are very much evident today.

This experiential aspect is itself a reason to consider teaching a course like this. We know that a deeper learning occurs when students experience, rather than merely listen to, the concepts we teach and we try to find ways to incorporate experiential opportunities to enrich the classroom experience. This can be hard and, too often, we revert back to traditional lectures. A study-abroad course like the ones I outline here is an opportunity to have our students actually live, albeit for a short time, what they have been reading and listening to in class.

My own career, now spanning almost four decades, has been as an economics faculty member in AACSB-accredited business schools. As Strow (2016) points out, current AACSB accreditation standards emphasize the global context of business. According to Di Gregorio (2015, p. 571), "(m)ore than one fifth of all US students studying abroad are business students." Yet, too often, these experiences are not focused on business or economics or are too often superficial, as when a faculty

22 Using Study Abroad to Teach the Fundamentals of a Market Economy in...

member takes students abroad for a series of factory visits that could just as well have taken place at home. As Di Gregorio (2015, p. 580) points out, "(s)hort-term programmes are often highly choreographed in order to make the most of limited time, as well as to make sure that students stay on the programme (and avoid getting into trouble). In my experience, this may lead students to be overly passive." My study-abroad courses have very specific learning objectives with a significant experiential component and time for independent exploration and learning, which canned programs are unlikely to provide.

International experience is an aspect of faculty, as well as student, learning and development, as McCannon (2011) and Strow (2016) point out. This has been particularly the case for me as my own research and teaching interest is the socialist and post-socialist economies. Teaching these courses helps me to maintain academic connections and to continually gain new insights that enliven both my teaching and research. My course on the post-socialist economies of Europe has resulted in a Fulbright for me and a Fulbright for a European colleague whom I hosted. It even resulted in my hosting the Polish economist Leszek Balcerowicz, father of Poland's highly successful 'shock therapy' transition and twice deputy prime minister, finance minister, president of the central bank, and now special assistant to the president of Ukraine, who addressed the entire Citadel Corps of Cadets on lessons learned on the road from socialism to a market economy. Definitely a highlight of my career!

Finally, one might consider teaching a study-abroad course because it is enormously satisfying. As much as I enjoy my interactions with students in my other classes, these interactions are limited to class times and the occasional office visits. It is hard to really get to know these students, to understand what they are really thinking, and the degree to which they really care about what I am teaching them. In the regular classroom setting, I find many students to be somewhat reticent about expressing themselves. During the intense and highly focused experience abroad, that reticence disappears and I discover whole new dimensions to these students that I did not know existed. I find them intensely interested and eager to discuss and explore their discoveries and new insights gained during the trip. And they open up about who they are, what their goals are, and what they are interested in. I find that very rewarding.

On the other hand, it is, as I have mentioned, a lot of work. In addition to all the work that is associated with our regular classes, a study abroad requires organizing the program abroad, the lodging, and the transportation. One could offload these tasks to an agent, of course, but I would be wary of that unless you are satisfied with a highly generic and unfocused program and, in the case of Cuba, one that is designed to convince the students that Cuba is a socialist paradise and that all Cubans are devoted socialists, a lesson I learned once and will never repeat.

For me, this extra work includes time I spent in each of the three locations (Cuba, the Czech Republic, and Poland) before taking students there. My first trip to Cuba was in 1998. I went there as a guest of a University of Havana economics professor. He introduced me to many of the academics who would later become the backbone of my program in Havana. My first few years teaching the course (starting in 1999), we worked together on the program and the University of Havana made all the arrangements for lodging and ground transportation. I was later forced to work through an agent because of a new rule prohibiting Cuban universities from working directly with foreigners on study-abroad programs such as mine. However, by then, my contacts were well established and I was able continue with my program design.

I continued teaching the Cuba course through 2004. Later that year, the George W. Bush administration issued new rules on faculty-led study-abroad programs in Cuba (including a minimum 10-week stay in Cuba) that made it impossible to continue. That summer, I travelled to Prague to work with a faculty member at the University of Economics to develop a program in the Czech Republic and, in 2005, taught my first class on the post-socialist economies of Europe. In 2006, I visited a colleague at Collegium Civitas in Warsaw to develop a program in Poland. From 2007 to 2013, I taught this course each year alternating between the Czech Republic and Poland. In the fall of 2013, I moved to my current institution, The Citadel, and have returned to the Cuba course, the restrictive rules of the Bush years having been dropped by the Obama administration. While I do work through an agent (Cuba Educational Travel), that agent does an excellent job of implementing my program design and arranging housing in casas particulares, privately-owned houses that are rented to tourists.

Another addition to the standard teaching workload is the time spent recruiting students, which is not something we have to worry about normally. At least at the institutions where I have worked, the course fee and airfare are very significant costs for most students. I make presentations in my classes and ask my colleagues to market the class to their students and advisees. I send email to colleagues in the other Citadel schools. I put flyers on every classroom and restroom door and bulletin board. I twist arms. It is a lot of work. As my two payment deadlines approach and pass, I inevitably have to deal with students who are unable to make payments on time or who have grants or scholarships that make payments on their own timelines. Meanwhile, I have payments that have to be made for lodging, transportation, and the program abroad.

All of this, setting up the trip, recruiting, dealing with students' payments, making payments, requires coordination between our study-abroad office, our finance office, financial aid, and the dean's office. This amounts to many hours of work during the fall semester and the first half of the spring semester. Even after returning from the trip, there are still two more extra tasks—expense reimbursement and budget reconciliation.

Finally, there is an element of risk. Our students are adolescents. They will do stupid things, especially when alcohol is involved. I have had to spring a student from a Polish jail. I have had to leave a student behind for a day in the care of my faculty co-leader after he got so drunk during a long layover that the airline would not let him board the next flight. I have had to deal with the police after students caused minor damage to our hotel. I have had a student talk his buddies into joining him for a swim through rapids during a snow storm. I have had to take a student to have his foot sewn up after slicing it open on broken glass playing baseball barefoot in a village outside Havana. Students have gotten sick. I have gotten sick.

Having taught a study-abroad course 16 times, this list is really not all that long and most trips go off without any such problems. But problems can happen and one has to be prepared to deal with them. One way is to make sure to always have a colleague who can help handle emergencies. Another is to make sure that all participants bring the antibiotic Cipro, which is cheap and highly effective.

While alcohol is often a common denominator in these problems, I do not prohibit drinking. The students are legal adults even if their behavior sometimes belies that fact. The drinking age in most countries is 18 or lower. It's 16 in Spain and most of Switzerland. China has no minimum drinking age. That means that the students are not breaking the law when they drink. I do, however, impose consequences for bad behavior. Any missed event (lecture, cultural activity, field trip) costs half a course letter grade. Falling asleep during any event costs half a course letter grade. Behavior that is sufficiently egregious results in being sent home and a course grade of F, though I have never had occasion to apply this penalty. I want them (and me!) to have a good time but they have to be responsible.

Let us turn now to the specifics of my study-abroad courses.

22.3 Course Specifics

As I mentioned above, the class is offered during the spring semester with the trip taking place over spring break. The course is a regular elective course in business and economics. In addition to the tuition the students pay every semester, there is a course fee that covers the costs of the academic program, lodging, ground transportation, all breakfasts and lunches, and two dinners, and the fixed costs of the two faculty leaders' expenses. That fee is currently $1850 for the Cuba course (I do not have current costs for the course on the post-socialist economies of Europe as I have not taught it in several years). The fee does not include airfare to Havana, currently a little under $500 from Charleston, SC.

As I indicated in the introduction, my primary goal in both courses, The Cuban Economy and The Post-Socialist Economies of Europe, is for my students to understand the miracle that is the uncoordinated market economy. I accomplish this by teaching them about planned socialism, a non-market economic system, and then taking them to a country that operates under the planned-socialist system (Cuba) or one that has emerged from that system (the Czech Republic or Poland). I accomplish this goal by contrasting the market system with the planned-socialist system and then taking them to experience this contrast for themselves.

The more specific objectives of the Cuba course are to:

- define the characteristics of the three modern economic systems: capitalism, planned socialism, and market socialism
- assess economic performance of economies and economic systems
- describe the workings of a typical planned-socialist economy
- outline the economic history of socialist Cuba

- analyze the reforms of both the Fidel Castro and the Raul Castro regimes and the very new Díaz-Canel regime
- offer predictions about Cuba's economic prospects

The objectives of the course on post-socialist Europe are similar except that the Cuba-specific objectives are replaced with understanding transition and case studies of transition in the Czech Republic, Hungary, Poland, and Russia.

The graded outputs are quizzes, an exam, a journal, and a term paper. In addition, I give credit for active participation while on the trip. The specific weights are in Table 22.1.

Both courses have a very similar format. The first 8 weeks are lecture-intensive. This is followed by the 10-day trip, which includes lectures by local economists, historians, and political scientists, as well as visits to museums and other cultural activities. Because of the contact time during what would otherwise be their spring break, I do not hold classes after the trip, with the exception of one class for general discussion and reflection. The students spend this time after the trip on the remaining graded outputs.

The lectures are organized in modules, more or less in the order of the course objectives above. Each module is self-contained with a narrative posted in the LMS course site, readings, all of which I provide as downloads, an audio-over-PowerPoint lecture that supplements our classroom lecture and discussion, and the PowerPoint notes for that module. Finally, each module ends with a quiz.

Table 22.2 reproduces the schedule and readings for the 8 weeks prior to the trip for the most recent offering of the Cuba course.

The program in Havana includes lectures by Cuban academics on various topics including economic reforms in Cuba, agriculture, Cuba-U.S. relations, Cuban foreign policy, health care, and current events. There are numerous visits to firms in the emerging private sector, as well as non-profit entities providing community support, and cultural activities. There is even a day trip to visit a family in a rural village for a pig picking and a pickup baseball game. Finally, there is substantial time for independent exploration and reflection. For instance, only two dinners (a welcome dinner and a departure dinner) are included in the program. This forces the students to separate from the large group and explore, preferably in small groups of three or four.

The appendix reproduces the itinerary for the trip that was supposed to take place in March of 2020, a trip that was canceled a week before departure, a victim of the emerging COVID-19 pandemic.

Table 22.1 Weighting of course assignments

Assignment	Percent weight
Quizzes	20%
Exam	30%
Journal	20%
Paper	25%
Participation	5%

22 Using Study Abroad to Teach the Fundamentals of a Market Economy in... 279

Table 22.2 Sample course modules and readings

Module	Dates	Topic	Readings
1	1/12–1/18	Introduction to comparative economic systems	Neuberger (1989)
2	1/19–1/25	Assessing economic performance	Bornstein (1989)
3	1/26–2/1	Outline of the typical planned-socialist system	Brown and Neuberger (1989)
4	2/2–2/8	Capitalism: The role of prices	Hayek (1945)
		Capital and fairness	Okun (2015, Chapter 2)
5	2/9–2/15	A brief economic history of the Cuban socialist economy	Mesa-Lago (1981, pp. 7–36)
			Mesa-Lago (2000, pp. 199–200; 264–288)
			Pérez-López (2003)
			Hernández-Catá et al. (2012)
6	2/16–2/22	Economic reform: Introduction	Mesa-Lago (2000, pp. 289–339)
			Pérez-López and Travieso-Díaz (1998, pp. 3–54)
			Trumbull (2000)
			Trumbull (2001)
			Mesa-Lago et al. (2005)
7	2/23–2/28	Economic Reform under Fidel	Same as Module 6
8	3/1–3/7	Economic reform under Raúl—Cuba in transition?	Bye (2014)
		Cuba in Transition?	Pujol (2009, 2013, 2014)
			Pérez-López (2010)
			Henken (2015, including Fact Sheet)
			Hakim (2016)
9	3/8–3/13	World democratization: How did Cuba get left out?	Huntington (1968, pp. 1–59)
		The Cuban Political System	Fukuyama (2014, pp. 1–19)
			Rabkin (1991, pp. 9–34)
			Domíinguez (2009, pp. 457–508)
			Gershman and Gutierrez (2009, pp. 36–53)
	3/14–3/23	Trip	

The program for the course on the post-socialist economies of Europe is very similar with the exception that firm visits are primarily to former state-owned enterprises that have been privatized as part of the transition from the former socialist to the current market-based (capitalist) system. Privatization is a major component of transition, and perhaps the most difficult.

I expect (and grade) the students to be active participants during lectures and field trips, to ask questions and make comments during the events and to discuss them afterwards with me and among themselves. I want the students to take an active part in every event and to have ample opportunity to reflect on what they have learned. In general, I have been very pleasantly surprised by their participation, especially because I am so used to the reticence that they so often display in a regular classroom setting. At the beginning, they are sometimes nervous about asking questions or making comments that may appear critical, especially in Cuba. I have seldom encountered a presenter, even among government officials, who was unwilling to answer any question or debate any critical comment as long as they are offered respectfully. This may not be all luck, since most of the Cuban experts I use have had extensive experience in the U.S. and are not going to be surprised by very many of the attitudes expressed by American students.

After the trip, the students have three more graded outputs to complete: a journal, a term paper, and an exam.

The students are expected to keep a daily journal while on the trip. The journal is in two parts. First, I want to see their detailed notes on all lectures and field trips. Second, I expect thoughtful commentary on all their other experiences. I look for insight outside the classroom. I want them to have conversations with locals wherever they go and to write about what they learned from those encounters. I want this to be an opportunity for reflection about what they are going through. (Of course, what they really want to write about is how cool the nightclubs and bars are. That's fine. I just don't give them a lot of points for that!) After the trip, they type up their journals and submit them for a grade.

I have experimented some with the timing of the exam. One possibility is to give the exam right before the trip so as to focus them on what they have learned so that they go on the trip as knowledgeable as possible about the country and its economy. However, they are just too excited about the impending trip and getting ready for it that this sort of focus is hard on them. Furthermore, there is not sufficient time between the last module and the trip to give them adequate time to study. I have settled on giving them the exam a week after the trip. This serves as an early final, as I give them no new material after the trip.

The last graded product is a short term paper. For the Cuba course, the topic is of their choosing as long as it relates in some way to the economy. Recent topics have included have included health care, ending the embargo, tourism, the impact of the coronavirus, whether Cuba is really in transition, education, and U.S.-Cuba relations. For the course on the post-socialist economies of Europe, I ask them to write on transition in a country other than the ones we focused on in the course (that is, not Russia, the Czech Republic, Hungary, or Poland). Note that these assignments, the journal, paper, participation, and even the exam (now that I have decided that it is best to give it after the trip), are opportunities to reflect on and apply the concepts learned, that is, to connect the dots. Eyler (2009, p. 30) emphasizes the importance of reflection and application: "The most critical factor for achieving powerful learning outcomes from experiential-learning programs is the inclusion of opportunities for feedback and reflection."

22.4 Concluding Remarks

Being able to offer my study-abroad course as a regular spring semester course has several advantages. It allows me to offer the course as part of my normal teaching load, eliminating the need to add a summer stipend to the fixed charges incorporated in the student fee, which would amount to approximately $1000 per student. That kind of fee would likely deter so many students that the course would not draw a sufficient number.

Almost all Citadel students are in military training (The Citadel being a military college) or are working during the summer and cannot take the time off to go abroad. Again, it would be hard to recruit a sufficient number of students during the summer.

The trip, being over spring break, gives me 8 weeks to teach the students what I want them to learn about the planned-socialist system, the comparison between the planned-socialist and capitalist systems, and a little about the history and politics of the place. When my students get to Cuba, the Czech Republic, or Poland, they are already educated about the country and its economy. And when they return, they still have 5 weeks to complete the reflective assignments (exam, journal, and term paper).

The first 2 years I taught the Cuba course (1999 and 2000), I did offer it over a 5-week summer term. It was frustrating. I front-loaded the course during the first week, meeting more than the normal class time for a summer class. After the trip, we had only two and a half weeks left, which is not sufficient. To make matters worse, because we were no longer meeting as a class, the students all scattered to summer jobs and tried to get their assignments in while their focus was elsewhere. The results were not good!

Another advantage, at least for the Cuba course, is that the weather in Havana is perfect in March. Almost without fail, the sky is clear, the temperature very warm but not uncomfortable, and the humidity low. During June, there is much more likely to be rain and both the temperature and humidity are very high. The weather in Europe is better in the summer, of course, but airfares and lodging are much more expensive. Actually, in my experience, the seasons are shifted earlier than here, with the result that I have always been able to have at least a coffee at an outdoor café, even in Warsaw.

By the way, I would not recommend the semester model for the fall semester, even at those schools that have a full week off at Thanksgiving. I suspect it would be a hard sell, since Thanksgiving for most is an important family event. Also, there is so little time after Thanksgiving and students are focused then on completing assignments and studying for finals.

I am lucky to have been able to align my study-abroad courses with my particular teaching and research expertise. That allows me to do a lot—if nothing else, to enliven my lectures with war stories of my time in the Soviet Union, and in Ukraine and Hungary during the early years of their transitions. It also means that I know people with whom I can collaborate in putting together each class.

It is not necessary that the instructor be a subject expert. McCannon (2011) describes a course that he offered in Vienna that was focused on Austrian economics, a subject in which he was interested but did not have a deep expertise. However, he was able to make use of a facility owned by his university and the expertise he needed on site. He reports a valuable learning experience for both students and instructor. As I mentioned above, what I would be wary of is an overdependence on agents or study-abroad organizations that provide generic study-abroad experiences that are little more than tourist excursions. To quote Di Gregorio (2015, p. 572): "Study-abroad experiences that entail extensive travel and brief, superficial engagements with specific foreign contexts may amount to no more than 'academic tourism', and may even serve to reinforce existing stereotypes and create a false understanding."

I am quite certain that my courses are much more than academic tourism!

Appendix

Itinerary in Havana

- Saturday, March 14

  - Arrival to Havana
  - Meet CET guide at the exit of the Terminal and transfer to accommodations.
  - Check-in at a bed and breakfast in Vedado, known as 'casas particulares,' or 'private homes.' (Since the 1990s Cuban families have been permitted to rent rooms out of their family homes to foreigners.)
  - Orientation meeting: overview of the agenda, discussion about local transportation, nearby markets, internet access and other logistics, safety, cultural norms and current events in Cuba
  - Evening Welcome dinner at your Bed and Breakfast.

- Sunday, March 15

  - Discussion with Jorge Mario Sanchez, renowned Cuban economist, about the current process of economic reform. Sanchez, who has authored several important books on the Cuban economy, has taught at Harvard, Columbia and several other U.S. universities. He will share his views on the Cuban governments 'updating' of the economic model.
  - Tour of an agricultural market with economist Giulio Ricci to learn about purchasing power and consumption in Cuba.
  - Lunch and discussion with a family of artists, AltaMira art loft. A few years ago, Edel Bordón and his family embarked on a journey to establish an art collective in their apartment building. Spearheaded by his wife Yamilé Pardo, the family created the AltaMira art space, which features an exhibition and workspace off of the main lobby and collaborations with neighbors.

- Afternoon of independent study/research.
- Monday, March 16
  - Discussion with Carlos Alzugaray, former Cuban diplomat, about Cuban foreign policy and international reforms.
  - Walking tour of Old Havana's Historic Center, a UNESCO World Heritage Site since 1982. Wander through the Plaza de Armas, a scenic tree-lined plaza formerly at the center of influence in Cuba. It is surrounded by many of the most historic structures in Havana as well as important monuments. See the Plaza de San Francisco, a cobbled plaza surrounded by buildings dating from the eighteenth century, dominated by the baroque Iglesia and Convento de San Francisco dating from 1719. Visit the Plaza Vieja, surrounded by sumptuous houses of the Havana aristocracy from the eighteenth and nineteenth centuries. Visit Plaza de la Catedral de San Cristóbal de La Habana.
  - Lunch at Tatagua, a new paladar (private restaurant) and art gallery in Old Havana situated on the famous Prado Promenade. Named for one of the Cuban words for butterfly, the modern restaurant and bar offers delicious international food within a photography gallery.
  - Visit to the Museum of the Revolution, which holds hundreds of artifacts from pre- and post-revolutionary times and highlights the tense relationship between the U.S. and Cuba.
  - Meet with the Barrio Habana team, a nonprofit organization that leads a community sports-arts program in Old Havana for children, at-risk youth and elderly people, while also contributing to preserve the heritage of the city.
- Tuesday, March 17
  - Driving Tour in Nostalgic Cars. Hop into 1950s classic and take in the scenery. Visit the workshop to meet the owners. This husband and wife couple has become the face of entrepreneurship in Cuba, taking advantage of the new economic changes to restore and operate these American beauties.
  - Meeting with Tostonet, a software development company, and discussion with entrepreneurs about their private business.
  - Visit Vinilos Decorazon, a small private business that specializes in home decorations. Discussion about the private sector in Cuba, challenges and opportunities.
  - Lunch at your casa.
  - Afternoon Independent study/research.
- Wednesday, March 18
  - Day trip to rural Havana (Corralillo, south of Bauta) enjoy a Pig Roast lunch with locals. Stops on the way to visit the Shrine of Saint Lazarus (an important site for both Catholics and followers of Santería).
- Thursday, March 19

- Discussion with Raul Rodriguez, director of the Center for the Study of the United States at the University of Havana, about bilateral relations between the United States and Cuba.
- Lunch at your casa.
- Afternoon Independent study/research.

- Friday, March 20

  - Discussion with Dr. Marcelino Feal, a Professor of General Surgery at the University Hospital Calixto García. Dr. Feal will provide an overview of the Cuban health care system, followed by a discussion.
  - Visit a centuries-old mansion in Vedado neighborhood. Step inside this stately residence to discover what lies behind the crumbling facades of Havana's impressive mansions. Josie, who has lived in the house for over 60 years, will show us around and explain its rich history.
  - Lunch at Grados, a private restaurant defender of the traditional Cuban cuisine rescued from Mambi books and stories, paired with a unique style of preparation. Meet its owner and chef Rulito Bazuk, another example of Cuba's young, up and coming entrepreneurial class of creative professionals pursuing their dream.
  - Visit to a family home and discussion with locals about the ration card and purchasing power in Cuba.
  - Discussion with La Reyna y Real, a female hip hop/jazz duo. The group's music focuses on breaking down stereotypes in Cuban society, including machismo, healthy relationships, gender relations and race. They will share info about their interesting musical journey and insight into the challenges and opportunities young Cubans face.

- Saturday, March 21

  - Independent study/research.

- Sunday, March 22

  - Independent study/research.
  - Lunch and discussion with Collin Laverty, president of Cuba Educational Travel and a senior manager at Havana Strategies about private business in Cuba. He will also touch on current events such as the relationship with the U.S. and how young Cubans view the future.
  - Discussion with expert Reynaldo Cruz about baseball in Cuba.
  - Farewell dinner at Mas Habana, a modern private restaurant in Old Havana which has become very popular amongst locals and visitors.

- Saturday, March 21

  - Check out and depart for airport.

References

Bornstein M (1989) The comparison of economic systems. In: Bornstein M (ed) Comparative economic systems: models and cases. Richard D. Irwin, Homewood, IL

Brown A, Neuberger A (1989) The traditional centrally planned economy and economic reforms. In: Bornstein M (ed) Comparative economic systems: models and cases. Richard D. Irwin, Homewood, IL

Bye V (2014) Political implications of recent economic reform trends in Cuba: The 2014 status. Cuba Transition 24(1):40–58

Di Gregorio D (2015) Fostering experiential learning in faculty-led study-abroad programmes. In: Taras V, Gonzalez-Perez MA (eds) The Palgrave handbook of experiential learning in international business. Palgrave MacMillan, London, pp 569–584

Domíinguez J (2009) Cuba: order and revolution. Harvard University Press, Cambridge, MA

Eyler J (2009) The power of experiential education. Liberal Educ 95(4):24–31

Fukuyama F (2014) Political order and political decay: From the industrial revolution to the globalization of democracy. Macmillan, New York, NY

Gershman C, Gutierrez O (2009) Can Cuba change? ferment in civil society. J Democr 20(1):36–53

Hakim P (2016) The future is coming: Observations and reflections on Cuba. The Dialogue: Leadership for the Americas 11 January

Hayek FA (1945) The use of knowledge in society. Am Econ Rev 35(4):519–530

Henken T (2015) One year later: Cuba's Cuentapropistas. World Policy Blog. 17 December 17

Hernández-Catá E et al (2012) The growth of the Cuban economy in the first decade of the XXI century: Is it sustainable? Cuba Transition 22(1):88–101

Huntington SP (1968) Political order in changing societies. Yale University Press, New Haven, CT

McCannon BC (2011) Teaching Austrian economics in Austria as a non-Austrian: A note. J Econ Finance Educ 10(2):82–86

Mesa-Lago C (1981) The economy of socialist Cuba: A two-decade appraisal. University of New Mexico Press, Albuquerque, NM

Mesa-Lago C (2000) Market, socialist, and mixed economies: comparative policy and performance–Chile, Cuba, and Costa Rica. John Hopkins University Press, Baltimore, MD

Mesa-Lago C et al (2005) The Cuban economy in 2004–2005. Cuba Transition 15(1):1–18

Neuberger E (1989) Classifying economic systems. In: Bornstein M (ed) Comparative economic systems: models and cases. Richard D. Irwin, Homewood, IL

Okun AM (2015) Equality and efficiency: The big tradeoff. Brookings Institution Press, Washington, DC

Pérez-López J (2003) The Cuban economy in 2002–2003. Cuba Transition 13(1):1–13

Pérez-López J (2010) Dashed expectations: Raúl Castro's management of the Cuban economy, 2006–2010. Cuba Transition 20(1):78–87

Pérez-López JF, Travieso-Díaz MF (eds) (1998) Perspectives on Cuban economic reforms. Arizona State University, Center for Latin American Studies, Tempe, AZ

Pujol J (2009) The Cuban economy in a world of uncertainty. Cuba Transition 19(1):1–13

Pujol J (2013) Where is Cuba going? economic policies that have been adopted and results thus far. Cuba Transition 13(1):77–98

Pujol J (2014) Cuba's perplexing changes: Is the society in crisis? Cuba Transition 24(1):1–8

Rabkin RP (1991) Cuban politics: The revolutionary experiment. Praeger Publishers, New York, NY

Strow C (2016) Teaching the economics of ecotourism, trade, healthcare, education, poverty, and immigration as a study abroad experience in Costa Rica. J Econ Finance Educ 15(3):83–94

Trumbull C (2000) Economic reforms and social contradictions in Cuba. Cuba Transition 10(1):305–320

Trumbull C (2001) Prostitution and sex tourism in Cuba. Cuba Transition 11(1):356–371

Chapter 23
Study Abroad in the Transitional Economies

Travis Wiseman

Abstract This paper offers a guide to developing and executing a short-term, faculty-led study abroad program, focusing on the economics of institutional change. While I will primarily discuss my experience with programs in the Transitional Economies—e.g., Czech Republic, Poland, Hungary. I have used the same basic format to organize programs in other parts of the world—e.g., Cuba, Chile, and Peru. I will highlight course objectives, provide a course outline with reading list, and discuss both academic and non-academic benefits of carrying out instruction beyond the classroom.

23.1 Introduction

Studying institutional variation provides students with insights into the fundamental structures of the world's economies—and the importance of rules, formal and informal, in determining political, economic, and social outcomes. From minor variations in rules that one experiences when traveling across developed countries—e.g., a lower, legal drinking age (popular among U.S. undergraduates traveling abroad!)—to much larger variations experienced when traveling from developed to under- or un-developed regions, for students and faculty alike, stepping into these differences brings the course to life! The Transitional Economies—e.g., Czech Republic, Poland, Hungary, Estonia, Germany, etc.—are unique in that they offer a first-world international experience coupled with a history of large-scale institutional adjustment.

First, my background. I am currently Director of the International Business Program at Mississippi State University. This position is part of a dual assignment, as my directorship is a college-level assignment, wherein I advise nearly 200 students, each working towards both a business and a language degree—all of whom

---

T. Wiseman (✉)
Department of Finance and Economics, Mississippi State University, Mississippi State, MS, USA
e-mail: travis.wiseman@msstate.edu

© The Author(s), under exclusive license to Springer Nature Switzerland AG 2021
J. Hall, K. Holder (eds.), *Off-Campus Study, Study Abroad, and Study Away in Economics*, Contributions to Economics,
https://doi.org/10.1007/978-3-030-73831-0_23

are required to complete both a study abroad program, and an internship, domestic or foreign. I came to this position in 2014 after teaching for the 2013–2014 academic year as an instructor in MSU's Finance and Economics Department—my second assignment. I teach primarily for that department to this day. My annual course offerings typically include Comparative Economic Policy, International Economics, and a study abroad course. I came to MSU with a PhD in Economics from West Virginia University, with field emphasis in international and developing economies, and public economics. As an undergraduate, I studied abroad in the Czech Republic. As a graduate student, I moved to Estonia to work on my dissertation.

Much of my research focuses on institutions and entrepreneurship—including off-the-books (or shadow economy) entrepreneurship. And, my experience in the transitional economies motivated this interest. It was after my first trip to Central and Eastern Europe that I decided to pursue a PhD and study institutional change. My international experience as a student solidified my appreciation and understanding of the value of study abroad. While there are many general 'how-to' resources available to those interested, I do not cite any of those here, as the programs I've developed at MSU have been developed around my personal experiences traveling abroad as both a student and a professional scholar. I've packed into my programs those things I recall capturing my attention as a student and omit those that I least enjoyed.[1]

For most MSU students their study abroad experiences mark their first ever departure from the U.S. With that (and my own interest in traveling) in mind, I began developing short-term, faculty-led study abroad programs in the Spring of 2014. All programs are launched in either the spring or summer semesters. And all are economics courses designed to focus on institutions.

23.2   Program Design and Objectives

Since the programs are offered during the spring and summer semesters, the courses are typically structured such that in-person classes are taught on campus at MSU prior to departure, with one or two meetings after we return. The time abroad varies in length, depending on the semester. During the spring semester, we travel over spring break, typically borrowing a day or two from the weeks on both sides of the break, so that we get at least 10 days on the ground abroad. If the course is a summer

---

[1] Among the most beneficial: spend time with your students outside the program itinerary. Offer to go out for dinner and drinks on free evenings, and/or show them around town—visiting museums, explore the culinary scene, etc. Not all will want to participate in this, but several will jump at the opportunity to hang out with their professor. Among the least beneficial: avoid spending too much time on tour buses around town. Buses are fine for transport between cities, and day trips away from your hotel, but jumping on and off buses all day, every day is tiresome—and if feels a bit too 'touristy'. Spend time navigating the city on foot. (Note: warn your students about lots of walking—encourage them to bring comfortable shoes).

offering, it is typically planned for our 'Maymester,' which is a 3-week semester. I usually plan for 15 days on the ground abroad in this case.

My objective in designing study abroad courses is to provide students with the following:

- An understanding of the importance of institutions. The course begins as a study of Comparative Systems, in which we identify the characteristics of capitalism, planned socialism, market socialism, and mixed economies.
- An understanding of the historical transitions to socialism, and subsequently from socialism to market-based systems.
- An understanding of the unique experiences of the Transitional Economies—e.g., we highlight the pros and cons of Shock Therapy vs Gradualism, etc.
- An opportunity to interact with persons and businesses who lived through the transitions.
- Fun cultural excursions.
- General lessons in navigating the world—as, for many of my students, this is their first time traveling out of the US. For several, it may be the first time traveling to any major city—so, general lessons in navigating public transportation, etc., are in order.
- Plenty of free time for students to explore on their own.
- And, I like to introduce students to places they've never considered traveling to. Depending on the size of the group I aim to attract to the program, it is sometimes useful to include a 'bait city' in the program. I ultimately want students to experience places like Prague or Budapest or Krakow, but these usually aren't high on students lists of places to visit. Including a large, well-known city in the program usually garners a bunch of attention. Amsterdam is always a popular one—and its Schiphol Airport is a common stop for those traveling to Central Europe. (Not to mention, the layovers are typically either 4 h or 8 h in length). I've included a brief stop in Berlin, also. Plan to stay a night or two in a major city somewhere along the way. There are always relevant activities to engage in.[2]

For the sake of brevity, I will outline here only the structure of my spring semester offering. For summer programs, the condensed nature of the course requires that students do more reading outside of class—and often I ask them to complete readings before the semester begins and/or during their time on planes, trains and buses while traveling abroad.

The course output typically consists of an exam, a journal, a discussion forum and a research paper.

---

[2]The Anne Frank House in Amsterdam is a poplar activity that fits in with the course material. Be sure to book tickets in advance for this one, though. The lines for same-day ticket purchases are unreal. A half-day Berlin City tour is great, also, with stops at all the major government buildings and the Berlin Wall. There is a great museum set up in the old SS headquarters building, located at the Berlin Wall monument.

Exam The exam is given prior to departure for the trip and covers all readings and lecture material up to the trip.

Journal I require that students keep a daily journal while traveling, to document their personal experiences—from their experiences in the airports, coming and going, to notes from their program lectures and field trips. I ask that they document their impression of everything they can—the people they meet, cultural things, the economy, politics, music and art, language, and anything else of interest. After the trip, I ask the students to type out their journal notes and submit to me, along with supplemental material—such as fun pictures they may have captured during their adventures.

Discussion Forum Throughout the course, I ask that students participate in a web-based threaded discussion. This provides a great opportunity to read and talk about current events in countries of interest. It's made even better if you can get participants involved from the countries they'll be visiting.

Research Paper I often experiment with this assignment. Sometimes I ask students to author a paper on the experiences of some transitional economy(ies) other than the one(s) we visited during our program. Other times, I've given them complete freedom to choose their topic related to transition and ask simply that they dive deeper into something that we perhaps gloss over either in class or during any part of the program itinerary. I like doing this because it informs me on what students find most interesting among their experiences abroad, and often gives me enough material to include in future iterations of the course. In any case, I typically ask that the papers be no shorter than 10 pages (double-spaced, 12-point Times New Roman font, 1-inch margins all around).

A general course outline is provided in Table 23.1. In addition to the readings in the table, students are asked to read Marx and Engels (1848[2005]), Hayek (1945), Lucas (2009), and another book—usually a novel, or history book that reads like a novel (past examples of books include Smith (2008), Larson (2011), Gjelten (2008)), as well as various current events op-eds from the *Wall Street Journal* and other sources. Coverage of 'Socialism' and 'Capitalism' on the syllabus combine info from Gros and Steinherr (2004), Hayek (1945), and Marx and Engels (1848[2005]), as well as some basic info from recommended principles-level texts—such as Gwartney et al. (2017). I also suggest that week 8 is a great time to get faculty from the History or Language departments involved.

For programs catering to larger groups (>10 students) I find it's best to use a provider company to help organize the itinerary. Doing so will save tons of leg work for you on the international side of the program, and free up your time to focus on the administrative stuff at home—Study Abroad Office program applications and proposals, securing the appropriate permission and signatures from all relevant university offices, and marketing your program! If it is your first time organizing a study abroad program, especially one attached to a specific discipline—e.g., economics—and no one has laid that groundwork ahead of you, plan to build in

23 Study Abroad in the Transitional Economies

Table 23.1 Course outline

Week	Topic	Readings
1	Introduction to the course and principles review. Introduction to comparative economic systems	Neuberger (1989)
2	Classification of economic systems. How economists assess economic performance	Bornstein (1989), Gros and Steinherr (2004, Chapters 1–2)
3	Assessing performance continued	None
4	Marx's vision and the typical planned socialist system	Marx and Engels (1848[2005])
5	Socialism continued. Capitalism	Hayek (1945)
6	Capitalism continued	None
7	Transition: an introduction. Transition in Central and Eastern Europe	Gros and Steinherr (2004)
8	Transition in Central and Eastern Europe, continued. The Baltic States. A word about Cuba	Lucas (2009)
9	History and culture of the [host country]. Travel tips and safety	None
10	Spring break trip	
11	Debrief: lessons learned and discussion of [assigned book]	
12–15	No class meetings. It is expected that students will dedicate this time to polishing up the journal and finishing the research paper	

extra time for proposals to your university's curriculum committee, to get the study abroad course on the books.

I've had great success with Society for Legal and Economic Education, headquartered in Prague, Czech Republic. They will cater nearly any demand, and can organize programs built entirely of cultural excursions, programs with daily lectures in foreign university classrooms, or some mix of that. They will help you put together single- or multi-country programs (they're not just a Czech focused company).

Below, I provide an itinerary from a recent trip to the Czech Republic.[3]

- Day 1—Arrival in Prague

  - Arrival at Vaclav Havel Airport
  - Bus transfer to the hotel

---

[3]Thanks to Tomáš Říčka and Radovan Kačín for organizing the international leg of the program. This itinerary is their design, with only minor input from me about desired site visits and lecture time and material.

292 T. Wiseman

- Short tour to get everyone downtown and oriented
- Welcome drink and dinner

- Day 2—Prague

  - Guided walking tour of Lesser Town, Castle, and Charles Bridge
  - Free afternoon

- Day 3—Kutná Hora[4]

  - Bus transfer to Kutná Hora (1 h 15 min)
  - Bone church (Ossuary Sedlec)
  - Guided walking tour of the town
  - Bus transfer to Prague
  - Free evening

- Day 4—Prague

  - Lecture: History of the Czech Republic I
  - Lecture: History of the Czech Republic II
  - Lecture: Transformation after 1989
  - Free afternoon

- Day 5—Terezín, Mělník[5]

  - Bus transfer to Terezín (1 h)
  - Terezín Memorial
  - Bus transfer to Mělník (40 min)
  - Free afternoon in Mělník
  - Bus transfer to Prague

- Day 6—Prague

  - Guided walking tour of the Jewish Quarter
  - Guided walking tour of Strahov Library
  - Free evening

- Day 7—Southern Bohemia—Český Krumlov[6]

  - Bus transfer to Český Krumlov with stop in Pisek town (visit castle) on the way (2 h 42 min)
  - Check-in at hotel
  - Dinner in Medieval restaurant
  - Guided walking tour of Krumlov by night

---

[4]UNESCO sites, medieval mining town, 'bone church' always a hit with students.

[5]Even if Terezín concentration camp was 'less severe' than Mauthausen, Auschwitz, it personifies the history of the twentieth century.

[6]Český Krumlov, a UNESCO site, is a highlight on every itinerary of the region. For comparison we make a stop in another historical town that is not as popular yet.

23 Study Abroad in the Transitional Economies 293

- Day 8—Southern Bohemia—Český Krumlov, České Budějovice

  - Guided walking tour of Český Krumlov
  - Bus transfer to uCeské Budějovice (45 min)
  - Budweiser Brewery tour
  - Bus transfer to Prague
  - Hotel check-in and farewell dinner

- Day 9—Prague, US

  - Check out of hotel
  - Bus transfer to the airport
  - Flight to the United States

When planning a program in Central and Eastern Europe, know that the climate will be similar to that of the Central/Eastern U.S., if only off by a couple weeks. One really must monitor weather patterns up to the day of departure to make an accurate assessment about what clothing to pack. I've been to CZ in mid-March on several occasions, and nearly each experience has been different. I've delighted in warm, sunny spring weather; and I've experienced rain and snow!

23.3 Program Costs

I've discovered a remarkable drop in interest for short-term, faculty-led programs once total costs to the student surpass $3200. I try to keep charges for the academic portion of my programs at or below $2500, and give students freedom to secure their own flights to/from Europe—which has given me some play in the pricing.[7]

The program fee generally includes:

- Office of Study Abroad Application Fee
- International Health and Emergency Assistance Insurance
- Accommodations (typically 2–4 students per room)
- In-country transportation (excluding Uber/taxis during free evenings. But they usually get a metro/rail pass good for their entire visit)
- Entrance fees for all included program activities (museums, tours, etc.)
- Some meals (daily breakfast, some lunches, a few dinners)

Not included in the program fee:

- University Tuition and Fees
- Airfare
- Some meals

---

[7]This works well for a number of reasons. Some students are able to save money by flying out of various airports located close to home, if home is outside of the university area. Some secure flights using their parent's airline points.

23.4 Conclusion

This short paper on studying abroad in the Transitional Economies is intended to aid anyone interested in developing similar programs. It is not an all-inclusive guide to program, development; rather a sample of course objectives, reading material and output, along with some tidbits of advice, that have provided great results for me. Much like preparation for any new course, first-time offerings require a substantial amount time and dedication. And, each university will offer its own set of challenges in getting similar programs off the ground. I hope the information here will provide some shortcuts in that process. I encourage anyone interested in acquiring more detail about my courses, experiences with study abroad, or foreign contacts, to please contact me.

Acknowledgments I owe a huge thanks to Dr. William Trumbull (Dean, School of Business, The Citadel), whose courses on Comparative Economic Systems and Transitional European Economies at West Virginia University piqued my interest in the study of institutional change, and study abroad. I have structured my study abroad programs after those of his that I participated in while a student at WVU.

References

Bornstein M (1989) The comparison of economic systems. In: Bornstein M (ed) Comparative economic systems: models and cases. Richard D. Irwin, Homewood, IL

Gjelten T (2008) Bacardi and the long fight for Cuba: The biography of a cause. Penguin, New York, NY

Gros D, Steinherr A (2004) Economic transition in Central and Eastern Europe: Planting the seeds. Cambridge University Press, Cambridge, MA

Gwartney JD, Stroup RL, Sobel RS, Macpherson DA (2017) Economics: Private and public choice. Cengage, Boston, MA

Hayek FA (1945) The use of knowledge in society. Am Econ Rev 35(4):519–530

Larson E (2011) In the garden of beasts: love and terror in Hitler's Berlin. Random House, New York, NY

Lucas E (2009) The fall and rise and fall again of the Baltic states. Foreign Policy 173:72–79

Marx K, Engels F (1848[2005]) The communist manifesto and other writings. Barnes and Noble Classics, New York, NY

Neuberger E (1989) Classifying economic systems. In: Bornstein M (ed) Comparative economic systems: models and cases. Richard D. Irwin, Homewood, IL

Smith TR (2008) Child 44. Grand Central Publishing, New York, NY

Printed in the United States
by Baker & Taylor Publisher Services